MODERN LEGAL STUDIES

LAW AND EDUCATION

Regulation, Consumerism and

the Education System

AUSTRALIA
The Law Book Company
Brisbane ● Sydney ● Melbourne ● Perth

CANADA
Carswell
Ottawa ● Toronto ● Calgary ● Montreal ● Vancouver

AGENTS
Steimatzky's Agency Ltd., Tel Aviv;
N.M. Tripathi (Private) Ltd., Bombay;
Eastern Law House (Private) Ltd., Calcutta;
M.P.P. House, Bangalore;
Universal Book Traders, Delhi;
Aditya Books, Delhi;
MacMillan Shuppan KK, Tokyo;
Pakistan Law House, Karachi, Lahore

MODERN LEGAL STUDIES

LAW AND EDUCATION
Regulation, Consumerism and the Education System

by

NEVILLE HARRIS

Senior Lecturer in Law
University of Liverpool

LONDON
SWEET AND MAXWELL
1993

Published in 1993 by
Sweet & Maxwell Ltd. of
South Quay Plaza
183 Marsh Wall London E14 9FT
Computerset by
P.B. Computer Typesetting
Pickering, N. Yorks.
Printed and bound in Scotland

A CIP catalogue record
for this book is available
from the British Library

ISBN 0 421–474009

PREFACE

The stimulus for writing this book came from my own long-standing academic interest in education law. But I was also aware of the increasing interest in legal developments in the field of education being shown by scholars of public law and family law. My aim in writing the book was to open up this field by analysing the important and often controversial legal and policy developments of recent years which are transforming the education system in England and Wales. In doing so I was concerned to give prominence to what I see as the key themes in these developments — themes centred on regulation and consumerism, such as control, privatisation, central-local government relationships, accountability, choice, participation and redress. Consumerism in particular is an area that has come increasingly to the fore in the development of government policy towards public services, yet has received little attention to date from legal writers. In relation to family law, there are a number of issues of particular relevance, including the public-private divide and child autonomy, especially in the context of the curriculum and the enforcement of discipline at school and in relation to the issue of whether parents and/or children are the true "consumers" of education.

In preparing the text I was mindful of some readers' possible unfamiliarity with some or much of the legal terrain. With so few up to date works on this subject in print it was necessary to seek to present a fairly comprehensive statement of the areas of the law under examination, incorporating the now extensive case law and selected areas of international human rights law. I aimed to combine my exposition of the law with exploration of the policy issues and broad themes under analysis, covering the historical context where relevant and speculating about possible future developments. Although principally concerned with the schools system, the book also explores aspects of regulation and consumerism in the further and higher education sectors.

The book covers legal developments up to and including the Education Act 1993. The Act received The Royal Assent on July 27, 1993. At the time of completing the text only one commencement order had been issued (S.I. 1993 No. 1975, bringing about 45 sections into effect on or by October 1, 1993 including most of the provisions on school attendance and those on identification of schools requiring special measures). Nevertheless, I decided where appropriate to cite all relevant sections of the Act, on the assumption that by publication of the book many of the provisions would (or would shortly) be in force. In any event I have endeavoured to explain the pre- and post-Act positions.

Subject to the above, the law is stated as at August 5, 1993. A few subsequent policy developments were included at proof stage.

I would like to express particular thanks to Professor Alan Page of the Modern Legal Studies editorial board for his most helpful suggestions concerning the structuring of the book in the initial stages of preparation; to Mr Clive Griffiths of the Department for Education for statistics on education complaints; to Derek Way and Wendy Neale of the Law Faculty Library for assisting with my hunt for cases and other materials; to the editorial department at Sweet and Maxwell for their friendliness and co-operation; and above all to my wife Marie, for her support and tolerance.

Neville Harris   September 6, 1993
Faculty of Law
University of Liverpool

CONTENTS

TABLE OF CASES

TABLE OF STATUTES

TABLE OF STATUTORY INSTRUMENTS

ABBREVIATIONS

Choice and Diversity	Secretaries of State for Education and Wales, Choice and Diversity—A new framework for schools (1992) Cm. 2021 (White Paper)
CNAA	Council for National Academic Awards
CRE	Commission for Racial Equality
DES	Department of Education and Science
DFE	Department for Education
EA	Education Act
EAC	Education appeal committee
E(No. 2)A	Education (No. 2) Act
ESA	Education (Schools) Act
EWO	Education welfare officer
FE	Further education
FA	Funding authority
FHEA	Further and Higher Education Act
GM	Grant maintained
HEFC(E)	Higher Education Funding Council (for England)
HMI	Her Majesty's Inspectorate/Inspector
ILEA	Inner London Education Authority

LEA   Local education authority

OFSTED   Office for Standards in Education

RRA   Race Relations Act

SACRE   Standing advisory council on religious education

SATs   Standard Assessment Tasks

SDA   Sex Discrimination Act

SEAC   School Examinations and Assessment Authority

T.E.S.   *Times Educational Supplement*

INTRODUCTION

♪

Since 1980, the Government has legislated in the field of education on an unprecedented scale, to give effect to radical and far-reaching reforms. All sectors of the education system have been affected. Seven major statutes since 1980, the most recent of which (the EA 1993), with over 300 sections, is the longest education measure ever enacted in the U.K., have introduced major changes to the education power structure. Out, it is said, goes producer domination, as the vested interests of hitherto all-powerful local education authorities are swept aside and teachers' professional autonomy is undermined. In comes "parent power" and greater institutional autonomy and diversity. Consumer choice becomes the key to the operation of a quasi-market structure in which schools, colleges and universities are in effect forced to compete with each other to attract the pupils and students on whose numbers levels of funding increasingly depend. But central government's wish to control the development and operation of the education system as a whole has resulted in a substantial increase in regulation, which has taken diverse forms (see Chapter 1).

Regulation and consumerism have become dominant themes in the fundamental reform of the education system in England and Wales in the 1980s and 1990s, and they provide the main themes of this book. Particular attention is given to consumerism, which, in a legal context, has so far been a relatively unexplored area.

The nature of consumerism in education is discussed in detail in Chapter 1. It will be shown to have arisen out of the opportunities created by education legislation for consumer choice, participation, representation, access and redress. The philosophy of consumerism in relation to public services is premised, in large part, on the notion that competition between providers and the exercise of individual choice by consumers, in other words the operation of a relatively free market for the service in question, results in greater quality and efficiency (which is to the greater public good) and maximised individual satisfaction. Consumerism in its more secondary forms — participation, representation and redress — is also claimed to preserve or enhance public accountability, although there is disagreement as to the extent to which it does so.

The Government has acknowledged that since 1980 it has been "intent on widening parental choice, and entrenching parental influence and control."[1] Consumer power has been increased in stages. The EA 1980 began the process, with its requirement that a parent's preference for a school be granted save on specific grounds (the Act, according to the Government, "rightly reversed the burden of proof"[2]). The Act also conferred on parents an associated right of appeal and sought to facilitate the exercise of choice of school through requirements on the publication of information by schools and LEAs. Although less consumerist in emphasis, the EA 1981 gave parents of a child with special educational needs opportunities for involvement and redress in respect of decisions concerning the child's education. The E(No. 2)A 1986 tackled the lack of parental representation on school governing bodies and required governors to report to parents. As governing bodies were also given considerably increased powers over the management of schools, the consumer interest was to be represented in all major decision-making at school level. "Parent power" gained yet further ground with the ERA 1988's provisions on parental ballots concerning GM status and a new regime of "open enrolment," which, in simple terms, required schools to admit pupils up to the limit of the school's physical capacity in response to parental demand.

Although the ERA 1988 reflected a "vision of a consumer democracy,"[3] it did not represent the high water mark of consumerism, and additional measures have followed. The ESA 1992 introduced further requirements on the publication of information, relating to the comparative performance of schools ("league tables," which are also to be introduced in the FE sector, under the FHEA 1992), and gave parents a role in the school inspection process. Most recently, the EA 1993 has extended opportunities for opting-out and strengthened the rights of parents in respect of children with special educational needs. It has also facilitated greater diversity in educational provision, designed to enhance parental choice.[4]

The fostering of educational consumerism in its various forms is claimed to have as its overriding social objective an improvement in the quality of educational provision.[5] This is linked to a wider economic objective concerned with changing the principal basis for the

---

[1] *Choice and Diversity*, para. 1.17.

[2] *Ibid.*

[3] S. Ranson, "From 1944 to 1988: Education, Citizenship and Democracy," in M. Flude and M. Hammer (eds.), *The Education Reform Act 1988: Its Origins and Implications* (1990) p. 1.

[4] *Choice and Diversity*, para. 1.49.

[5] *Ibid.* para. 2.1.

distribution of public financial resources. The theory is that consumer choice will help to determine what is good and worth supporting via public funds, thereby also identifying what is bad and, if necessary improvement does not occur, what should be allowed to wither away. However, this basic theory gives rise to practical difficulties (for example in hindering local planning of provision) and potentially undesirable social consequences, as shall be shown.

Responsibility for what is bad and inefficient has, according to the Government, rested with LEAs. Thus a wider political objective has been to weaken LEAs' influence, which may be seen as part of a sustained policy of reducing the role of local government[6] and exerting new forms of control over local authorities.[7] For nearly 40 years the EA 1944 provided more or less the entire legal framework for educational provision at school and FE level in England and Wales. The education service was a national one, locally administered. In the partnership between central and local government, the former was expected to play only a minimal, supervisory role. LEAs, on the other hand, were free to dominate key aspects of local educational provision, planning and management. They controlled the secular curriculum and senior staff appointments and were able to exert substantial influence on school governing bodies. They were responsible for overall planning, which meant that they decided how the local service should be organised (although in some cases needing the approval of the Secretary of State for reorganisation proposals).

However, as shall be shown, LEA domination has been curtailed by the reforms of the 1980s and early 1990s. Part of the rationale for the new, complex and all-pervading regulatory framework for the provision of education in England and Wales,[8] which has enabled central government to exert firmer control over provision, is the need to provide a safeguard against abuse of power by institutions freed from LEA control and enjoying far greater independence and autonomy.[9] Key elements in this framework are the centrally regulated National Curriculum and the new funding regimes, operated by government appointed funding councils, in the further and higher education sectors.

Central regulation has also become a major weapon in the Government's bid to quell the radicalist element among the teaching

---

[6] P. John, *Recent Trends in Central-Local Relations* (1990). The Care in the Community system introduced under the National Health Service and Community Care Act 1990 offers perhaps the only major exception to the general trend.

[7] M. Loughlin, "Law, Ideologies, and the Political-Administrative System" (1989) 16 *Journal of Law and Society* 21 at p. 35.

[8] There is separate provision for Scotland.

[9] But see the problems in respect of governing bodies of GM schools, discussed in Chap. 3.

profession. "Progressive" teachers were blamed for many of the ills, and in particular falling standards, which the introduction of the National Curriculum, with its prescribed content and administrative arrangements (for example, governing assessment and pupils' records of achievement), aimed to eradicate. As in England and Wales, there is also considerable regulation of teaching in the United States, operating at state and federal levels. Regulation by state authorities, which extends to such matters as textbook selection and the curriculum, is said to provide "a check on the discretion of local boards of education, administrators and teachers."[10] But it has been argued that this regulation has created resentment and loss of esteem among teachers by undermining their professional autonomy, and that it is in any event unnecessary in achieving the desired goal of maximising quality and effectiveness in educational provision.[11] The teaching unions' boycott of National Curriculum assessment tests in England and Wales in the summer of 1993 was clearly in part a reaction against the effects of excessive regulation.

It has been suggested that the co-incidence of extended freedom of consumer choice with greater central regulation and control, for example in relation to the curriculum ("parents are to be free to choose a school for their children but not free to choose what is taught there, which is the exclusive territory of the Secretary of State"), constitutes one of the major ideological contradictions inherent in recent education reforms in England and Wales.[12] This holds true, but only to a degree. For, as shall be shown, individual freedom of school choice is not guaranteed, and central control of the curriculum, while pervasive, is not absolute.

Regulation and consumerism find a common role in relation to accountability, itself an important theme of this book. The Government has been particularly keen to emphasise the accountability that flows "downwards," to consumers, rather than that which permeates "upwards," via central control. Accountability to the consumer dominates the Government's perception of public accountability in the field of education, and there are numerous references to it in the 1992 White Paper. For example, when complete results of individual schools' National Curriculum assessments of pupils and public examinations are published, parents will be able to "hold schools to account for their

---

[10] M. G. Yudof *et. al.*, *Educational Policy and the Law* (2nd ed. 1982) p. 381.

[11] W. H. Clune, "The deregulation critique of the federal role in education," in D. L. Kirp and D. N. Jersen (eds.) *School Days, Rule Days* (1986) p. 187. The general trend in the U.S. of questioning the need for regulation of services is noted in R. Baldwin and M. Mcrudden, *Regulation and Public Law* (1987) pp. 330–331.

[12] D. Coulby, "The Ideological Contradictions of Educational Reform," in L. Bash and D. Coulby, *The Education Reform Act 1988: Competition and Control* (1989), p. 114.

performance."[13] Schools will have to respond to "the broadening of choice of schools, which will enable parents to act on information about schools' relative performance . . ."[14] As we shall see, this view, which is evident throughout the *Citizens' Charter*[15] programme, is concerned more with accountability via consumer choice in the market-place rather than internal accountability within schools or the remedial rights of consumers. Nevertheless, it is accepted that other elements of consumerism may operate as a regulatory and constraining force which increases accountability in other ways. For example, the need to conduct a ballot of parents on whether a school should seek GM status, the duty to consult parents over proposed changes to a school's starting or finishing times and the presence of parents (with full voting rights) on school governing bodies, impose constraints on the autonomy of education institutions and some "internal accountability requirements."[16] Similarly, individual consumers can call institutions and education authorities to account by exercising statutory rights of redress, including rights of appeal over school choice or exclusions and rights to complain in respect of curricular provision. As these elements of consumerism are based on forms of democratic participation, they have given rise to the notion of "consumer-citizenship," which is discussed in Chapter 1.

Regulation and consumerism thus operate to sustain the new market-led, yet centrally directed, education system which the legislation has created. As these concepts provide key themes to the book, Chapter 1 examines them in more detail and tackles the question "who is the consumer?" Chapters 2 and 3 look at the evolving legal structure of education in England and Wales, with specific reference to central-local government relations and professional and institutional autonomy. Primary, secondary, further and higher education are all covered. Chapter 4 considers the opportunities for consumers to influence the pattern of local educational provision (for example, to save a school from closure, to secure state funding for a school, to take a school out of LEA control and to widen opportunities for single sex schooling). Individual choice of school is the theme of Chapter 5, which also covers rights of appeal. Chapter 6 examines the development of quality assurance in the schools and higher education sectors, in which regulation and consumerism are playing key roles. In Chapter 7 there is a review of the regulatory framework to curricular provision and consumer rights in

---

[13] *Choice and Diversity*, para. 2.7.
[14] *Ibid.*
[15] H.M. Government, *The Citizens' Charter* (1991) Cm. 1599.
[16] P. Birkenshaw, I. Harden and N. Lewis, *Government By Moonlight: The Hybrid Parts of the State* (1992) pp. 205–206.

relation to the content of children's education. Chapter 8, which is the
final chapter, offers some broad conclusions and considers whether the
limits of consumerism in the education system have yet been reached.

1

REGULATION AND CONSUMERISM IN EDUCATION

1. INTRODUCTION

The present degree of regulation in the education system seems on the face of it inconsistent with the general move towards the development of a quasi-market for education, based on competition and consumer choice. The introduction of these free market principles suggests, on the face of it, a relaxation of governmental control. State domination at local level, which is said to have given rise to near-monopolistic supply conditions in relation to educational provision, has certainly been reduced. This has been achieved by providing for, *inter alia*, an element of individual choice, increased freedom to establish more diverse forms of institution providing education (including GM schools and CTCs: see Chapter 2), and greater autonomy among institutions — all at the expense of LEA power. Adler explains that the reforms leading to creation of this quasi-market can be seen:

> "as the first stage of a two-stage deregulation of the educational system which sought to undermine the role of the local authority and replace bureaucratic and political forms of accountability with market-like relationships between schools and parents. In this two-stage process, the second stage comprises the delegation of powers and responsibilities from education authorities to individual schools and parents in their management."[1]

Yet despite these elements of deregulation there has been considerably more central government activity, and significantly more regulation, than ever before. The power of regulation has been used by central government in the assertion of greater authority and control over the system (in a way that McAuslan and others have suggested has serious

---

[1] M. Adler, *An Alternative Approach to Parental Choice*, National Commission on Education Briefing No. 13 (1993), p. 2.

constitutional implications[2]). Indeed, it has even been used to force those responsible for the management of institutions to play the 'market game.' This has been achieved, for example, by controlling the content of local schemes of financial management, so that pupil numbers have a major bearing on school budget allocations, and by requiring the publication of information relating to school and college performance, which can engender competition. Furthermore, the EA 1993 now, in effect, *requires* the Secretary of State to legislate in a way consistent with the development of a market system: he must "in the case of his power to regulate the provision made in educational institutions . . . exercise his powers with a view, amongst other things, to . . . encouraging diversity and increasing opportunities for choice."[3]

Of course, as a major part of the Government's exertion of greater overall political control has involved taking power away from LEAs and devolving it to educational institutions themselves, central government has had to find a way of controlling the activities of governing bodies and the teaching profession more closely. This has resulted in significant central controls in the distribution of funds. It has, along with general public concern about falling standards of attainment by pupils, also led to strict control of the content of the school curriculum. Central regulation has also been important in offering some (albeit limited) public safeguards in areas where privatisation has been in evidence (see below).

The overall position, therefore, is that there has been simultaneous regulation *and* deregulation. Both have begun to change the nature of the relationship between schools, colleges and universities and the users of their services. The basis of this relationship is increasingly that of producer-consumer. Educational consumerism is a phenomenon which is explored later in this chapter and elsewhere in the book.

2.   REGULATION OF EDUCATION

Central government has always regulated the education system, either directly or through its general controls over local authorities, which have increased considerably since the early 1980s, especially in financial matters. But in recent years, regulation of education has not only grown in scale but has taken increasingly diverse forms. Whilst the traditional

---

[2] The principal concern seems to be the undermining of the principle of the separation of powers, given the absence of effective constitutional checks: see P. McAuslan, "The Constitution: Does the Bill Offend it?," in J. Haviland (ed.), *Take Care Mr Baker* (1988), pp. 266–267, and B. Simon and C. Chitty, *SOS — Save Our Schools* (1993), Chap. 4.

[3] EA 1993, s. 2(2).

means of regulation, such as the use of legislative powers and the long-standing regime of administrative regulation via departmental circular, memoranda and codes of practice,[4] continue to be employed, less traditional forms have become important. These include agency regulation, the use of performance indicators and licensing. The legislative powers in the European Communities have had little impact on educational provision in the U.K. to date but may also become increasingly relevant in this field.[5] There are already a number of measures relevant to: programmes for exchange; recognition of qualifications and vocational training, such as the ERASMUS, Tempus and PETRA programmes;[6] and access to education for children of Community workers.[7] Among the important legal developments is the decision of the European Court of Justice in *Gravier* v. *City of Liege*,[8] which confirmed that conditions of access to vocational training fall within the scope of the Treaty of Rome (Article 128); so it would be unlawful discrimination (under Article 7) for a Member State to charge higher course fees for EC nationals from other Member States than those charged to its own nationals.

The ERA 1988 is said to have given the Secretary of State for Education over 200 separate powers. The EA 1993 is said to have added another 40 or so. A number of these powers are far-reaching, and decisions made under them difficult to challenge, as in the case of the power to confer GM status on a school (see Chapter 2). Many are legislative powers, which have been used to regulate a wide variety of functions, including the conduct of school government, the provision and publication of data and, most strikingly, the operation of the school curriculum. Thus there have been some 40-plus sets of regulations and orders regulating the National Curriculum since 1989. One writer has referred to this as "education by prescription."[9] Among the means of enforcing the responsibilities imposed as a result of the use of legislative powers are the long-standing default powers contained in sections 68 and 99 of the EA 1944, which are discussed in Chapter 2. These are in

---

[4] See G. Ganz, *Quasi-Legislation* (1987).
[5] For discussion of the relevant EC law, see J. Lonbay, "Education and Law: the Community Context" (1989) 14 *European Law Review* 363; J. Shaw "Education and the European Community" (1991) 3(1) *Education & the Law* 1; and C. Barnard, "The Maastricht agreement and education: one step forward, two steps back?" (1992) 4(3) *Education and the Law* 123.
[6] See N. Harris, "Social Citizenship and Young People in Europe," in B. Jackson and D. McGoldrick (eds), *Legal Visions of the New Europe* (1993) at pp. 209–210.
[7] H. Houghton-James, "The Implication for Member State of the Development of an Education Policy by the Court of Justice" (1993) 5(2) *Education and the Law* 85.
[8] [1985] E.C.R. 593.
[9] H. Iven, "Clarke's Prescription" (1991) 177 *Education* 358.

addition to new general directory powers under recent legislation; for example, under the ESA 1992 the Chief Inspector of Schools must "have regard to such aspects of Government policy as the Secretary of State may direct,"[10] and the new School Curriculum and Assessment Authority must "comply with any directions given by the Secretary of State."[11] The Secretary of State also appoints the relevant office-holders. It is easy to see why much concern has been expressed about the constitutional implications of the concentration of so much power in central government. [12]

The concerns apply just as much to the role played by the various agencies such as the Training Agency[13] (in relation to vocational training) and the Higher Education Funding Councils (HEFCs)[14] (in respect of university education), most significantly through the attachment of conditions to the funding of institutions. [15] The latest of these regulatory agencies are the non-statutory Office for Standards in Education (OFSTED), which regulates the recently privatised schools inspection service, and the funding authorities created by the EA 1993, which could take over all or part of LEAs' role in relation to specific functions and whose members are appointed by the Secretary of State (see Chapter 2). As later discussion will show, among the problems with these regulatory agencies is their lack of both accountability and independence from government. [16]

Regulatory agencies increasingly use performance indicators in the allocation of resources. Performance indicators and targets now form an important element in the quality control regimes for public services. [17]

---

[10] ESA 1992, ss. 1(6) and 4(6).

[11] EA 1993, s. 245(3)(*a*).

[12] *e.g.* McAuslan *op. cit.*

[13] Funds for training and NAFE (non-advanced further education provision) have been channelled to LEAs and colleges through the Training Agency (the grandchild of the Manpower Services Commission, which directed the Youth Training Scheme in the 1980s). The Training Agency has in fact been able to exert considerable control over the direction of vocational training in further education. Yet it has only a quasi-autonomous existence from the Department of Employment.

[14] See FHEA 1992, ss. 62–70 and Sched. 1.

[15] So far as the higher education is concerned, Griffith has commented that "the explicit and overriding aim of Government is to bring universities within the detailed control of state agencies." J. Griffith, "The Education Reform Act 1988: abolishing the independent status of the universities" (1990) (3) *Education & the Law* 97 at p. 106.

[16] See N. Lewis and D. Longley, "Accountability in Education, Social Services and Health," in *Accountability to the Public* Papers presented at European Policy Forum Conference (1992) p. 20. This problem is not peculiar to regulation of education: see, *e.g.* R. Baldwin and C. McCrudden, *Regulation and Public Law* (1987) at pp. 30–31.

[17] See T. Prosser, *Nationalised Industries and Public Control* (1986), pp. 176–183 and N. Lewis and P. Birkenshaw, *When Citizens Complain: Reforming Justice and Administration* (1993) pp. 34–35.

They are employed to measure quality and value for money in higher education (under the aegis of the HEFCs), vocational training (under Training Agency contracts with Training and Enterprise Councils (TECs) — see below) and the privatised schools inspection service (under OFSTED). The Further Education Funding Council is currently considering performance indicators for the FE sector.[18] Performance indicators for local authorities are being laid down by the Audit Commission as part of the *Citizen's Charter* programme,[19] with separate indicators for each local authority service, including education.[20]

Agency regulation has been particularly evident in areas of service provision where there has been privatisation. Relevant developments in privatisation in the area of education reflect two particular aspects: contracting out and liberalisation (the introduction of competition to break up monopoly power).[21] One example is the conditional public funding of vocational training by private companies. Local TECs, which are comprised of representatives of business organisations of various sizes and voluntary and other organisations operating in a particular locality, sub-contract training connected with awards of National Vocational Qualifications (NVQs[22]) to local providers, including accredited private training organisations and further education corporations (representing colleges).[23] Many large employers, such as Marks and Spencer and British Rail, have been granted Approved Training Organisation status as well as being accredited to run programmes by the awarding bodies. It has been suggested that as a result of this new system, "vocational qualifications have, in essence, been privatised."[24] These organisations have, in effect, been licensed to provide training at public expense

---

[18] See DFE Press Release 68/93 March 4, 1993. Student drop-out rates will be one of the indicators.

[19] See Local Government Act 1992, s. 1.

[20] See Audit Commission, *Citizen's Charter Performance Indicators* (Consultation Paper) (1992), pp. 50–57. The Audit Commission will in due course publish "league tables of performance": The Prime Minister, *The Citizen's Charter First Report: 1992* (1992) p. 55.

[21] See A. Gamble, "Privatisation, Thatcherism and the British State" (1989) 16 *Journal of Law & Society* 1, at p. 9.

[22] The award of NVQs is based on skills-based competence criteria which in essence have to be assessed in a workplace setting. NVQs cover a range of qualifications awarded by bodies such as City and Guilds, RSA and BTEC (the Business and Technician Education Council). Colleges may also offer their own General NVQ (GNVQ) courses.

[23] The role of TECs was first described by the government in the Department of Employment's White Paper *Employment for the 1990s* Cm 540 (1988) Chap. 5. TECs control how the public money allocated to training in their locality is spent, on the basis of their plan for meeting local training needs.

[24] L. Unwin, "Learning to Live Under Water: The 1988 Education Reform Act and its Implications for Further and Adult Education," in M. Flude and M. Hammer, *The Education Reform Act 1988: Its Origins and Implications* (1989), at p. 252.

(TECs presently handle over £2 billion of public money a year). The TECs operate under a contract with the Department of Employment's Training Agency.[25] The question of public accountability in relation to such contracts will become increasingly important and may require new legal and constitutional solutions. As Harden points out, there is a danger that the basic contractual framework within which public services are increasingly provided may diminish their essentially "public" aspect, which may need to be reinforced through measures to safeguard the public interest.[26] At present, TECs are regulated only by the terms of their contracts and a mere expectation that they will publish an annual plan and report. There is, for example, no requirement to publish contracts, which Harden would consider "the bare minimum in terms of structuring the discretion of those whose decisions constitute the 'demand' for public services."[27]

There is a similar contractual basis to the funding of assisted places in independent schools. The assisted places scheme aims to enable children "who might not otherwise be able to do so to benefit from education at independent schools,"[28] by providing for the cost of tuition and other fees up to a prescribed amount, and subject to a contribution based on a means test, to be met by the DFE. Around 34,000 assisted places are financed by the DFE at present. Institutions may only offer places under the scheme if they have a participation agreement with the Department.[29] There is also a contractual basis to the provision of school inspection services by private inspectors, who operate under agreements with OFSTED, secured via competitive tendering. Other services which have been privatised, such as school cleaning and grounds maintenance, have also been subjected to a competitive tendering

---

[25] The contract specifies "programme and management standards and... quantifiable outcome measures relating to target groups to be served, such as qualifications to be obtained, acceptable job replacement rates, business support activities, and unit cost requirements": Department of Employment (1988) *op. cit.* at para. 5.15.

[26] See I. Harden, *The Contracting State* (1992). This is equally true of the privatised school inspection service. Inspectors registered under the ESA 1992 will be hired under contracts issued by the Chief Inspector of Schools — see Chap. 6. For general discussion of the weak accountability of non-departmental public bodies (NDPBs), see N. Lewis, "Regulating Non-governmental Bodies: Privatization, Accountability and the Public-Private Divide," in J. Jowell and D. Oliver (eds.), *The Changing Constitution* (2nd ed. 1989) pp. 219–245.

[27] *Op. cit.* p. 74.

[28] EA 1980, s. 17. For a study of the operation of the scheme, see T. Edwards *et. al., The State and Private Education: An Evaluation of the Assisted Places Scheme* (1989).

[29] Provision is made by the 1980 Act for termination of a participation agreement by either party if certain conditions are met: Sched. 4. Three years' notice is needed, unless the Secretary of State is terminating the agreement because educational standards are not being maintained at the school, or because a condition under the agreement or relevant regulations is not being met.

process.[30] As Harden explains, "if the outside tender is successful the service is contracted out."[31] Recently, the possibility of contracting out the marking of National Curriculum tests was under consideration in the wake of the teaching unions' boycott of assessments and the High Court's ruling (later upheld by the Court of Appeal) that teachers have no statutory duty to test pupils.[32]

Another example of partial privatisation has been government support for the two types of city technology college (CTC). This is provided under agreements whereby the Secretary of State will make payments towards the establishment and running costs of city technology colleges or city colleges for the technology of the arts. These CTCs (there are 15 at present) are classed as independent schools.[33] The Government argued that much of their funding would come from private industrial sponsorship; but it seems that increasing amounts of government money have been required, prompting the comment from the Opposition's education spokesperson that "the government's original intention of setting up private schools with private money has now changed to setting up private schools with public money."[34]

In fact, the assisted places scheme, the CTCs and the new and expanding GM schools sector are said to have blurred the boundaries between public and private schooling, in addition to widening the scope of privatisation within education.[35] Perhaps the most recent development is the provision in the EA 1993 for the establishment of GM schools by private sponsors (see Chapter 4). The Government has conceded that this could enable some independent schools to become state-funded schools.

Licensing is another form of (administrative) regulation. It may be seen as a means of ensuring some measure of government control over

---

[30] Local Government Act 1988, s. 2 and Sched. 1. See S. Bailey, *Cross on Local Government Law* (8th ed., 1991), paras 4.91–4.94.

[31] I. Harden, "Money and the Constitution: Financial Control, Reporting and Audit" (1993) 13 *Legal Studies* 16, at p. 27.

[32] *Wandsworth L.B.C.* v. *N.A.S./U.W.T.* (1993) *The Times*, April 7 (Q.B.D.), April 26 (C.A.); "Marking exams may be privatised," *The Times*, April 15 1993. Wandsworth L.B.C. subsequently announced plans to hire additional staff to conduct the summer 1993 tests for 14 year olds: *The Independent*, April 29, 1993.

[33] ERA 1988, s. 105(1).

[34] Cited in *Education*, July 8, 1988; see N. Clough *et al.*, "Restructuring the Education System?," in L. Bash and D. Coulby (eds), *The Education Reform Act: Competition and Control* (1989) at pp. 41–44.

[35] M. Flude and M. Hammer, "Opting for an Uncertain Future: Grant-Maintained Schools" in M. Flude and M. Hammer *op. cit.*; and G. Whitty and I. Menter, "Lessons of Thatcherism: Education Policy in England and Wales 1979–88" (1989) 16 *Journal of Law & Society* 42, at p. 48.

competitive provision of essential services and utilities. In this respect it is most closely associated with specific areas of largely private commercial activity such as civil aviation and other transport services.[36] Developments in privatisation and corporatism make this means of control particularly relevant to specific areas of education and training provision which have a commercial basis. For example, private education and, as shown above, training, are also in effect subject to licensing control. For the operation of an independent school to be lawful it must be registered on the register maintained by the Registrar of Independent Schools.[37] However, permission to operate such a school is contingent upon the school maintaining appropriate standards of educational provision, staff and premises.[38] Moreover, the welfare of children in independent boarding schools is now intended to be safeguarded by the regulatory regime imposed by the Children Act 1989.[39] The regulations governing qualified teacher status also provide for a licensing regime,[40] for the same purpose that "licensing agencies screen doctors, lawyers . . . to weed out the safe or the unfit."[41] Often qualification depends on having attended an approved training course (that is, one approved by the DFE). The licensing element in entry to the teaching profession has been reinforced by the Government's introduction of the "licensed teacher" scheme, which has made it possible for unqualified teachers to enter teaching and train on the job.[42]

It can be seen, therefore, that a wide range of regulatory measures has been applied to the education system to give effect to and/or underpin recent reforms.

---

[36] See D.R. Miers and A.C. Page, *Legislation* (2nd ed., 1990) pp. 216–217.

[37] EA 1944, s. 70(1). An independent school is a school providing full-time education for five or pupils of compulsory school age which is neither LEA-maintained, GM or a special school not maintained by a LEA: EA 1944, s.114(1) as amended. The Secretary of State may approve an independent school as suitable for the admission of pupils for whom statements of special educational needs are maintained: EA 1993, s. 189.

[38] EA 1944, s. 71(1). See *R. v. Secretary of State for Education and Science ex p. Talmud Torah Machzichei Hadass School Trust* (1985) *The Times,* April 12. Ultimately, and subject to the right of appeal to the Independent Schools Tribunal, the school may be struck off the register if it is considered by the DFE to be "objectionable" on certain grounds. Whitty, however, sees independent schools as subject to less regulation than the privatised utilities: G. Whitty, "The New Right and the National Curriculum," in M. Flude and M. Hammer *op. cit.* pp. 27–28.

[39] ss. 63–66 and 87 and Sched. 6 (note amendments to s. 63 made by EA 1993 s. 292); Children's Homes Regulations 1991 SI 1991 No. 1506; Inspection of Premises, Children and Records (Independent Schools) Regulations 1991 SI 1991 No. 975.

[40] Education (Teachers) Regulations 1989 SI 1989 No. 1319.

[41] S. Breyer, *Regulation and its Reform* (1982) p. 71.

[42] *Supra* (n. 40) Sched. 4.

3. CONSUMERISM

(a) Consumerism, citizenship and public services

Consumerism is said to provide a means of redressing the imbalance of power which exists between the providers and consumers of goods and services,[43] which results from providers' inherent advantages of corporate power and control of resources. It has come to prominence in recent years under initatives designed to provide a new basis for the distribution of public resources for essential services such as education, health and transport. Indeed, the entire *Citizen's Charter*[44] concept in public services policy rests on the notion of consumer empowerment. Choice is the central element of the "competitive market model" which is being employed. Under this model, "consumers' interests are supposed to be protected and promoted by the fact that producers need to compete with each other for custom."[45] In theory, consumers have the "power of exit": if dissatisfied they can "take their business elsewhere."[46] In this way, consumer choice can facilitate the most effective distribution of resources for public services, as these resources can be directed towards providers who satisfy consumer demands (provided they also meet the efficiency and other performance standards set by regulation). The various ways in which, in the context of education, these free market principles have been applied and reinforced through legal rights and duties, are examined at various points throughout the book.

Consumerism in relation to public services is a more diverse concept than it is in the context of a private enterprise market system. Potter suggests that in the public sector there are "five key factors which provide a structural underpinning of consumerism . . . access, choice, information, redress and representation."[47] These are common themes in theoretical and empirical studies of the development of public services consumerism across Europe and beyond.[48] It is clear that, in the public sphere, consumerism rests on the broader notion of "participation." Although the exercise of consumer choice is one facet,[49] participation also involves having a "voice."[50] Public service consumers have a stake

---

[43] I. Ramsay, *Consumer Protection* (1989) p. 12.

[44] H.M. Government, *The Citizen's Charter* (1991) Cm 1599.

[45] P. Woods, "Parents as Consumer-Citizens," conference paper, University of North London, September 1992, pp. 4–5.

[46] R. Hambleton and P. Hoggett, "Rethinking consumerism in public services" (1993) 3(2) *Consumer Policy Review* 103 at p. 104.

[47] J. Potter, "Consumerism and the Public Sector: How Well Does the Coat Fit?" (1988) 66 *Public* Administration 149–164, p. 150.

[48] See J. Epstein, *Public Services: Working for the Consumer* (1990).

[49] P. Woods, "A strategic view of parent participation" (1988) 3 *Journal of Educational Policy* 323.

[50] R. Hambleton and P. Hoggett *op. cit.*

in local services such as education and health and are deemed to have a right to participate in decisions which shape the services on which they depend. Furthermore, although the way that services are provided may be governed by the operation of a quasi-market, there is a need for the public element of these services to be reflected in a degree of public accountability, in which access to information may play a role. Accountability and voice can be provided through various forms of participation, for example consultation and representation. Thus consumers may be represented on the boards and committees that make decisions, as in the case of elected parent governors of schools. The ability to obtain redress is another important element of this wider notion of participation, especially as regards accountability.

These kinds of participation may be seen as the practice of *citizenship*, which is said to be important "in establishing a 'civil society' independent of the state, thereby contributing to pluralism and a dispersal of power, important attributes of a democratic system."[51] Although the enjoyment of citizenship is dependent upon *rights* of participation, since the 1980s Conservative politicians, through the employment of the concept of "active citizenship," have sought to emphasise the *responsibilities* of citizens.[52] Through the active citizenship concept, those on the Right have challenged the strong emphasis on citizens' rights and entitlements in the concepts of citizenship developed by liberal theorists such as Marshall, Plant and Lister.[53] Nevertheless, active participation of the kind that parents may now enjoy in the public education context, fostered by New Right policies on education, is supported by a wide range of rights (as shall be shown).

Yet there is a contradiction, in the sense that some aspects of consumerism, notably the expression of individual choice, seem inimical to this broader notion of citizenship, which has a more collectivist orientation.[54] Thus Ranson distinguishes between the self-interest of the consumer and the public-spiritedness or altruism of the citizen. A consumer, he argues, "expresses self-interest registered privately and

---

[51] D. Oliver, *Government in the United Kingdom: The Search for Accountability, Effectiveness and Citizenship* (1991) p. 32.

[52] See, *e.g.* John Major's Foreword to *The Citizen's Charter* (1991). See D. Oliver, "Active Citizenship in the 1990s" (1991) 44(2) *Journal of Parliamentary Affairs* 157.

[53] T.H. Marshall, *Citizenship and Social Class* (1950); R. Plant, *Citizenship, Rights and Socialism* (1988); R. Lister, *The Exclusive Society: Citizenship and the Poor* (1990).

[54] McHarg argues that the *Citizen's Charter* "is essentially about consumerism rather than citizenship: it tolerates the public sector, but only if it is made to act more like the private sector through competition or competition substitutes": A. McHarg, "The Competition and Services (Utilities) Act 1992: Utility Regulation and the Charter" (1992) P.L. 385–396, 386. See also N. Lewis and P. Birkenshaw, *When Citizens Complain: Reforming Justice and Administration* (1993) p. 37.

with uncertain (though often malign) public consequences."[55] He cites
as an example, the possible deleterious consequences of the private
expression of individual choice for an education "product," a school,
involving a denial of choice to others and economic damage to less
popular schools. The citizen, on the other hand, "has a concern for the
well-being of others as well as the health of society."[56] If this definition
is accepted, the extent to which participation in education decision-
making by parents forms a basis to citizenship will depend on whether
parents' involvement is motivated principally by personal gain or
community advancement. Making this distinction could be extremely
problematic, especially in cases where parents exercise choice collectively. Woods seeks a solution to this problem in his concept of the
"consumer-citizen," which acknowledges the differences between public
(state-citizen) and private (producer-consumer) aspects.[57]

Public policies which have advanced the consumer interest owe their
success to their popular appeal, which in turn has flowed from the
satisfaction of natural desire which the policies have supported. The
classic example is the wish to own one's own home, to which the policy
of selling council houses to their tenants has appealed. In the field of
education, policies advancing parental choice and involvement have
appealed to parents' natural desire to see that their children gain as
much as possible from their education. Thus, establishing a right of
parental choice and involvement has involved little more than
legitimising a deeply felt moral right.[58] Golbey *et al.*, writing about
empirical research into parent governors of schools, note that "the
parents seek a moral right to exercise influence on schools in partnership
with those who know and work closely with pupils."[59]

The Government has emphasised the right of parents "to choose the
schools best suited to their children's needs," stressing in emotive terms
that "parents know best the needs of their children — certainly better
than educational theorists or administrators, better even than our mostly
excellent teachers."[60] However, what this signifies is that despite
exhortations to active and responsible citizenship, the Government has
been particularly keen to promote the opportunities for *personal* gain that
flow from being an education consumer. There has thus been a shift in
focus from "ways to make schooling effective through local community

[55] S. Ranson, "From 1944 to 1988: Education, Citizenship and Democracy," in M. Flude
and M. Hammer (eds) *op. cit.* p. 15.
[56] *Ibid.*
[57] P. Woods (1992) *op. cit.* pp. 9–10.
[58] M. Sutherland, *Theory of Education* (1988), p. 64.
[59] M. Golbey *et al.* (eds), *The New Governors Speak* (1990), p. 22.
[60] *Choice and Diversity*, paras 15.3 and 1.6 respectively.

forms of political participation to those concerned about individual parental involvement as consumers."[61]

(b) Consumerism and education

It was noted earlier that consumerism in relation to public services has been said to combine five key elements: access, choice, information, representation and redress. Examples of developments in the field of education relevant to each of these elements are given below. The discussion is introductory; more detailed analysis occurs in later chapters.

i. *Access*

Access focuses on the idea that a public service should be accessible, and thus truly available, to all who need to make use of it. In theory, every child is guaranteed a state education. But curiously, and in marked contrast to the position in many states with a written constitution (for example, the Netherlands), there is no specific "right" to education enshrined in law in England and Wales. This was demonstrated most graphically in the case of *R. v. I.L.E.A. ex p. Ali and Murshid.*[62] The case, discussed more fully in Chapter 2, concerned a legal challenge based on the LEA's failure to provide a sufficient number of teachers to ensure that all children of primary school age could be offered a school place. The action failed because it was concluded, by Woolf L.J., that the LEA's duty under the EA 1944 to provide "sufficient" schools was merely a "target duty," which this LEA had striven to meet but had been prevented from fulfilling by lack of resources; there had been no illegality. Of course, if access to education can be denied in this way (over 300 children were left without a school place), compliance with the European Convention on Human Rights 1950 and the UN Charter on the Rights of the Child 1989 may be called into question. Both provide for a right to education.[63]

Other aspects of the law relevant to access include the requirement that basic educational provision in state schools must be free,[64] that

---

[61] M.E. David, *Parents, Gender and Education Reform* (1993), p. 115.

[62] (1991) *The Times*, February 21.

[63] See Chap. 7. See also Article 13 of the International Covenant on Economic, Social and Cultural Rights, discussed by D. Feldman in *Civil Liberties and Human Rights* (1993) Chap. 18. Note that Feldman regards the "sufficient" schools duty as in fact giving rise to an implicit "right" to education and argues that this duty, in combination with the duty of parents to ensure their children receive education, means that such international treaty obligations *are* being fulfilled by the U.K.

[64] ERA 1988, s. 106(2). Schools and LEAs can charge for some forms of provision, *e.g.* individual music tuition (s. 106(3)(*a*)): see Chap. 6.

racial or sexual discrimination in admission to or exclusion from an educational institution or in relation to the content of education is unlawful[65] and that access to buildings by disabled persons should be facilitated.[66] Access to education is also affected by the provision of transport[67] and financial support. Thus, so far as the latter is concerned, the freezing of mandatory awards and removal of social security entitlement from most students are said to have hindered access to higher education for students from low income families, despite the provision of loans and discretionary hardship funds.[68]

The degree of access in any particular case may increasingly depend upon the capacity to exercise choice. As later discussion will show (see Chapters 4 and 8), one of the major difficulties with the operation of a market model of choice and competition in education is the differential impact on the educational opportunities of various individuals and groups of consumers.

ii. *Information*

It was stated earlier that consumerism is a means of giving more power to the users of public services. But, as Pearce argues, "consumer power depends on knowledge for choice and accountability."[69] In fact, a wide range of education information must now by law be made available to parents and others. There is the information which LEAs and schools must publish relating to various aspects of the service that they provide.[70] There is also the information that relates to performance indication — following the ESA 1992 (section 16), publication is required of comparative tables of schools' examination and National Curriculum assessment results, truancy rates and pupil destinations. This information is intended to help parents judge the standards being achieved by their local schools and enable those selecting a school to make an informed choice. It is intended to facilitate competition and accountability to the consumer.

Other requirements enable parents to obtain or receive information relating to their child's performance, through annual reports of

---

[65] Race Relations Act 1976 ss. 17–19 and Sex Discrimination Act 1975 ss. 22–25.

[66] Chronically Sick and Disabled Persons Act 1970 s. 3.

[67] LEAs have a legal duty to make arrangements for the provision of free transport for children of compulsory school age living a prescribed distance from school, under s. 55 of the EA 1944, as amended.

[68] See N. Harris, "Social Security, Student Loans and Access to Education" (1991) 54 M.L.R. 258.

[69] P. Pearce, "Access to Information," in N. Harris *et al.*, *The Legal Context of Teaching* (1992) at p. 94.

[70] EA 1980 s. 8, Education (School Information) (England) Regs 1993, SI 1993 No. 1502; ERA 1988 s. 22, Education (School Curriculum and Related Information) Regs 1989 SI 1989 No. 954 as amended. See further Chap. 5.

achievements or via access to their child's school records.[71] Also important is the information which must be provided on rights of redress, since it contributes significantly to the consumer empowerment and public accountability resulting from the provision of information.[72]

iii.   *Choice*

As noted above, choice lies at the heart of consumerism. Selection of a desired product or service forms the basis for a free market economy for the production, supply and consumption of goods and services. But there will always be a question as to whether there can ever be a free market for public services such as education and whether consumer choice can be translated into an absolute right. This is because it is impossible to operate a public service on the basis that consumer choice will be the sole driving force behind the allocation of resources,[73] and because choice is constrained by such factors as the total public investment in the service and the extent of access (above) and local availability.[74] These factors are to some extent politically determined. To take one example, the Government's policy of exerting pressure on LEAs to remove surplus capacity from schools can have a limiting effect on choice. The necessary limitations to choice are implicitly acknowledged in the Government's aim to "secure the optimum balance between choice, diversity and the effective use of resources."[75]

Nevertheless, choice of school has been promoted in various ways. For example, the EA 1980 introduced the right to express a preference for a particular school, which preference can only be denied on limited grounds,[76] coupled with a right of appeal. The ERA 1988 introduced open enrolment (in effect requiring that pupils seeking places at a school continue to be admitted to the limit of the school's physical capacity). Most recently, via the EA 1993, the Government has pursued a policy of diversity in educational provision (see Chapter 2).

Pressure from elements of the Conservative Party for the introduction of a voucher system in the schools system failed (in the mid-1980s) to overcome resistance to what would have amounted to a potentially disruptive and enormously expensive system. Vouchers were seen by

---

[71] Education (Individual Pupils' Achievements) (Information) Regulations 1990 SI 1990 No. 1381, as amended; Education (School Records) Regulations 1989 SI 1989 No. 1261.

[72] *e.g.* school prospectuses must contain information on the local complaints procedure established under s. 23 of the ERA 1988.

[73] J. Potter *op. cit.* p. 150.

[74] As, for example in the availability of places at special schools for children with special educational needs: see Chap. 7. See R. Hambleton and P. Hoggett, *op. cit.* p. 106.

[75] *Choice and Diversity*, para. 4.1.

[76] EA 1980 s. 6, as amended; see Chap. 5.

their proponents, such as Rhodes Boyson and Sir Keith Joseph (who is said to have admired the writings of Hayek and Friedman, both of whom had objections to the principle of state controlled education)[77] as a means of moving education further into the market place. The idea behind a voucher system is that the consumer can 'purchase' a place at the institution of his or her choice up to the nominal value of the voucher. Some versions of this principle recognise the consumer's right to supplement this amount and use the voucher in purchasing a place at an independent school. It can be argued that in the post-ERA 1988 schools sector the combination of open enrolment and local management of schools (LMS) could achieve the same objective as a voucher system.

Despite the potential difficulty with, and it seems, lack of necessity for, the operation of a voucher system in the schools sector, the Government has brought in such a system in the further education sector. The aim, announced in a White Paper, *Education and Training for the 21st Century*, in May 1991, is to provide, by 1996, all 16- and 17-year-olds with a "training credit" enabling them to select a programme of training up to a certain value (currently set at £1,000) from those offered by (in effect) competing NVQ suppliers. Rather than "vouchers," the scheme introduced (called "Futures") in fact involves the provision of a special training "credit card."

Parental choice in respect of the content of the school curriculum is also relevant. Among the issues discussed in Chapter 7 are parents' rights in respect of religious education, collective worship, sex education, special education and examination entry. As will be shown, there is little scope for the exercise of individual choice over the content of education as compared with the (albeit restricted) opportunities to secure choice of school.

iv.   *Representation/Participation in Decision-making*

> "We must give the consumers of education a central part in decision-making."[78]

There is a liberal democratic tradition of local community participation in the education system.[79] Within this, the involvement of parents is seen to be beneficial to children by ensuring that home and school work in partnership and that schools are responsive to parental wishes and promote community interests. This tradition, as opposed to the

---

[77] D. Lawson, *Education and Politics in the 1990s* (1992) p. 40.

[78] H.C. Debs., Vol. 123, col. 772 (December 1, 1987), Mr K. Baker M.P., Secretary of State for Education and Science.

[79] See N. Beattie, *Professional Parents* (1985), which gives an account of this tradition in a comparative study of four countries, including England.

consumerist empowerment/accountability policy dimension, provided much of the impetus for the introduction of parental representation on school governing bodies.[80] However, the consumerist policies of late have also given rise to increased opportunities for participation in some decision-making processes.

There are a number of ways in which participation by parents enables the consumer interest to be represented in the decision-making processes in education.[81] Examples of collective participation in decisions include parental ballots on opting out (GM status) and consultation over school closures, changes to school starting finishing times, etc. Individual participation is also important and may occur in the context of decisions concerning an individual parent's own child, as for example under the regulated assessment and statementing procedures under the EA 1993 for a child with special educational needs. It may also take the form of representing parents as a whole on school governing bodies (see Chapter 3) or serving on an education appeal committee (see Chapter 5).

Evidence backs up claims that parental involvement in education should be seen in a positive light.[82] But the practical reality, as shown in later chapters, is that parents in general fail to capitalise on the opportunities for individual involvement provided by their rights in this area. Indeed, the assumption that parents want to participate may be rash. As Beresford says, it can logically be argued that "people may *not* want such a say," and the argument continues thus: "Why burden them with all the difficulties of developing and providing services when all they want is to *use* them?"[83] Collective participation is more likely to occur, since the opportunity to participate in this way usually arises in the context of proposed fundamental changes to local schools, which often generate considerable local opposition.

The extent to which the opportunities for representation/participation have provided any real empowerment for education consumers, both individuals and groups of consumers, will be considered in later chapters.

v. *Redress*

Redress mechanisms not only provide a potential legal remedy for consumers; they may also have a quality control effect, with providers of services being made aware of "any underlying problems in their

---

[80] P. Woods (1988) *op. cit.* p. 325.

[81] See M. E. David, *Parents, Gender and Education Reform* (1993) pp. 99–102 for typologies of parental involvement.

[82] See J. Sallis, *Schools, Parents and Governors: A New Approach to Accountability* (1988), and S. Jowett *et al. Building Bridges — Parental Involvement in Schools* (1991).

[83] P. Beresford, "Consumer Views: Data Collection or Democracy?" in I. White *et al.*, *Hearing the Voice of the Consumer* (1988) at p. 42.

management systems, policies and practices."[84] In contributing to accountability by providers of public services they have some constitutional significance. Until recently there were relatively few avenues of redress available to education consumers; but since 1980 the scope for challenging decisions and securing a remedy has widened considerably.[85]

The courts, through judicial review procedure, have become increasingly involved in education disputes between parents and LEAs or governors. However, as the courts can only consider the legality of action taken or proposed, such proceedings have not proved a particularly useful means of challenging decisions, because the legislation has tended to confer considerable discretion on education providers.[86] For many years, the availability of an administrative remedy via intervention by the Secretary of State under the default powers in sections 68 and 99 of the EA 1944, powers which he has been extremely reluctant to use, has generally been regarded by the courts as precluding their intervention.[87] Moreover, the absence of a constitutional court and a Bill of Rights in the U.K. has inhibited the courts' involvement in matters of general principle, such as those which have been considered by the U.S. Supreme Court.[88]

The most significant development in the area of redress in education has been the inception of statutory appeal systems. The appeal committees established under Schedule 2 to the EA 1980 have jurisdiction in school admissions cases and cases involving permanent exclusion from school. The EA 1993 has sought to address the problem of lack of independence in these committees through changes to their composition (see Chapter 5). Also under the 1993 Act, appeals by parents concerning provision for children with special educational needs, for example over the content of statements of special educational needs, lie to a new Special Educational Needs Tribunal.[89]

Special educational needs cases have also been prominent among the Commission for Local Administration's case-load. Within the limitations

---

[84] J. Potter *op. cit.* p. 153. See also N. Lewis and P. Birkenshaw, *op. cit.*, p. 27.

[85] For evaluation of the mechanisms currently available, see National Consumer Council, *When Things Go Wrong at School* (1992).

[86] See, *e.g. Meade* v. *Haringey* [1979] 2 All E.R. 1016 and *Secretary of State for Education and Science* v. *Tameside M.B.C.* [1977] A.C. 1124, discussed in Chap. 2.

[87] See N. Harris "Education By Right? Breach of the Duty to Provide 'Sufficient' Schools" (1990) M.L.R. 525–536 for a review of the cases. See also the discussion of ss. 68 and 99 in Chap. 2. These powers may be used "on complaint. . . or otherwise."

[88] An example, on racial segregation in schooling, is the historically important decision of *Brown* v.*United States* (1954) 347 U.S. 483.

[89] See EA 1993, ss. 169 and 170. The 1993 Act has extended special educational needs appeal rights: see Chap. 7.

placed upon it,[90] the Local Government Ombudsman system has provided an important mechanism for the investigation and resolution of a range of education complaints.[91]

Redress of grievance is one of the principal elements in the *Citizen's Charter*, and the Government has emphasised that among the available avenues should be "well-publicised complaints procedures."[92] One education complaints procedure has been introduced by section 23 of the ERA 1988. Each LEA has had to establish a procedure for the investigation and resolution of complaints concerning the discharge by a governing body or LEA of its legal responsibilities in connection with the school curriculum or the provision of information.[93] No complaint on these matters may be entertained by the Secretary of State under sections 68 or 99 of the 1944 Act unless it has first been disposed of by the local complaints procedure.[94] Recent research, discussed in Chapter 7, has revealed flaws in the procedures and ignorance among consumers of the right to complain.

Despite their limitations, these new avenues of redress have been of considerable importance to the development of consumerism in education. The remedies offered not only enable education consumers' rights to be enforced; the various rights of appeal and complaint have also become key elements in promoting a culture of consumerism. Research has revealed parents' willingness to complain if dissatisfied with schooling (although very few actually do so).[95] Moreover, over 15,000 school admissions appeals have been lodged in each of the past few years and several thousand complaints reach the Secretary of State each year, for possible intervention under sections 68 or 99 of the 1944 Act.

---

[90] See P. Birkenshaw, *Grievances, Remedies and the State* (1985) pp. 140–147. See also the judgment of Woolf L.J. in *R.* v. *Commissioner for Local Administration ex parte Croydon London Borough Council and Another* [1989] 1 All E.R. 1033 in upholding the jurisdiction of the Commissioners in respect of school admissions appeals committees. Note that the Local Government Ombudsmen have no jurisdiction over the curriculum, discipline and other internal affairs of a school: Local Government Act 1974, Sched. 5. N. Lewis and P. Birkenshaw (*op. cit.* p. 136) comment that "this presents many anomalies," for example complaints about a child's treatment in a local authority home are within the Commissioners' jurisdiction whereas those about treatment in a state school are not.

[91] See, *e.g.* the role of the Local Government Ombudsmen in special educational needs cases, as shown in Chap. 7.

[92] (1991) Cm 1599, p. 42.

[93] ERA 1988, s. 23(1).

[94] *Ibid.* s. 23(2).

[95] N. Harris, *Complaints About Schooling: The Role of Section 23 of the Education Reform Act 1988* (1992) p. 116.

(c) Who is the consumer?

The existence of consumerism in education is beyond doubt. But, as one writer asks, who exactly are the consumers?[96] In higher education, students themselves can be regarded as the consumers (although if one takes graduates to be the 'product' of the system, employers may also be consumers). So far as schooling is concerned, it tends to be assumed that the parent (and perhaps also the future employer) rather than the child is the consumer of education, largely because this is the way that policy makers and most commentators[97] have seen it. While it is not within the scope of this book to explore at length the principle of child autonomy, it is important to consider whether it is appropriate to deem the parent to be the consumer, especially given the emphasis on children's independent rights and the paramountcy of the child's welfare under certain other areas of the law (notably the Children Act 1989). We must also consider whether gender assumptions are implicit in the notion of parent as consumer.

The assumption that it is the parent alone who is the consumer derives from the traditional protective role that parents are expected to play in respect of their children. This role is often assumed by large sections of society and by policy makers to be the mother's rather than the father's. It has been argued that participation by parents in their children's education is predicated upon gender assumptions, differentiating between mothers and fathers in their respective traditional roles in relation to child-rearing and employment. David considers that this has been true of the liberal-democratic tradition of parental involvement and the strategic development of parent participation under consumerist policy.[98] It may for example, apply to individual involvement in a child's schooling or representative involvement, as a parent governor (for, as shall be shown in Chapter 3, women outnumber men as parent governors).

In any event, responsibility for the development of the child may be shared between parent and state. For example, as regards the attendance of a child at school, parents have a duty to ensure that their children receive an efficient, full-time and suitable education,[99] and the state has a duty to ensure that education is provided. Through such educational provision the education system shares with parents the role of social reproduction, via the inculcation of the values and ideals of the majority or dominant culture. This can sometimes lead to conflict between parent

---

[96] L. Bash, "Education goes to market," in L. Bash and D. Coulby (eds.) *supra* (n. 34) at p. 20.
[97] *e.g.*, R. Deem, "The Reform of School Governing Bodies," in M. Flude and M. Hammer *op. cit.*, pp. 161–162.
[98] M. E. David, *op. cit.*, pp. 158–160.
[99] EA 1944, s. 36.

and state, over such matters as religious education, discipline or sex education, which is not surprising given the centrality of these matters to parents' own cultural values. In essence it is a conflict between parents' and the state's right to decide what is best for the child.[1]

For example, in the dispute between a group of white parents and the LEA in Dewsbury over the authority's decision to place the children at a school where 83 per cent. of the children were of Asian origin, the LEA's decision to back down in the face of a challenge to the legality of their admission procedures was hailed as a victory for parental rights by the parents and their supporters.[2] Similarly, in the *Cleveland* case, when the High Court held that it had not been unlawful discrimination or segregation for an LEA to permit a child to be transferred at her parent's request away from a school with many Asian children to a different school, the parent's solicitor claimed that the case had shown that "parental wishes are paramount."[3]

The concept of parental rights may be in general serious decline: "it has become increasingly difficult to reconcile its existence with the predominant emphasis which the law now places on the welfare of children."[4] The Children Act 1989 has given primacy to children's interests. Yet in the sphere of education the concept of parental rights is flourishing. Calren *et al.* note that "the consumer within the market is generally assumed to be the parent, not the child. There is no mention of children's rights to set alongside the repeated emphasis on parental choice."[5] It has been suggested that parents may legitimately be regarded as the "child's representatives"[6] or, in the context of consumerism, as "consumers by proxy, acting on behalf of their children."[7] It is certainly true that many of the Dewsbury parents claimed to have been acting for the sake of their children. But it is still not clear primarily whose interests or rights were upheld. The rights being asserted may in reality be a reflection of parental responsibility to ensure that a child receives a suitable education, but this raises questions as to whether parents are the best judges of what is suitable. In the light of this Adler argues that "since parents act as agents of their children but are not all equally effective in this regard, children's

---

[1] P. Marson, "Parental Choice in State Education" (1980) *Journal of Social Welfare Law* 193.

[2] *The Times*, July 14, 1988.

[3] *Daily Telegraph*, October 19, 1991. The case was *R. v. Cleveland County Council and others ex p. Commission for Racial Equality* (1991) *Independent* 25 October. Macpherson J's decision was upheld by the Court of Appeal (1992) July 31. This case is discussed in detail in Chap. 5.

[4] A. Bainham, *Children, Parents and the State* (1988) p. 5.

[5] P. Carlen *et al., Truancy — the politics of compulsory schooling* (1992), p. 59.

[6] A. Bainham, *op. cit.*

[7] P. Woods (1988) *op. cit.* p. 323.

interests need to be considered directly."[8] The rapid development of educational consumerism, with its emphasis on parental rights and involvement, may be one of the forces that has actually hindered the development of independent rights for children in the context of education.

Morgan argues that "if there is a consumer, it is most properly the child."[9] Of course, very young children would be expected to be able to enjoy education rights only vicariously, through their parents. But even older children lack the independent rights to participate as education consumers. There are numerous examples of rights enjoyed by parents but not by children themselves. Children have no right to express a preference for a particular school; choice of school is seen as the parent's prerogative. They cannot become school governors (the minimum age for governorship being 18). A child under 16 has no right to see his/her school record. A person aged under 18 has no independent right of appeal against his/her permanent exclusion from school. Only a parent, not the child him/herself, can authorise a child's withdrawal from religious education.

As noted earlier, children's rights are, by contrast, recognised under the Children Act 1989. These include rights as consumers. For example, section 26 of the Act specifically provides that complaints against social services departments may be made by children as well as parents. But, in contrast, the local curriculum complaints procedures under section 23 of the ERA 1988 are generally considered to be for parents alone (the section is actually silent on the matter but the guidance issued by the DES[10] refers to parents but not children). The National Consumer Council recently recommended that all young people aged 16 or over should have an independent right of complaint in education cases.[11]

Research suggests that when section 23 education complaints are investigated and heard there is no attempt to elicit the views of children.[12] By contrast, the courts in family proceedings now have a legal duty to have regard to the "ascertainable wishes and feelings of the child concerned (considered in the light of his age and understanding)."[13] Similarly, the United Nations Convention on the Rights

---

[8] M. Adler, *An Alternative Approach to Parental Choice* (1993) *op. cit.* p. 3. See also M. Adler, "Parental Choice and the Enhancement of Children's Interests" in P. Munn (ed.) *Parents and Schools: Customers, Managers and Partners* (1993).

[9] I. Morgan, "The Politics of Parental Involvement," in F. Macleod (eds) *Parents and Schools: The Contemporary Challenge* (1989) at p. 148.

[10] DES Circular 1/89.

[11] See National Consumer Council *supra* (n. 85).

[12] N. Harris (1992) *supra* (n. 95) p. 54.

[13] Children Act 1989, s. 1(3)(a).

of the Child 1989, now ratified by the UK Government, states that
children should be heard in all matters affecting them, "their views
being given due weight in accordance with their age and understanding."[14] In the recent case of *Re P (A Minor) (Education)*, where the
court had to determine a dispute between parents as to the school which
a boy aged 14 should attend, Butler Sloss L.J. acknowledged that "older
children often have an appreciation of their own situation which is
worthy of consideration by, and the respect of, the adults, and
particularly the courts."[15] All this suggests that the views of children,
especially older children, should be sought in the determination of
questions about schooling. This argument is reinforced by research
findings showing that the choice of GCSE options is generally made by
14 year olds themselves rather than their parents.[16]

The Government acknowledged in the 1992 White Paper that:

"Children themselves, as they grow older and more mature, often
have a well developed sense of their needs and a good grasp of the
quality of teaching they receive. Listening to their views, both
through their parents and directly, can help schools in improving
the standards of their service."[17]

Nevertheless, this is as far as the Government has gone towards
recognising children as consumers in addition to their parents. Indeed,
the Government resisted an attempt to include in the recent Education
Bill a legal duty for the wishes of the children concerned to be taken
into account (i) in relation to any school matter affecting them and (ii)
in decisions on whether they should be taught in a mainstream school or
a special school.[18] However, the new statutory Code of Practice on
special educational needs will, at least, "make provision for LEAs to
take into account a child's wishes and feelings, considered in the light
of his or her age and understanding."[19]

---

[14] Article 12.
[15] [1992] 1 F.L.R. 316, at p. 321. This is in fact a pre-Children Act case. See also *Re* S.
[1992] 2 F.L.R. 313 and M. *v.* M. (Minors) (Jurisdiction) (1993) Fam.Law. 396.
[16] S. Jowett *et al., supra* p. 34.
[17] *Choice and Diversity,* para. 1.6.
[18] See (i) H.L. Debs., Vol. 547, col. 68 (June 21, 1993) and (ii) Official Report, House
of Commons Standing Committee E, col. 1105 (January 26, 1993); in response to
arguments that the Government were resisting an approach affirmed by the Children
Act 1989 (in particular s. 1(1)), the minister said that there was "a difference between
taking full account of a young person's attitudes and responses in a social welfare
context, and asking the child to make a judgment, utter an opinion or give a view on
his or her educational requirements": col. 1108, Mr E. Forth M.P.
[19] H.L. Debs., Vol. 545, col. 489 (April 29, 1993) *per* Baroness Blatch.

4. CONCLUSION

Regulation and consumerism constitute underlying themes in the development of the law in this area, which is intended to give effect to the Government's radical policies for changing the framework of educational provision and many of the control mechanisms within it. Consumerism, which has been shown to be a multi-faceted concept, is a relatively new (and increasingly engendered) phenomenon in the area of public educational provision. Regulation has long been employed in this field, but has increasingly emanated from central government, as LEAs' role has been reduced, and has become more pervasive and taken additional forms.

Although the broad pattern is one of increased regulation, there are exceptions. Attention has, for example, been drawn to the relative lack of regulation in areas such as teachers' and schools' disciplinary authority.[20] There have also been elements of internal regulation inherent in the institutional autonomy which many of the recent education reforms have precipitated, for example in relation to the running of GM schools.[21] Nevertheless, central government and agency controls seek to ensure that schools, colleges and other institutions operate under strict financial constraints. Institutions must also comply with their significant statutory responsibilities. Even so, as schools become increasingly independent of, and in greater competition with, each other, and as greater diversity of provision and publication of a wider range of information enhances choice, there may in the long term be perceived by the Government to be less need for central regulation and even more scope for self-regulation and accountability via consumerism and the marketplace. For example, despite the provision made for more regular and rigorous school inspections and the introduction of stricter central powers in respect of "failing schools," the Government has been keen to emphasise that quality assurance is "in the first instance a matter for governing bodies themselves and their head teachers. They are directly accountable to parents for the performance of their schools."[22] Similarly, the new funding authorities established under the EA 1993, which are responsible for administering funds to GM schools, are expected to keep regulation to a minimum,

---

[20] See Lord Elton (chair), *Discipline in Schools* (1989), para. 72. During the passage of the Education Bill, there was a call for a a "tight legal framework" governing the circumstances when pupils may be excluded from school; and it was said that "parents must know where they stand": Official Report, House of Commons Standing Committee E, Education Bill col. 573 (December 8, 1992), Mr G. Pope M.P.

[21] See H.C. Debs., Vol. 213, col. 661 (November 9, 1992), comments of Mr G. Steinberg M.P.

[22] *Choice and Diversity* para. 3.13.

for the most part.[23] Instead they will operate within a legal framework intended to "permit powers and responsibilities to be devolved to individual schools to the maximum extent possible."[24] The dangers inherent in this approach will be considered in later chapters.

---

[23] But note that a late amendment to the Education Bill requires them to arrange for value-for-money studies of GM schools in appropriate cases: EA 1993, s.8.
[24] *Ibid.* para. 3.7.

2

CONTROL OF THE SCHOOLS SYSTEM

1. INTRODUCTION

In the development of the education system of England and Wales, the broad picture, at least since the 1960s and more especially since the 1980s, has been one of conflict and change. There has been an ideological and political struggle in which central government, local authorities and teachers have been the main combatants. Parents and governors have also been willing to enter the fray to defend their local interests, when threatened. The experience of the most recent past, in which power has increasingly been taken away from LEAs and in which the teaching profession's autonomy has been weakened, is a far cry from the co-operative spirit in which the formative EA 1944 was enacted. That Act is said to have been "the product of war-time bi-partisan optimism and consensus about a better post-war world."[1] Certainly there was no serious opposition to any of the Bill's clauses as it progressed through Parliament.[2] As shall be shown, many of the changes wrought by that Act still provide the basic institutional framework regarding schools provision. But the power relationships within the system have radically altered.

This chapter focuses on the evolving relationship between central government, local authorities and the teaching profession in the control of the schools system. In the next chapter there is analysis of the independence and autonomy of educational institutions, focussing on the changed relationship between government and schools, colleges and universities.

2. EDUCATION AND CENTRAL AND LOCAL GOVERNMENT

(a) The 1944 Act 'partnership' between LEAs and central government

i. *A 'national service, locally administered'*
One of the most notable features of the recent reforms has been a

---

[1] D. Lawton, *Education and Politics in the 1990s: Conflict or Consensus?* (1992) p. 32.
[2] See B. Simon, *Education and the Social Order 1940–1990* (1991) pp. 71–78.

considerable increase in central government control. This has tended to weaken considerably the spirit of partnership between central and local government fostered by the 1944 Act. The 1944 Act resulted in a education system based on a 'national service, locally administered'. The intention was that central government would have a broad directory function, but that responsibility for planning and making provision, and for maintenance and staffing, would be performed by LEAs.[3] It has been argued that the legislators were conscious of the need to diffuse power over education decision-making and avoid concentrating too much control in any particular direction; they were also concerned that power was organised in a way that was appropriate to the functions of the system as a whole.[4]

Under section 1(1) of the Act the Secretary of State for Education was given a duty to:

> "promote the education of the people of England and Wales and the progressive development of institutions devoted to that purpose, and to secure the effective execution by local authorities, under his control and direction, of the national policy for providing a varied and comprehensive educational service in every area."

The section on the face of it placed wide power in the hands of the Secretary of State. But the Minister, R.A. Butler, argued that although central government should play a leading role, the partnership which had developed between it and local authorities should not be weakened or destroyed. Nevertheless, there were fears that the section "could open the door to an educational dictatorship,"[5] and an amendment was proposed (but not carried) to remove the words "under his control and direction" from section 1(1). However, if authoritariansim has developed, it is not the result of this sub-section. In the 1980s far more powerful central controls were introduced, as shown below. Moreover, section 1(1) of the EA 1944 has now been replaced by sections 1 and 2 of the EA 1993, which not only restate the Secretary of State's promotional duty (s. 1), but also confer on him a more pro-active general responsibility to "exercise his powers with a view, among other things, to improving standards, encouraging diversity and increasing opportunities for choice" (s. 2(2)).

---

[3] Defined in s.6, as subsequently amended, as the county councils, district councils in former metropolitan councils and outer and (following the abolition of the Inner London Education Authority in April 1990) inner London boroughs.

[4] See S. Ranson, "From 1944 to 1988: Education, Citizenship and Democracy," in M. Flude and M. Hammer (eds), *The Education Reform Act 1988: Its Origins and Implications* (1990), at p. 3.

[5] H.C. Dent, *The Education Act 1944* (1969) pp. 5–6.

Section 67 of the 1944 Act also gave powers (still subsisting) to the Secretary of State to arbitrate disputes between governing bodies and LEAs and to determine a dispute between two or more LEAs as to which of them (if either any) is responsible for the education of a child.[6] Section 67 has not proved to be of major importance in practice. However, the mediating role of the Secretary of State has since been extended — for example into disputes over the instrument of government for a voluntary school[7] or concerning admission arrangements made between the governors of certain schools and the LEA.[8]

LEAs, on the other hand, were given a broad duty by section 7 (still in force) to, so far as their powers allowed:

"contribute towards the spiritual, moral, mental and physical development of the community by securing that efficient education throughout [primary, secondary and further education] stages shall be available to meet the needs of the population of their area."

They were also required, by section 8, to ensure the provision of sufficient schools in their area (see below). LEAs also had notional control of the school curriculum under section 23 of the 1944 Act (repealed by the E(No. 2)A 1986); but curriculum development and appropriate teaching methods were considered to be in the main matters for the teaching profession.[9] Teachers were thus the third 'partner,' sharing with LEAs the role of determining the content of secular education.

Although laying down the broad functions of LEAs, the law played only a limited role in ordering their structure. It constituted local authorities as LEAs — presently district councils, in the case of former Metropolitan counties, county councils, outer London boroughs and inner London boroughs (formerly comprised in one LEA, the Inner London Education Authority, whose demise under the ERA 1988 is discussed below). It required LEAs to have education committees (whose members had to include persons with experience of education and local education conditions).[10] (The EA 1993 has now abolished the requirement to establish an education committee.[11]) LEAs also had to have a chief education officer.[12] Otherwise they were free to develop their own internal structures.

---

[6] s.67(1) and (2).
[7] See E(No. 2)A 1986 s.2(5)–(7).
[8] EA 1980, s.6(7)–(9), added by the EA 1993 s.270.
[9] S. Ranson, *op. cit.* at p. 3.
[10] EA 1944 s.6(2) and Sched. 1. paras 1 and 2; see *R.* v. *Croydon LBC ex p. Leney* (1987) 85 L.G.R. 466 on qualification for education committee membership.
[11] EA 1993, s.296; see below.
[12] EA 1944, s.88.

The division of the statutory system of education into three "progressive stages to be known as primary education, secondary education and further education"[13] (recognising that "education is a continuous process conducted in successive stages"[14]) has survived all the subsequent legislative changes. The only amendment has been the creation of an optional "middle-school" sector, spanning the primary and secondary stages, under the EA 1964.[15]

ii. *The "sufficient" schools duty*

Also surviving from 1944 is LEAs' duty in section 8 of the 1944 Act. Section 8(1) provides that LEAs must ensure that there are available in their area "sufficient schools" for primary and secondary education (but note the provision in the EA 1993 for transferring to funding authorities responsibility for ensuring the provision of sufficient school places: see below). Further education (FE) was excluded from this basic duty, but an amendment to the 1944 Act by the ERA 1988 required LEAs to ensure "adequate facilities" for FE in their area. Since then, however, sixth form colleges and further education colleges have become further education corporations independent of LEAs, and responsibility for most FE provision has been transferred to the Further Education Funding Councils.[16]

The duty to ensure the provision of sufficient schools does not imply that LEAs actually have to provide all schools necessary in the area.[17] Indeed, CTCs, GM schools and, of course, the private sector are all outside LEA control, and LEA provision is set to shrink further following the EA 1993 (see below).

The "sufficient schools" duty in section 8 means that the schools in the LEA's area must be sufficient in "number, character and equipment" to provide "for all pupils opportunities for education . . . such as may be desirable in view of their different ages, abilities and aptitudes and of the different periods for which they may be expected to remain at school . . ."[18] The idealism surrounding this provision is perhaps best captured

---

[13] *Ibid.* s.7. The definitions of each stage are contained in s.8(1)(*a*) (primary education), 8(1)(*b*) (and s.14 of the FHEA 1992) (secondary education) and a combination of s.41 of the 1944 Act and s.14 of the FHEA 1992 (further education).

[14] White Paper *Educational Reconstruction* (1943) para. 2.

[15] See the EA 1964, s.1, and the Education (Middle Schools) Regulations 1980 SI 1980 No. 918. Such schools will be designated as primary or secondary schools depending upon whether the majority of registered pupils are of primary or secondary school age.

[16] These changes, introduced by the FHEA 1992, are discussed in Chap. 3.

[17] "The duty of securing that sufficient schools are available for providing . . . education of a suitable kind is a different duty from a duty to provide such schools," *per* Neill L.J. in *R.* v. *Birmingham City Council ex p. Equal Opportunities Commission (No. 2)* (1992) *The Times*, October 27 (C.A.).

[18] s.8(1). In an amendment introduced by the EA 1981, regard also has to be had to any special educational needs of pupils: see EA 1944 s.8(2)(*c*).

by the words of Harold Dent, an influential educationalist who had campaigned vociferously for reform prior to the 1944 Act; he said that section 8 "should be hung up in the meeting-room of every local education committee and learned by heart by every citizen... [P]roperly interpreted it will find an appropriate educational opportunity for every boy and girl throughout the period of compulsory schooling and, if desired, beyond it to age 19."[19]

The extent of the responsibility imposed on LEAs by the "sufficient" schools duty in section 8 has long been open to debate. In *Meade* v. *London Borough of Haringey*[20] (discussed more fully below) and *R.* v. *Liverpool City Council ex p. Ferguson and Others*[21] it was held that the duty extended to the provision of staff. However, in *R.* v. *Inner London Education Authority ex p. Ali and Murshid*,[22] which arose out of an alleged breach of section 8 by a LEA which had insufficient teachers to staff its schools, resulting in some 300 pupils being deprived of a primary school place, it was held that the section imposed a "target" but not an "absolute" duty. Provided the LEA was doing all that it reasonably could to rectify the situation, within the financial constraints it had to operate under, and was not acting *ultra vires*,[23] the court had no basis to intervene (*per* Woolf L.J.). This approach is consistent with other judicial interpretations of section 8, under which the sufficient schools duty is seen to be couched in broad and general terms to allow LEAs to have regard to a wide range of considerations which might affect its performance.[24] In *Meade*, for example, the Court of Appeal considered that there might not be a breach of section 8 if the LEA was genuinely doing its utmost to enable its schools system to continue to function efficiently and in the best interests of the children and accordingly decided to close its schools for a time during a caretakers' strike — to avoid provoking a situation which could be detrimental to children's education in the long run. In other words, "the local education authority are entrusted with the duty of running the schools, and if what they do is genuinely directed to that end and is a legitimate

---

[19] H.C. Dent *op. cit.*, p. 13. Dent's book was first published in 1944.

[20] [1979] 2 All E.R. 1016 at 1020 *per* Denning M.R.

[21] *The Times*, November 20, 1985.

[22] *The Times*, February 21, 1990; *The Guardian* March 8, 1990.

[23] *per Associated Provincial Picture Houses Ltd.* v. *Wednesbury Corporation* [1948] 1 K.B. 223 and *Council of Civil Service Unions* v. *Minister for the Civil Service* [1985] A.C. 374.

[24] See the *dictum* of Lord Diplock in *Secretary of State for Education and Science* v. *Tameside Metropolitan Borough Council* [1976] 3 All E.R. 665 at p. 695 and of Denning M.R. in *Meade op. cit.* at p. 1024. In *R.* v. *Hereford and Worcester LEA ex p. Jones* [1981] 1 W.L.R. 768, which concerned a challenge to an LEA's decision, taken in the face of severe financial restraints, to make music tuition an optional extra subject to a fee, the duty in s.8 was held to cover the provision of a basic curriculum of which music tuition could not be said to form a part.

choice of the various options they would not be in breach of that duty."[25] The extent of the discretion surrounding the manner of exercise of the section 8 duty has been emphasised by decisions confirming that when the LEA makes policy decisions on allocating school places[26] or on whether to provide selective or non-selective schools,[27] such decisions are not amenable to legal challenge provided the authority acts *intra vires* and consistent with its other duties, such as those under the Sex Discrimination Act 1975[28] (see Chapter 4).

Section 8 was regarded as a key provision, since it provided in law for secondary education for all, replacing the system of elementary schools that, after the EA 1918, provided elementary education to the age of 14. As Ranson explains, the 1944 Act "realised for the first time Tawney's[29] ideal of universal free secondary education for all directed to the needs and capacities of youngsters rather than dependent upon material well-being, status and power of their parents."[30] But, as Dent acknowledged, "no one could pretend that it is easy to achieve this ideal."[31] It can be seen from the cases on section 8 that the wording of the section itself has meant that LEAs' failure to provide schooling may, in certain circumstances, not be unlawful. Thus while it may be true to say that in broad terms "the Act established the universal right to personal development through education,"[32] such educational opportunity as may be provided to citizens is not founded on an absolute right to education as such, as the *Ali* case in 1990 so emphatically illustrated.

As noted above, the sufficient schools duty takes account of the period for which pupils are required or expected to remain at school. Part of the process of extending provision for pupils of secondary school age involved raising the school leaving age. Section 35 of the 1944 Act set that age at 15, but provided that the minister might raise it to 16

---

[25] *per* Eveleigh L.J. at 1028.

[26] *Cumings* v. *Birkenhead Corporation* [1972] Ch. 12.

[27] See *Equal Opportunities Commission* v. *Birmingham City Council* 1 All E.R. 769 (H.L.), *per* Lord Goff at p. 775.

[28] See *R.* v. *Secretary of State for Education and Science ex p. Keating* (1985) 84 L.G.R. 469; *Equal Opportunities Commission* v. *Birmingham City Council op. cit.; Equal Opportunities Commission* v. *Birmingham City Council (No. 2)* (1992) 90 L.G.R. 492 (Q.B.D.) and *The Times,* October 27, 1992 (C.A.). All of these cases are discussed in Chap. 4.

[29] R.H. Tawney drafted the Labour Party's 1922 education manifesto *Secondary Education for All* and was the Chairman of the Council for Educational Advance set up by the labour movement and teachers in 1942, which campaigned for "immediate legislation to provide equality of education for all children, irrespective of their social or economic condition": stated policy aim, cited in B. Simon *op. cit.* p. 67.

[30] S. Ranson *supra* (n.4) at p. 4.

[31] H.C. Dent *supra* (n.5).

[32] S. Ranson *op. cit.*

by Order in Council when he was "satisfied that it has become practicable" to do so. The school leaving age was, in fact, not raised to 16 until 1972.[33] It was, in any event, assumed that all young people would receive continuing education until the age of 18,[34] although this became a neglected area in the decades that followed. Only in very recent years has the Government begun to address the relatively low education staying-on rate in England and Wales, which is now beginning to improve,[35] and put further education on a proper statutory footing.

iii. *The default powers in sections 68 and 99*

Perhaps the most significant powers given to the Secretary of State by the 1944 Act are contained in sections 68 and 99 — the default powers. The powers have helped to define the relationship between central and local government in education, despite the meagre use made of them and some uncertainty about their role.

Section 68 empowers the Secretary of State, where he is of the opinion that an LEA or the governors of a school are acting or are proposing to act "unreasonably," to give "such directions as the exercise of . . . the performance of [a] duty [under the Act] as appear to him to be expedient." In *Secretary of State for Education and Science* v. *Metropolitan Borough of Tameside,* the House of Lords held that if section 68 directions were issued to an LEA the authority would be statutorily bound to comply with them and could be forced to do so by an order of *mandamus.*[36] *Section 99(1)* states, *inter alia,* that if the Secretary of State is satisfied that the governors or LEA have "failed to discharge any duty imposed on them by or for the purposes of this Act," he make an order declaring them to be in default and "giving such directions for the purpose of enforcing the execution thereof as appear to [him] to be expedient." Unlike section 68, this section states specifically that these directions are enforceable via *mandamus.* These powers may be exercised on complaint by "any person" (section 68) or "any person interested" (section 99) or at the Secretary of State's own intitiative. The DFE has

---

[33] Raising of the School Leaving Age Order 1972 SI 1972 No. 444. Dates on which a person might be deemed to have reached school leaving age were laid down by the EA 1962 s.9, amended by the Education (School Leaving Dates) Act 1976 s.1. The EA 1993, s.235, now provides that such dates may be fixed by the Secretary of State by order.

[34] White Paper *Educational Reconstruction* (1943) para. 3.

[35] In 1987–88 only 50 per cent. of 16 year olds continued at school or in full-time further education; by 1991–92 the figure was approaching 70 per cent. Over the same period the proportion of 17 year olds continuing in education rose from 33 to 50 per cent.: *Choice and Diversity* para. 2.2.

[36] [1976] 3 All E.R. 665 at p. 681 (*per* Lord Wilberforce).

said that the Secretary of State currently receives "thousands of letters a month, a 'huge proportion' of which consists of potential section 68 or 99 cases."[37] This may be one reason why it was provided in the ERA 1988 that curriculum complaints can not be entertained by the Secretary of State unless and until they have been pursued through the local complaints procedure.[38] The ERA 1988 also extended the scope of sections 68 and 99 to cover decisions by governors of GM schools, special schools[39] maintained by an LEA, and LEA-maintained institutions providing further or higher education (or both).[40] Section 9(4) of the EA 1993 has extended their scope still further, to include the actions of the new funding authorities created by that Act (discussed below).

When reviewing the role of the default powers over 10 years ago, the House of Commons Education, Science and the Arts Select Committee found that the DES regarded them as principally for the purpose of assisting the Secretary of State to carry out his broad promotional duty (as regards national education policy) in section 1 of the 1944 Act (above). The Select Committee called, however, for greater default powers to be made available in circumstances in which a "nationally agreed guaranteed provision is at risk."[41] It was concerned at the Department's view that the powers were difficult to enforce and, in any event, a matter of last resort. In response to the call for extending these central powers, the Government said that it was against this because it would be contrary to the notion of partnership between central and local government which the 1944 Act had created[42] — which seems somewhat ironic in the light of recent centralising education reforms.

Prior to the establishment of a detailed legal framework for curriculum delivery and assessment, under the ERA 1988, the principal legal duties in respect of which the default powers were likely to be invoked were those contained in the "sufficient schools" duty in section 8 (above). For example, there were many complaints about inadequacy of provision during the 1980s resulting from cutbacks in local authority

[37] See National Consumer Council, *When Things Go Wrong at School: Redress procedures in the education service* (1992) p. 5.
[38] ERA 1988, s.23(2). The s.23 procedures are discussed in Chap. 7.
[39] For a definition of special school, see p. 43 n. 10 below.
[40] ERA 1988, s.219. Until amendment of s.219 by the FHEA 1992, Sched. 9, the powers in ss.68 and 99 extended to higher education corporations. Sections 68 and 99 are made applicable to the Further Education Funding Council and FE corporations by FHEA 1992, Sched. 8.
[41] *Second Report (1981–82) The Secondary School Curriculum and Examinations* HC 116–1 paras 9.16 and 9.17.
[42] *Initial Observations on the Second Report from the Education, Science and the Arts Committee Session 1981–82* Cmnd 8551.

expenditure.[43] A line of cases going back to 1955 has established that in most cases complaints concerning breach of section 8 should be pursued via sections 68 or 99 rather than via applications for judicial review. In one case, where there was a successful challenge to the Secretary of State's failure to intervene in the case of a boy with dyslexia whose special educational needs were not being met by the LEA, Woolf J. (as he then was) commented that if the Secretary of State exercises his functions properly under sections 68 and 99 "that should have the beneficial effect of avoiding the courts getting involved in education matters, which they are much less equipped to deal with than the Secretary of State."[44]

The earliest case was *Watt* v. *Kesteven County Council*.[45] The plaintiff had argued that the LEA had acted unlawfully under section 8 in failing to fund places for his twin sons at the independent Roman Catholic grammar school of his choice. Both Denning and Parker L.JJ. emphasised that the duty in section 8 was enforceable only via complaint to the minister under section 99.[46] In *Bradbury* v. *London Borough of Enfield*,[47] one of several cases arising out of LEAs' introduction of comprehensive schools in the 1960s (see below), Diplock L.J.[48] compared section 99 with a section of the Public Health Act 1875 which contained a similar default power and which the House of Lords had therefore held deprived the aggrieved citizen of a remedy in the courts in respect of nonfeasance.[49] It was clear, however, that the court could intervene if there had been direct contravention of a specific duty contained in the Act. Thus the LEA's failure to give the required notice (under section 13 of the 1944 Act) of ceasing to maintain eight of its schools, part of its process of establishing a system of comprehensive schools, was justiciable. There was an express statutory prohibition against implementation of the changes without the approval of the Secretary of State, and the failure to give the appropriate public notice rendered ineffective the approval which had been given in the instant case. However, part of the plaintiffs' case was that the premises of the other schools affected by the proposed changes would not be of the standard required by the 1944 Act. This aspect was considered by

---

[43] See, *e.g.* the campaign in Northamptonshire in the early 1980s, discussed in P. Meredith, *Government, Schools and the Law* (1992) Chap. 4.

[44] *R.* v. *Secretary of State for Education and Science ex p. Chance* (1982) July 26, unreported, but set out in P. Liell and S.B. Saunders, *The Law of Education* 9th ed. p. F[77].

[45] [1955] 1 All E.R. 473 (C.A.).

[46] At pp. 477 and 480.

[47] [1967] 3 All E.R. 434.

[48] *Ibid.* at p. 442.

[49] *Pasmore* v. *Oswaldtwistle Urban District Council* [1898] A.C. 387.

Lord Denning M.R. to be within the Secretary of State's exclusive
jurisdiction under section 99.[50]

The exclusivity of the remedy in section 99 was considered further by
the Court of Appeal in *Meade* v. *Haringey L.B.C.*[51] The case centred on
a decision by the LEA to close all of its schools from a particular date
on which a strike by school caretakers and ancillary staff was to
commence. Seven days after the closures the authority issued a statement
indicating that it was in sympathy with the strike but had sought to
lessen its impact on the schools by negotiating concessions from the
trades unions involved and by following a conciliatory line. After three
weeks, when the schools had not re-opened, a parent issued a writ
against the authority, seeking a declaration that the authority was in
breach of section 8 of the 1944 Act and an interim injunction forcing it
to re-open the schools. By the time the case came to trial the unions
had modified their stance and the schools were closed on only one day
per week. The trial judge refused to grant an interim injunction,
holding that the authority's failure to open the schools amounted to
nonfeasance, which was non-justiciable. There had been no improper
motive or failure to take account of relevant factors. In the Court of
Appeal, Denning M.R. pursued the same line of reasoning as the court
adopted in *Bradbury*, although he emphasised that the existence of the
administrative remedy in section 99 did not preclude intervention by
the courts where the LEA "flies in the face of the statute, by doing
something which the statute expressly prohibits, or failing to do
something which the statute expressly enjoins, or otherwise so conducts
itself, by omission or commission, as to frustrate or hinder the policy
and objects of the Act."[52] Where there was, what Eveleigh L.J. in the
instant case referred to as a "simple failure," a complainant would be
left with recourse under section 99 only. Eveleigh L.J. in fact felt that
there had not been a simple failure but rather a situation "where
educational facilities exist and are being used by all concerned [and] the
authority take a decision positively to stop production as it were . . .
bringing the system to a halt."[53] In the event, however, the court
declined to award a declaration in what were interlocutory proceedings,
or an injunction. In their Lordships' view such remedies (which are, of
course, discretionary) would, on the balance of convenience, have been
difficult to enforce and would have amounted to an undesirable
interference in an industrial dispute.

The role of section 99 in remedying an alleged breach of the
"sufficient" schools duty in section 8 was considered most recently in

---

[50] *per* Lord Denning M.R. at p. 441. See also Diplock L.J. at p. 450.
[51] *Supra* (n.20).
[52] *Ibid.* at p. 1024.
[53] *Ibid.* at p. 1028.

the case of *Ali and Murshid*,[54] referred to above, which arose out of teacher shortages in the London Borough of Tower Hamlets and a consequential lack of school places for some 300 or more children. Woolf L.J. confirmed that the jurisdiction of a court to review a decision of a public authority was not ousted by the existence of a statutory complaints procedure; but in the instant case there were no grounds for judicial intervention because the authority, in trying its utmost to remedy the situation, was not, to borrow Denning M.R.'s phrase, "flying in the face of the statute." This conclusion was in large part inevitable, given the nature of the duty itself. Failure that might fly in the face of section 8 would, for example, be a failure to ensure the provision of *any* primary schools. But the "sufficient" schools duty is essentially broad and general in nature, and the courts have regarded a mere failure of the broad aspect of the duty as non-justiciable.

The existence of default powers such as those in sections 68 and 99 is often taken to imply the exclusivity of the administrative remedies offered by them, as noted above. Professor Wade has suggested that the courts' view that statutory default powers can provide a substitute for ordinary legal remedies is based on a perception that "the nature of the duty made it unsuitable for enforcement by private action or that, in other words, Parliament did not intend to make it a duty owed to individuals personally."[55] In *Ali,* Woolf L.J. felt that one of the applicants' claim for damages arising out of the alleged breach of section 8 must fail because the section was "intended to enure for the public in general and not intended to give the individual litigant a cause of action."[56] So, as Wade says, it is "reasonable to suppose that the general obligations of public authorities in the areas of health, education and welfare are not intended to be enforceable at the suit of individuals,"[57] although, as he goes on to point out, the courts have recognised on several occasions that the default powers do not supply an adequate remedy in every case — in particular where there has been defiance of "a direct prohibition in the Act of certain acts by a local education authority" (*per* Lord Denning M.R. in *Bradbury*[58]), or a failure in respect of a very specific duty, or where an authority has acted *ultra vires* in reaching its decision and exercising its discretion.[59]

---

[54] *Supra* (n.22).
[55] H.W.R. Wade, *Administrative Law* (6th Ed., 1988) p. 749.
[56] For another illustration of this approach see *Calverley* v. *Chief Constable of Merseyside* [1988] 3 All E.R. 385 (C.A.).
[57] *Op. cit.* at p. 750.
[58] *Op. cit.* at p. 440.
[59] *Meade* v. *Haringey L.B.C. op. cit.* at 1024–1025 *per* Lord Denning M.R. See also *R.* v. *Secretary of State for the Environment ex p. Ward* [1984] 2 All E.R. 556 at p. 566, *per* Woolf J.

A final question relating to section 99, and section 68 for that matter, concerns the extent of the Secretary of State's discretion in the use (or non-use) of these default powers.[60] As noted earlier, there has been a general reluctance on the part of the Secretary of State to use these powers — in some cases despite great public pressure, as for example in the Dewsbury dispute.[61] Similarly, in *Ali and Murshid*,[62] the Secretary of State refused to use his power in section 99 and declare the LEA to be in default, a decision vindicated by the court's eventual conclusion that the authority was not in breach of section 8. When the Education Bill was before Parliament in 1944 the Government resisted pressure to make these powers subject to judicial scrutiny. Lord Selbourne commented that as decisions taken under section 68 were "a matter of administration" it would be inappropriate to enforce such a check on the Secretary of State's powers.[63] Thus, in *Bradbury*, Diplock L.J. commented that if the Secretary of State "fails to take steps which are available to him under section 99 of the Act of 1944 he is responsible to Parliament, but not to this court."[64] Similarly, in *Tameside*,[65] the House of Lords said that evaluation of an LEA's act or omission was for the Secretary of State alone; the court could not substitute its view for his. The court might have an inherent jurisdiction to review a minister's subjective decision, but it could not interfere if the Secretary of State had "directed himself properly in law and had in consequence taken into consideration the matters which on a true construction of the Act he ought to have considered and excluded from his consideration matters that were irrelevant to what he had to consider."[66] In only one case so far, *R. v. Secretary of State for Education and Science ex p. Chance*,[67] has there been a successful challenge to the Secretary of State's refusal to use one of the two default powers. There the Secretary of State had failed to intervene via section 99 on behalf of the parents of a dyslexic boy, despite a clear breach by the LEA of its duty to secure that there was provision in respect of the child's special educational needs.

The Secretary of State's reluctance to use these default powers may, in the past, have resulted from an overly-modest estimation of their potential for control.[68] But a minister recently commented that "section

---

[60] A power similar to that in s.99, relating to local authority social services departments, may be found in s.84 of the Children Act 1989.
[61] See Chap. 4.
[62] *Op. cit.*
[63] H.L. Debs., Vol. 132, No. 72, cols. 960–961 (July 18, 1944).
[64] *Supra* (n.47) at p. 440.
[65] *Supra* (n.24).
[66] *Ibid.*, *per* Lord Diplock at p. 695; see also Lord Wilberforce at pp. 681–682.
[67] *Supra* (n.44).
[68] B. Salter and T. Tapper, *Education, Politics and the State* (1981) p. 106.

68 is powerful and all-embracing."[69] There has been a rapid move away from a consensual approach in education policy-making in recent years, with central government acquiring many new powers of control and regulation, and this has resulted in the Secretary of State's far greater assertion of power over the education system. Thus any reluctance to use the default powers may stem from the courts' insistence that the 1944 Act only contemplates intervention by the Secretary of State under these powers in somewhat extreme cases.[70]

(b) Education Act 1993: funding authorities and control and rationalisation of the supply of school places

The creation of funding authorities (FAs) under the EA 1993 threatens LEAs' future role under section 8 of the 1944 Act, discussed above. The FAs, in England the Funding Agency for Schools (FAS) and in Wales the Schools Funding Council for Wales, will have between 10–15 and 8–12 members respectively, appointed by the Secretary of State, who, in appointing the members, must have regard to the desirability of including persons with the prescribed experience in, or who have demonstrated capacity in, (i) primary or secondary education, (ii) provision in denominational schools, (iii) industrial, commercial or financial matters, or (iv) special educational needs and provision.[71] Although their principal functions are those which were previously carried out by the DFE in relation to GM schools, most particularly the payment of grants, they could also take over certain functions from LEAs. The role of LEAs, which will in any event be undermined by reductions in the number of schools maintained by them as GM status spreads, will be particularly threatened by the Secretary of State's power to transfer to the FAs all or part of the responsibility for ensuring that there are sufficient school places in the area. He can order joint responsibility once more than 10 per cent. of pupils in state primary and/or secondary schools in an area are being educated in GM schools.[72] A complete transfer of this responsibility to a funding authority may be ordered where that proportion has risen to 75 per cent.[73] Transference can be effected in primary and secondary sectors separately.[74]

---

[69] Official Report, House of Commons Standing Committee E., col. 636, (December 10, 1992), Mr E. Forth M.P. (Under-Secretary of State, Schools).

[70] But see the threatened use of the default powers against LEAs which use intimidation to discourage support for opting out — below.

[71] ss.3 and 4. (ii) applies only to state sector schools.

[72] s.12(1)(a) and (4)(a). Special schools are not included in this calculation.

[73] s.12(1)(b) and (4)(b) Sched. 2, para. 5.

[74] s.12(2)(c); see Official Report, House of Commons Standing Committee E, col. 440 (December 3, 1992).

If all of the responsibility is transferred, LEAs will only be able to establish a new school if it is to replace an existing one.[75] This is a most severe restriction on the long-standing role of LEAs as providers of schools. It is not merely intended to limit the role of LEAs but is part of the Government's strategy for rationalisation of school places which, the Government argues, tends to be hindered by local political considerations.[76] In the past the Government has used persuasion (via departmental circular), reinforced by financial pressure, to encourage the removal of surplus capacity at a time of falling school rolls, especially in inner-city areas.[77] Many authorities have responded positively; for example, Gloucestershire reduced provision and shed 60 teaching posts in 1991–92 after the Government accused the authority of carrying several thousand surplus places.[78] Already, some of the performance indicators for education set by the Audit Commission under the *Citizen's Charter* programme refer to the minimisation of surplus capacity (although they indicate that a little surplus capacity is desirable in the interest of maximising parental choice).[79] But now that up to 1.5 million surplus places exist nationwide[80] — described as "a significant and unacceptable waste of resources"[81] — the Government has decided that stern measures are needed. The 1993 Act has given the Secretary of State a power to compel a reduction of surplus capacity by directing the funding authorities and/or LEA/governing body of a voluntary aided school to present him with proposals for rationalisation; and he can set a timetable for this.[82] He can also present a rationalisation scheme himself.[83] Any such rationalisation proposals will, however, have to be considered at a public inquiry.[84] These changes are discussed further in Chapter 4.

---

[75] Sched. 2 paras. 6 and 7.

[76] *Choice and Diversity*, paras 4.1 and 4.2.

[77] Meredith (1992) *op. cit.* pp. 115–127 assesses the impact of the use of circulars to encourage rationalisation of school places.

[78] *T.E.S.*, October 23, 1992.

[79] The Audit Commission can require local authorities to publish information giving relevant information on performance: ss.1 and 2 of the Local Government Act 1992. Indicators are set out in Audit Commission, *Citizen's Charter Performance Indicators* (Consultation Paper) (1992); see especially pp. 52 and 53.

[80] The Association of Metropolitan Authorities has argued that the Government has overestimated the total by some 500,000: *T.E.S.* October 23, 1992.

[81] *Choice and Diversity*, para. 4.2.

[82] EA 1993, s.232. See also the power to direct an LEA or governing body of a voluntary school to bring forward proposals for *additional* provisions where this is required: s.233, discussed in Chap. 4.

[83] s.234.

[84] s.235.

The creation of the FAs represents a further weakening of local accountability for educational provision.[85] They join the growing list of Government appointed regulatory agencies which are accountable only to the relevant Secretary of State (although, through him/her, also to Parliament). Some may question the appropriateness of the resolution of disputes between LEAs and the FAs over their remit, and the determination of complaints about FAs' activities, being the Secretary of State's responsibility.[86] Although the FAs are subject to the broad duty in EA 1944 section 76 to have regard to parental wishes, it is well known that this section is of merely token significance as regards accountability to parents (see Chapters 4 and 5).

(c) Education in London

In may respects the Government's antagonism towards the Labour controlled Inner London Education Authority (ILEA) was symptomatic of a wider distrust of LEAs. Immediately prior to ILEA's abolition, the basis for this antagonism was the alleged shortcomings of the authority itself — said by the Government to be its excessive size, remoteness and bureaucracy, its inefficiency, the poor educational standards in its schools, and its financial and curricular extravagance. Yet at the heart of the matter was the sheer dominance of the Authority. This dominance was rooted in the establishment of an independent education body for London in the 19th Century. Prior to its abolition under the EA 1902, educational provision for the children of London was under the control of the London School Board. The Board had set in motion the pioneering tradition of education in London. Furthermore, it had been prepared to invest large sums in a bid to help tackle the social problems of the working-class slum areas of London, and at one point education spending per child in London was around 50 per cent. higher than in the rest of the country.[87] From 1902–1965 education in London was the responsibility of the London County Council, which "became a showcase for progressive policies."[88] It was during this period that the political tension between Conservative central government and the Labour dominated County Hall took root.

The ILEA was established in 1965, as a "special committee" of the Greater London Council (GLC). Many of the areas it served were areas of extreme social deprivation, with large immigrant communities. The

---

[85] See generally M. Grant, "Central–Local Relations," in J. Jowell and D. Oliver (eds.) *The Changing Constitution* (2nd ed., 1989) pp. 247–272. See also the comments of Opposition M.P.s during the Committee stage of the Education Bill: Official Report, House of Commons Standing Committee E cols 439–442, (December 3, 1992).

[86] EA 1993, ss.20 and 9(4) respectively.

[87] S. Maclure, *Education Reformed* (2nd ed., 1989) p. 115.

[88] *Ibid.* p. 116.

ethnic mix, in combination with the left-wing political idealism of the 1960s and 1970s, was instrumental in the development of anti-racism policies, which the Conservatives later argued had, in common with other policies, signified self-indulgence, profligacy and political interference with the curriculum. In 1975, the "William Tyndale affair" brought education in one part of London in disrepute, helping to create a climate of concern in which the Prime Minister, James Callaghan, delivered his famous speech at Ruskin College in 1976 about the importance of achieving higher educational standards for the nation's children. This precipitated the so-called Great Debate about the future of education in England and Wales. The Tyndale affair concerned a small primary school in Islington, the teachers in which were, despite intense parental opposition, not only firmly wedded to a notion of child-centred education but also were "possessed by an apocalyptic vision of the role of education in achieving social change."[89] Parents took their children away from the school as egalitarian pupil-teacher structures were introduced and "the media coverage of the affair brought into public prominence for the first time the idea of the so-called 'loony-left' teacher."[90] When the ILEA carried out an inspection the teachers went on strike. Subsequently, adverse media coverage prompted the ILEA to hold a public inquiry.[91] The Tyndale affair helped to foster a lasting spirit of mistrust about the teaching profession among those on the political Right. Although a report by HMI in 1980[92] seemed to suggest that the lessons of the Tyndale affair had been learnt by the ILEA, the avowed intention of the Conservative Government elected in 1979 to attack the vested interests in local government eventually led it to consider ways of reducing or removing the power of the ILEA.

The Local Government Act 1985, which abolished the GLC, enabled the ILEA to survive as a directly elected single purpose education authority. However, Government attention was turned to the ILEA after the 1987 general election and following publication of a report on education in London by the Senior Chief of HMI. This, while now considered to be reasonably balanced between criticism and support,[93] contained sufficient ammunition for opponents (for example it found that 40 per cent. of lessons in secondary schools were unsatisfactory or poor). Critics of the ILEA, including many leading Conservatives, pointed to the poor standards being achieved at high costs. A poll of

---

[89] B. Simon, *Education and the Social Order 1944–1990* (1991) p. 445.

[90] C. Jones, "The Break-up of the Inner London Education Authority," in L. Bash and D. Coulby, *Education Reform Act: Competition and Control* (1990), p. 88.

[91] R. Auld, *William Tyndale Junior and Infants School Public Inquiry* (1976).

[92] DES, *Report by HM Inspectors on Educational Provision by the Inner London Education Authority* (1980).

[93] D. Lawton, *supra* (n.1) p. 59.

parents came out in favour of the retention of the ILEA, but the authority was doomed.[94]

The ERA 1988 made individual inner London boroughs responsible for education in their own areas. It also gave considerable control to the Secretary of State in the transition period in which power and authority were transferred from the ILEA to the boroughs. Provision had to be made for the transfer not only of functions, but also personnel and property. The 1988 Act gave the Secretary of State powers to regulate these transfers via statutory instrument.[95] The ILEA itself was abolished on April 1, 1990.

The Government found it convenient to give the London Residuary Body, which had been set up under the Local Government Act 1985 to take over certain of the functions of the GLC, a key role. It was put in control of the disposal of ILEA property, the payment of compensation and redundancy pay to ILEA employees, and the administration of staff pensions and the ILEA's final accounts.[96] A Staff Commission was appointed to advise the Secretary of State on various aspects of staffing under the changes. Categories of staff (and individuals) were transferred to the LEAs (with no break in continuity of service) if designated;[97] otherwise staff were made redundant.[98] During the transition period there were controls over contracts worth over £15,000 and restrictions on the disposal of property by the ILEA, in that any such transactions required the Secretary of State's express approval.[99] Each inner London borough had to prepare a development plan detailing the schools and property formerly controlled by the ILEA that it proposed to maintain after 1990.[1] There had to be consultation over the plan and account had to be taken of guidance issued by the Secretary of State, who had the ultimate say over which schools were designated to which authority.[2]

Given its antipathy towards the way education had been managed in London in the past, the Government was determined to leave nothing to chance in its bid to ensure that new, sounder practices were introduced. The Act required all the boroughs' management structures for education

---

[94] C. Jones, *op. cit.* p. 94.

[95] s.231. See DES Circular 6/88 *The Transfer of Responsibility for Education in Inner London* (1988).

[96] ERA 1988, ss.176–186.

[97] *Ibid.* s.172.

[98] For other provision on staff transfers, including compensation for lost employment, see ERA 1988, ss.173–175, 178 and 179 and a long list of orders.

[99] ERA 1988, ss.188–191; the Education (Inner London Education Authority) (Property Transfer) Order 1990 SI 1990 No. 124; Amendment Order 1990 SI 1990 No. 313; and (No. 2) Order 1990 SI 1990 No. 772.

[1] s.165(1) and (2).

[2] Education (Inner London Education Authority) Schools Designation Order SI 1989 No. 1280 and Amendment Order SI 1990 No. 480.

to be approved by the Secretary of State.[3] Furthermore, the boroughs were required to consult the Secretary of State over their choice of chief education officer or holder of other designated posts.[4] Consultation for this purpose was defined as sending the Secretary of State a proposed appointee's curriculum vitae.[5] The process of vetting was reinforced by a power of veto where the Secretary of State was of the opinion that the person selected was "not a fit person to hold the appointment in question."[6] Such consultation and control is required until April 1, 1995. The Secretary of State has been able to exert other controls, such as a power to block inner London staff pay increases if he considers that the new rate would be "excessive" having regard to levels of remuneration paid to local authority employees engaged in comparable work.[7]

Thus while the abolition of the ILEA was a decision for Parliament in the 1988 Act, the process of transference has been closely regulated and controlled by the Secretary of State.

The abolition of the ILEA was clearly a major landmark in the transformation of central-local government relations and, more particularly, in the changing pattern of control of the schools system.

(d) Uniformity versus diversity

i. *Introduction*

"As we approach the next century our education system will be characterised not by uniformity but by diversity."[8]

This statement by a Government minister illustrates the emphasis in current government education policy on breaking down the barriers to choice which uniformity of provision, associated most closely with the LEA-maintained sector, is claimed to represent. There are already two new forms of state school, both outside LEA control — the GM school and the CTC. The Secretary of State now has a statutory duty to encourage diversity of provision[9] and is currently promoting greater specialisation among schools (see below).

In fact, the 1944 Act itself had provided for diversity of provision. In addition to the county schools (which today approximately three-quarters of children in the maintained sector attend) and special schools,

---

[3] s. 169.
[4] s. 169(4)–(6).
[5] s. 169(7).
[6] s. 169(8).
[7] s. 170.
[8] H.C. Debs., Vol. 213, col. 769 (November 10, 1992), Mr N. Forman M.P. (Under Secretary of State for Further and Higher Education).
[9] EA 1993, s.2(2), *op. cit.*

the Act gave religious denominations the opportunity to run, in the state sector, schools of a particular religious character (called "voluntary" schools, of which there are presently 8,000 altogether).[10] As will be shown in Chapter 3, voluntary schools have enjoyed a degree of independence from LEAs whilst receiving most of their funding from the state. There is, of course, also an independent sector, which, whilst at various times threatened by the Labour Party with abolition or nationalisation, has survived and presently caters for over half a million children. Indeed it has benefited from the element of privatisation that occurred with the introduction of the "assisted places" scheme under the EA 1980.[11]

Despite the different categories of school in the state sector, there has tended to be a high degree of uniformity — in the case of secondary schools, most particularly after the introduction of comprehensive schools in the 1960s. As will be shown, Government reaction against uniformity today reflects in part a continuing rejection of the comprehensive schools policy developed in that era.

ii. *Comprehensive schools*

One of the most testing periods in central-local relations on education matters prior to 1979 occurred in the mid to late 1960s, when the Labour Government promoted the introduction of non-selective comprehensive schools in the secondary sector. This policy precipitated not only localised conflict over the closure or change of character of a particular school, but also an ideological conflict over the issue of selection which continues to this day.

The 1943 Norwood Report[12] had recommended a system that would cater for the differing needs of pupils, which it concluded could be met in three different types of secondary school, each of which would enjoy "parity of esteem": "Grammar" (providing academic education for those destined for the professions, business or white collar appointments); "Technical" (specialising in education for the more technologically minded); and "Modern" (offering a more varied curriculum for the less

---

[10] EA 1944, ss.9 and 15. County schools are LEA-maintained and non-denominational. Voluntary controlled schools are also LEA-maintained, but have foundation governors and are denominational (most are Church of England). Voluntary aided schools (most of which are Roman Catholic) are similarly constituted but have to find 15 per cent. of certain of their maintenance costs (EA 1944 s.15(3)). Special agreement schools, of which there are about 100, are also mostly state-funded — on the basis of an agreement between the LEA and the school. Special schools are specially organised to make special educational provision for pupils with special educational needs and must be approved for that purpose: EA 1993, s.182(1).

[11] See *supra* p. 6.

[12] *Report of the Committee of the Secondary Schools Examination Council on Curriculum and Examinations in Secondary Schools* (chair: Cyril Norwood) (1943) pp. 1–15.

academically able). Although the tripartite system was not legislated for in the 1944 Act, LEAs were encouraged by ministerial circular and pamphlet to organise their schools along these lines. Technical schools did not prove viable, however, and for the most part a bipartite system developed.[13]

Although, initially, the secondary modern schools were popular with teachers, especially those imbued with a pioneering spirit, they eventually suffered low esteem as a result of being discouraged from offering academic courses and receiving a disproportionately lower share of funding than grammar schools. Furthermore, it became apparent that the secondary schools system reflected and reinforced social divisions. In a system based on selection, the importance of achieving success in the 11-plus tests was considerable and the tests were thus a cause of anxiety for parents and children. It was clear, however, that because the 11-plus was a local examination there were variations in the standard required for a pass. Furthermore, there was evidence that around 10 per cent. of children were being allocated to an unsuitable type of school.[14] Although the Conservative Government's White Paper in 1958 proposed the preservation of grammar schools (but modifications to secondary modern schools), political pressure for the removal of selection was mounting, reinforced by a "social movement of some significance."[15] From 1962–64, the major local authorities, especially those in the North of England, determined to introduce non-selective "comprehensive" schools. A partial recognition of the impetus for change occurred with the Conservatives' EA 1964, which made possible the introduction of "middle" schools for children in the 8–13 age range (as noted above).

Initially it looked as though the Labour Government would seek to make it compulsory for all secondary schools to be turned into comprehensives. The Labour Party Conference report for 1963 noted an agreed commitment to achieve comprehensivisation by "converting existing permissive legislation into compulsory legislation binding upon local authorities."[16] In the event, however, the Labour Government elected in 1964 chose encouragement and persuasion.

DES Circular 10/65 (July 1965) aimed to encourage LEAs which had not reorganised to prepare and submit proposals by July 1966. However, by the autumn of 1965, 12 LEAs were defiantly refusing to submit plans or were postponing them indefinitely. A second circular (10/66) threatened the withholding of central government grants for capital projects in respect of school building inconsistent with the

---

[13] P. Sharp and J. Dunford, *The Education System in England and Wales* (1989) p. 21.
[14] A Yates and D.A. Newnes, *Admission to Grammar Schools* (1957).
[15] B. Simon, *supra* (n.89) p. 271.
[16] Cited in *ibid.* at p. 275.

national policy of comprehensivisation. This might have been amenable to legal challenge but was never subjected to it.[17] However, a series of legal challenges to local decisions on schools reorganisation were mounted in the late 1960s by parents and governors;[18] but they were mostly unsuccessful and failed to halt the tide of comprehensivisation. By January 1969, only six LEAs retained selection. A Bill was prepared to force these authorities into compliance, but the election of a Conservative Government in 1970 sank it at the committee stage. The new Government withdrew Circular 10/65, replacing it with Circular 10/70 which indicated that change for change's sake in local schooling was to be avoided.

The return of a Labour Government in 1974 saw renewed pressure on LEAs to eliminate selection.[19] This time school building projects would only be funded where actually needed for comprehensive reorganisation, and legislation would be introduced if it proved necessary.[20] There had been only 262 comprehensive schools in 1965, but by 1976 there were 3,387.[21] Nevertheless, in February 1975 around one quarter of pupils still sat the 11-plus.[22] When political control of Tameside LEA changed, in 1975, shortly before it was due to introduce comprehensive schools, and the authority's new Conservative administration decided to abandon the reorganisation plans, the Secretary of State issued a direction to the LEA under section 68 of the 1944 Act (above). But when the dispute was taken to the courts, the House of Lords held that, for a variety of reasons, and in particular the fact that the LEA's abandonment of the proposals was supported by the electorate and parents, there were no grounds upon which the Secretary of State could legitimately base her assertion of unreasonableness on the part of the LEA.[23] In any event, the Government had determined on drastic action against recalcitrant LEAs and introduced a Bill that became the EA 1976. LEAs could thenceforth be required to submit plans for comprehensive reorganisation to the Secretary of State.[24] As Ganz has explained, "Parliament was used as a weapon of last resort when persuasion backed up by financial sanctions failed."[25]

---

[17] G. Ganz, *Quasi-Legislation: Recent Developments in Secondary Legislation* (1987) p. 18.

[18] See Chap. 4.

[19] DES Circular 4/74 (1974).

[20] B. Simon, *supra* (n.89) p. 433.

[21] DES, *The Growth of Comprehensive Education* Report on Education No. 87 (March 1977) p. 5.

[22] B. Simon *op. cit.* p. 439.

[23] *Secretary of State for Education and Science* v. *Tameside Metropolitan Borough Council* [1977] AC 1014.

[24] ss. 1–3.

[25] *Op. cit.* p. 18.

Before any of the rebellious authorities could be compelled to abolish selection, however, the Conservatives were elected to office in 1979 and promptly steered the short EA 1979 through Parliament. As a result of this Act, not only could LEAs retain their selective system, but those which had abandoned it could reintroduce it.

The battle over comprehensivisation had been, at times, a bitter struggle. Although it would be inappropriate to view this particular cause of conflict as the sole factor behind the breakup of the central-local partnership established by the 1944 Act, it was certainly influential. Indeed, Ganz cites the comprehensive schools saga as a classic illustration of the wider breakdown of central-local relations.[26] It led to an increasing preparedness on the part of the government to use its power in Parliament to ensure that its will on matters of educational policy would prevail. It also engendered a determination to use this power to bury uniformism and re-establish and extend diversity.

iii.   *City technology colleges*

With the promotion of two new types of school, the CTC and the GM school (see below), the Government was able to combine an assault on LEA domination of provision with an extension of the populist concept of "parental choice."

CTCs are intended to be centres of excellence in business and technological sciences or in the performing arts. Each must follow a "broad curriculum," but with an emphasis on science and technology (in the case of a "city technology college") or on technology in its application to the performing arts ("city colleges for the technology of the arts").[27] The Government originally intended that there would be around 20 CTCs, which would receive substantial amounts of funding from the private sector. Sensibly, from the Government's point of view, the ERA 1988 ensured that public money, which is now the principal source of funding, could be provided.[28] Yet these institutions are officially classed as "independent" schools,[29] enabling them to be free from LEA involvement and not statutorily bound to follow the National Curriculum. LEAs regard CTCs as undermining their role as local planners and deliverers of education.

---

[26] *Ibid.* pp. 76 and 77.

[27] ERA 1988, s.105(2)(c).

[28] ERA 1988, s.105(1) and (4); see also the Education (Grants) (City Colleges) Regulations 1987 SI 1987 No. 1138. The cost of setting up ADT City Technology College in Wandsworth, which is sponsored by a car auctions and security systems company, was £11 million of which 80 per cent. was contributed by the Government, just under 10 per cent. by ADT and rest by other private sponsors: *The Guardian*, August 18, 1992.

[29] ERA 1988, s.105(1).

Critics have argued that although only 15 CTCs have been founded so far, they stand out as elitist institutions demanding huge sums of public money to equip and maintain them while neighbouring LEA-maintained schools are, by comparison, starved of resources. The Government, however, says that the schools are not elitist, arguing that the most gifted children will not be creamed off by CTCs. The Act, says the Government, requires the CTCs to cater for pupils with "different abilities."[30] But it is clear that there is selection, even if, as the Government claims, mere competence will be all that will be looked for in a potential entrant.

The CTCs are quite different in character and financial structure to other schools. Indeed, teachers may well find that they receive higher salaries (although probably in return for longer hours).[31] Thus in *Bostock* v. *Kay*[32] it was held that on the question of whether it would be lawful for teacher governors to participate in the governing body's vote concerning the establishment of a CTC in place of their school, these teachers were not entitled to vote because they had a direct pecuniary interest in the outcome. However, on a similar question in later case,[33] this time concerning a vote on seeking GM status, *Bostock* was distinguished on the ground that the change would be far less fundamental than a change to CTC status.

iv.   *Grant-maintained schools*
Rationale   The rationale for the introduction of GM schools as presented by the Government was greater parental choice and greater effectiveness as a result of freedom from LEA control.[34] Consumer choice was to operate in two directions: first, collectively, as parents would be balloted on the question of GM status for the school; and secondly, individually, in that greater diversity of provision would give parents a wider variety of schools from which to select a place for their child. By being offered the chance to take a school 'out of local authority control,' parents were in effect receiving an implied message that education would be better outside the framework of LEA provision. Indeed, the weakening of the LEA monopoly on public sector schools provision was justified with reference to the likelihood of improved standards in *all* schools. It was suggested that as things stood, LEAs could not meet the expectations of many parents, who were concerned about the policies of

---

[30] *Ibid.* s.105(2)(*a*) and (*b*). Pupils must be drawn wholly or mainly from the urban areas in which these schools must be located.
[31] See S. Maclure, *Education Re-formed* (3rd ed., 1992) p. 129.
[32] (1989) *The Times*, 20 April.
[33] *R.* v. *Governors of Small Heath School ex p. Birmingham City Council* (1989) *The Times*, August 14; *The Guardian*, 19 September (C.A.).
[34] DES, *Grant-maintained Schools — A Consultation Paper* (1987) p. 1.

extremist councils and falling standards in schools. GM schools would
be funded by central government rather than depending on a share of
the LEA's schools budget and would be run by governing bodies
without LEA involvement (see Chapter 3). Free from LEA interference,
these schools would, according to the Consultation Paper, be expected
to provide "a stimulus for higher standards in all schools" as other
schools competed with them.[35]

The progress of opting out   Initially, the possibility of applying to opt out
was available to governing bodies of all county and voluntary secondary
schools and primary schools with at least 300 pupils.[36] Potential GM
status was extended to all other primary schools in November 1990.[37]
The smallest school to have been given GM status to date had just 12
pupils at the time. Nursery schools and schools in the process of
closure, remain ineligible.[38] (For recent changes making the creation of
GM special schools possible, see below.)

   The procedure for acquisition of GM status laid down in the 1988
Act, which is explained in greater detail in Chapter 4, was weighed
heavily in favour of achieving an opt-out. For example, the procedure
could be initiated by a simple majority vote of the governing body or
by a written request by parents whose number equalled 20 per cent. of
the number of registered pupils at the school.[39] If less than 50 per cent.
of the persons eligible to vote voted in the first ballot, a second ballot
had to be held within 14 days; at the second ballot a simple majority
would determine the issue.[40] The governors would then have to publish
opting out proposals and submit them to the Secretary of State, who
could approve them with or without modifications or reject them.[41] As
will be shown below, LEA attempts to challenge the Secretary of State's
approval of GM status in the courts have been largely fruitless.

   The progress of opting out has been slow but steady. By June 1991,
only 80 schools had been granted GM status, including just one
primary school. By November 1992, 340 schools (1.5 per cent. of the

---

[35] *Ibid.*
[36] ERA 1988, s.52.
[37] Education (Eligibility of Primary Schools for Grant-maintained Status) Order 1990 SI
      1990 No. 2031.
[38] ERA 1988, s.52(5), (8) and (9), now replaced by EA 1993, s.23.
[39] ERA 1988, s.60(1) and (2). In November 1992 a governing body at a Sussex school
      agreed that a two-thirds majority would be needed on a resolution to ballot parents on
      opting out. This prompted a legal row, because the regulations dealing with
      proceedings at governors' meetings, the Education (School Government) Regulations
      1989 (SI 1989 No. 1503), were silent on this question: *T.E.S.,* November 27, 1992.
[40] ERA 1988, s.61.
[41] *Ibid.* s.62.

total) had been given GM status (out of 676 schools which had held ballots[42]). There was a disparate pattern, with no ballots having been called for in a significant number of LEAs.[43] Thus, 69 schools in Kent and 73 in Essex, both Conservative controlled authorities, had opted out by January 1993; their combined total exceeded the total sum of opt-outs in all Labour authorities added together.[44] The Government hopes for a more rapid expansion in the GM sector over the next few years. The 1992 White Paper suggested that by 1996 "most of the 3,900 maintained secondary schools, as well as a significant proportion of the 19,000 maintained primary schools, could be grant-maintained."[45]

The EA 1993 has added fresh impetus to opting out. The basic rules on eligibility for GM status have not changed,[46] nor has the proportion of parents whose request can initiate the procedure.[47] However, the requirement for governors to approve opting out at a second resolution has been removed. More controversially, at a time when LEAs' attempts to dissuade parents and schools from opting out are being severely curtailed by legislation (see below), the 1993 Act has empowered the governing body to "promote (otherwise than as part of the arrangements made for the ballot) the case for seeking grant-maintained status for the school."[48] This clarifies the position, which had been at issue in the cases of *R.* v. *Governors of Small Heath School ex p. Birmingham City Council* and *ex p. Khan*.[49] Here the principal question had been whether a resolution in favour of opting out by the governing body of a school was invalidated by the fact that two teacher governors had voted.[50] However, at an earlier hearing before the High Court, concerning the governors' decision to hold the ballot on opting out,[51] Popplewell J. (while refusing on the balance of convenience to grant an interlocutory

---

[42] H.C. Debs., Vol. 213, col. 494w (November 6, 1992).

[43] *Ibid.* cols 477w–488w.

[44] Official Report House of Commons Standing Committee E, col. 725, Jan. 12, 1993.

[45] *Choice and Diversity* para 3.2.

[46] See s.23.

[47] See s.26(2).

[48] s.28(6).

[49] *The Times*, May 31, 1989 (Q.B.D.); August 14, 1989 (C.A.).

[50] The argument, rejected by the Court of Appeal (see above), was that the consequences of the change to GM status meant that these teacher governors had a direct pecuniary interest in the proposals; persons with such an interest were barred from participating by the Education (School Government) Regulations 1987 SI 1987 No. 1359 — since replaced by 1989 Regulations *op. cit.* The Government believes that there should be no restriction on head teachers voting, as governors, on a resolution concerning GM status, because there is no certainty of personal financial gain or loss by the change of status: Official Report House of Commons Standing Committee E, cols 708–709, January 12, 1993.

[51] *R.* v. *Knight and Others ex p. Khan and Another* (1989) *The Times*, February 2, 1989.

injunction to halt the ballot) said that when the head teacher sent a letter out to parents via pupil post advocating opting out he was in breach of section 45 of the E(No. 2)A 1986. This section requires schools to offer "a balanced presentation of opposing views" when political issues are brought to the attention of pupils. It had also been alleged, but not proved either way, that the school assembly had been used as a forum for persuading the children of the virtues of opting out. In any event, Popplewell J. said, *obiter*, that the head teacher and governors would not be precluded from presenting their views as "private individuals."

As noted above, the 1993 Act now permits the governors to promote the case for opting out, provided this is done separately from any communications concerning the ballot itself. In doing so the governing body must "take into account any guidance given by the Secretary of State as to the action he considers appropriate for the purpose."[52] This requirement enables the Secretary of State to exert considerable influence over the process.

A greater incidence of opting out may also be precipitated by the provision (via regulation) enabling two or more primary schools to opt out as a group (to be under one governing body).[53] It is believed that this provision may help to ensure the survival of some of the smaller rural primary schools, whose financial viability has become increasingly in doubt following the introduction of formula funding under local management of schools (see Chapter 3). The EA 1993 also enables regulations to make provision for the governing body of a maintained special school to submit proposals for GM status.[54] A further important change is the possibility that *new* schools may be established as GM schools. Under the ERA 1988 existing schools could become GM schools but new schools would have to be county or voluntary (or special). However, where the Secretary of State has wholly or partly transferred the "sufficient schools" responsibility from the LEA to a funding authority (see above), the FA may propose the establishment of new GM schools[55] and "promoters" may also promote such a school.[56] As a promoter could be the proprietor of an independent school, this makes it theoretically possible for such schools to achieve GM status (see further Chapter 4).[57]

---

[52] s.28(6).
[53] The regulations will be made under EA 1993, s.127.
[54] EA 1993, s.186.
[55] *Ibid.* s.48. The new GM schools can include GM special schools: s.183.
[56] *Ibid.* s.49. Promoters cannot establish a GM special school.
[57] Official Report, House of Commons Standing Committee E, col. 294, Nov. 26 1992, Mr E. Forth M.P. (Under-Secretary of State).

A proposed Opposition amendment to the Education Bill in the House of Lords (April 1993) would have enabled GM schools to 'opt back' into the LEA sector (after holding GM status for a minimum of five years). It was rejected by peers, avoiding a potential hindrance to the growth of the GM sector.

A significant change of character?   Some governors may be attracted to opting out as a route to changing the character of the school. The possibility of a significant change of character (see further Chapter 4) exists as before,[58] and there are already signs of a relaxation of the Government's policy of not approving such a change of character within five years of the school opting out. The Secretary of State has said that, contrary to Opposition assertions, the 1993 Act will not result in the introduction of "selection by the back door," but at the same time has stressed that he is "always happy to consider applications for changes of character from any schools in this country on their merits."[59] In March 1993, permission was given to the governors of a GM school in Penrith, Cumbria, to operate selection; three other GM schools have been given permission to select half their intake by ability.[60] Under the EA 1993, governing bodies of county schools can, when applying for GM status, now apply simultaneously for a change of character or enlargement of premises in order to ensure that there is "consistency in the provision made in the area of the [LEA]" if published LEA plans for a change of character to a school or schools in the area are implemented.[61]

Funding   As noted earlier, the EA 1993 set up funding authorities, which are to provide GM schools with annual maintenance grants and, in appropriate cases, special purpose grants and capital grants (up to 100 per cent.).[62] The funding authorities are taking over this role (and possibly others[63]) from the DFE, a necessary reform in view of the planned expansion of the GM sector. The 1993 Act continues to base a GM school's annual maintenance grant on the budget share the school would have received had it remained in LEA control, supplemented by

[58] ss.96–98, which, *inter alia*, replace s.89 of the 1988 Act. See p. 105 for a definition of "change of character".
[59] H.C. Debs., Vol. 213, col. 636 (November 9, 1992).
[60] *The Times*, March 19, 1993. Cumbria LEA subsequently failed in a judicial review application to have the Secretary of State's decision quashed for inadequacy of consultation: see *The Times*, July 3, 1993.
[61] EA 1993, s.272(1) and (2).
[62] EA 1993, ss.81–83.
[63] See EA 1993, s.17, which enables the Secretary of State to confer certain functions on the funding authorities by order.

an amount to cover costs for services previously provided centrally by the LEA.[64] But the Secretary of State is to have a discretion to introduce a common funding formula for GM schools in an LEA's area; this would give GM schools a share of the Government's Standard Spending Assessment for the LEA concerned.[65]

All the way along, the Government has stressed that the acquisition of GM status will have a financially neutral effect on a school.[66] Certainly in the past the Government claims to have followed an even-handed approach.[67] Nevertheless, the Secretary of State has always had the power to extend the range of the special purpose and capital grants, leading to a suspicion that he would offer more favourable treatment to GM schools.[68] Furthermore, the provision of maintenance grants has favoured schools which become GM, as they are likely to receive a generous transitional grant when they first opt out. Maclure comments that "a secondary school which opts out may well receive an immediate six figure increase in its annual budget."[69] It has been argued that "much of the pressure on schools to become grant-maintained has come from the promise of an extra funding."[70] Government funding allocations for 1993–94 show that the GM sector will receive £77m worth of capital grants; this represents nearly 13 per cent. of the total of capital grants for schools even though only around 2–3 per cent. of children attend GM schools. A recent report by OFSTED, based on inspections of the first 143 schools to have acquired GM status, has confirmed the financial advantages of opting out.[71]

Impact on local education authorities[72]   The introduction of GM schools is certain to have the most profound effect on LEAs of all the reforms since 1979. It is not so much the transfer of staff and property attached to

---

[64] EA 1993, Chapter VI, and grants regulations (when made) will regulate funding of GM schools.

[65] *Choice and Diversity*, paras 13.7 and 13.8. On the potential impact of a common funding formula in respect of GM schools, see House of Commons Education Select Committee, Second Report, Session 1992–93, *Some Aspects of the Funding of Schools* H.C. 419 (March 1993) paras. 15–25.

[66] See, for example, DES Circular 10/88 para. 53.

[67] *Ibid.* para. 60. The then Secretary of State, Mr Kenneth Baker M.P., referred to "an equality of public resourcing" as between GM and LEA-maintained schools: H.C. Debs., Vol. 123, col. 788 (December 1, 1987).

[68] See P. Meredith, "The Education Reform Act 1988: Grant-maintained Schools" (1989) 1(3) *Education and the Law* 1(3) 95 at p. 98.

[69] S. Maclure, *Education Re-formed* (3rd ed., 1992) p. 76.

[70] H.C. Debs., Vol. 213, col. 645 (November 9, 1992) A. Taylor M.P.

[71] Office for Standards in Education, *Grant-maintained Schools* 1989–92 (1993).

[72] For an empirical study, see M. Feintuck, unpublished Ph.D thesis (University of Sheffield) (1993).

the schools that opt out.[73] Much more important is the effect on the role of LEA as principal provider and strategic planner. The impact of opting out has already been felt where LEAs have sought to reorganise provision, something which the Government has in recent years been urging them to do with a view to removing surplus capacity in schools. The position is complicated by the fact that LEAs may, initially at least, continue to be responsible for rationalisation of school places even where some of their schools have opted out. (Note that GM schools handle their own admissions. The weakening of a central admissions system can create barriers to choice, even though the Government's intention is to extend it, and cause instability: see Chapter 5.)

The inter-relationship between the relevant provisions is such that when opting out is sought as a means of avoiding a LEA's reorganisation/closure scheme, the Secretary of State can give the application for GM status priority. Section 73 of the ERA 1988 laid down the following rules (now contained in section 273 of the ERA 1993):

(i) No proposals concerning the establishment, significant alteration or closure of a county school (under section 12 of the EA 1980) or establishment or alteration of a voluntary school (under section 13 of the 1980 Act) could be published where a school had been given approval by the Secretary of State to become GM;

(ii) If such proposals had already been published, an application for the acquisition of GM status would be treated as a statutory objection to them (which would have the effect, in cases where the Secretary of State's approval of the proposals would not, under the terms of the section, have been necessary, of making his approval a requirement);

(iii) If an application for GM status was made while such proposals were awaiting approval, both sets of proposals would be considered together "on their merits";[74] but the

---

[73] See EA 1993, ss.38–47. In broad terms the property and contractual rights and liabilities of the local authority and the existing governing body will vest in the new governing body from the date GM status commences. There are excepted items. Responsibility for ensuring that property is transferred to the governors by the due date rests with the Education Assets Board: s.198 ERA 1988. There are restrictions on entering contracts and disposal of property liable to be transferred on GM status. In general, staff will be transferred to the employment of the new governing body. There is continuity of employment and the change of employer and to the school's status cannot, without more, be considered to amount to a substantial change to an employee's working conditions to his or her detriment such as could constitute termination of the contract of employment by the employer.

[74] See DES Circular 10/88 para. 37.

Secretary of State could not consider the sections 12 or 13 proposals until he had made a decision concerning GM status — and if he had approved GM status the proposals had to be rejected.

The question of how far the rules in (iii) might jeopardise an LEA's schools reorganisation scheme was at issue in the Bath litigation.[75] The background was the planned reorganisation of six secondary schools in Bath whose numbers of pupils on roll had declined from 6,248 in September 1978 to 5,753 in September 1983, with a projected further decline to 4,360 by September 1992. Given this situation, and the exhortations in a series of government circulars to remove surplus capacity in schools,[76] the LEA (Avon) published proposals in 1984, involving: the closure of Beechen Cliff Boys School; the age range of the other five schools being restricted to 11–16; a sixth form college being established on the Beechen Cliff premises; and one of the schools, a girls' school, becoming co-educational. The proposals were in fact rejected by the Secretary of State in 1986. In July 1987 a consultation process was commenced in Bath concerning a further, similar, reorganisation plan (this time seemingly justified by the contents of Circular 3/87,[77] which urged reorganisation to meet the problems of falling rolls and under-sized sixth forms). With public support seemingly in favour of the proposals, and after further consultation with the governing bodies of the schools affected, a final decision was made by the council in January 1989 to proceed with the proposed reorganisation. Although two schools (of which Beechen Cliff was one) opposed the plan, the other four supported it.

Meanwhile, Beechen Cliff school decided to ballot its parents on GM status. Two-thirds of parents voted, and of those voting 55.4 per cent. voted in favour and 44.6 per cent. voted against. The education committee said that Beechen Cliff's opting out would be to the detriment of the secondary education of other children in Bath, whose education was already suffering from the confusion and uncertainty about the city's schools and the inadequacy of sixth form provision. There was also concern that the LEA's much needed schools reorganisation plans would be completely undermined. On August 17, 1989, the DES informed the authority that the reorganisation plans had been rejected, and informed the governors of Beechen Cliff school that, provided they brought forward by three weeks the date of implementation, the school could have GM status. No reasons for the

---

[75] R. v. *Secretary of State for Education and Science ex p. Avon County Council* (1990) 88 L.G.R. 716 (Q.B.D.) and *ex p. Avon* (No. 2) 737 (C.A.).

[76] DES Circulars 2/80, 2/81 and 4/82 and Admin. Memorandum 4/82.

[77] *Providing for Quality: the Pattern of Organisation to Age 19.*

decision were stated, other than that "the merits of the application by the governors of Beechen Cliff school for grant-maintained status outweighed those of the authority's proposals."

The central basis to the LEA's challenge was that the Secretary of State had failed to consider the case for the reorganisation and the case for GM status independently before reaching his decisions, and had ignored relevant considerations, including the LEA's legitimate and responsible response to the problem of falling rolls and their impact on education in the city. Hutchinson J. considered that it could not have been Parliament's intention that a planned reorganisation could effectively be frustrated by one school "provided only that it could make a good case for grant-maintained status . . . viewed in isolation."[78] He also concluded that at the stage of weighing one proposal against the other the Secretary of State had failed to have regard to "the most important factor, the consequences that rejection of the council's proposal would have in terms of disruption, delay and prolonged uncertainty for the majority of children and their parents in Bath."[79] Hutchinson J. decided to quash the decisions even though change of status at Beechen Cliff school was well underway.

However, the Secretary of State was entitled to reconsider the matter. He did so, and, on March 30, 1990, confirmed that he had reached an identical conclusion. On this occasion he set out his reasons at some length.[80] These stated that not only were there sound reasons for leaving Beechen Cliff, a successful school, with its sixth-form, but there was in any event considerable room for improvement with the LEA's reorganisation plans. Indeed several alternatives that the LEA might consider for the five remaining schools were set out. Again the LEA mounted a legal challenge, heard by the Court of Appeal exercising original jurisdiction. Ralph Gibson L.J. saw the LEA's principal grounds as being that the Secretary of State (i) had wrongly treated the GM application as "paramount"; (ii) had incorrectly taken into account various options as feasible when, in the light of the decision to allow Beechen Cliff school to opt out, they would not be; and (iii) had failed to take into account the delay and uncertainty that would arise from his decision on the reorganisation proposals. These arguments, and a fourth, alleging that the Secretary of State had failed to have regard to the fact that the LEA would face particular difficulty in meeting its obligations under the SDA 1975, were rejected. It was felt that the Secretary of State alone was the judge of the feasibility of the various schemes, and there was insufficient evidence of irrationality. So far as the paramountcy

---

[78] *Supra* (n.75) at p. 722.
[79] p. 735.
[80] These are not set out in the L.G.R. report (*op. cit.*) but are in the Lexis report.

argument in (i) was concerned, Ralph Gibson L.J., referring to the fact that the Secretary of State had to weigh one proposal against the other, said that the Secretary of State was entitled to "have a policy and to apply his policy preference in considering the proposals."[81] In other words, if he believed that GM schools offered a better form of provision, and there was a rational basis to this conclusion, then that was a legitimate consideration for the Minister to apply. Ultimately, then, it was for the Minister, having considered both sets of proposals together, to follow a process of "judgment and evaluation." It included

> "judgment of the future course of events by reference to existing facts, to the accumulated knowledge and experience available to the Minister in his department, to his policy for securing the objects of the legislation, and to his assessment of the prospects for success of that policy in achieving those objects."[82]

In any event, there was nothing to prevent the Secretary of State from giving greater weight to any one or more of the various factors which he had to take into account.[83]

It is interesting that this case in some ways reinforces the argument for the application of the doctrine of proportionality in English public law.[84] Under the proportionality principle, the court would consider, *inter alia*, whether the Secretary of State had maintained a proper balance between purpose achieved by his decision and the impact the decision would have on the rights and interests of those affected by it. It could be argued in relation to the *Avon* case that those interests were disproportionately affected by the chaos, confusion and uncertainty which the decision to allow Beechen Cliff School to opt out caused in Bath. So far as the implications for central-local government relations are concerned, the Court of Appeal's decision confirmed the Secretary of State's relatively unimpeded power to make ever deeper inroads in the role of LEAs by conferring GM status — even where this undermines LEA attempts to comply with the Government's own policy of promoting reorganisation of schools to remove surplus capacity and inefficiency.

This conclusion is reinforced by the decision in *R.* v. *Secretary of State for Education and Science ex p. Newham L.B.C.*[85] Here Stratford School in Newham applied for GM status after a narrow vote in favour by parents. Approving the application, the Secretary of State attached more weight

---

[81] At p. 740.
[82] *Ibid.*
[83] *per* Nicholls L.J. at p. 742.
[84] See J. Jowell and A. Lester Q.C., "Proportionality: Neither Novel Nor Dangerous," in J. Jowell and D. Oliver, *New Directions in Judicial Review* (1988) pp. 51–72.
[85] (1991) *The Times*, January 11; Lexis CO/2521/90.

to the need for greater parental choice in this inner city area than to the LEA's legitimate claim to be offering a viable and cost-effective reorganisation plan. Schiemann J. accepted that local variation to the national policy of removal of surplus capacity was within the remit of the Secretary of State's powers. He also accepted the Secretary of State's argument concerning enhancement of choice, on the basis that GM schools were different from LEA schools because of their independence from LEA control and direct government funding.

The problems in Bath and Newham are part of a broader picture of disruption to local planning resulting from the possibility of GM status.[86] Similar problems have arisen elsewhere.[87] Looking at the schools which have opted out, reasons for seeking GM status have in many cases included avoidance of closure or merger under a reorganisation scheme, or, where grammar schools are concerned, the possibility of changes to selection policy or future introduction of comprehensive schools.[88] (Ironically, in Kent, which has selective entry, some schools have opted out in order to change their status to comprehensives.[89]) Of the first 340 schools to opt out, 63 had been threatened with closure under a reorganisation scheme.[90] Concerned about the detrimental impact on LEAs' efforts to reduce surplus capacity, the Government has, however, recently announced that new guidelines will indicate that applications for GM status to avoid closure will normally be rejected.[91]

The impact of the SDA 1975 in this context also needs to be considered. In Birmingham, the LEA was forced to reorganise its schools after the House of Lords ruled that provision of unequal numbers of single sex places for boys and girls at voluntary aided grammar schools, with the result that it would be more difficult for a girl to secure a place, was contrary to that Act.[92] The LEA considered

---

[86] As noted above, the provisions which were the subject of the *Beechen Cliff* and *Newham* cases have been re-enacted in the EA 1993, s.273 — see p. 105 below.

[87] *e.g.* in Dudley, where the LEA was seeking a wholesale reorganisation involving a variety of schools of different sizes and age ranges: M. Flude and M. Hammer, "Opting for an Uncertain Future," in M. Flude and M. Hammer *op. cit.* p. 60.

[88] The threat of being converted into a comprehensive school persuaded Bacup and Rawstenstall Grammar school to seek GM status: see *The Guardian*, August 29, 1989.

[89] *The Guardian*, August 4, 1991.

[90] H.C. Debs., Vol. 213, col. 651 (November 9, 1992), A. Rumbold M.P. Of the schools holding ballots by April 1993, 114 had been in receipt of an EA 1980 s.12 closure notice; 85 of these schools voted to opt out, of which 42 were given approval to do so: H.L. Debs., Vol. 544, col. 1775 (April 22, 1993).

[91] *The Times*, June 19, 1993. Over-rigidity in the application of such a policy might, of course, amount to unlawful fettering of discretion.

[92] *Equal Opportunities Commission* v. *Birmingham City Council* [1989] 1 All E.R. 769; [1989] A.C. 1155, discussed in Chap. 4 at p. 119.

various options and preferred one that involved closing Handsworth
Grammar School for Boys. But, following a parental ballot, the school
applied for and was granted GM status. The council, following
consultation, rejigged entry to the remaining single sex schools so that
there would be more or less equal numbers of places at the boys' and
girls' schools. However, as one of the girls' schools was non-selective, it
was still harder for a girl to obtain a grammar school place, because a
higher exam mark would be needed to guarantee entry. When the Equal
Opportunities Commission challenged the reorganisation via judicial
review proceedings,[93] the council conceded that on that count there was
unlawful sex discrimination.[94] However, the Divisional Court held that
the LEA's duty to ensure that the provision of "sufficient" schools
occurred without sex discrimination meant that the availability of places
for boys at Handsworth school had to be taken into account by the
authority. The decision was upheld by the Court of Appeal.[95] The
remaining voluntary aided grammar schools in Birmingham have
regarded opting out as a means of avoiding possible merger (as co-
educational schools) or comprehensivisation.[96] If all these schools acquire
GM status it will put the LEA into an impossible position as regards its
duties under the SDA 1975, although following the enactment of the
EA 1993, the involvement of the FAS, which will have a parallel non-
discrimination duty under sections 23C and 25 of that Act, might lead
to a resolution of such a difficulty. (The impact of the SDA 1975 on the
pattern of local schools provision is considered further in Chapter 4.)

LEA anti-opt out campaigns   While the Government has been accused of
mounting a campaign of "glossy propaganda to promote grant-
maintained schools,"[97] LEAs are claimed to have sought "to undermine
governing bodies' attempts to inform parents properly about the GM
option"[98] and to be "bombarding parents on their doorstep and at
school gates with anti-grant-maintained literature."[99] There have also
been complaints of implicit or explicit warnings by LEAs to staff
concerning their future career if opting out occurs.[1] Despite the lack of

---

[93] R. v. *Birmingham City Council ex p. Equal Opportunities Commission (No. 2)* (1992) 90
L.G.R. 492.
[94] In the light of the decision in *In re Equal Opportunities Commission and the Sex
Discrimination (Northern Ireland) Order 1976 Nos 1 and 2*, cited in *ibid.*
[95] *The Times*, October 27, 1992.
[96] See *The Times*, May 18, 1992.
[97] H.C. Debs., Vol. 213, col. 643 (November 9, 1992), Mrs A. Taylor M.P.
[98] *Choice and Diversity*, para 7.6.
[99] H.C. Debs., Vol. 213, col. 631 (November 9, 1992), Dame Angela Rumbold M.P.
[1] Referred to in letter sent by Secretary of State to LEAs on November 3, 1992. The
letter threatens possible use of the default powers in EA 1944, ss.68 and 99.

a consistent approach in the case law,[2] Local Government Circular 20/88, which offers general guidance to local authorities on the provision of information, warns against over-simplification or biased presentation of issues. But this does not mean that LEAs are prohibited from presenting their view to parents.[3]

The 1992 White Paper announced that LEA expenditure on "staying in" campaigns would be limited to that which the governing body itself might be helped (via state funds) to incur: each would be able to produce and distribute the equivalent of one leaflet to parents.[4] Although the EA 1993 contains no such restrictions on the number of leaflets, etc., section 36(3) provides that an LEA may not make payments "for the purpose of influencing the outcome of ballots ... if the aggregate of the payments for that purpose ... would exceed the limit" (which may be set by the Secretary of State by regulation).

Note also the power (referred to above) for governing bodies to put the case for opting out to parents.

Other issues relating GM schools, including the new powers of the Secretary of State to replace governors, are discussed in Chapter 3. Opting out procedure is examined further in Chapter 4.

v. *Specialisation*
The Government has advanced another concept designed to bury still deeper the uniformism of the 1960s and 1970s — specialisation. The idea is to enhance parental choice while enabling a school to "play to its strengths."[5] A school would be permitted to offer a greater emphasis on particular areas of knowledge and skills (technology has been identified as the first priority area) while retaining its obligation to meet the requirements of the National Curriculum. The Government intend to build on the technology schools initiative (under which, in 1992–93, 100 state schools received additional capital allowances out of an extra allocation of £25m) to enhance technological facilities and promote a greater vocational emphasis. Created along with technology schools might be maintained technology colleges (not to be confused with CTCs above), which could be voluntary aided.

No doubt anticipating the criticism that these proposals were simply another attempt to (re-)introduce selection 'by the back door,' the Government argued that the technological or other specialist bias of

---

[2] *Meek* v. *Lothian R.C.* (1983) S.L.T. 494, and *R.* v. *I.L.E.A. ex p. Westminster C.C.* [1986] 1 All E.R. 19.

[3] See *Report by the Local Government Ombudsman on an Investigation into Complaint No. 91/C/0045 Against Kirklees M.B.C.*

[4] *Choice and Diversity*, para. 7.6.

[5] *Ibid.* paras. 1.45 and 10.1.

these schools would not mean that pupils would be selected in the way that grammar schools select pupils: specialisation, it was said, is "separate from the issue of selection."[6] But clearly governors of these schools will want some reassurance that a child has the aptitude to benefit from the particular form of education in which the school specialises, especially in view of the publication of league tables of schools' examination results. There was a hint that selection may be sanctioned: "It is not the Government's intention either to encourage or to discourage ... applications [for a significant change of character]."[7] In any event, up to 10 per cent. of the intake could be selected on the basis of aptitude without this amounting to a significant change of character requiring DFE approval.[8]

vi. *Failing schools*

Although LEAs overall role has been reduced significantly by recent reforms, they are being given additional powers in respect of those of their schools which are providing education which is below acceptable standards. However, schools which do not improve as a result of LEA intervention may be taken over by an Education Association, whose members will be appointed by the Secretary of State.[9] The school would only be released from Education Association control by becoming GM (apparently without any need for a parental ballot) or being discontinued.[10] The LEA would thus have a clear incentive to make its intervention tell. But because LEAs are being given no additional resources to lever-up standards in failing schools, they may in reality face the prospect of net *loss* of power overall even in this context. The failing schools provisions are considered further in Chapter 6.

(f) LEAs in the future

Until very recently the Secretary of State's broad duty in promoting education was to secure the "effective execution by local authorities ... of the national policy" (see above). This duty, in section 1 of the EA 1944, has been replaced by one which refers to "those bodies in receipt of public funds" which provide education.[11] The symbolic significance of this change lies in the omission of any direct reference to LEAs. It emphasises that LEAs' strategic and operational roles will become of

---

[6] *Ibid.* para. 1.48.
[7] *Ibid.*
[8] See Official Report, House of Commons, Standing Committee E, December 10, 1992, Mr E. Forth M.P. (Under-Secretary of State).
[9] EA 1993, s.218. There must be at least five members of an Association.
[10] ss.224 and 225.
[11] EA 1993, s.2(2).

increasingly marginal importance.[12] This is further reinforced by the removal of the requirement that LEAs have education committees (above); these are now seen as becoming unnecessary given the expectation of LEAs' much reduced role in the future.[13] Furthermore, there is even the prospect that the private sector may take over some of the remaining areas of the LEA provision, such as school library services or peripatetic music teaching.[14] Policy research indicates, however, that despite the transfer of power away from them, downwards to schools and colleges and upwards to central government and its agencies, LEAs could still play an important role in assessing local needs and working out the services that are required.[15] But it is possible that the creation of the funding authorities will remove even that possibility save in relation to a small number of specific areas of provision, such as special education or pupil referral units.[16]

3.　THE THIRD PARTNER: TEACHERS

The third partner in the 'partnership' that was to be responsible for the future development of the education system of England and Wales under the EA 1944 was the teaching profession.[17] As noted earlier, the teachers were to be entrusted with the important role of developing the curriculum and teaching methods.

However, in the post-1980 reforms the Government appears to have taken every opportunity to resist teacher influence. The Schools Council, a curriculum advisory body consisting of teachers, has been abolished. Teacher representation on many of the new bodies created to advise government and monitor standards has been minimised or removed. On school governing bodies, teachers' membership has been limited to one or two (see Chapter 3); and the increasing representation of the local business and other service providers has shifted the focus from the producer/professional perspectives of teachers to the consumer/community interest. Experience as a teacher is not a pre-requisite for

---

[12] *cf.* Audit Commission, *Losing an Empire, Finding a Role — the LEA of the future* (1989).
[13] See H.C. Debs., Vol. 213, col. 765 (November 10, 1992), Mr N. Forman M.P. (Parliamentary Under-Secretary of State for Further and Higher Education).
[14] *Choice and Diversity*, para. 6.7 and 6.8. LEAs are, however, to retain responsibility for special educational needs and school attendance in all maintained (including GM) schools.
[15] See P. Cordingley and M. Kogan, *Meeting Educational Needs* (1993).
[16] See EA 1993, s.298 and Sched. 18. A "pupil referral unit" is an establishment providing suitable full-time or part-time education for pupils who are not attending school due to illness, exclusion from school etc.
[17] See D. Lawton, *Education and Politics in the 1990s* (1992) p. 115.

appointment as a registered inspector of schools. Furthermore, there is no requirement that any members of an inspection team should be former teachers; and one member must be a person "without personal experience in the management of any school or the provision of education in any school"[18] (see Chapter 6).

Although the School Curriculum and Assessment Authority (SCAA) must include persons having relevant knowledge of and experience in education,[19] the Secretary of State has the final say on matters within its remit (such as the content of National Curriculum programmes of study and assessment arrangements) and can disregard the professional view. This has happened on a number of occasions, described in Chapter 7. In an account of his experience as chair of the National Curriculum Council (replaced along with the School Examinations and Assessment Council by the SCAA), Graham explains that much of the ministerial antipathy towards the curriculum and assessment councils and their work has stemmed from a perception that they are being dominated by narrow professional self-interest.[20] Maclure notes that "Ministers have not hesitated . . . to put it about that the Councils were unregenerate organs of the Educational Establishment when they have failed to come to heel."[21]

As in the case of other professions, especially social workers and doctors employed in the National Health Service,[22] government regulation has impinged on professional autonomy. The establishment of a National Curriculum laid down by law (see Chapter 7) has regulated teaching and put the Government in control of subject content and methods of pupil assessment. As with other developments resulting in reduced teacher autonomy, this control has been justified with reference to the need to raise standards, but it is currently meeting stern resistance through the boycott of National Curriculum assessments by teaching unions. A partial reversal of Government policy now seems in prospect in the light of the interim report of the Dearing review of the National Curriculum (August 1993), which recommends putting more faith in teachers' ability to assess their own pupils' progress and giving teachers more flexibility as regards curriculum content.

Teacher autonomy has also been challenged by consumer rights such as parental access to information. For example, parents have a right to inspect their child's school record and to examine schemes of work followed at the school.[23] Generally, the closer involvement of parents in their children's schooling has posed little threat to teacher autonomy.

---

[18] ESA 1992, Sched. 2 para. 3(2)(a)(i).
[19] EA 1993, s.244(4).
[20] D. Graham with D. Tytler, *A Lesson for Us All — The Making of the National Curriculum* (1992).
[21] (1992) *op. cit.* p. 10.
[22] See M. Moran and B. Wood, *Doctors, Regulation and the State* (1992).
[23] See N. Harris, *The Law Relating to Schools* (1990) pp. 141–146.

Indeed, recent research has shown a continuing positive attitude among teachers towards parental involvement in children's curricular and other school activities.[24] Nevertheless, many of new consumer rights in education, such as rights to information, give more emphasis to accountability than partnership. (The concept of partnership appears only at the end of the *Parent's Charter* (1991), after sections on the right to know, right to choose and rights of redress.) Regardless of the position in practice, teachers are increasingly being made to *feel* that they are answerable to parents.

Entry to the teaching profession has been subjected to greater regulation, as the Government has exerted firmer control over teacher training, introduced an appraisal scheme (under section 49 of the E(No. 2)A 1986) and promulgated more detailed regulations governing qualified teacher status. One of the changes introduced under these regulations has been the "licensed teacher" scheme, under which a person aged 26 or over who is deemed to be a "suitable person to be a teacher" can be employed as a teacher at a school (effectively as a trainee) despite his/her lack of a teaching qualification.[25] The scheme has been criticised by most of the teaching unions, since its introduction in 1989, for undermining the status of teaching as a profession. The unions have also reacted negatively to recent Government proposals for non-graduates to be able to qualify as teachers of infants after one year's training. In addition to regulating entry to the teaching profession, the Secretary of State regulates teachers' conditions, via the national Teachers' Pay and Conditions Document, first introduced following the Teachers' Pay and Conditions Act 1987.[26]

4. CONCLUSION

It is becoming increasingly inappropriate to talk of the partnership between central and local government as the dominant feature of the structure of education administration in England and Wales. This partnership was undermined during the 1980s, when the powers of the Secretary of State, parents and governors were increased. The changes introduced under the EA 1993, especially those involving greater centralisation and diversity and a reduced role for LEAs, continue a trend which "marks a step back from the electoral principle; in place of the universal provision of education by elected local authorities [is] . . . the differential provision of education by appointed bodies in which the

---

[24] S. Jowett *et al.*, *Building Bridges: Parental Involvement in Schools* (1991).

[25] Sched. 4 to the Education (Teachers) Regulations 1989 SI 1989 No. 1319.

[26] See now the Teachers' Pay and Conditions Act 1992, which created a pay review body but left the final say with the Secretary of State.

elected element is in the minority and a specific group [ministers etc.]
. . . is accorded a privileged place in appointments."[27] Also threatened,
according to many commentators, has been the profession autonomy of
teachers, the third partner.[28]

The overall picture from the 1960s onwards, but more especially
since the 1980s, has been one of major restructuring. The changes
introduced in the 1960s and 1970s were reflective of political and
ideological change in which egalitarianism and social justice under-
pinned institutional reforms. The political Left, many members of
whom were teachers in the state sector or in the majority on LEAs,
seized the opportunity, at a time of major social change, to put ideology
into practice. But from the 1980s the political Right were able to
capitalise on the dissatisfaction with producer-domination emanating
from some quarters and consumer pressures for increased rights and
accountability.[29] As one educationalist notes, "what crashed . . . was the
belief that professional educationalists and the persons within the system
itself could deliver the hoped for educational goals without the need for
either state or parental accountability."[30] This failure by education
providers helped to fuel many of the radical reforms introduced under
the legislation of the 1980s and early 1990s.

---

[27] P. McAuslan, "The Constitution: Does the Bill Offend It?," in J. Haviland (ed.), *Take Care, Mr Baker* (1988) p. 267.

[28] See, *e.g.* D. Lawton *Education and Politics in the 1990s: Conflict or Consensus?* (1992) p. 115.

[29] See J. Sallis, *Schools, Parents and Governors: A New Approach to Accountability* (1988) Chap. 5.

[30] D. Reynolds, "Parents and the Left: Rethinking the Relationship," in F. Macleod (ed.) *Parents and Schools: The Contemporary Challenge* (1991) p. 171.

3

GOVERNMENT AND AUTONOMY OF EDUCATIONAL INSTITUTIONS

1. INTRODUCTION

A key element in the changes to the education system since 1979 has been the devolution of elements of power, and in particular a degree of budgetary control, to educational institutions. Together with the centralisation of power discussed in Chapter 1, greater institutional autonomy has been achieved at the expense of LEA control. At the same time there has been a major reform of the structures of governance within institutions, providing for greater consumer representation and reductions in the scope for political influence to be brought to bear by local authorities. The legal changes to the governance of schools, in particular, are of vital importance given the range of responsibilities now resting with governing bodies. Important developments have also occurred in relation to the government and independence of further and higher education institutions. In particular, the ERA 1988 and FHEA 1992 have removed all LEA involvement in higher education and left LEAs with only a residual role in further education. The legislation has also provided the Secretary of State with more comprehensive powers over the two sectors, a fact barely hidden by the increased autonomy of colleges and former polytechnics.

2. SCHOOLS

(a) School governing bodies: membership and decision-making

i. *Historical background: pre-Education (No. 2) Act 1986*
The Elementary Education Act 1870 marked the beginning of the state education system. The aim of the Act was to support the universal provision of elementary education. To this end it was a requirement that where church (and other) schools were insufficient to meet local needs, a

school board (with elected members) was to be formed for each district, whose function was to "maintain and keep efficient every school" provided by it.[1] The Act empowered boards to delegate functions relating to "the control and management of a school" to "a body of managers appointed by them, consisting of not less than three persons."[2]

The role of the school boards was taken over by LEAs under the Education Act 1902. The appointment of managers of elementary schools (not normally more than six per school) become compulsory.[3] The EA 1944 required the appointment of managers (termed governors after 1980) of primary schools and governors of secondary schools.[4] As shown below, the 1944 Act distinguished between voluntary (denominational) schools, which had a number of foundation governors (appointed by the religious foundation under which the school was established) in addition to LEA governors, and county schools, which had boards of governors appointed by the LEA. It was possible for governors to be appointed to serve a large number of schools and for a number of schools to be grouped under one governing body. This undoubtedly limited the accountability of governing bodies to parents and provided scope for local party political manipulation of them.[5]

During the 1960s and 1970s there was growing pressure for change. In 1967 the Plowden Report on primary schools recommended that parents should be represented on boards of managers.[6] By the 1970s there was a major impetus for change arising out of the intensifying debate about educational standards and mounting consumer pressure.[7] There was a "rising tide of consumerism which encouraged the idea of more direct participation by parents."[8] The introduction of comprehensive schools (see Chapter 2), aiming to serve the whole of the local community, added further weight to the case for closer school–community ties, in which governing bodies would play a key role. But for the most part the system of school government was "moribund," with unrepresentative boards who lacked accountability to parents.[9] However, some LEAs restructured governing bodies in the late 1960s and early

---

[1] ss.6 and 18.
[2] s.15.
[3] EA 1902, s.6(1).
[4] ss.17 and 18; EA 1980, s.1(1).
[5] See J. Sallis, *Schools, Parents and Governors: A New Approach to Accountability* (1988), pp. 109–110.
[6] Lady Plowden (chair), *Children and their Primary Schools* (1967) Vol. 1, para. 1150.
[7] A. Richardson, *Participation* (1983), p.38; N. Beattie, *Professional Parents* (1985) pp. 194–205; J. Sallis *op. cit.* p. 113.
[8] S. Maclure, *Education Re-formed* (3rd ed. 1992) p. 139.
[9] J. Sallis, *op. cit.* at p. 128.

1970s, with Sheffield LEA leading the way by appointing parent governors, teacher governors and representatives of voluntary organisations and by encouraging governors to become actively involved in their schools.[10] By 1975, some 85 per cent. of LEAs claimed to appoint parent governors.[11] Nevertheless, there was continuing dissatisfaction, not least with the political domination of boards.

The Government responded by appointing a Committee of Enquiry, under the chairmanship of Tom Taylor (later Lord Taylor of Blackburn), which reported in 1977.[12] It found considerable party political influence and a failure in many key areas of responsibility, while identifying improvements in representation after 1969 with the appointment of more parent and teacher governors. The Committee made a number of key recommendations,[13] several of which were subsequently adopted in the EA 1980: the term "manager" should be dropped (see above); each school should have its own governing body and grouping should therefore be prevented (this was not implemented, although grouping was later limited); and there should be equal representation on governing bodies of four parties — LEAs, parents (and older pupils in secondary schools), teachers (and non-teaching staff in larger schools) and the local community. (Equal representation was not implemented, although there were reforms.) It was also recommended that governors should be given a more active role in relation to various matters, including staff appointments and curriculum aims.[14]

The report therefore contemplated greater parental involvement in the management of schools, through representation on governing bodies enjoying extended powers. LEAs and teaching unions lined up in opposition to the report, the former because of the prospect of having reduced influence and the latter because of the threat to teachers' control of the curriculum. However, at national level, interest among the political parties in legitimising parent participation was growing. Prior to its defeat in the 1979 general election, the Labour Party had made plans to give legal effect to some of the Taylor Committee's recommendations. The in-coming Conservative Government, conscious of the fact that consumer pressure for increased representation was emanating largely from middle-class parents, saw an opportunity to gain political capital by rewarding many of its traditional supporters. The EA 1980, which also introduced the important choice of school provisions (see Chapter 5), required all maintained schools to have two parent

---

[10] *Ibid.* p. 115.
[11] N. Beattie, *op. cit.*
[12] *A New Partnership for Our Schools.*
[13] *Ibid.* Chaps. 3 and 4.
[14] *Ibid.* Chaps. 8 and 6 respectively.

governors, both (in the case of county schools) elected by secret ballot of parents (as had been recommended by the Taylor Committee as a means to maximising participation[15]). It also required teacher representation (although limited it to one or two teachers, depending on the size of the school) and reduced the scope for grouping of schools. It also empowered the making of regulations governing procedure at governors' meetings (see below).

The 1980 Act has been described as a "diluted" response to the Taylor Committee's report.[16] Nevertheless, by making parental representation on school governing bodies compulsory, together with its provisions on choice of school and the publication of school information, it signified the beginning of a new era of parental participation and consumerism.

In 1984, a DES-commissioned study of school governing bodies[17] showed that parent governors were frequently unrepresentative of parents and unable to make an effective contribution. Parents were in effect dependent on professional and LEA inputs rather than acting in true partnership or even taking the lead.[18] Despite the doubts about the effectiveness of parent governorship, the Government proposed a radical reform, going much further than the Taylor recommendations; it involved putting parents into the majority on governing bodies. The proposals, set out in Education Secretary Sir Keith Joseph's Green Paper of May 1984,[19] were condemned as flawed in principle and unworkable in practice. Even organisations representing parents were critical of the principle of parental control rather than partnership envisaged by the proposals.[20] But the Government was committed to reform, articulating the view that the involvement of parents, both generally and as school governors, would put pressure on schools and LEAs to improve standards.

In the 1985 White Paper, *Better Schools*, fresh proposals were published, closer to those originally contained in the Taylor Committee's report in that the basic approach was that "no single interest will predominate."[21] The proposals were given legal effect by the E(No. 2)A 1986. The Act provides that the constitution of the governing body, to be determined in accordance with the relevant

---

[15] *Ibid.* paras 4.20–4.23.
[16] J. Sallis, *op. cit.* p. 133.
[17] M. Kogan (ed.), *School Governing Bodies* (1984).
[18] *Ibid.* pp. 81 and 90.
[19] DES, *Parental Influence at School* (1984) Cmnd 9242.
[20] J. Sallis, *op. cit.* p. 135.
[21] Cmnd 9469 para. 221.

provisions of the Act, is to be set out in an instrument of government for the school.[22] Separate provision in relation to GM schools was made in the ERA 1988 and is now contained in the EA 1993 (see iii. below).

ii. *Constitution, membership and decision-making following the Education (No. 2) Act 1986 (LEA-maintained schools)*

The 1986 Act has put LEA representatives into the minority and has widened local representation, through co-opted business community members and elected parent governors. Teacher representation is limited to one (if a school has fewer than 300 pupils) or two members per board (elected by the teaching body as a whole). The head teacher has a choice over whether to serve as a governor (ex-officio). There is no requirement for pupil governors; if a pupil were co-opted onto the governing body s/he would have to be at least 18 years old, the minimum age for appointment as a school governor.[23]

Prior to the 1986 Act, the governing body in aided or special agreement schools consisted of two-thirds foundation governors and one-third LEA governors. The Act provided for flexibility, yet kept the foundation governors in the majority and provided for parent and teacher representation. It also provided for grouping of schools under one governing body, with disputes to be resolved by the Secretary of State.[24]

Composition of school governing body for county, controlled and maintained special schools (s.3)

Size of School	Representation on governing body					
No. of pupils	Parents	LEA	Teachers	Co-opted	Head	*Tot*
Less than 100	2	2	1	3	1	9
100–299	3	3	1	4	1	12
300–599	4	4	2	5	1	16
600 or more	5	5	2	6	1	19

---

[22] s.1(1).

[23] E(No. 2)A 1986, s.15(4). All but one of the members of the Taylor Committee wished to see pupils eligible for governorship at the age of 16: *op. cit.* para. 4.26.

[24] ss.2(5) and (6), 9 and 10. On the extent of the Secretary of State's power to order grouping of schools, see *R.* v. *Secretary of State for Education and Science ex p. Inner London Education Authority* (1989) *The Times,* September 19, 1989. The category of school, for the purpose of the composition of the governing body, shall be determined under s.9(3).

Note:

In controlled schools all bar one (or two, in the largest category of school) of the total shown for co-opted governors must be foundation governors. For example, a school of 300–599 pupils will have four foundation governors and one co-opted governor.

Parent governors must be elected from amongst their own number by secret ballot organised by the LEA (or, in the case of voluntary aided, special agreement or GM schools, by the governing body).[25] There is no prescribed method of election — schools are free to decide whether to use a first past the post or single transferable vote system, or whatever other system they wish.[26] In the event of there being an insufficient number of parents standing for election, the governors must appoint parents to the vacancies.[27] The governors must look to the local business community when seeking to co-opt governors.[28] In maintained special schools a co-opted governor (or two, if the school has at least 100 pupils) may be appointed by a voluntary organisation (or by two jointly).[29]

The scope for party political manipulation of governing bodies of the above schools has clearly been lessened considerably. LEA members constitute only one quarter of the entire membership. Nevertheless, there is evidence that party politics may influence the nomination of governors by LEAs. In 1990 there were reports that three LEAs had refused to nominate (or had withdraw nomination from) opposition councillors. The shadow Education Secretary presented a private member's bill aimed at requiring nominations to reflect the political complexion of the LEA concerned, although it was not supported by the Government and did not progress.[30] Attempts to remove governors who did not follow party policy led to the important *Brunyate* litigation, discussed below.

---

[25] E(No. 2)A 1986, s.15.

[26] See DES Circular 7/87 Annex 9 para. 22.

[27] E(No. 2)A 1986, s.5.

[28] s.6. A Leverhulme study found that 66 per cent. of the co-opted governors were male (see *Education* December 23, 1988). For discussion of the kinds of people co-opted, see R. Deem, "The Reform of School Governing Bodies: The Power of the Consumer over the Producer?," in M. Flude and M. Hammer (eds), *The Education Reform Act 1988: Its Origins and Implications* (1990) at pp. 161–162.

[29] E(No. 2)A 1986, s.7.

[30] See *The Times*, February 8, 1990.

Composition of school governing body for voluntary aided or special agreement school (s.4)

Size of School No. of pupils	Representation on governing body				
	Parents	LEA	Teachers	Found'n	Head
Less than 300	1(min.)	1(min.)	1(min.)	6	1
300 or more	1(min.)	1(min.)	2(min.)	7	1

Note:
The size of the governing body will obviously depend on the numbers chosen in each category. As shown, the law lays down the *minimum* number of parent, teacher and LEA governors. The number of foundation governors must be such as will mean that they outnumber the other governors by two, or by three where the size of the governing body as a whole will be 19 or more: s.3(3)(*a*). Aided secondary schools may now also have sponsor governors: s.4A (added by EA 1993, s.271).

The provisions on election of teacher and parent governors outlined earlier apply also to voluntary aided and special agreement schools. The 1986 Act also provides that at least one of the foundation governors must, at the time of his or her appointment, be a parent of a pupil registered at the school.[31]
So far as *all* categories of LEA-maintained school are concerned, the election of parent governors has been problematic in several respects. First, there has been the question of eligibility to vote. The LEA or governors must take all reasonably practicable steps to ensure that those eligible to vote are informed of the vacancy and of their eligibility to stand for election.[32] (The governors' annual report to parents must also give information about forthcoming parent governor elections.[33]) To be eligible to vote a person must fall within the definition of "parent" in s.114(1) of the EA 1944, as amended. This now includes, following the Children Act 1989, persons with "parental reponsibility" for a child — such as a person in whose favour a residence order has been made.[34] As that person need not be the child's natural or adoptive parent, it is possible for more than two persons to be eligible to vote as an EA

---

[31] E(No. 2)A 1986, s.4(3)(*b*).
[32] *Ibid.* s.15(6).
[33] *Ibid.* s.30(2)(*g*).
[34] See s.12(4) of the Children Act 1989, which states that where a residence order is made the court shall make an order conferring parental responsibility on the applicant (unless s/he already has it).

"parent." LEAs and governors are advised that they need not seek to
trace every person who falls within the definition of parent "but ...
cannot rule ineligible anyone known to them to be a parent."[35] An
indeterminate constituency may be undesirable, but it is difficult to see
what else could be advised in the circumstances.

A second problem is the elected parent governor's term of office.
Governors may generally hold office for up to four years.[36] Teacher
governors must relinquish office on leaving the school. But elected
parent governors may remain as full members of the governing body
even though their child may no longer be registered there. Governors
can be disqualified from office on such grounds as: being an
undischarged bankrupt; being sentenced to a term of imprisonment, in
the previous five years, of at least three months (suspended or not); and
receiving a sentence of imprisonment, in the previous 20 years, of at
least two and a half years.[37] Some of the rules on disqualification were
tightened up in 1992. For example, a person is disqualified from
holding governorships at more than two schools (previously four) and is
disqualified from continuing to hold office if s/he fails to attend any
governors' meetings over a continuous period of six months (previously
twelve months).[38]

Another problem has been the difficulty of finding a sufficient
number of persons to serve on governing bodies. Following the 1986
Act, elections took place in county, controlled and special schools in
1988 and in voluntary aided and special agreement schools in 1989. By
1992 the first batch of appointees had come to the end of their four year
term of office (although may have been eligible for re-election[39]). There
is evidence that of those who resigned early, many did so because of the
strain of the work. In a survey by a group of northern England LEAs,
the 569 governors who had resigned in the first six months of 1991
gave their principal reason as lack of time (29 per cent.), or the
responsibilities of financial control (25 per cent.) or the high level of
overall responsibility (16 per cent.).[40] Faced with the possibility of a
shortfall in recruitment, the DFE mounted a publicity campaign aimed
at attracting the 75,000 governors needed. A booklet, *Schools Need
Governors*, was published, and a week in June 1992 was designated
"National Governors' Week." In addition to these general difficulties in
recruitment, there has been under-representation of ethnic minorities
among parent and other governors.[41]

[35] DES Circular 7/87 para. 12.
[36] E(No. 2)A 1986, s.8(2).
[37] Education (School Government) Regulations 1989 SI 1989 No. 1503, regs. 6 and 7.
[38] *Ibid.* regs 5 and 8.
[39] E(No. 2)A 1986, s.8(3).
[40] *The Guardian*, June 9, 1992.
[41] R. Deem, *supra* (n.28) at p. 164.

Finally, there have reportedly been irregularities in a small number of elections. The Divisional Court has held that if it is alleged that the election was carried out in a defective manner, the appropriate recourse would be to the Secretary of State via complaint under section 99 of the 1944 Act rather than to the courts.[42]

With parent governors having equal voting rights, there are, on the face of it, enormous opportunities for advancement of consumer interests at school level. As the Department's publicity material on school governorship puts it, the legislation "gives local people the opportunity to become involved in the running of local schools and to have a real stake in the education service."[43] Now that so much power has been devolved to schools, very many important decisions have to be taken by the governing body, and parent governors can make an influential contribution. In governors' meetings, decisions may be taken on most matters by a simple majority vote,[44] and with the quorum being relatively small,[45] it is possible for a determined group of parent governors to sway the matter in their favour. Furthermore, as a meeting may be requisitioned by any three (or more) members of the governing body, the parent governors in most county and voluntary controlled schools could call a meeting to present a particular issue and put it to the vote.[46] Parent governors may also be eligible to chair the governing body (the governors must generally elect their chairman/woman and vice-chairman/woman at the first meeting of the school year[47]) and to be members of its delegated committees, which are permitted to make decisions on certain matters.[48] The only circumstances in which

---

[42] R. v. *Northampton County Council ex p. Gray* (1986) *The Times,* June 10, *per* Mann J.

[43] *Schools Need Governors* (1992) p. 2.

[44] Education (School Government) Regulations 1989 *op. cit.,* reg. 14(1). If the votes for and against the motion are equal in number, the chairman/woman has the casting vote.

[45] Reg. 13 provides that, with a few limited exceptions (e.g. decisions on the co-option of governors other than foundation governors), where quorum is three-quarters of those entitled to vote, the quorum is either:

    (i)   three governors, or, if greater, one-third of the total membership (rounded up where necessary); or

    (ii) the quorum specified in the instrument of government if greater than the figure in (i), provided that it is not more than two-fifths of the total membership (rounded up where necessary).

[46] Governors' meetings must be held at least once a term (reg. 12(1)), and in practice tend to be held more frequently.

[47] Education (School Government) Regulations 1989 *op. cit.* reg. 9(1). All categories of governor, apart from teacher governors (reg. 9(5)), are eligible for these offices.

[48] *Ibid.* regs 25 and 26. The use of these committees, under such titles as "finance and general purposes," "staffing and curriculum," and "buildings and maintenance" etc., has grown in line with the increased responsibilities of governing bodies. For the purposes of delegation of decision-making, the regulations in effect divide governors'

—continued on next page

participation would be proscribed would be where the governors were discussing a matter relating to a governor's own child in particular, for example in connection with a disciplinary matter. In the heavily regulated regime for the conduct of governors' business, there are in fact detailed rules covering withdrawal from meetings, and non-participation in voting, in circumstances where any member's personal interests, including defined pecuniary interests, are involved.[49]

On the whole, then, there is considerable potential for real participation by parent governors in the running of schools. Parent governors are being helped to acquire the necessary skills through programmes of governor training,[50] which have received fairly generous government financial support via Education Support Grants. Although, as noted earlier, a 1984 study showed that parent governors' contribution was not particularly effective, the size of parental representation on governing bodies has grown since then; and, more importantly, the consumer interest has been advanced in so many different ways that schools must now perceive the importance of eliciting the consumer view and ensuring that they are responsive to it. As a result, parent governors' views may carry more weight than previously.

But how much influence can and do parents exert through their parent governors? Parent governors are representatives rather than delegates, representing the collective consumer interest in education. However, there is recent evidence of parent governors' reluctance or inability to express the "parent" view, for example in relation to a

---

[48] *—continued from previous page*
functions into three categories: (i) those which may not be delegated (reg. 25(2)) (*e.g.* curricular responsibilities, decisions on starting and finishing times of school day); (ii) those which may be delegated to a committee only (reg. 25(3) and (4)) (*e.g.* reinstatement of an excluded pupil); and (iii) those which may be delegated to a committee, a member of the governing body or the head teacher (any which do not fall within (i) or (ii)). See further DES, *Amendments to the Education (School Government) Regulations 1987* Consultation Document (1989).

[49] Education (School Government) Regulations *op. cit.* reg. 14 and Sched. 2. As noted in Chap. 2, the courts held that teacher governors would have a direct or indirect pecuniary interest in a decision on whether to apply for city technology college status, because of the significant differences in working conditions and possibly pay (*Bostock* v. *Kay* (1989) *The Times,* April 20), but would not where the decision was whether or not to ballot parents on GM status (*R.* v. *Governors of Small Heath School ex p. Birmingham City Council* (1989) *The Times,* August 14). The regulations were amended in 1989, in line with the *Small Heath* decision, to provide that teacher and head teacher governors should not be deemed to have a pecuniary interest in an opting out vote.

[50] Training is provided for by the E(No. 2)A 1986, s.57(*b*). It has been funded at the rate of 70 per cent. Education Support Grant (ESG) paid under the Education (Grants and Awards) Act 1984. The 70 per cent. limit has been removed by s.278 of the EA 1993, which has also renamed ESGs as "grants for education support and training."

school's charging policy.[51] Furthermore, although the DFE's Booklet, *Schools Need Governors*, suggests that parent governors can play an important role in supplying information to parents, communication between parent governors and their "constituency" is often poor.[52] It has been suggested that better channels of communication between governors and parents should be provided by schools, although there has been some resistance to this among head teachers.[53] Parent governors can also take up individual cases on parents' behalf.[54] But in research by the author, in which 440 parents were questioned about, *inter alia*, the person whom they would approach first with a complaint about their child's schooling, only *four* parents selected the parent governor compared with over 400 who selected the head teacher or teacher.[55]

iii. *Governing bodies of grant-maintained schools*
The rules concerning the constitution of governing bodies and the election, appointment and dismissal of governors, are in some respects more elaborate in the case of GM schools than for other maintained schools. In part this is because the acquisition of GM status involves reconstituting the governing body, although with reference to the school's previous status as a county, controlled, aided or special agreement school.[56] For example, if the school was previously voluntary aided it will have a number of foundation governors, but possibly a different number when it becomes GM. Extending opportunities for opting out by enabling schools to gain GM status as a group, or by enabling sponsors to establish a new GM school, discussed in Chapter 2, have added further separate provisions on constitution and related matters.

Whatever the school's previous status or the arrangements under which it acquired its GM status, its instrument of government must incorporate the requirements of the relevant parts of the 1993 Act which deal with the constitution of the governing body.[57] The composition of the governing body of a GM school (but not of a GM special school) is to be as shown below.

---

[51] K.J. Brehony and R. Deem, "Charging for free education: an exploration of a debate in school governing bodies" (1990) 5 *Journal of Education Policy* 333.

[52] See M. Golbey, "Parent Governorship in the New Order," in F. Macleod (ed.), *Parents and Schools: the Contemporary Challenge* (1989), p. 143.

[53] J. Sallis *op. cit.* p. 159.

[54] *Ibid.*

[55] See N. Harris, *Complaints About Schooling — The role of section 23 of the Education Reform Act 1988* (1992) pp. 116 and 117.

[56] See Chap. 2. p. 43 n.10 for a description of these categories.

[57] EA 1993, s.55(2).

Composition of governing body of GM school[58]

	Primary school	Secondary school
Parents	3–5	5
Teachers	1 or 2	1or 2
Head teacher[a]	1	1
First or foundation governors[b]	6–9	6–9
(Sponsor governors[c])	(4)	(4)

Note:

a.   The head teacher is a governor ex-officio. Unlike in LEA-maintained schools the head teacher *must* serve as a governor: EA 1993, s.62(1).

b.   The Act simply states that the instrument of governors should provide that the number of first or foundation governors (defined below) must be sufficient to outnumber the rest of the governors: EA 1993, ss.63(2) and 65(2).

c.   A secondary school may have up to four sponsor governors: EA 1993, s.66. A sponsor governor is a person appointed as a governor by a sponsor of the school: *Ibid.* Sched. 7 paras 9 and 14.

Parent governors and teacher governors are to be elected in the same way as in other maintained schools.[59] GM primary schools may have between three and five parent governors, whereas secondary schools must have five.[60] The number of parent, teacher or first or foundation governors is not related to the number of pupils at the school, unlike in the LEA-maintained sector (above).

If the school was a county school before it acquired GM status, or if (by virtue of the new powers contained in the 1993 Act) it is a new school established as a GM school by a funding authority, the school has "first" governors. At least two of the first governors must be parents of children at the school and at least two must represent the local community; and among the first governors the "local business community" must also be represented.[61] GM schools which were classed as voluntary schools or which are new schools established by promoters under the 1993 Act[62] will have "foundation" governors rather than first

---

[58] *Ibid.* ss.59–67 and Sched. 7. On GM special schools, see Sched. 11.

[59] *Ibid.* s.60(3) and (5) and 61(3).

[60] *Ibid.* s.60(2) and (7).

[61] *Ibid.* s.63(3).

[62] s.49 permits voluntary bodies or other promoters to establish new GM schools. Unlike voluntary aided schools, which receive grants covering 85 per cent. of capital costs, a school established as a GM school under s.49 will have 100 per cent. of capital costs covered: see *Choice and Diversity*, para. 4.11.

governors. There is a general rule that at least two foundation governors must be parents of children at the school.[63]

Note that up to two *additional governors* may be appointed by the Secretary of State if it appears to him that the governing body "are not adequately carrying out their responsibilities in respect of the conduct or management of the school"[64] (see below). If this power is exercised, the foundation/governing body can appoint up to the same number of additional foundation or first governors.[65] There are also rules concerning the constitution of governing bodies of grouped GM schools, which have "core" governors.[66]

(b) Institutional autonomy in the schools sector

i. *County, voluntary and special schools*

Introduction In the space of some seven years, since the E(No.2)A 1986 began the process, the role of school governing bodies has been almost totally transformed. No longer do these bodies have a "mainly decorative" function.[67] Today, the 300,000 or so school governors in England and Wales have important powers and responsibilities in the running of their schools. The changes introduced under local management of schools (LMS), discussed below, mean that, by 1994, budgetary and management control of most maintained schools in England and Wales will rest with their governing bodies, although in practice exercised in partnership with head teachers.[68] Furthermore, the "conduct of the school" is under the governors' direction.[69] They have overall responsibility for the organisation of the secular curriculum at the school and, together with the head teacher, for school discipline and the implementation of the National Curriculum, religious education and other curricular requirements. Governing bodies also have important responsibilities concerning staffing. All these legal responsibilities

---

[63] EA 1993, s.65(6).

[64] *Ibid.* s.67(1). Note also the power to replace governors (below).

[65] *Ibid.* s.67(2).

[66] *Ibid.* s.122 and Sched. 8.

[67] S. Maclure *Education Re-formed* (3rd ed. 1992) p. 139.

[68] *e.g.*, in relation to expenditure, the expectation is that the governors and the head teacher will together produce a development plan and that the head teacher will play "a key role . . . in securing its implementation": DES Circular 7/88 *Education Reform Act: Local Management of Schools* para. 22. One author has in fact concluded that a result of the ERA 1988 is that "in the main, power has shifted from local authorities to rest with head teachers, not governing bodies": L. Field, "Power brokers in the ERA of autonomy" *T.E.S.*, July 10, 1992, p. 17. Research has certainly shown that considerable strain has been imposed on head teachers as a result of financial delegation to schools: M. Arnott *et al.*, *The Impact of Local Management on Schools* (1992).

[69] E(No. 2)A 1986, s.16(1).

relating to the conduct of the school must be laid down in articles of government, approved by the Secretary of State.[70] Governors have other responsibilities concerning, for example, the provision of information to parents and the investigation of complaints about schooling. Furthermore, with parental approval they can apply for the school to acquire GM status.

As most of these responsibilities are discussed in other chapters, it is necessary to concentrate here on only one area, probably the most important one — LMS — which involves financial and personnel management.

Local management of schools (LMS) The principle behind the LMS provisions of the ERA 1988 is simple: "maximum delegation," to governing bodies, of the finances needed to run a school and powers of management over those resources and any contracts governed by them. The Government had argued that governors were far better placed than LEAs to judge the real needs of the school and that LEAs' many tiers of bureaucracy often hindered their responsiveness to the expenditure needs of schools. The Coopers and Lybrand report on LMS, which the Government circulated to schools as guidance, emphasised that LMS would produce a more responsive and effective schools system.[71] The Government also saw LMS as a way to wrest much of the control of schools from LEAs by giving schools independence on financial matters.[72] It also viewed LMS as a means of encouraging greater competition between schools and strengthening the market approach reflected in many of its reforms by making pupil numbers at the school the principal determinant of a school's budget share. With artificial admissions limits being removed as a result of the 'open enrolment' provisions of the ERA 1988 (see Chapter 5), each school would have a major financial incentive to recruit as many pupils as the school could accommodate.

Pilot schemes in Cambridgeshire and Solihull had shown that LMS worked in practice, and plans to introduce it in all areas were announced in a consultation document in 1987 and given legal effect by the ERA 1988. All LEAs had to publish delegation schemes by September 30, 1989. Since April 1, 1993, maximum delegation under schemes already in force has applied to primary schools with 200 or more pupils and all secondary schools (apart from those in inner London boroughs, which will experience maximum delegation in 1994).

---

[70] *Ibid.* s. 1(1). The articles must not contain any provision which is inconsistent with any enactment: s. 1(5)(*a*). If a school operates under a trust deed its articles of government and instrument of govenment must be in compliance with it: s1(5)(*b*).

[71] Cooper and Lybrand, *Local Management of Schools* (1988).

[72] S. Maclure, *op. cit.* pp. 44–45.

Smaller primary schools, together with special schools,[73] will also be covered by delegation schemes, from April 1, 1994.

Only county and voluntary schools maintained by LEAs have to be covered by an LMS scheme. (LMS does not apply to GM schools.) Nursery schools are not included, but children under the age of five who are registered at a primary school (whether in a reception or nursery class) are to be taken into account in determining the size of a school's budget.

The transition to full LMS is being closely regulated. All schemes have had to be approved by the Secretary of State, who has the power to modify a scheme and/or attach conditions, and to substitute his own scheme if he considers that an LEA has unreasonably departed from the guidance on the preparation of schemes.[74] He also has the power to revise the whole or part of an operative delegation scheme by issuing (after consultation with the LEA and others) a direction to the LEA.[75] The 1988 Act and regulations provide for the publication of schemes and regular financial statements concerning the principal allocations and expenditure under them.[76] Such publication is seen as providing an element of public accountability.

Under LMS schemes, each school's budget allocation is put at the disposal of the school governors to spend in such a way "as they think fit for the purposes of the school."[77] The constraints imposed by the requirements of the National Curriculum and general expenditure needs will, in practice, leave governors with little additional freedom. As Maclure comments: "financial delegation will take place within fairly tight financial and educational constraints. Experience suggests the scope for redirection of spending, initially at least, is modest — of the order of two or three per cent."[78]

The overall sum available to the governors will depend on a number of factors. The first factor is the total amount available for expenditure by the LEA on its schools (the *general schools budget* — GSB). This is dependent on, inter alia, the amount allocated to the local authority in accordance with its standard spending assessment (SSA). In 1990, when the community charge was introduced under the Local Government

---

[73] See ERA 1988, s.43 (as substituted by the EA 1993, s.276).

[74] *Ibid.* s.34(5) and (6). The LEA must take into account the guidance: s.34(2).

[75] *Ibid.* s.35(7) and (8) (as substituted by s.274 of the EA 1993).

[76] *Ibid.* s.42 as amended by EA 1993, s.275; Education (Publication of Schemes for Financing Schools) Regulations 1989 SI 1989 No. 2335; Education (Pre-Scheme Financial Statements) Regulations 1989, SI 1989 No. 370.

[77] ERA 1988, s.36(5)(*a*).

[78] S. Maclure *op. cit.* p. 55. A recent Audit Commission report noted that "the room for manoeuvre within school budgets is often small": *Adding up the Sums: Schools' Management of their Finances* (1993) para. 38.

Finance Act 1988, one effect of the charge-capping of 20 local authorities (for exceeding their SSA's) was that the general schools budget was reduced and it was impossible to provide schools with the budget share they had already been promised by their LEA. An unsuccessful legal challenge in the High Court to the Secretary of State's action was brought by the local authorities concerned together with the National Union of Teachers and the chairs of governors of two schools. Appeals to the Court of Appeal and House of Lords failed.[79]

The next stage in assessing the allocation to schools involves the determination of how much is left (this residue forms the *aggregated schools budget* — ASB) after the excepted items (the *mandatory* and *discretionary exceptions*) have been deducted from the GSB. Finally, the budget share formula within the scheme allocates, from the ASB, a budget to each school (see below).

The *mandatory* exceptions, deducted from the GSB (as noted above), comprise, *inter alia*, capital expenditure and interest payments on debt, expenditure supported by central government grants of particular description and EC grants.[80]

The Government's policy on LMS has throughout been that "provision should be delegated unless there is a clearly identified need for the LEA to retain control."[81] This policy has led to restrictions on the amount LEAs can withhold from the GSB as *discretionary* items. The guidelines provided that for the first three years of a scheme some discretionary items should in aggregate amount to not more than 10 per cent. of the GSB. Thereafter they should be reduced progressively to seven per cent. Schools' repairs and maintenance costs, and items that could most effectively be provided centrally — including the education welfare services, peripatetic teachers and services in respect of pupils with special educational needs — were among the major items subject to this limit. Those not subject to the 10 per cent. limit included one of the most expensive items, school meals services, and premature retirement compensation and dismissal costs.

In 1991 the DES introduced a new concept: the *potential schools budget* (PSB).[82] The PSB consists of the remainder of the GSB after deduction of the mandatory exceptions and only few discretionary items: home to school transport, school meals and (during a transition period) school cleaning and grounds maintenance. LEAs should now aim to delegate at least 85 per cent. of the PSB, which produces greater delegation overall

---

[79] *Hammersmith and Fulham London Borough Council* v. *Secretary of State for the Environment* [1990] 3 All E.R. 589 (Q.B.D., C.A. and H.L.).

[80] Prescribed by s.38(4) of the 1988 Act and the Education (Financial Delegation to Schools) (Mandatory Exceptions) Regulations 1989 SI 1989 No. 1352.

[81] DES Circular 7/88, para. 63.

[82] See DES Circular 7/91, paras. 27–30.

than the previous target of 90 (rising to 93) per cent. of the GSB in respect of most of the discretionary items (above).

As noted above, a scheme's *budget share formula* will determine how much an individual school actually receives. Pupil numbers are the central determinant: 75 per cent. of the ASB was to be allocated on this basis, but the DFE have recently raised this minimum to 80 per cent. Weighting is given in accordance with the different ages of pupils (a secondary school pupil is more expensive to educate than a primary school pupil, so attracts a higher unit of resource[83]) and (following the 1991 revision of the guidance) any special educational needs.

One of the main probems with the budget share arrangements has been the averaging of teaching costs (which tend to amount to around 70 per cent. of a school's costs) across all the LEA's schools. This means that a school would have to meet its actual salary costs even though these might be higher (because the school might have older and more experienced staff) than the average. A survey by one of the major teacher unions in 1989 showed that over 50 per cent. of schools would be worse off. The Secretary of State has now allowed LEAs to compensate schools for these extra inherited costs.[84] Also taken into account in determining a school's budget allocation are the extra pro-rata costs in maintaining necessary subject expertise in small schools and the additional costs resulting from the location (*e.g.* much vandalism), the design of buildings (*e.g.* extra heating needed) and general social deprivation in the school's area.

The degree of budgetary power now resting with school governing bodies (despite the limited scope for redirecting resources noted earlier) raises questions about how governors can be made accountable. This issue is discussed below.

Control of staffing is the other main area to have been devolved to governing bodies under LMS. Previously LEAs generally had the final say on all staff appointments and dismissals (with the exception of RE teachers at voluntary schools or where the articles of government at a voluntary aided school provided otherwise), although the E(No. 2)A 1986 had provided for greater consultation of governors and more governor participation on staff selection panels, in addition to regulated

---

[83] On average 50 per cent. more was spent per secondary school pupil than per primary school pupil in England in 1990/91, which S. Byers M.P. regards as highlighting unjustifiable neglect of the primary sector: "Conspiracy of silence" *The Guardian*, April 13, 1993.

[84] DES Circular 7/91, paras. 43–48. The House of Commons Education Committee has called for more protection for such disadvantaged schools: Second Report, Session 1992–93, *Some Aspects of the Funding of Schools*. H.C. 419 (March 1993), paras. 1–14. However, to take full account of actual teaching costs would be extremely problematic, according to the Audit Commission *supra* (n.78) paras. 12–16.

recruitment procedures. Schedule 3 to the 1988 Act (and section 45 in the case of voluntary aided schools) has put control of all teaching staff (and most non-teaching staff) appointments and dismissals in the hands of governing bodies, with the LEA having no power of veto (other than on the ground that a teacher is not professionally qualified).[85] Curiously, the position where the employee is found by an industrial tribunal to have been unfairly dismissed is that the award must be made against the LEA even though it had no power to dismiss.[86]

ii. *Grant-maintained schools*

GM schools are, as noted above, independent of LEAs. Their governing bodies enjoy considerable autonomy. Section 68(4) of the EA 1993, for example, provides that the governors have "the power to do anything which appears to them to be necessary or expedient for the purpose of, or in connection with, the conduct of the school ..." The governing body has control of the school's budget and staffing. But they are, of course, dependent on the central government or funding authorities for their annual maintenance grant (and for any additional special purpose or capital grants) and must comply with any requirements relating to such grants laid down in the regulations.[87] Moreover, in certain cases powers are available to the Secretary of State to replace governors or order the closure of the school. The power of the Secretary of State (in section 53(5) of the ERA 1988) to replace up to two members of the governing body (exercised in the Newham dispute discussed below) has been extended. Under section 64 of the 1993 Act the Secretary of State can now replace all or any of the governors in cases of: "persistent failure to comply or secure compliance with any requirement ... under any enactment"; where an inspector's report reveals unacceptable standards of education which the governors have not remedied or are unlikely to remedy; or where action is proposed or has been taken by the governors which is "prejudicial to the provision of education by the school." It may be noted that county or voluntary schools' governance can, on similar grounds, be taken over by an Education Association appointed by the Secretary of State (see Chapter 6).

Government of the school The Education (School Government) Regulations, which regulate the conduct of business by governing bodies (above), do not apply to GM schools. Instead, the instrument of government must set out the rules on such matters as disqualification

---

[85] See further N. Harris, *The Law Relating to Schools* (1990) pp. 73–84.

[86] Education (Modification of Enactments Relating to Employment) Order 1989 SI 1989 No. 901. art. 4.

[87] See s.84. At the time of going to press the regulations to replace the Education (Grant-Maintained Schools) (Finance) Regulations 1989 SI 1989 No. 1287 had not been made. The funding of GM schools was discussed in Chap. 2.

from governorship and the conduct of meetings, within the framework laid down in the EA 1993.[88] It is appropriate to call it a framework because several matters prescribed elsewhere in respect of other schools' governing bodies are, in the case of GM schools, left to the governing body itself to determine — for example the quorum and voting procedure. Subject to any specific requirements laid down in the Act or instrument of government, "the governing body of a [GM] school may regulate their own procedure."[89]

Governing bodies of GM schools have virtually the same managerial role as their counterparts in LEA-maintained schools which have financial delegation. Many of their responsibilities and powers are set out in the articles of government, which must comply with the 1993 Act.[90] There are some important differences, arising out of the fact that there is no LEA involvement. Thus, for example, the LEA does not have to be consulted over staffing matters and there is no division of responsibility, between school and LEA, over repairs and maintenance. Similarly, the governing body has complete autonomy over disciplinary matters. The differences have important consequences for the accountability of GM schools, which the Government acknowledged in the 1992 White Paper (see below).

(c) Accountability and removal of school governors

i. *Aspects of accountability*

With the degree of institutional autonomy that now exists in the schools sector, the question of accountability becomes extremely important. Accountability in the running of schools operates at various levels. One of the key areas at present is accountability to the consumer for the performance of the school. The reforms of the 1980s and 1990s have placed great emphasis on this. Among the relevant requirements are those on the publication of performance data, discussed in Chapter 5. This is essentially marketplace accountability, in that schools which fail to meet parents' expectations may lose consumer support. The notion of consumer accountability is also emphasised through the attempt to present school governing bodies as 'boards of directors' which must present accounts and hold an annual meeting with the 'shareholders' (parents) to review the past year's activities. Financial and personnel control, incorporation of governing bodies of schools[91] and the

---

[88] Sched. 5.
[89] *Ibid.* para. 12.
[90] *Ibid.* Sched. 6. The powers of the governing body as regards the conduct of the school, employment of staff and entry into contracts and other matters are set out in s.68.
[91] EA 1993, s.238.

requirement to have business community governors, all suggest that the business organisation analogy is not inapt.

There is also the question of direct *legal* accountability. It would be unreasonable to expect school governors to undertake their (unpaid) responsibilities and hold themselves accountable to education consumers without some protection from legal liability. Governing bodies may incur premises liability (for example for breach of statutory duty in respect of the Education (School Premises) Regulations (SI 1981 No. 909) or breach of the Occupier's Liability Acts of 1957 or 1984)[92] or liability under the Health and Safety at Work, etc., Act 1974. It is a condition of financial delegation schemes that LEAs ensure that there is provision for governors' liability insurance in respect of such matters. The operation of a delegation scheme will itself be subject to the risk that sometimes inexperienced governors, responsible for a budget which could be in excess of £2 million (in the case of the larger secondary schools), could make mistakes resulting in funds being misapplied. The fact that governing bodies are to be incorporated (as noted above) offers individual governors some general protection from personal liability, but in any event individual governors have protection under section 36(6) of the ERA 1988, which provides that "the governors of a school shall not incur any personal liability in respect of anything done in good faith in the exercise or purported exercise of their [control of the school's budget]."

However, it is necessary for there to be broader public accountability and safeguards, because governing bodies are administering public funds. A recent authoritative review by the Audit Commission has revealed that in *practice* the accountability of governing bodies in respect of financial management under LMS is worryingly weak in a significant minority (40 per cent. in the Commission's survey) of schools. The principal causes revealed by the report (see n.78 above, paras. 54–57) are a lack of expertise (and in some cases a lack of interest) in financial management among governors and a tendency to surrender to head teachers the formal controls that would act as safeguards (such that some head teachers have been given "unlimited authority to spend money"). There are, however, some important safeguards provided by the legislation. For example, in relation to LMS, there are the requirements

---

[92] Liability may depend on whether it is the LEA or governing body which is responsible for the buildings: see N. Harris, (1991) 3(3) *Education and the Law* 125 and P. Leighton, *Schools and Employment Law* (1992) p. 157. On breach of statutory duty for the inadequacy of a glass panel in a school door, see *Refell* v. *Surrey County Council* [1964] 1 All E.R. 743. For a recent case on liability under the 1957 Act, in respect of a failure to clear frozen snow from a path leading into a school, see *Murphy* v. *Bradford Metropolitan Council* (1991) *The Times*, February 2.

concerning publication of financial statements of proposed and actual expenditure, referred to above. (In the case of GM schools, production of similar statements may be a condition attached by a funding authority to the making of a grant.[93]) LEAs are required to monitor the operation of their LMS scheme, and may, where they find that a governing body has "been guilty of a substantial or persistent failure" in respect of the requirements of the scheme, or has not been managing funds "in a satisfactory manner," suspend financial delegation.[94] Usually one month's notice must be given, but this can be dispensed with in a severe case.[95] Suspension is subject to a right of appeal to the Secretary of State.[96]

In GM schools, grants could be withdrawn, where the Secretary of State considers that the school is "unsuitable to continue" as a GM school because "the governing body have been guilty of substantial or persistent failure to comply or secure compliance with any ... enactment" (EA 1993, section 109(1)(b)). The school would in effect be discontinued by order of the Secretary of State. But so politically uncomfortable could such an eventuality be for the Government that it has tended to down-play the possibility of these schools being badly run. Note that the sections of the 1993 Act empowering the establishment of an Education Association to take over the running of a school which is failing its pupils badly (see Chapter 6) apply only to LEA-maintained schools. Nevertheless, the lack of accountability of governing bodies of GM schools highlighted by the dispute centring on Stratford School in Newham prompted a Government response, in the form of the introduction of a power for the Secretary of State to replace all or any of the first governors (see below).

ii.   *The Stratford School saga and the Government's response*
The Stratford School case hit the headlines in February 1992. Although some of the media coverage sought to present the dispute between the governors and the head teacher as a racial conflict, the real issue was the power of governors of GM schools. As noted earlier, Stratford School acquired GM status in April 1991, after a bitter dispute between members of the local community and the LEA, which was seeking permission to establish two new secondary schools in the Docklands area and wished to close the school to remove surplus capacity. According to *The Independent on Sunday,* the dispute at the school began after the governing body as a whole selected a white woman for the headship and

---

[93] EA 1993, s.84, depending on provision in grants regulations.
[94] ERA 1988, s.37(1).
[95] *Ibid.* s. 37(3).
[96] *Ibid.* s.37(8) and (9).

turned down a Sikh.[97] There were reported to be a series of rows between some members of the governing body and the head teacher over staff appointments and the running of the school.[98]

In the face of what was becoming a politically embarrassing row for the Government,[99] given that the dispute centred on an opted out school, the Secretary of State used his powers under section 53(6)(*a*) of the ERA 1988 to appoint two additional governors. This power could be exercised where it appeared to the Secretary of State that "the governing body of the school are not adequately carrying out their responsibilities with respect to the conduct or management of the school." The two additional governors were Eric Bolton, former Chief of HMI, and Daphne Gold, former head teacher at a school in the neighbouring borough of Tower Hamlets.

Commentators said that in the pursuit of their aim to give GM schools as much independence as was possible in the state sector and to make governing bodies supreme, the Government had left head teachers in a vulnerable position and had given governors relatively unchecked power. Maclure suggested that the Government had exploited "the rhetoric of governor power ... as a weapon in its campaign to undermine local authorities" and in doing so had left GM schools subject to fewer and less precise legal controls than other schools.[1] The *Independent on Sunday* posed the question "will the crisis at Stratford [School] be repeated elsewhere, and will the Secretary of State again find himself struggling to control other rebellious groups of governors?"[2]

The only other powers available to the Secretary of State had been to order discontinuance of the school or to issue directions under section 68 of the 1944 Act on the grounds of unreasonableness, use of which would have been even more embarrassing politically (Maclure commented that by closing the school the Government would have been "slaughtering one of its firstborn"[3]) and could have been open to legal challenge. In the 1992 White Paper, the Government commented, that the powers available where to order closure of the school would be "unjustified" or "inappropriate" were limited and can be only partially effective in the face of an intransigent or divided governing body."[4] It was proposed that the Secretary of State should have the power to replace any or all of the first governors (see above) where the governing

---

[97] "Parent Power Turns Sour" *The Independent on Sunday*, February 16, 1992.
[98] "Head must go, crisis school chairman insists" *Independent on Sunday*, February 1992.
[99] See, *e.g.* "Key speech puts more pressure on race dispute head", *The Times*, February 10, 1992.
[1] S.Maclure, "Beware the power of governors" *The Times*, February 17, 1992.
[2] February 9, 1992.
[3] S. Maclure *supra* (n.1).
[4] *Choice and Diversity*, para. 3.15.

body was persistently or substantially failing in its duty, or where the school inspectors had identified the school as being at risk and it was likely to remain so, or where the governing body's actions were such as to "prejudice the effective provision of education to the school's pupils."[5] These provisions would apply only to ex-county GM schools, and not therefore in the case of foundation governors in ex-voluntary schools (because "it would not be consistent with the principle of partnership with voluntary schools for the Secretary of State to have the power to be able to remove foundation governors"[6]). The Government hoped that the foundation of a former voluntary school, which has a power to remove governors (see below), would take "tough action where there are continuing and grave problems at a school."[7] The EA 1993 contains a new power to remove governors in former county GM schools (or in new GM schools established by a funding authority) and incorporates the pre-existing power to appoint two additional governors to the governing body of any GM school.[8]

iii. *Removal by appointing authorities:* Brunyate *and other decisions*
There has been important litigation concerning the exercise by appointing authorities (LEAs or foundations/trustees) of their power to remove governors from office.[9] Foundation governors of aided schools and co-opted governors (other than foundation governors) in other LEA-maintained schools may be removed under this power; but elected governors, governors appointed by the governing body where there are too few candidates for an elected post, and ex-officio governors, may not be.

The Government said in 1987 that it hoped that the power of removal would be used "only in exceptional circumstances."[10] Nevertheless, there is still scope for political manipulation, and it was reported in 1989 that the ruling Labour group on one LEA had been systematically removing 135 non-socialists from school governing bodies.[11] However, such a practice is undoubtedly illegal.

In *R. v. Brent L.B.C. ex p. Assegai*[12] Woolf L.J. said he "rejected the argument that having regard to the wide discretion of the authority in relation to the appointment and removal of governors . . . governors

---

[5] *Ibid.* para. 3.16.
[6] *Ibid.*
[7] *Ibid.*
[8] EA 1993, ss.64 and 67.
[9] See s.8(5) E(No. 2)A 1986, which states in very stark terms that "any governor . . . may be removed by the authority by whom he has been appointed."
[10] DES Circular 7/87, para. 5.5.1.
[11] "Heads angry after governors sacked" *The Guardian,* October 25, 1989.
[12] (1987) *The Times,* June 18 (Q.B.D.).

held office at the pleasure of the authority and could be removed at will." His Lordship said that Parliament had intended the power of removal to be exercised "fairly and not unreasonably or capriciously and in the interests of the school." However, the issue in the instant case was whether the LEA should have invited and heard representations from Dr Assegai before deciding to dismiss him. Woolf L.J. held that they acted illegally in removing him without having done so.

In *Brunyate* v. *Inner London Education Authority*,[13] the main issue was simply whether the LEA had acted lawfully in dismissing two of the governors it had appointed to the governing body of two grouped voluntary controlled schools. The reason for their dismissal had been their failure to support the LEA's policy of opposition to a possible application for GM or CTC status by the schools and its proposals for an extension to the period of consultation over the issue. The Divisional Court[14] (*per* Glidewell L.J.) held that the LEA was entitled to have a policy on the future of the local voluntary schools and to take that into account in the exercise of its statutory power to remove the governors that it had appointed as a means of promoting its policy. The Divisional Court had applied Simon Brown J.'s reasoning in an earlier decision, *ex p. Mars*.[15] In that case, Simon Brown J. had refused to overturn a decision to remove two foundation governors who would not support the trustees' scheme for reorganisation of a Catholic school:

> "I have to conclude that it is a legitimate use of power and thus lawful to remove foundation governors whose conscientious discharge of their role thwarts the trustees' policy . . . Clearly upon appointment the trustees can select as governors those sympathetic to their policies; it is not readily to be thought that Parliament intended to preclude such a consideration upon their exercise of the power of dismissal."

The Divisional Court's decision in *Brunyate* was overturned by the Court of Appeal.[16] The Court held that while the LEA's policy could legitimately be brought to bear in its selection of appointees, it could not provide the sole or main basis for removing governors in mid-term (cf *Mars* above). Having chosen particular individuals as governors, the LEA could not use the power of removal "for reasons which did not involve any possible criticism of the governors as to the way they had

---

[13] [1989] 2 All E.R. 417 (H.L.).

[14] (1989) *The Times*, February 1, reported *sub nom. R.* v. *Haberdashers' Aske's Hatcham School Governors, ex p. I.L.E.A.; R.* v. *I.L.E.A., ex parte Brunyate.*

[15] *R.* v. *Trustees of the Roman Catholic Diocese of Westminster, ex p. Mars* (1988) 86 L.G.R. 507.

[16] (1989) *The Times*, March 7.

performed their duties" (*per* Woolf L.J.). The intention behind the legislation was that govenors would be removed only "to the extent that was necessary to prevent the policy of the Act being frustrated" and that LEAs and governors "should have independent spheres of responsibility." The same view prevailed when the LEA appealed to the House of Lords. Lord Bridge stated that the appointed governors were not delegates of the authority; once appointed they were completely independent of the appointing authority. Thus "to allow removal . . . of non-compliant governors on the grounds of their non-compliance with the wishes of the authority is inevitably to allow a usurpation of the governors' independent function."[17]

In the light of the House of Lords' decision in *Brunyate*, the Court of Appeal in *ex p. Mars* (pursued to appeal *sub. nom. ex p. Andrews*[18]) overturned Simon Brown J.'s decision.

The *Brunyate* decision has told us much more about the circumstances in which removal of governors by appointing authorities may take place than when it may not. Only in the Court of Appeal, when Woolf L.J. suggested that the power of removal might be used solely where there is a legitimate concern about the way the governors have performed their duties, do we have a clear indication of the scope of the power of removal. However, Lord Bridge's judgment in the House of Lords does deal with the important point concerning the independence not only of the governing body as a whole, but also of individual governors. He said that "independent governors, so long as they hold office as such, have both the right and the duty to exercise the function of their office independently in accordance with their own judgment."[19] This emphasises that individual governors, whether elected or not, may speak freely in accordance with their conscience, even if this can create the kind of dissention witnessed in a number of cases. This freedom may be seen as essential in order that governors are able to participate fully in policy making at school level.

3. COLLEGES OF FURTHER EDUCATION AND SIXTH FORM COLLEGES

(a) Institutional autonomy and government following the ERA 1988

Institutional autonomy was brought to the further education (FE) sector in two stages. First, the ERA 1988 introduced arrangements intended

---

[17] *Supra.* (n. 13) at p. 421.
[18] (1989) *The Times,* August 18.
[19] *Supra* (n. 13) at p. 420.

to give institutions a similar degree of self-government and independence from LEAs as the schools sector under LMS. LEAs had to prepare
financial delegation schemes for FE colleges (apart from those with fewer
than 200 full-time students),[20] with funding to be based on a formula.
As with LMS, financial delegation brought with it control of staffing.

For the first time, the basic constitution of governing bodies of
colleges was prescribed by law. A governing body could have no more
than 25 governors. Of these, no more than 20 per cent. could consist of
persons selected and appointed by the LEA. Local business, professional
and other groupings, (*e.g.* trade unions) also had to be represented.[21] As
with schools, provision was made for withdrawal of financial delegation
in cases of failure or mismanagement.[22]

At the same time as giving colleges greater autonomy, the 1988 Act
also conferred more clear-cut responsibilities on LEAs concerning the
provision of further education (FE).[23] LEAs were required to ensure that
there were adequate facilities for FE in their area, and in determining
whether facilities were adequate had to consider, *inter alia*, the
requirements of those aged 16 or over with learning difficulties.[24]

(b) The Further and Higher Education Act 1992 and the FE sector

Hardly had the reforms under the ERA 1988 come into effect than the
Government announced, in a two-volume White Paper published in
May 1991,[25] a substantial restructuring of post-16 provision. The
Government argued that one of the means of improving education and
training opportunities for young people was to "give colleges more
freedom to expand their provision and respond more flexibly to the
demands of customers."[26] As a means of achieving this, colleges of FE
would be removed from local authority control. Sixth-form colleges
would also cease to be part of the LEA-maintained sector, the idea being
to enable them to continue with their academic traditions while
extending increasingly into vocational education, on which the White
Paper laid great emphasis. All colleges would be funded through central
councils (appointed by the Secretary of State). The funding regime
operated by the councils would be designed to provide "a powerful
incentive to recruit additional students and reduce unit costs."[27]

---

[20] ERA 1988, ss.139–144. See also DES Circular 9/88.
[21] ERA 1988, s.152(1)(*b*).
[22] *Ibid.* s.150.
[23] EA 1944, s.41(2), as substituted by s.120(2) of the ERA 1988.
[24] EA 1944, s.41, as substituted by s.120 ERA 1988.
[25] *Education and Training for the 21st Century* (1991), Cm 1536.
[26] *Ibid.* Vol. 1, para 1.5.
[27] *Ibid.* para. 9.5.

Colleges would also continue to be funded partly through TECs (see Chapter 1).

Thus what was planned, and has now been given legal effect under Part I of the FHEA 1992 (as from April 1, 1993), is a system which combines devolved authority with greater centralisation of power. The former results from colleges having corporate status, as further education corporations, with most property and staff transferred into their ownership and employment respectively.[28] The constitution of a corporation and the legal framework for the management of the institution are laid down in the instrument and articles of government, which are to be as prescribed by regulations, although some room for flexibility has been left — for example, over the size and composition of the corporation and the academic board.[29] At the same time, the creation of the Further Education Funding Councils (one for England, which has regional advisory committees, and one for Wales), appointed by the Secretary of State,[30] has resulted in centralised control over the FE sector. The Councils allocate and administer central government funds to institutions (and "will only fund the kinds of education they consider appropriate to be made by [a] college"[31]). They must provide information and advice requested by the Secretary of State.[32] They have also taken over LEAs' legal duty to secure the provision of sufficient facilities for FE and all full-time education for persons over the age of 16, including those in school sixth forms (for the most part leaving LEAs with responsibility only for adult education and organised leisure time occupation).[33] The Councils also have a role in the assessment of the quality of education provided by institutions, and each has to have a Quality Assessment Committee (also appointed by the Secretary of State) for this purpose.[34]

---

[28] FHEA 1992, ss.15–25. See also the Further and Higher EA 1992 (Commencement No. 1 and Transitional Provisions) Order 1992 SI 1992 No. 831, as amended by an amending order, SI 1992 No. 2041.

[29] See ss.20 and 89(4) of, and Sched. 4 to, the FHEA 1992; the Education (Government of Further Education Corporations) (Former Sixth Form Colleges) Regulations 1992 SI 1992 No. 1957; and the Education (Government of Further Education Corporations) (Former Further Education Colleges) Regulations 1992 SI 1992 No. 1963. Academic boards may have up to 30 members. Note that under the regulations the membership of a former sixth-form college that is a further education corporation may include a maximum of two parents. In any further education corporation there may be one student member, nominated and elected by the students. Persons under the age of 18 are eligible to be student members of further education corporations, whereas school governors who must be at least 18 years old (see above).

[30] FHEA 1992, s.1.

[31] Cm 1536, *op. cit.*, Vol. 2 para 4.14.

[32] FHEA 1992, ss.6–8.

[33] *Ibid.* ss.2, 3, 10, and 11 and Sched. 2.

[34] *Ibid.* s.9.

Section 7 enables the Secretary of State to attach terms and conditions to the provision of grants to the Funding Councils. The Secretary of State also has the power[35] to issue directions both to the Councils (including directions as to the provision of financial support to institutions) and, in a case of default of duty by an institution, to the institution concerned. If the governors of an institution are found to be mismanaging its financial affairs, the Secretary of State can remove and replace any or all of them.[36] Thus while the FE sector and sixth form colleges have joined GM schools and the former polytechnics in being 'liberated' from LEAs,[37] their new controllers are in essence central government, albeit exerting less overt authority than LEAs.

4. HIGHER EDUCATION

(a) Introduction

As with the further education sector, the reforms to higher education have combined devolved power and local independence with greater central control. They must be viewed in the context of an official Government policy of "cost effective expansion [via] greater competition for funds and students."[38] The funding of higher education is a complex matter, and it is not proposed to include here a detailed discussion of the way that institutions' allocations are determined. Nevertheless, as it is principally through funding controls that central authority over higher education is exerted, it is necessary to explain the legal framework surrounding funding allocations. The Government has regarded tight control of funding as particularly important in view of the continuing expansion of student numbers, to which it first committed itself publicly in a 1987 White Paper.[39]

The potential impact of the expected expansion (from 677,000 full time equivalent students in 1987 to 1,170,000 in 2000 — approaching one in three of 18–19 year olds) on the mandatory awards system led to the freezing of student grants at their 1989/90 level and the introduction of the student loans system (under the Education (Student Loans) Act 1990). Much more fundamental, however, were the changes

---

[35] *Ibid.* ss.56 and 57.

[36] *Ibid.* s.57(1).

[37] A further illustration of reduced LEA influence over colleges is the limit on local authority membership of further education corporations — a maximum of two councillors or council employees, who can only serve as co-opted members (SI 1992 No. 1957 *op. cit.* Sched. 1 para. 3; SI 1992 No. 1963 *op. cit.* Sched. 1 para. 3).

[38] Secretary of State for Education and Science, *Higher Education: A New Framework* (1991) Cm. 1541.

[39] *Higher Education: Meeting the Challenge* Cmnd 9691.

to the structure of the higher education system itself. As with further education, there were two distinct phases.

(b) Higher education under the Education Reform Act 1988

The Robbins Committee in 1963 had commented that while it was desirable to secure "the removal of any designations or limitations that cause differentiation between institutions that are performing similar functions," it was important to recognise that "with the wide field of higher education there is a need for a variety of institutions whose functions differ."[40] In the period after Robbins the emergent polytechnic sector developed a different type of higher education, with an emphasis largely on technical and vocational education, until the establishment of the Council for National Academic Awards paved the way for the polytechnics to introduce undergraduate and postgraduate courses equivalent to those offered by universities.

The ERA 1988 left the binary line intact. But the universities' independence, derived from the Royal Charters under which they were established,[41] was seen as becoming increasingly under attack through greater funding controls. Furthermore, lecturers' academic freedom was regarded as threatened by, *inter alia,* the abolition of tenure for new and promoted staff.[42] The Act introduced a new funding body for the university sector, the Universities Funding Council (UFC), which was responsible for administering central government grants to institutions, for research, teaching and associated activities.[43] It replaced the

---

[40] Robbins Committee, *Report of the Committee on Higher Education Vol. 1: Report* (1963), p. 8.

[41] On the scope and role of such a charter in prescribing the internal legal regime for the conduct of a university, see *Pearce* v. *University of Aston in Birmingham (No. 2)* [1991] 2 All E.R. 469 at 472–474, *per* Browne-Wilkinson V-C. The arcane world of internal university regulation was penetrated momentarily in a number of cases concerned with the jurisdiction of University Visitors over personnel disputes. Although the House of Lords upheld the general exclusivity of this jurisdiction (*Thomas* v. *University of Bradford* [1987] 1 A.C. 795), it has been cut down by the ERA 1988 — for example in respect of dismissal through compulsory redundancy (see *Pearce* v. *University of Aston in Birmingham* [1991] 2 All E.R. 461 (C.A.)) — in cases where a dispute has not been referred to and accepted by the Visitor (see A. Khan "University visitor revisited. Part 2" (1991) 3(4) *Education and the Law* 179 at p. 183). See further ERA 1988, ss.202–206, and, on the question of *res judicata* in respect of a decision prior to the coming into force of the relevant sections of the ERA 1988, *Hines* v. *Birbeck College (No. 2)* [1991] 4 All E.R. 450 (C.A.). *R.* v. *Lord President of the Privy Council ex p. Page* [1993] 1 All E.R. 97 (H.L.) limits the courts' judicial review jurisdiction over Visitors' decisions; see H. W. R. Wade, "Visitors and Errors of Law" [1993] 109 L.Q.R. 155.

[42] J. Griffith, "The Education Reform Act: abolishing the independent status of the universities" (1990) 2(3) *Education and the Law* 97.

[43] ERA 1988, s.131

University Grants Committee (UGC), which had had no statutory basis but which for over half a century had allocated funds to universities and "allowed the universities to retain an arms-length relationship with the Treasury (and later the Department of Education and Science)."[44] In 1981, the UGC, dominated by academics, had sought to defend academic standards in the face of severe Treasury-imposed cuts in funding. It is said that at the same time it had allowed a disproportionate burden of the cuts to fall on some of the newer universities which tailored courses to the industrial and commercial sectors.[45] Unpopular with the Government because of differences in its and ministers' priorities, and increasingly out of favour with the universities as a result of its implementation of the Government's higher education funding cuts, the UGC had been on a downward slope. The Government wanted greater control, and the 1988 Act provided it.

The UFC, created by the 1988 Act, had 15 members, all appointed by the Secretary of State. Between six and nine members could be drawn from higher education, but the remainder would normally be comprised of persons with experience of, and capacity in, "industrial, commerical or financial matters or the practice of any profession."[46] On the other side of the binary line, funds were administered to the polytechnics and colleges by the identically constituted and appointed Polytechnic and Colleges Funding Council (PCFC).[47] Each of Funding Councils had the power to attach conditions to the making of grants. Funds were provided to the Councils by the Secretary of State, who could attach conditions (but not in relation to the funding of any specific institution).

The changes in the funding of higher education produced an unprecedented degree of central control over the university sector at the expense of institutional autonomy. This control was, for the most part, exercised via the UFC.[48] The UFC had to operate within the policy framework laid down by the Secretary of State. The Council controlled most land and building acquisitions and disposals and required the universities to present accounts and provide various forms of output information. It was also empowered to keep each institution's level of

[44] S. Maclure, *Education Re-formed* (2nd ed., 1989) p. 93. The Croham Committee (*Review of the University Grants Committee* Cm 81 (1987)) recommended the establishment of a statutory University Grants Council, which would have operated along similar lines, although with less Government control, to the UFC established by the 1988 Act: see G. Williams, "Higher Education," in M. Flude and M. Hammer, *The Education Reform Act 1988: Its Origins and Implications* (1990) at p. 264.
[45] S. Maclure, *op. cit.*; G. Williams, *op. cit.*
[46] ERA 1988, s. 131(3).
[47] s. 132.
[48] See ss. 131–134.

balances under review. In UFC Circular 19/89, the Council made it clear that funding would be determined on a competitive basis, with universities having to bid for funds (although price would not be the only consideration in allocating funds; managerial requirements relating to, *inter alia*, performance indication and quality assessment, would also be used). So what was being introduced was a kind of "contract" system for the funding of institutions.[49] Universities would have to meet all the terms and conditions laid down and would, in any event, be forced to seek ever greater cost-effectiveness by the competitive element.

Griffith commented that through the 1988 Act the Government "provided itself with the detailed powers . . . necessary to control the activities of the universities to the extent that [it] thinks fit."[50] Such control was unprecedented. As Maclure says:

> "It is difficult to exaggerate the magnitude of the change in the management of British higher education implicit in these sections of the Act . . . The foundations have shifted. The idea of universities as independent centres of research, capable of standing out against government and society . . . is discarded. Instead universities are made servants of the State and its priorities."[51]

Similar controls were introduced in the polytechnics sector.[52] They did not produce the same degree of controversy, perhaps because this sector had already been subject to elements of funding regulation through the National Advisory Body (abolished by the Act[53]) and the DES. Nevertheless, the controls introduced under the Act went considerably further, as shown above. Even so, the polytechnics did gain greater independence than they had previously enjoyed. The Government applauded their relative cost-effectiveness and responsiveness to the needs of industry. In some fields, such as business and technology, polytechnics were leading the way. The polytechnics had 'come of age.' These were arguments that were later used to justify the conferment of

---

[49] See DES, *Changes in Structure and Planning for Higher Education: Contracts Between Funding Bodies and HE Institutions* (May 1987) and G. Zellick, "British Universities and the Education Reform Act 1988" [1989] *Public Law* 513.

[50] *Supra.* (n.42) at p. 106.

[51] *Supra* (n.44) p. 96. However, section 202(2)(a) of the 1988 Act seeks to preserve academic freedom by enabling academics to "question and test received wisdom, and put forward new ideas and controversial or unpopular opinions, without placing themselves in jeopardy of losing their jobs or privileges they may have."

[52] ss.132 and 134. See P. Sharp, "The Education Reform Act 1988: the provisions for further and higher education" (1990) 2(3) *Education and the Law* 109.

[53] s.136. The NAB allocated funds to LEAs and consisted largely of representatives of local authorities. It enabled the Government to exert "some planning control over the local authority sector" (to which polytechnics then belonged): G. Williams *op. cit.* pp. 261–262.

university status on polytechnics. For the time being the polytechnics and colleges had to be satisfied with their freedom from LEAs; each would, subject to meeting the conditions laid down in the Act, be run (and still are run) by a higher education corporation (HEC).[54] At least half of the initial membership of a corporation[55] had to comprise "independent members," and not more than three of the "initial" members could be nominees of local authorities.[56] The initial members were appointed by the Secretary of State; subsequent appointments were to be made by the corporation or, in the case of independent members, by the existing independent members or the corporation (depending on when the appointment was to be made).[57] With the corporation having such a range of functions — providing higher education courses, carrying out research, employing academic and non-academic staff, borrowing money, supplying goods and services and so on — there was a dependence on strong government of the institution and a presupposition of "energetic and time-consuming participation" by local businesspersons.[58] Although the scope of the Secretary of State's default power under section 68 of the EA 1944 was extended to HECs by section 219 of the 1988 Act, there was no specific power for the Secretary of State to remove a member of a corporation.

(c) Higher education following the Further and Higher Education Act 1992

The ERA 1988 instituted a transitional phase which the FHEA 1992 has concluded. The 1992 Act has empowered the Privy Council to authorise polytechnics' use of the word "university" in their title.[59] It has also abolished the Council for National Academic Awards (through which polytechnic degrees were awarded)[60] and has empowered

---

[54] The Secretary of State designated the qualifying institutions by order and conferred corporate status under ss.121 and 122 of the Act. The powers of HECs and provision for transfer of property and staff were laid down in ss.124–128.

[55] The initial members were the Principal of the institution, unless he or she chose not to be a member, plus 24 other members.

[56] See N.A. Bastin, "The appointment and removal of independent members of higher education corporations under the Education Reform Act 1988" (1990) 2(4) *Education and the Law* 151.

[57] Sched. 7 para. 7. Once a corporation was appointed it had to make a determination (under Sched. 7 para. 6) as to its membership in each "variable" category. In the case of independent members, if the appointment was made within three months of a determination the corporation made the appointment; otherwise the existing independent members were to make it.

[58] S. Maclure *supra* (n.44) pp. 87 and 102.

[59] FHEA 1992, s.77.

[60] *Ibid.* s.80.

polytechnics to award their own degrees.[61] More flexibility in the constitution of HECs is now permitted, and the requirement for HECs to have members who are local authority, teacher or general staff nominees has been removed.[62] There are still academic nominees, so teaching staff may continue to be represented as nominees of the institution's academic board, and there may now be up to two student nominees (previously there could only be one). The instrument now requires the approval of the Privy Council (rather than the Secretary of State),[63] as is the case with changes to chartered universities' statutes. Furthermore, in line with the suggestion in the White Paper, approval of the articles of government or of any revocation or variation of them also now rests with the Privy Council.[64]

The removal of the binary line between the former polytechnic and university sectors was achieved via the creation of the Higher Education Funding Councils (one for England and one for Wales[65]) in place of the UFC and PCFC.[66] Their members (10–15 in England and 8–12 in Wales) are appointed by the Secretary of State.[67] The HEFCs administer teaching and research funds to institutions.[68] The amount of grants made to the HEFCs, and the terms and conditions to which payment of grants may be subject, may be determined by the Secretary of State, who may impose requirements as to the funding of institutions or classes of institution.[69] However, a House of Lords amendment prevented the Secretary of State from controlling funding for individual subject programmes: the Act provides that terms and conditions attached to grants "may not be framed by reference to particular courses of study or programmes of research."[70] This restriction also applies to the "criteria for the selection and appointment of academic staff and for the admission of students." Nevertheless, the Councils must comply with any directions made to them by the Secretary of State in an order.[71] With the Government's aim being to ensure that institutions

---

[61] *Ibid.* s. 76.
[62] New Sched. 7A (replacing 7) of 1988 Act, inserted by Sched. 6 to the 1992 Act.
[63] ERA 1988, s.124A, inserted by FHEA 1992, s.71(1).
[64] Cm 1541 *op. cit.* para. 93; ERA 1988, s.125(1) and (5), as amended by FHEA 1992, s.71(2).
[65] See also the Further and Higher Education (Scotland) Act 1992, which, in s.37, created the Scottish Higher Education Funding Council.
[66] See N.A. Bastin "Further and Higher Education Act 1992 — the end of the binary line" (1992) 4(4) *Education and the Law* 163.
[67] FHEA 1992, s.62(2) and (3). The HEFC for England currently has 13 members.
[68] *Ibid.* ss.65 and 66. Research is also supported by research council funds.
[69] *Ibid.* s.68.
[70] *Ibid.* s.68(3).
[71] *Ibid.* s.81. There is also a power to give directions to the Councils in respect of an institution which is mismanaging its affairs: s.81(3).

are publicly accountable for the funds paid to them and that quality of
provision will be one of the factors determining funding,[72] the Councils
have also been given an important responsibility for quality assessment[73]
(discussed in Chapter 6). HECs themselves, have (under the model
articles) to operate internal audit procedures and may commission
efficiency studies "designed to improve the economy, efficiency and
effectiveness in the management or operation of an institution."[74] They
must also prepare proper accounts.[75]

The strong competitive element in funding allocation is set to
continue. As noted above, in the 1991 White Paper the Government
stated its belief that if cost-effective expansion was to be achieved it
would be necessary to introduce greater competition for funds and
students.[76] Under this policy, institutions will increasingly be forced to
attract more students in order to maintain (or perhaps improve) levels of
funding, and this will engender more of a market system. One of the
implications will be greater pressure to introduce shorter ('fast track')
degree programmes as well as more flexible modularized arrangements
for those who need to take time off from studying during their
degree.[77] The HEFCs have it within their power to force institutions
progressively down this road as and when the Secretary of State decrees.

5.   CONCLUSION

A broad framework of greater central government control has been
created in all sectors of education, in many cases through the funding
agencies and councils. But, leaving aside the chartered universities, it
has not prevented a considerable increase in the scope for decision-
making by institutions themselves (at the expense of LEAs' traditional
control). In schools, the increasing regulation of the decision-making
processes themselves does not detract from the power and autonomy
which governing bodies now enjoy. Consumers may have benefited from
this regulation — from the guarantee of increased representation
(although it is not clear that parent governors are truly representative of
the local community) and participation. Important decisions are taken at
the school level in which in the consumer interest is strongly

---

[72] Cm 1541 *op. cit.* Chap. 5.
[73] s.70.
[74] s.83(1).
[75] ERA 1988, s.124B.
[76] Cm 1541 *op. cit.* para. 17.
[77] *Ibid.* para. 16. See "Students call for flexible two-term academic year" *The Times* December 5, 1992.

represented. (In both schools and colleges, the business governors, as potential employers, may also represent consumer interests.) The changes which have occurred form part of the process noted elsewhere in this book towards empowerment of consumers at the expense of producers, although where school governing bodies are concerned the line between 'producer' and 'consumer' becomes somewhat blurred. This is because both sets of interests are represented on governing bodies — sometimes, for example in the case of the many parent governors who are also teachers, by individual governors.[78]

However, the increased involvement of consumers in the running of schools presents a number of problems. There is the practical problem of how parents and businesspersons can cope not only with the lack of expertise in specific areas but more particularly with the burdens of time and responsibility which the role of governor involves. Evidence suggests that this burden may leave some consumers content, or forced, to leave the running of schools substantially in the hands of full-time professionals: "consumers have been given the potential to control; however, in practice they may prove unequal to the task, by being either unable or unwilling to control producers."[79] An illustration of this is the often poor attendance at the governors' annual meeting with parents (under E(No. 2)A 1986, section 30); in a survey by HMI in 1990 of nearly 30 primary and secondary schools, no meetings in secondary schools, and only three in primary schools, were quorate.[80]

Ultimately, the influence that consumers as a whole will be able to exert over the running of schools will flow not so much from the opportunities for participation afforded to a small number of elected representatives on governing bodies, but rather from consumers' 'economic' power in the market-place for education. The development of consumer choice in education, whether parental choice of school, student choice of further or higher education institution or employer preference for a particular institution, may be the most important factor.

The changes to higher education have brought the two formerly separate sectors together under one funding body. However, the "new" universities have different management structures (within higher education corporations) to those of the chartered universities, despite other changes which have created greater parity. Although the new combined university sector will continue to comprise independent institutions, whose discreteness will be emphasised by their increasing

---

[78] See R. Deem, "The Reform of School Governing Bodies," in M. Flude and M. Hammer (eds.), *The Education Reform Act 1988: Its Origins and Implications* (1990).
[79] *Ibid.* p. 169.
[80] H.M.I., *Parents and Schools: Aspects of Parental Involvement in Primary and Secondary Schools 1989–90* (1991), p. 1.

competition for teaching and research funds, there is now closer external regulation as a result of the Acts of 1988 and 1992.[81] This legislation has subjected higher education as a whole (and further education) to considerable central government control and a combination of greater accountability and consumerist forces.[82]

---

[81] Note the comment by N.A. Bastin that "given this type of regulatory framework, the use of the term 'autonomous' in any description of a higher education corporation seems somewhat inappropriate": unpublished MA thesis Univ. of Leeds (1993), p. 103.

[82] A further development in this regard is the DFE's publication, as consultation texts, of the draft *Charter for Further Education* and *Charter for Higher Education* (both May 1993).

4

COLLECTIVE CONSUMER INTERESTS AND THE PATTERN OF LOCAL SCHOOLS PROVISION

1. INTRODUCTION

Seen in terms of school availibility, for the purposes of exercising choice, the pattern of local provision is likely to be of great importance to parents. But *all* members of the local community may claim a legitimate interest in the way education is provided in their locality. Thus participation in decision-making over significant changes to local schools, including school closures, may be a key element in local democracy. Traditionally, the local community's collective voice has been represented by its democratically elected municipal authority. Throughout much of this century LEAs have had a free hand, as well as an electoral mandate, to plan provision and to reorganise it as and when they see fit to do so, although ministerial approval has sometimes been necessary. Local electors who object to an authority's proposals have, of course, generally enjoyed a statutory right merely to submit objections, which have to be taken into account when the final decision is made. They will have similar rights in relation to proposals made by a funding authority (see below).

Changes to local provision tend to promote conflict between members of the local community and the authorities. But the scope for legal challenge is limited. Moreover, the cases have merely tended to confirm doubts, in this context, about the degree of consumer empowerment and the extent of the law's recognition of the interests of particular groups of consumers. At a time when decisions by public authorities are, in general, becoming more amenable to challenge under various avenues of redress, and there are significant moves towards greater accountability among education providers, one might expect parents and other members of the community to enjoy more rights in respect of changes to schools than they presently do. Furthermore, as consumerism has already made rather more telling incursions into this area, through the opportunities to vote on 'opting out' (GM status), one might expect rather closer recognition of collective consumer interests in respect of other decisions affecting the pattern of local schools provision. The fact that non-elected funding authorities will in the near future be in the position of proposing the establishment or closure of schools emphasises the importance of this issue.

2.   ESTABLISHMENT, CLOSURE AND REORGANISATION OF SCHOOLS

(a)   Introduction

The law on the establishment, reorganisation and closure of schools stands somewhat in isolation from the economic and political forces, both national and local, which influence the pattern of local educational provision. In general, and subject to the *ultra vires* doctrine, the law is not concerned with the underlying reasons for plans to close a school or remove its sixth form. Nevertheless, any assessment of the law's recognition of consumer interests must take account of the wider economic, political and social context to the wholesale reorganisation of schooling in many parts of the country over the past ten years.

Schools reorganisation and individual school closures have become a necessary consequence of central government pressure (reinforced, throughout the 1980s by a succession of circulars and other cajoling tactics[1]) to achieve greater economic efficiency at a time of falling school rolls.[2] The introduction of strict legal requirements concerning the curriculum, laid down in the ERA 1988, has made educational efficiency a highly pertinent consideration, in that smaller schools may struggle to find the staffing resources (providing the range of skills) needed to fulfil the statutory requirements. Furthermore, larger schools have greater economic viability,[3] especially under the LMS formula funding system (see Chapter 3).

---

[1] See P. Meredith, *Government, Schools and the Law* (1992) pp. 117–123. By 1987, 1.25 million places had been eliminated (S. Maclure, *Education Re-formed* (3rd edn. 1992) p. 34). However, in that year Circular 3/87 (*Providing for Quality: the Pattern of Organisation to Age 19*) urged the reduction of a further one in two surplus places in primary schools and three in five in secondary schools by 1991. As noted in Chap. 2, the 1992 White Paper reported that there were still some 1.5 million surplus places (*Choice and Diveristy*, para. 4.2).

[2] *Supra* p. 38. Maclure (*op. cit.* p. 33) comments that "Demography always has a bearing on educational planning and administration — usually a bigger part than ideology."

[3] A. B. Atkinson, *The Economics of Education* (1983), p. 133.

The potential conflict between the two government policies of widening parental choice and achieving greater efficiency through the elimination of surplus capacity is all too evident. As the Audit Commission recognised when framing its *Citizen's Charter* performance indicators for education recently, "for reasons of efficiency, schools should be well filled, but if parents are to be able to choose schools there must be enough capacity to allow them to do so."[4] Ironically, under the open enrolment provisions of the ERA 1988, LEAs cannot use economic efficiency as a reason for limiting the intake to a school if it means denying parental preference.[5]

The policy of minimising surplus capacity has had a particular impact on the opportunities of ethnic or religious minorities to secure the provision of denominational state funded schools which uphold their cultural or religious traditions. This is part of a broader question, to which we shall return in Chapter 5, of how well served by the Government's policy of choice and diversity in education are these minority groups.

(b) Cultural and religious diversity and the establishment of schools

The Government has argued that diversity of educational provision is fundamental to the concept of parental choice. That choice may be exercised by parents partly on the basis of an assessment of the general quality of the school but also on the suitability of provision in relation to a whole range of specific factors. In many cases the key factor will be the religious character of the school or the cultural traditions upheld by it. This may be true for parents following majority or minority religious or cultural traditions. Thus parents may wish their child to attend a denominational school, such as Roman Catholic or Church of England school, or may prefer that their child attends a single sex school.

Although this may be a matter of individual choice, there are identifiable groups of education consumers with common beliefs and cultural identities. For them, the availability of a school of a particular religious character affects not only individual choice but also, and perhaps more importantly, a collective sense of community. In some cases, such a school is seen by religious or ethnic groups as helping to preserve their traditions and safeguard their cultural identity.

The EA 1944 sought to retain the link between Church and State in the provision of education, while recognising the legitimate demands of

---

[4] Audit Commission, *Citizen's Charter Performance Indicators* (Consultation Document) (1992) p. 52.
[5] See ERA 1988, s.26(9). See further Chap. 5.

religious groups to run schools, with state funding, in accordance with a particular religious ethos.[6] These "voluntary" schools, of which there are around 8,000 altogether, are established by religious foundations.[7] Voluntary aided schools (which, unlike the voluntary controlled schools, have to bear part of their maintenance costs) enjoyed a degree of independence from the LEA even before LMS, including greater power than any other state schools over staff appointments and the use of school premises. Voluntary schools have foundation governors who, in aided and special agreement schools, will be in the majority (see Chapter 3). Often they must be run in accordance with the terms of a trust deed. They are generally able to give admissions preference to pupils of the denomination. In other respects they are part of the state sector, and must follow the National Curriculum.

It has proved difficult for some of the minority religious communities to secure voluntary aided status for existing independent schools (or proposed schools), as the *Islam* case, discussed below, illustrates. But there has been growing political support for a change in the law to make it easier for such schools to acquire maintained status as voluntary aided schools. In 1991 an all-party group of peers supported an Education (Amendment) Bill, which had such an aim. The Bill progressed no further than its second reading. In the course of a lengthy debate in the upper chamber[8] there were several references to the fact that the European Convention on Human Rights provides for states to respect parents' rights to have their children educated in conformity with their religious and philosophical convictions.[9] One of the Bill's proposers, Baroness Cox, said that the chief reason that tended to be given by the DES for rejecting a voluntary aided status application was that there already existed surplus capacity in the area. The Bill aimed to amend the law to prevent denial of voluntary aided status on this ground alone.

There are, of course, surrounding educational and philosophical arguments about the separation or integration of ethnic or religious minorities and the kind of education provided,[10] some of which are referred to in Chapter 7. But, leaving these aside, one can argue that if the Government is truly committed to diversity of provision it follows

---

[6] See A. Bradney, *Religion, Rights and Laws* (1993) pp. 60–52.

[7] These schools are defined in ss.9 and 15 of the EA 1944; see above, p. 43, n.10.

[8] H.L. Debs; Vol. 526, cols. 1247–1308 (March 4, 1991).

[9] Article 2 First Protocol.

[10] See E. Hulmes, *Education and Cultural Identity* (1989) pp. 28–31; S. Poulter, *English Law and Ethnic Minority Customs* (1986) pp. 203–4; P.Cumper, "Muslim Schools: The Implication of the Education Reform Act 1988" 16(3) *New Community* 379; D. Anderson, *Sunday Times* April 29, 1990; and A. Bradney, *op. cit.*

that the aspirations of these minorities as regards the preservation of their religious and cultural identity can and should be recognised. The new possibility of independent denominational schools acquiring GM status, of a change in religious character of a GM school, or of new denominational GM schools being established (see below) may, however, improve the situation.

(c) Establishment, closure and significant changes to schools: procedure

i. *County and voluntary schools*

The statutory procedures for the establishment or closure of a county or voluntary school, or for a significant alteration to its character or premises, are laid down in sections 12 and 13 of the EA 1980. Proposals may be made by an LEA (section 12) or governing body of a voluntary school (section 13 — which applies only to the establishment of or significant change to a school).

"Significant" is not defined. The question whether a change is significant is referable to the Secretary of State.[11] The definition of change of character appears not to be exhaustive, for the 1980 Act says that a change of character shall:

> "include, in particular, changes in character resulting from education beginning or ceasing to be provided for pupils above or below a particular age, for boys as well as girls or for girls as well as boys, or from the making or alteration of arrangements for the admission of pupils by reference to ability or aptitude."[12]

The Government's view is that the introduction of a limited amount of selection (up to 10 per cent. of the intake), on the basis of ability or aptitude in, for example, music, art or physical education, would not amount to a significant change of character.[13]

The Government's desire to maximise the use of opting out led to the inclusion of important provisions in the ERA 1988, now contained, in amended form, in section 273 of the EA 1993. Section 273(1) provides that before the LEA formulates any proposals for ceasing to maintain a county or voluntary school or for a significant change/enlargement of a county school, it must, if the school is eligible for GM status, consult

---

[11] EA 1944, s.67(4), as amended by ERA 1988 Sched. 12 para. 4(3) in respect of GM schools.

[12] EA 1980, s.16(2)

[13] Draft DFE Circular, *Admissions to Maintained Schools* (December 1992), discussed in Chap. 5.

the governing body of the school. The purpose of this provision, previously contained in section 73(1) of the ERA 1988, is said to be "to allow the governing body time to consider whether the LEA's plans are such that the parents' views should be sought on the advisability of preparing an application for grant-maintained status."[14] It therefore aims positively to encourage governing bodies to consider opting out as a means of avoiding closure or reorganisation. As we saw in Chapter 2, many of the applications for GM status have just such an object in mind.

The remainder of section 273 deals with the situation where proposals are published which conflict with an application by a school for GM status. It comes into play in the following circumstances:[15]

    (i)   where proposals for the closure, establishment[16] or significant alteration of a school are published under section 12 or 13 of the 1980 Act but have not yet been determined or withdrawn, and at this stage proposals for the acquisition of GM status are published by the governing body; or

    (ii) where proposals for GM status have been published, but before they have been determined or withdrawn

        (a) proposals under sections 12 or 13 are published, or

        (b) proposals (under EA 1993, section 272) to make a significant alteration to the character of the school or the size of its premises are made by the governing body.[17]

In these cases, the Secretary of State must consider the proposals for closure, alteration etc. simultaneously with the GM proposal, but must not make a determination with regard to the former until he has determined the latter.[18] The operation of this provision, previously contained within section 73(4)(b), was partly the subject of the litigation arising out of schools reorganisation in the city of Bath (the *Avon* cases), discussed in Chapter 2. Approval of the opting out means automatic rejection of a closure proposal; but the Secretary of State may

[14] DES Circular 10/88, para.33.
[15] s.273(3), which re-enacts parts of ERA 1988, s.73, as discussed in Chap. 2., at p. 53.
[16] In this case, it could be establishment resulting from the creation of a new school which arises from the amalgamation of two or more former schools.
[17] The governing body may make such an application only where the LEA has published plans to change the character, etc., of one or more schools in its area. The idea is that the governing body of a school which is intending to become GM will be able to seek approval for plans to alter the character of the school or size of premises in order to be consistent with provision in the area if the LEA's plans are implemented (see s.272(1)(c).
[18] EA 1993 s.273(4)(b).

in limited circumstances, approve a significant change in character or enlargement at the same time as approving the opting out proposals.[19]

Proposals under sections 12 and 13 of the EA 1980 must be sent to the Secretary of State[20] and be published in the prescribed manner.[21] Details of the proposals must appear in a newspaper distributed in the area and must be posted in at least one conspicuous place. The published proposals must contain sufficient, accurate details to enable parents and others to understand their effect.[22] Parents and other members of the local community are thereby put on notice of the proposed changes. (In the case of closure of a voluntary school at the instance of the governing body, two years' notice must be given under section 14). The 1980 Act in effect gives objectors a right to submit their objections to the proposals to the LEA. Consideration must be given to the objections provided there are 10 or more objectors.[23] In *Milne* v. *Wandsworth L.B.C.*[24] the Court of Appeal held that separate objections or groups of objections could not constitute a statutory objection for the purposes of closure of a school unless they were made by 10 or more persons collectively. Here, although there had been 14 objections, they had emanated from two independent sources. The Court held that they must come from one source, or each group should make explicit reference to the other(s), so that objections were endorsed by at least 10 persons in all. According to Stuart-Smith L.J., the purpose of the requirement was "clearly to ensure that frivolous objections, which do not command the respect of at least 10 electors, are not submitted to the Secretary of State."[25] However, as Beldam L.J. noted, there is "no express requirement for reasons to be given for objections."[26] The perverse logic of all this is that 10 or more objectors must, in effect, indicate their concurrence with each other even though the basis of their individual objections may be quite distinct. If nothing else, this case has confirmed that objection to school changes involves truly collective action by consumers.

---

[19] *Ibid.* s.273(5).

[20] EA, 1980, ss.12(1) and 13(1).

[21] Education (Publication of School Proposals) (No.2) Regulations 1980 SI 1980 No.658. In *Coney* v. *Choyce* [1975] 1 W.L.R. 422 the court refused to uphold a legal challenge based on the LEA's failure to comply fully with the publication requirements, holding that no-one had been prejudiced by it.

[22] See *Legg v I.L.E.A.* [1972] 3 All E.R. 177. The admissions total for the school and the date on which the proposals would take effect must be stated: EA 1980 s.12(2), as amended.

[23] s.12(3) and 13(3). Note that if a funding authority is in operation in the area (see Chap. 2. p. 37), it too may object to proposals made by the LEA: EA 1993, s.229(3).

[24] (1992) 90 L.G.R. 515.

[25] *Ibid.* at p. 523.

[26] *Ibid.* at p. 524.

There is no strict requirement to hold a public meeting to hear objections and consider the issues, although there is now a statutory duty to consult appropriate persons.[27] In practice, meetings between education officials and parents are generally called, especially where a school closure is planned.[28] These are often very heated affairs, and, while arguably offering an element of local accountability through the consultation process, have no statutory significance.

The Secretary of State's approval of an LEA's proposals or, in the case of voluntary schools, those of governors, is required in certain circumstances — and always where objections have been submitted to the LEA by 10 or more local government electors within two months of publication of the proposals.[29] In any event, the Secretary of State may insist that his approval be obtained, if he gives notice to this effect to the LEA within two months of submission of the proposals to him.[30] The Secretary of State has the power to approve the proposals (with or without modifications) or reject them.[31] In other cases, where Secretary of State's approval is not required, the LEA must decide within four months whether it wishes to implement the proposals, and must notify the Secretary of State of its decision.[32]

There has never been an express statutory obligation on the Secretary of State to give reasons for his decision on school changes. However, fairness or natural justice may demand that he does so, depending on the circumstances of the case.[33] In practice, the Secretary of State may take account of a wide variety of factors in coming to his decision. He may put a high priority on rationalisation in the interests of improving local cost-effectiveness (see below). But, ironically, approval of GM status for some schools faced with closure or substantial change is being granted despite the fact that the proposed closures or changes are the result of LEAs' efforts to rationalise provision in the light of falling rolls, as encouraged by the Government. As discussed in Chapter 2, the

---

[27] EA 1980, s.12(1A) and (1B), inserted by s.299(1) of the EA 1993, and s.230(1) and (1C), inserted by s.230(1) of the 1993 Act. Under these amendments, the Secretary of State may produce guidance (which must be published); the LEA or governing body proposing the changes must have regard to it.

[28] One such meeting was held in Birmingham when a school closure was planned. The school concerned was in a multi-ethnic area and there was an unsuccessful legal challenge, based on procedural unfairness and breach of the RRA 1976, arising out of the LEA's failure to provide an interpreter in one of the languages spoken by parents: *R v. Birmingham City Council ex p. Dashan Kaur* [1991] C.O.D. 21.

[29] EA 1980, ss.12(4) and (5)(*b*) and 13(4). The Secretary of State's approval is needed for certain changes to voluntary schools (for example a significant change in character).

[30] *Ibid.* s.12(5)(*a*).

[31] *Ibid.* ss.12(6) and 13(4).

[32] *Ibid.* ss.12(7) and (8).

[33] See P. Craig, *Administrative Law* (2nd edn; 1989), pp. 221–222 and 295 *et seq.*

courts have so far confirmed the Secretary of State's wide discretion as to the factors which are relevant for his consideration in these cases and in weighing up conflicting considerations.[34]

Among the important changes proposed in the Education Bill, as originally presented in 1992, was a new power for LEAs to propose a significant change of character (excluding religious character) or enlargement of a voluntary school. The Government explained that the purpose of this provision was to ensure "effective planning" by an LEA of county and voluntary schools provision, enabling it to "make sensible, comprehensive proposals concerning all its schools — essential if the most rational and effective use of resources is to be achieved."[35] Thus LEAs would have been able to include voluntary schools in schools reorganisation plans. However, representations from religious bodies and other persuaded the Government to drop these proposals. The Bill was amended to empower the Secretary of State to order a governing body of a voluntary school to put forward its proposals "for alteration of their school" where school places in the area are "excessive."[36] The Secretary of State can also now order an LEA to publish proposals for the establishment, alteration or discontinuance of a school (or schools).[37] In such a case he must, in the order which has been given, "require the proposals to apply such principles in giving effect to the direction as may be specified in the order."[38] This falls only a little way of short of complete control. Furthermore, the Secretary of State also has a power to put forward proposals of his own.[39] There is the standard provision for consultation and objection in these cases, but what is particularly interesting is the fact that if objections to the Secretary of State's proposals are made, these proposals, along with those of the LEA or governors of a voluntary school (if any), must be referred, together with the objections, to a *public inquiry*.[40]

The inquiry will be conducted in the same way as other public inquiries.[41] On the face of it, reference to a public inquiry implies that more serious regard may be given to the consumer's view. Certainly

[34] See *R* v. *Secretary of State for Education and Science ex p. Avon County Council* (1990) 88 L.G.R. 716 (Q.B.D.) and *ex p.* Avon (No.2) 737 (C.A.); and *R* v. *Secretary of State for Education and Science ex p. Newham L.B.C.* (1991) *The Times,* January 11. These cases were discussed at pp. 54–57 *supra.*
[35] *Choice and Diversity*, para. 4.5.
[36] See now EA 1993, s.232(1)(b).
[37] EA 1993, s.232(1)(a). This power may be used only if local provision is deemed to be excessive.
[38] *Ibid.* s.232(3)(b).
[39] *Ibid.* s.234.
[40] *Ibid.* s.235. See *Choice and Diversity*, paras 4.14–4.16.
[41] s.250(2)–(5) of the Local Government Act 1972 applies, by virtue of s.235(7).

there will be a greater likelihood of consumer involvement. Further-more, parents and others should be able to discover the weight attached by the inspector to their arguments, as the intention is that the inspector's report will be published.[42] However, the value of the inquiry from the consumer's viewpoint may be limited by virtue of the fact that the procedure will not come into operation until the Secretary of State has published proposals of his own. It seems unlikely that the Secretary of State, who will have the final say on any proposals (after considering the inspector's report), will want to risk the political embarrassment of a climb-down very often. If, however, he decides in the light of the inquiry to publish further proposals, these will not be subject to the public inquiry procedure. The inquiry process is in any event weighted in the Secretary of State's favour, in that it is not open to the inquiry to "question the principles" specified by the Secretary of State when he ordered an LEA or funding authority to make proposals (above).[43] As the White Paper stated, inquiry inspectors "will have to take as their starting point the criteria for the proposals set out by the Secretary of State."[44]

The Secretary of State's power to put foward proposals of his own must be seen as providing him with a far greater scope for central control than the power to modify proposals put forward by the LEA. It is difficult to view the public inquiry procedure other than as an attempt to disguise a very far reaching power which undermines local decision-making.

Further centralising powers may be found in the provisions enabling the Secretary of State to direct LEAs and (for alteration to premises only) governors of voluntary schools to publish proposals where there is shortfall of provision.[45] These powers apply only where a funding authority has sole responsibility for ensuring the availability of sufficient school places in the area.[46]

ii. *Grant-maintained schools*

Under the 1988 Act, GM schools could only be established from an existing school — where there had been a ballot in favour of opting out (see below). As noted in Chapter 2, however, there is now provision for establishment of *new* schoools as GM schools, at the instigation of promoters[47] or, if one has been established in the area, a funding

---

[42] *Choice and Diversity*, para. 4.16.
[43] EA 1993, s.235(6).
[44] *Choice and Diveristy*, para. 4.15.
[45] EA 1993, s.233.
[46] The funding authority may be given that responsibility where 75 per cent. of the children at maintained schools in an LEA area attend GM schools: see Chap. 2.
[47] EA 1993, s.49.

authority.[48] Voluntary bodies and, in theory, proprietors of independent schools, will now be able to establish new GM schools. However, this may only happen where at least 10 per cent. of pupils at state schools (excluding special schools) in the LEA area already attend GM schools. Those founding such a school will have the incentive of 100 per cent. state funding, instead of having to meet 15 per cent. of the cost of capital expenditure and external repairs if the school were to be voluntary aided. The acquisition of GM status by an independent school is, however, unlikely, in view of the additional public expenditure that would be involved and the difficulty of showing that there is a shortfall in local provision that cannot be met through an expansion of provision in existing schools. There is, nevertheless, a far greater likelihood of *new* denominational schools being established as GM schools rather than as voluntary aided schools; and, taken as a whole, these measures must be seen alongside those enabling clusters of primary schools to opt out[49] in facilitating the growth of the GM sector.

Any proposals concerning the establishment of new GM schools will be subject to similar procedural requirements to those applicable to LEA-maintained schools (above) — governing publication of the proposals, the raising and consideration of objections and the power of the Secretary of State to approve proposals (with or without modifications) or reject them.[50] However, a wider range of information must be made available to the public, including the detailed composition of the governing body and the name of the head teacher designate.[51] The list of those who may submit objections to the establishment of GM schools is also wider. As with county and voluntary schools, 10 or more local government electors may object within two months of publication of the proposals; but the list also includes any LEA concerned (not just the one for the area in which the school is situated) and governing bodies of schools affected by the proposals.[52]

Proposals for the closure of or significant alteration to GM schools must be handled in much the same way as those for county and voluntary schools. Here, a significant change of character or enlargement of school premises may be proposed by the governing body of the school concerned[53] or (once it has "sufficient school places" responsibility in

---

[48] *Ibid*, s.48.
[49] See *supra* pp. 50.
[50] EA 1993, s.51.
[51] Sched. 3, Part II. There is a duty to annexe a statement to the published proposals, briefly describing the character of the school: Sched. 3, para. 8.
[52] Sched. 3 para. 11.
[53] EA 1993, s.96(1).

the area[54]) the funding authority.[55] Changes to *religious* character may not be proposed by the funding authority and may only be proposed by the governing body if any trustees under any trust deed relating to the school have consented to the change.[56]

In each case there is a statutory duty to consult such persons as the proposers consider to be appropriate. Guidance on consultation issued by the Secretary of State must be taken into account.[57] There are the same rights of objection within two months of publication of the proposals as apply to the establishment of a new GM school (above). A decision by a governing body to publish proposals will be of no effect unless confirmed at a second meeting held not less than 28 days after the first.[58]

A change of character or enlargement proposed by the governing body always requires the Secretary of State's approval.[59] But where the proposal are made by the funding authority, approval is needed only if statutory objections are made or if the Secretary of State gives notice that his approval is necessary.[60] As noted earlier, in the case of a school applying for GM status it is also possible for proposals for a significant change in character (but not a change in religious character) to be considered and approved or rejected at the same time that the Secretary of State considers the opting out application.[61]

The procedures for the discontinuance of a GM school, including the duty to consult and take account of objections, and the circumstances in which the Secretary of State's approval is needed, are basically the same as those applicable to significant changes (above).[62] After the 1988 Act the Government expressed the belief that the discontinuance of a GM school would be "exceptional."[63] However, it now seems to be accepted that any rationalisation of provision in an area may require changes to GM schools as well as to LEA schools, especially once there are sufficient GM schools for a funding authority to be in operation there. In this regard, not only has a funding authority the power to propose the discontinuance of a GM school, but the Secretary of State may direct them to publish proposals if he considers there to be "excessive" provision in the area.[64] The Secretary of State also has a power, first

---

[54] An order under EA 1993 s.12(1)(*a*) or (*b*) must have been made: see p. 37.
[55] EA 1993, s.97(1).
[56] ss.96(2) and 97(3).
[57] s.96(3) and 97(4).
[58] s.96(8).
[59] s.98(1).
[60] s.98(2).
[61] ss.272 and 273.
[62] ss.104–107.
[63] DES Circular 10/88, para. 69.
[64] EA 1993, s.232.

introduced under the 1988 Act, to cease to maintain a GM school which he considers unsuitable to continue.[65]

It can be seen that the opportunities for consumers to influence a decision on changes to or closure of a GM school are no greater than is the case with county or voluntary schools. The formal requirements do provide for publicity and information, consultation and the consideration of objections, but they also give the Secretary of State considerable discretionary power — as also with decisions on approval or rejection of GM status itself (see Chapter 2).

(d) Legal challenges to local school changes

The courts may not consider the merits of proposals for changes to schools,[66] and challenges have mostly been based on alleged inadequacy of consultation, breach of anti-discrimination legislation and failure to take account of parental wishes.

i. *Failure to consult adequately*

As shown above, there is now a statutory duty to consult "appropriate" persons before publishing proposals for school changes or closures in both LEA and GM sectors. Although parents are not referred to specifically, it is clear that they fall within this definition. The Secretary of State's new guidance on consultation, to which, as we saw, those proposing the changes will have to have regard, is expected to emphasise that "when proposals are drawn up the views of *all* those with an interest in the proposals are considered."[67]

In any event, the insertion of a duty to consult into the statutory procedures means that consultation is now a mandatory requirement, so that failure to consult will amount to procedural *ultra vires*.[68] The effect of such a requirement was considered in *Lee* v. *Department of Education and Science*.[69] Here the Secretary of State had sought to rush through amendments to a school's instrument of government to remove that part requiring selection of pupils. Section 17(5) of the EA 1944 required the

---

[65] EA 1993, s.109(1)(a) (too few pupils) and (b) (badly run: see p.85).

[66] See e.g., *Lee* v. *Enfield L.B.C.* (1967) 66 L.G.R. 195 *per* Donaldson J (as he then was). More recently, in *R* v. *Secretary of State for Education and Science ex p. Banham* (1992), *The Times*, March 9, where judicial review was sought of a decision to approve the closure of three schools in Dorset, Macpherson J. emphasised that "before initiating proceedings for judicial review of school closure decisions, care should be taken to assess whether what was being sought was not an oblique appeal."

[67] *Choice and Diversity*, para. 4.17, emphasis added.

[68] See, e.g., *R* v. *Governors of Small Heath School ex parte Birmingham City Council* (1989) *The Independent*, June 30 (Q.B.D.). The consultation question was not pursued further in the Court of Appeal (*The Times*, August 14).

[69] (1968) 66 L.G.R. 211 (C.A.).

Secretary of State "to afford to the LEA and to any person concerned . . . an opportunity of making representations to him." Donaldson J. held that the time which had been allowed for representations, just four days, had been "wholly unreasonable, in the circumstances of this case"; it amounted to "a denial to the persons named in s. 17(5) of the rights conferred upon them by that sub-section."

Failure to comply with any of the statutory requirements, for example on publication of proposals, may constitute illegality. As Stuart Smith L.J. said in *Milne* v. *Wandsworth L.B.C.*,[70] "The local education authority have to get their tackle in order and it is necessary for them to comply with the technicalities and technical requirements . . . If they get it wrong, they are liable, as a matter of law, to be judicially reviewed."[71] However, even if there is illegality, the court has a discretion as to whether to grant a remedy, such as an injunction.[72]

The introduction (via amendment of the 1980 Act) of a statutory consultation duty probably stems from the decision in *R* v. *Brent L.B.C. ex p. Gunning.*[73] Here the LEA was contemplating closure and amalgamation of schools. Various proposals had been under consideration when the Director of Education prepared a short consultation document giving brief information about the possible changes. Copies were distributed via "pupil post" on the last day before half-term, May 24, 1984. Most parents were said not to have received the report until June 4 or 5. Public meetings were to be held on June 7, and written responses to the proposals had to be submitted to the education offices by June 15. The Director's report on the consultation exercise was considered by the education committee on July 5. The minutes of that meeting noted that the consultation had failed to give parents an adequate opportunity for discussion and that the consultation document had contained insufficient information. The authority met on July 12 and resolved in favour of the closure and amalgamation of four schools. The proposals by this stage differed from those on which consultation had taken place, but they were submitted to the Secretary of State for approval. The applicants were parents of three of the children attending schools included in the proposals. Hodgson J. said that the parents "had no statutory right to be consulted." But he concluded that "beyond question" they had "a legitimate expectation that they would be consulted."[74] In expressing this view, Hodgson J. noted that the various

---

[70] *Supra* (n.24).
[71] *Ibid.* at p. 522.
[72] See *Bradbury* v. *Enfield L.B.C.* [1967] 1 W.L.R. 1311 (C.A.), where an interim injunction was granted in respect of failure to comply with a statutory requirement on publication of proposals.
[73] (1985) 84 L.G.R. 168
[74] *Ibid.* at 187.

DES Circulars on rationalisation of school places had emphasised the importance of consulting parents, and noted also that in practice the Secretary of State will take account of the results of consultation when deciding whether or not to approve proposals.[75] He also referred to the House of Lords' recognition of the doctrine of legitimate expectation in *Council of Civil Service Unions* v. *Minister for the Civil Service*.[76] In that case Lord Fraser had explained that "legitimate, or reasonable, expectation may arise either from an express promise given on behalf of a public authority or from the existence of a regular practice which the claimant can reasonably expect to continue."[77] In *Gunning* the LEA had, in the past, consulted comprehensively on possible school changes.

It may be noted that where there is a legitimate expectation of consultation, it may be possible for a failure of consultation to, in effect, be put right when the proposals come before the Secretary of State. In *R* v. *Gwent County Council ex p. Bryant*,[78] Hodgson J. (although finding on the facts that the council had consulted properly over proposals to close two schools and establish one in their place) said that if the duty to consult was based not on statute but rather on legitimate expectation "then, although the decision-maker failed to comply with that duty, a later decision making process (... in this case, the Secretary of State) might rectify an earlier unfairness." Hodgson J. found that the Secretary of State, who had approved the LEA's proposals, had "had before him and considered most carefully the very full, articulate and persuasive submissions."

Gunning (above) also gave consideration to the *content* of consultation in the case of school changes. In the course of his judgment Hodgson J. seems to have accepted criteria put forward in argument by Stephen Sedley Q.C.:[79]

"[i.] ... consultation must be at a time when proposals are still at a formative stage ...

[ii] the proposer must give sufficient reasons for any proposal to permit of intelligent consideration and response ...

[iii] adequate time must be given for consideration and response and

---

[75] *Ibid.*

[76] [1985] A.C. 374. For discussion of recent developments with regard to legitimate expectation, see B. Schwer and P. Brown "Legitimate Expectation — Snuffed Out?" [1991] P.L. 163–170.

[77] At p. 401. See also the *dictum* of Lord Diplock at p. 408.

[78] (1988) *The Independent,* 19 April (Q.B.D.). See also *R* v. *Northampton County Council ex p. Tebbutt* (1986) June 26 (unreported).

[79] *Op. cit.* at p. 189.

[iv] the product of the consultation must be conscientiously taken into account in finalising any statutory proposals."

As the proposals which were put forward to the Secretary of State were different in certain material respects from those which had been considered at the meeting on June 7, there had been a failure to consult by the LEA. The consultation document itself and the time permitted for response to it were both held to be inadequate. Note that in the later case of *R* v. *Hertfordshire County Council ex p. George* it was held that once an adequate consultation period has expired there is normally no obligation on the LEA to consult further.[80]

Consultation, at whatever stage, clearly involves appraising those interested of all relevant information on which the decision may be based, so far as practicable. This had not been done in *Gunning*, when the proposals in their final form were different to those that had been the subject of the consultation exercise. Thus the objectors (and other potential objectors) had not been given an opportunity to respond to the additional points being made by the proposers. An analogous situation arose in *R* v. *Secretary of State for Education and Science ex p. Yusuf Islam*,[81] but here the responsibility for procedural impropriety rested with the Secretary of State. The case arose out of a decision of the Secretary of State to turn down the proposals submitted on behalf of the independent Islamia Primary School in Brent for the school to have voluntary aided status. The application, under section 13 of the EA 1944, had had the support of the LEA and there were no statutory objections. At the time the proposals were published, in 1986, there was an established need for additional primary school places in Brent. Moreover, the Secretary of State wrote to the applicants asking how the proposed school would help relieve a shortage of school places in the area, and sent a subsequent letter which gave the impression that only minor details were outstanding. According to Macpherson J., as a result of this letter the applicants were "lulled into a false sense of security." Matters were in abeyance until the Secretary of State asked (in 1989) for further information, including the numbers on the waiting list for the school. A few months later the LEA indicated that there was still a need for the school. However, in November 1989, almost out of the blue, the Secretary of State asked the LEA to confirm that there was now no need for the additional school places in the area. There were, in fact, surplus places. In May 1990 the Secretary of State rejected the application. It was indicated that the Secretary of State had also taken account of surplus capacity in neighbouring areas which were also served by the school.

---

[80] (1988) Lexis CO/856/87 (Q.B.D.)
[81] (1992) *The Times* May 22. The citations are taken from the transcript.

Macpherson J. noted that there was no statutory obligation on the Secretary of State to consult. He also firmly rejected the argument that there had been a legitimate expectation of consultation (describing legitimate expectation as an "overworked" doctrine). The principal reason appears to have been the absence in any previous dealings between the parties in this case of any indication of a promise of consultation, as opposed to a preparedness simply to "digest the facts, advice and opinions" presented by each other. However, by failing to appraise the applicants of the figures on which his decision ultimately was based and of giving them an opportunity to comment upon them, the Secretary of State had acted unfairly. The decision to turn down the application was quashed. However, Macpherson J. warned the applicants that there was no guarantee that the Secretary of State would be persuaded to change his mind: "Spare places cost the country an enormous amount of money, and the applicants must be well alive to the fact that this case is all about money and that when the case is reconsidered . . . the Secretary of State may reach exactly the same decision." This case, therefore, highlights yet again the limitations of judicial review as a means by which parent groups can secure the reversal of decisions on school changes.

ii. *Failure to comply with anti-discrimination legislation*
The inter-action of anti-discrimination legislation with the law governing educational provision is important. It is clear that if school changes would produce inequality of provision as between different ethnic groups or between males and females they could be struck down for illegality. Pertinent here are section 23 of the SDA 1975 and section 18 of the RRA 1976, which prohibit sex or race discrimination by LEAs in carrying out such of their functions as are not comprised within sections 22 and 17 of the respective Acts.[82] Also relevant is the general duty resting with LEAs "to secure that facilities for education provided by [them], and any ancillary benefits or services, are provided without [racial or sexual] discrimination."[83] Article 14 of the European

---

[82] s.22 of the SDA 1975 and s.17 of the RRA 1976 apply to discrimination in admission of pupils, access to benefits, facilities or services provided or exclusion or other detriment, which are not relevant to the discussion here but are considered elsewhere in this book (see Chaps. 5 and 7).

[83] s.25 of the SDA 1975 and s.19 of the RRA 1976. When considering the requirements of s.25 in *Equal Opportunities Commission* v. *Birmingham City Council* ([1989] 1 All E.R. 769), Lord Goff (at p.775–776) said he could see "no reason why [ss.22 and 23] should not, in the field of education, embrace all cases of unlawful discrimination as such"; thus the role of s.25 was different, being "not to outlaw acts of discrimination as such, but to place on [relevant] bodies a positive role in relation to the elimination of sex discrimination. The idea appears to have been that such bodies are, so to speak, put on their toes to ensure that sex discrimination does not occur in areas within their responsibility."

Convention on Human Rights forbids sex and race discrimination in relation to the various rights guaranteed by the Convention, including the right to education.[84]

As shown in Chapter 2, LEAs have a duty under section 8 of the EA 1944 (unless it is transferred to a funding authority) to ensure the provision of "sufficient" schools for primary and secondary education in their area. It is in relation to this duty that the relevant anti-discrimination provisions referred to above are most likely to be applied. After approval of school closure etc. proposals has been given by the Secretary of State, the legality of this decision may in turn depend on whether the implementation of the approved proposals would avoid unlawful discrimination in the performance of the section 8 duty.[85]

This section 8 duty is continuous and in fact applies whether or not changes to provision are planned or implemented. However, changes often highlight or produce unequal provision, and not surprisingly the litigation has generally arisen in this context.

In *ex p. Keating*,[86] the LEA's plan, drafted in the light of falling school rolls, had involved the closure of the sole single-sex boys' comprehensive school in Bristol. The alleged illegality was said to have arisen out of the fact that two single-sex schools for girls were to be retained. It was argued that the LEA's duty to provide sufficient schools should be read in conjunction with their duty not to discriminate on the grounds of sex under section 23 of the SDA 1975. Here there would be less favourable treatment of boys, as compared with girls. Taylor L.J. held that the fact that the desired option of single-sex education would not be available to boys meant that there was unlawful indirect discrimination.[87]

---

[84] Article 14. Note also the *Gravier* judgment on equal access to vocational training under EC Law: p. 3 *supra*.
[85] See *R v. Secretary of State for Education and Science ex p. Keating* (1986) 84 L.G.R. 469. In *R v. Secretary of State for Education and Science ex p. Malik* [1992] COD 31, where there was a challenge to the Secretary of State's decision to approve the closure of a single sex school for girls in Wandsworth, Rose J. confirmed that "If there was material before the Secretary of State showing an inadequate number of places in girls' single sex schools to meet demand in September 1991, that would . . . provide in itself a basis for striking down the Minister's decision." On the facts, however, there was felt to be no such evidence. But in *R. v. Northamptonshire County Council and the Secretary of State for Education, ex p. K.* (1993), *The Times*, July 27th (Q.B.D.) Hutchinson J. upheld the Secretary of State's decision to approve closure of the only boys' school in Kettering (leaving a girls' school as the only single sex school), holding that the Secretary of State had acted lawfully in weighing up the LEA's duty under the 1975 Act with the desperate need to remove considerable over-capacity resulting from falling rolls.
[86] *Op. cit.*
[87] *Ibid.* at p. 477. But see *ex. p. K. supra*, n.85.

The same issue arose in *Equal Opportunities Commission* v. *Birmingham City Council*,[88] where the EOC challenged the system of single-sex voluntary aided grammar schools in Birmingham. The basis for the challenge was unequal treatment, in that there were 540 places for boys at such schools but only 360 for girls. The selection system for determining entry meant that at identical test marks a girl would have a smaller chance of securing a place at one of these schools than a boy. It was alleged that there had been a similar breach of section 23 of the SDA to that which had occurred in *Keating*. The High Court and, in due course, the Court of Appeal and House of Lords, decided that the arrangements were illegal. Lord Goff said that the critical factor was the denial of choice rather than the denial of a particular form of education which might or might not be intrinsically superior.[89]

The decision caused immense problems for the LEA. In order to comply with the ruling it either had to make all of these schools single sex or convert some of the boys' schools to co-educational. When these possibilities were mooted, the parents and governors at at least one of the schools said that they were considering whether to initiate the opting-out procedure. In due course, one of the boys' schools, Handsworth, applied for and obtained GM status. The remaining schools provided 399 places for boys and 397 for girls — equal provision (*de minimis*). However, when the Equal Opportunities Commission pursued the matter further in the courts, it was held by the High Court, and subsequently the Court of Appeal,[90] that, in order to perform their "sufficient" schools duty without unlawful discrimination, the LEA had to take account of state provision available in their area as a whole. In other words, the provision available in Handsworth School, although out of the LEA's control, was relevant in determining whether there was inequality in the provision of places for boys and girls in single-sex schools. This flowed from the fact that the duty in section 8 of the EA 1944 was to secure that sufficient schools were *available* rather than to provide such schools.[91]

The transfer of responsibility for ensuring the availability of sufficient school places in an area to funding authorities, once a set proportion of children in an area attend GM schools, has necessitated amendments to the anti-discrimination legislation to impose the above obligations on these agencies.[92]

---

[88] [1989] 1 All E.R. 769.

[89] *Ibid.* p. 774.

[90] *R* v. *Birmingham City Council ex p. Equal Opportunities Commission (No. 2)* (1992) 90 L.G.R. 492 (Q.B.D.); (1992) *The Times* 27 October (C.A.). (On the ramifications of the ruling see "Ruling clouds equality law" *T.E.S.*, October 23, 1992.)

[91] *Ibid.* (C.A.), *per* Neill L.J. A similar case has since arisen in Northamptonshire.

[92] RRA 1976, ss.18C and 19(6)(*e*), and SDA 1975, ss.23C and 25(6)(*e*).

iii. *Failure to take account of particular matters*

Introduction   It is a familiar principle of public law that a public body
may be considered to have acted unlawfully if it has failed to take
account of a relevant consideration when exercising a statutory function
or discretion, as in *Gunning* (discussed at p. 114 above), where the LEA
had failed to take account of both the comparative costs involved in
their proposals and the difficulties with the plans for phasing in the
transfer of pupils as the changes were implemented.[93] One of the bases
of the challenge to the approval of GM status for Beechen Cliff school in
Bath, in *R* v. *Secretary of State for Education and Science ex p. Avon County
Council*[94] (not proven on the facts according to the Court of Appeal),
was that the Secretary of State had failed to take into account the
uncertainty as regards the future of the remainder of provision in that
city that would result from his decision.

LEAs are obliged by statute to have regard for particular matters
when exercising their functions concerning school changes (for example,
duties relating to sex and race discrimination (above)). However, one
such duty has now been removed. This was the requirement to
"consider a report from an education committee of the authority before
exercising any of their functions with respect to education . . ."[95] (LEAs
are no longer obliged to establish education committees.[96]) Alleged
failure in respect of the duty to consider an education committee report
had led to legal actions by a number of objectors looking for some
procedural illegality on which to base a challenge to school closure
plans.[97] The challenges were mostly unsuccessful, the courts taking a
surprisingly flexible view of the meaning of "report from an education
committee" for this purpose.[98]

We can now focus on an area which has formed the basis for a
number of challenges to decisions on school closures: the requirement to
take account of parental wishes.

To what extent must parental wishes be taken into account?   Section 76 of
the EA 1944, which is still in force, provides that LEAs must, in
carrying out their responsibilities,

---

[93] *per* Hodgson J. at pp. 196–197.

[94] (1990) 88 L.G.R. 716 (Q.B.D.) and *ex p. Avon (No. 2)* 737 (C.A.), discussed in Chap.
2, pp. 54–56.

[95] EA 1944, Sched. 1 Part II para. 7, removed by Sched. 21 to the EA 1993.

[96] EA 1993, s.245, as noted in Chap. 2.

[97] The reported cases are *R* v. *Kirklees M.B.C. ex parte Molloy* (1988) 86 L.G.R. 115;
Nichol v. *Gateshead M.B.C.* (1989) 87 L.G.R. 435 (C.A.) (where *Molloy* was applied,
but distinguished on the facts); and *R* v. *Secretary of State for Education and Science ex p.
Threapleton* (1988) *The Times* June 2 (Q.B.D.)

[98] *Ex p. Threapleton, op. cit.*

"have regard to the general principle that, so far as is compatible with the provision of efficient instruction and training and the avoidance of unreasonable public expenditure, children are to be educated in accordance with the wishes of their parents."

As a result of amendment of the section,[99] this duty now applies also to funding authorities. The principle of adherence to parental wishes in the educational context is also enshrined in the European Convention on Human Rights (see page 194 below).[1]

Reliance has been placed on section 76 by parents seeking to influence decisions on school changes. However, in *Wood* v. *Ealing L.B.C.*[2] Goff J. said that section 76 was not intended to require consideration of the wishes of parents in general. He said that "it would be wholly impracticable if section 76 meant the wishes of parents in general, since they would almost certainly not agree in most, if not all, cases and would be, moreover, a constantly fluctuating body."[3] In this case, a group of parents failed in their attempt to secure an injunction to restrain the LEA from proceeding with proposals for a scheme of reorganisation. So far as the claim that there had been a breach of section 76 was concerned, Goff J. was content to apply the *dictum* of Parker L.J. in *Watt* v. *Kesteven C.C.*, who had stated that an authority was required to do no more than "take into account the general principle, weighing it in the balance together with and against other considerations."[4] The same view prevailed in a later case concerning an equivalent provision in Scotland — section 28(1) of the Education (Scotland) Act 1980, as amended.[5] In this case the education authority had decided to close three out of six schools in Paisley because of falling rolls. Most parents in Paisley favoured a reduction to four schools rather than three and thus the retention of one of the threatened schools. The Lord President confirmed that the wishes of parents were only one matter which had to be taken into account by the authority. Furthermore, he said that "the fact that the education authority had made a decision counter to the wishes of the parents of the pupils at the school did not create a presumption that it had failed to have regard to the general principle in section 28(1)."

---

[99] Amendment made by EA 1993, Sched. 15 para. 10.
[1] 1950, Article 2 of the First Protocol, discussed in Chap. 7.
[2] [1967] Ch. 364.
[3] At p. 383.
[4] [1955] 1 Q.B. 408, cited by Goff J at p. 382. See also the *dictum* of Denning L.J. in *Watt* at p. 424: "Section 76 ... lays down a general principle to which the county council must have regard. This leaves it open to the county council to have regard to other things as well, and also to make exceptions to the general principle if it thinks fit to do so." See also *Darling and Jones* v. *Ministry of Education* (1962) *The Times*, April 7.
[5] *Harvey* v. *Strathclyde Regional District Council* (1988) *The Times*, October 13 and [1979] P.L. 160 (Court of Session, Inner House).

The courts have also confirmed that challenges based on breach of the section 76 duty would not normally be justiciable because of the availability of an avenue of complaint to the Secretary of State, under sections 68 or 99 of the EA 1944.[6]

According to Dent, prior to the introduction of the section 76 duty "it had often been complained ... that the interests of parents were neglected in educational legislation. This section was intended to remove that reproach."[7] However, the cases have demonstrated the extremely limited value of section 76 to parents and other seeking to influence or challenge decisions on school changes. This has been attributed to the "non-committal terms" in which the duty in the section is expressed.[8]

3. OPTING FOR GRANT-MAINTAINED STATUS

(a) Introduction

Although it is now possible for new schools to be established as GM schools (above), most GM schools will be schools moving from the LEA sector to this centrally administered sector. The basis for a school's transfer is a collective decision by the governing body and, more importantly, parents in favour of seeking approval for GM status from the Secretary of State. As the rationale for and implications of the introduction of GM schools were discussed in Chapter 2, it is possible to concentrate here on the mechanics of opting out. The law has been re-enacted, in amended form, in the EA 1993.[9] As noted in Chapter 2, all county and voluntary schools, other than those which are in the irreversible legal process of closure, are now eligible for GM status. To date (August 1993), however, there have been less than 1,000 ballots and there are currently less than 500 GM schools.[10]

(b) Initiation of the procedure

The ERA 1988 provided that opting out procedure could be initiated in either of two ways: first, by a resolution of the governing body to hold a ballot, which had to be confirmed at a second meeting within 28–42 days of the first;[11] and secondly, by a written request of a number of

---

[6] See *e.g. Lee* v. *Enfield L.B.C. op cit.* at p. 210 *per* Donaldson J. Sections 68 and 99 are discussed at pp. 31–37 above.

[7] H.C. Dent, *The Education Act 1944* (1969) p. 51.

[8] See R. J. Buxton, *Local Government* (1973) Chap. 8.

[9] ss.16–29 and Sched. 3 Part 1.

[10] On the past and possible future progress of opting out, see pp. 48–51.

[11] On the eligibility of teacher governors and the head teacher to participate in the governors' vote on the resolution, see pp. 49 and 74 (n.49) above.

parents equal in number to at least 20 per cent. of the number of registered pupils at the school. A ballot of parents had to be conducted within three months of the second resolution or the parents' request, save that no ballot could be conducted within 12 months of a previous ballot unless the Secretary of State gave written consent.

These basic rules relating to initiation of the procedure are now contained in section 18 of the EA 1993. However, there have been some important changes. The Government argued that the requirement for governing bodies to make a second resolution was causing "avoidable delay" and was "burdensome."[12] It has therefore been abolished by the 1993 Act. There has also been a reduction in the period from the governors' resolution in which the ballot must be held to 10 weeks; and the LEA no longer has to be consulted over a ballot, only given "notice" of it.[13]

(c) Preparation for the ballot

As noted in Chapter 2, the 1993 Act has restricted the scope for LEAs to campaign against opting out, although it has not removed it altogether. Governing bodies, on the other hand, are free to promote the case for opting out, but only where they do so "otherwise than as part of the arrangements made for the ballot" and provided they take account of any guidance issued by the Secretary of State.[14] In some cases parents may also wish to campaign over the issue. They are free to do so. Indeed, a parent is entitled, on request to the governing body, to have access to a list containing the names and addresses of the parents of all registered pupils at the school, provided the request is made in connection with the holding of an opt out ballot.[15] Although a parent can insist (by written request) that his or her name be excluded from such a list, concern has been expressed about the potential dangers arising from the availability of these lists to a large section of the local public. During the Committee Stage of the Education Bill in the House of Commons, M.P.s warned that persons such as paedophiles (given that the list would in effect contain the addresses of homes where children live) or violent ex-spouses might use the information for illicit and potentially dangerous purposes.[16]

Once it is certain that a ballot must be held, the governing body must ensure that all the necessary arrangements (for which the cost will

---

[12] *Choice and Diversity,* para. 7.4.

[13] ss.25(1) and 26(3).

[14] EA 1993,s.28(6).

[15] *Ibid.* s.27(1) and (2). A parent is entitled to a copy of the list; the governors may charge a fee in respect of the provision of such a copy: s.27(1)(*b*) and (4).

[16] Official Report, House of Commons Standing Committee E, col. 732–736, January 12, 1993.

probably be borne by the Secretary of State under section 35) are made[17] by the prescribed body.[18] They must involve the provision of the "prescribed information" to those entitled to vote. (At the time of writing the regulations prescribing the type of information have yet to be made.) The governing body must take all reasonably practicable steps to ensure that the prescribed body informs those eligible to vote of their right to vote and affords them all an opportunity to do so in a secret ballot.[19]

(d) Entitlement to vote

A person is entitled to vote in the ballot if he or she is a "registered parent of a registered pupil at the school."[20] "Parent" is defined as including guardians, persons with parental responsibility for a child or those who are simply caring for a child.[21] The fact that a parent's name was inadvertently omitted from the school register and in consequence s/he was not offered an opportunity to vote would appear not to constitute an irregularity such as would enable the Secretary of State to declare the ballot void (see below). The date from which eligibility to vote is determined appears to be 14 days after the process has been initiated by governors' resolution or written request from parents (above).[22]

One of the criticisms that may be made of the provisions governing eligibility to vote is that they enable parents whose children may shortly be leaving the school to vote but, in effect, exclude those whose children may shortly be joining the school and will therefore be affected by the decision taken. This seems unfair and patently undemocratic, but the Government has consistently argued that the situation here is no different from that in other areas of local democracy. For example, a registered elector is entitled to vote in a council election a few days before s/he is due to move to another part of the country.[23]

---

[17] EA 1993 s.28(1).

[18] The relevant regulation have not yet been made.

[19] *Ibid.* s.28(2) and (3).

[20] *Ibid.* s.29(1). The names of pupils and their parents must be shown in the school register: EA 1944, s.80(1A). A parent has only one vote. As the Minister has explained: "If there is only one child at the school the parents are getting one vote each . . . However, if the same parents happen to have three or four children at the school they will still have only one vote each. The number of parents produces the appropriate number of votes". H.L., Debs, Vol. 544, col. 1754 (April 22, 1993), *per* Lord Henley.

[21] EA 1944, s.114(1D) and (1E), introduced by the Children Act 1989, s.108(5) and Sched. 13 para. 10.

[22] EA 1993, s.29(2).

[23] This very analogy was drawn by Rose J in a case concerning to vote on GM status — *R v. Governing Body of Irlam and Cadishead Community High School ex p. Salford C.C.* (1992) Lexis CO/1919/92: "In a wide context, all electoral rolls are likely to be some extent out of date. This is unfortunate, but it cannot be regarded as flawing the democratic process."

The legality of this disenfranchisement was considered recently in *R v. Governing Body of Irlam and Cadishead Community High School ex p. Salford City Council.*[24] Here the governing body had passed their second resolution (as then legally required under the ERA 1988) on July 20, 1992. The parents who were eligible to vote were those on the register 14 days thereafter (August 3). Parents whose children were due to start at the school in the new school year commencing on September 2, 1992, were clearly excluded. The ballot was due to be conducted from October 1, 1992, with a view to the acquisition of GM status from April 1, 1993. Judicial review proceedings were commenced by the LEA, supported by the excluded parents. Among the central arguments advanced in favour of the application were that disenfranchisement of the new parents (i) frustrated the statutory purpose of the legislation (as *per Padfield* v. *Minister of Agriculture*[25]), which was intended to maximise participation; and (ii) was irrational, in that it was unnecessary for the governors to pass the resolution when they did (i.e. near the end of the school year) and contrary to the Secretary of State's guidance as to the timing of resolutions regarding opting out. These arguments were rejected by Rose J. He said that there was nothing in the Secretary of State's guidance or the legislation itself to indicate that maximisation of participation was to be pre-eminent. As to the timing of the second resolution, Rose J. said that the Secretary of State's guidance merely indicated that "disenfranchisement resulting from summer resolutions should be taken into account."

If there has to be a fresh ballot because the first has been declared void for irregularity,[26] and that ballot is to take place in the next school year, only parents whose names are on the school register at the date fixed for this fresh ballot will be eligible to vote.[27] This new provision was inserted following a dispute arising out of an extremely close vote on opting out concerning Caldy Grange Grammar School in West Kirby, Wirral. Parents had voted in favour of seeking GM status by 713 votes to 711 in May 1992. But the Secretary of State had declared the ballot void because of administrative errors in its preparation. He ordered a second ballot of the *same* parents, but this could only be held in the next school year. As a result, parents of 130 pupils who left the school in July 1992 were eligible to vote in the ballot (in November 1992), whereas the parents of 240 pupils who joined the school in

---

[24] *Ibid.*

[25] [1968] A.C. 997

[26] This arises where, *inter alia*, the requirements concerning the ballot have not been complied with, the governing body have acted unreasonably in connection with a ballot or the Secretary of State's guidance has not been followed: EA 1993, s.31(1).

[27] s.29(1) and 31(3).

September 1992 were ineligible. This meant that around one-fifth of parents whose children were attending the school at the start of the new school year were without a vote. There was widespread concern at the situation,[28] and this seems to have precipitated the introduction of the new provision on eligibility to vote in fresh ballots ordered by the Secretary of State.

(e) The vote

There was much debate during the Parliamentary stages of the Education Reform Bill about the size of the vote and the required majority in opting out ballots. As originally drafted, the Bill would have required a simple majority of those voting in the ballot to carry out the issue. There was some concern that this would enable the collective view of a small group of parent activists to prevail where, for whatever reason, a large proportion of the potential electorate did not vote. After various options were considered, the Government finally pushed through an amendment which required a second ballot to be held, within 14 days of the first, if less than 50 per cent. of the parents eligible to vote participated in the first ballot. An amendment to the Education Bill made it clear that a second ballot is also required where the vote of the first ballot is tied (see now EA 1993 s.30(1)). There was such a result at a Croydon school.

At the second ballot, a simple majority, irrespective of the number of votes polled, is all that is required. Maclure comments that "there must be a risk that the second poll will be thinner than the first,"[29] although he concludes that the Secretary of State is less likely to approve a scheme which does not have the firm backing of parents. In fact, the turnout has exceeded 60 per cent. in three-quarters of the opting out ballots held so far, but in over one-third of the second ballots which have been held the turnout has been below 50 per cent.[30]

(f) Publication and approval of opting out proposals

Within four months of an effective ballot in favour of opting out the governing body must publish the proposals and various statements in the prescribed manner[31] and submit them to the Secretary of State,

---

[28] See "New parents barred from second ballot on school's opt out" *The Times*, October 5, 1992.

[29] S. Maclure, *Education re-formed* (3rd edn 1992) p. 73.

[30] *Choice and Diversity*, para. 7.1; H.L., Debs, Vol. 544, col. 1757 (April 22, 1993).

[31] EA 1993, s.32(2) and Sched. 3 Part 1. The requirements are broadly the same as when proposals are published under ss.12 and 13 of the EA 1980 (above), save that the result of the ballot and the constitution of the initial governing body must be set out. Prior to the 1993 Act the governing body had six rather than four months in which to publish the proposals.

who makes the final decision on GM status.[32] Given the fact that parents have been able to have their say through the ballot, it is understandable that there is no statutory right at this stage for them to lodge objections. But members of the wider community, deprived of a vote on the opt out, may also have objections. It is possible that if objections are made which raise new issues of particular concern the Secretary of State may have a public law duty to give consideration to them.

4. CONCLUSION

Collective consumer influence over the shape of local schools provision continues to be restricted. As we have seen, the statutory machinery governing school closures offers parents a mere right to object (although there may also be a duty under statute or at common law to consult them, and others, about school changes). It has been argued that in practice the statutory machinery offers "little opportunity to present an effective case."[33] Legal challenges are quite rare, and have generally succeeded only on procedural grounds, such as failure to consult adequately. Parents therefore may turn to protest or other forms of political action, such as "save our school" campaigns, in their battle to change the LEA's collective mind or sway the Secretary of State's decision.[34] But in coming to his decision, the Secretary of State may legitimately give particular weight to factors which lie beyond the immediate concerns of parents.

It seems that the law gives parents more power to promote changes to provision, for example by initiating opting out procedure, rather than to preserve the status quo. Voting on opting out has been presented as a feature of local democracy. It may indeed be, but the voting system in opting out cases has several undemocratic features, as we have seen.

Despite the rhetoric of parental choice and involvement, the fact remains that, in decisions affecting the pattern of local educational provision, consumers' interests may often be subjugated to those of government. This may well mean that economy and efficiency in

---

[32] *Ibid.* s.33.

[33] See P. Meredith, "Falling Rolls and the Reorganisation of Schools" (1984) J.S.W.L. 208–221.

[34] For a compelling account of the battle to save one Liverpool comprehensive school, see P. F. Carspecken, *Community Schooling and the Nature of Power: the battle to save Croxteth Comprehensive* (1991).

educational provision are given a higher priority than local community wishes. So far as most ethnic minority groups are concerned, the opportunities to secure in the state sector the kind of schools in which their cultural or religious traditions and identity may best be preserved have been extremely limited. These groups may well perceive opting out (especially in schools where their children are in the majority) or the foundation of a new GM school as offering them the best hope so far of realising some of their aims in this context.

5

INDIVIDUAL CHOICE OF SCHOOL

1. INTRODUCTION

The principle of choice of school is at the heart of the Government's policy of reducing 'producer domination' and improving standards of education through competition and accountability to the consumer.[1] The policy of parental choice is part of a two-pronged attack on poor educational standards (ostensibly at little additional cost to the public purse[2]), complementing the increasing regulation of the school curriculum in this respect. The incentive to strive for higher standards comes from the responsiveness of parental demand to the perceived quality of provision by individual schools. Reinforcing the power of choice, the tending to promote greater accountability, has been the guaranteed availability of an increasing flow of information from schools and LEAs about the nature of educational provision and its 'output' (examination results, school-leaver destinations and so on).

In a free market, consumers are able to select and acquire a product at will, in accordance with the limits of their spending power. But in the public sector there has traditionally been producer sovereignty, flowing from the fact that the allocation of school places, like the allocation of council houses or home helps, has been regarded as an essential function of local authorities. The exercise of discretionary power in this way has been limited only by the ballot box and the rationality demanded by the law in determining and responding to local needs. Thus in order to give effect to a choice of school policy within the public sector, it has been necessary to give parents rights which challenge this domination. But the exercise of such rights can present local authorities with difficulties, since they have to respond to individual claims while at the same time having to consider the wider public interest and the impact of individual choice on schools provision as a whole. These obligations may be difficult to reconcile.[3] In any

---

[1] See, for example, *Choice and Diversity*, para. 1.66: "parental wishes through choice of school will drive improvements."

[2] M. Adler, A. Petch and J. Tweedie, *Parental Choice and Educational Policy* (1989) p. 31.

[3] See J. Tweedie, "Rights in Social Programmes: the Case of Parental Choice of School" [1986] P.L. 407–436.

event, there is a limit to the extent to which the claims of individuals can be accommodated. Local authorities (and governors of voluntary aided and GM schools) are entitled to have school allocation policies in order to present a rational basis for the allocation of school places and to make their task administratively achievable. Within these policies, allocation criteria may constrain parental wishes to a considerable degree.

The other major limiting factor lies on the supply side. Although the Government has made it easier for provision to be adapted in response to parental choice, it has had to recognise that the need to achieve an efficient use of resources may have a limiting effect. It has therefore increasingly placed an emphasis on fostering greater diversity of provision: "Diversity entails a range of choices available to parents. Parents can choose the school they believe best suited to the particular interests and aptitude of their children."[4]

Irrespective of the limitations on choice, the relevant rights continue to form an important element in the legal framework governing the allocation of school places. Furthermore, their exercise has brought broader benefits, in producing greater accountability and a tightening up of procedures.[5]

2.   BACKGROUND

(a)   Parental choice prior to the Education Act 1980

Section 76 of the EA 1944 has offered merely a general principle of adherence to parental wishes concerning the education of their children (as noted also in Chapters 4 and 7). The 1944 Act made this principle subject to the condition that adherence must be "compatible with the provision of efficient instruction and training and the avoidance of unreasonable public expenditure," indicating that parental choice would have to be subjugated to LEAs' wider concerns. As shown in Chapter 4, the courts have regarded this principle as but one of a number of factors to which LEAs might legitimately have regard in the exercise of their functions, including the admission of pupils. In *Watt* v. *Kesteven C.C.*[6] a parent based his case against his LEA, which refused to meet the full cost of his sons' education at an independent Roman Catholic boarding school, on section 76. It was held that the LEA had to fulfil its duty under section 8 of the 1944 Act to ensure the provision of sufficient

---

[4] *Choice and Diversity*, para. 1.49.
[5] T. Buck, "School Admission Appeals" (1985) J.S.W.L. 227–251, p. 247.
[6] [1955] 1 Q.B. 408. See also p. 121 *supra*.

schools (which it had done), but in doing so need only have regard to the general principle in section 76, leaving it open to the LEA:

> "to have regard to other things as well, and also to make exceptions to the general principle if it thinks fit to do so. It cannot therefore be said that a county council is at fault simply because it does not see fit to comply with the parent's wishes. And that is all that the father's complaint comes to in this case."[7]

This approach was followed in *Cumings* v. *Birkenhead Corporation*,[8] when a parent objected to the LEA's policy of allocating children who attended a Roman Catholic primary school to a secondary school of that denomination, and mounted an unsuccessful legal challenge.

Thus Ministry of Education Circular No. 83 (*Choice of Schools*, 1946) had been correct in stating: "At the onset it should be noted that section 76 does not confer on the parent complete freedom of choice." The Circular noted, however, that one of the factors that might count in the parent's favour was that his/her choice was based on the denomination of the school or the fact that it was non-denominational.[9] But, as *Cumings,* showed, even in such cases LEAs had virtually unfettered discretion.

Prior to the EA 1980, the LEA's allocation decisions were not subject to local appeal, but there was a route by which parents could refer a question of choice of school to the Minister. If the parent refused to send his or her child to the school named by the authority, and a school attendance order (SAO) was made, the LEA had to accede to the parent's request that a particular school be named in the SAO unless, *inter alia*, the LEA was of the opinion that "the proposed change of school is unreasonable or inexpedient in the interests of the child."[10] If the LEA refused to comply with the request the parent could refer the question to the Minister, who could give "such direction thereon as he thinks fit."[11] Parents could also challenge the reasonableness of the LEA's decision via complaint to the Minister under section 68 of the 1944 Act.[12]

Until the 1970s, parents were generally unwilling to use the limited rights that were then available.[13] But the impetus for greater parental

---

[7] *per* Denning L.J. at p. 424.
[8] [1972] Ch. 12.
[9] The others were the medium of education (for example Welsh) and particular curriculum followed.
[10] EA 1944, s.37(4).
[11] *Ibid.*
[12] Section 68 is discussed in Chap. 2 at p. 31 *et seq.*
[13] A. Stillman, "Legislating for Choice," in M. Flude and M. Hammer, *The Education Reform Act 1988 — Its Origins and Implications* (1990) at pp. 90–91.

involvement in the education system which began in the late 1960s
became increasingly felt in the area of choice of school. Giving parents
power to choose was advocated by the Plowden Report (1967). It was
argued that a parent might be more likely to support the school s/he
had chosen and that this in turn would help motivate his/her child.
Furthermore, there was, some 25 years before *Choice and Diversity*
presented the same argument, an expectation that parental choice could
drive up standards: "Whenever a school is unpopular that should be an
indication to the authority to find out why and make it better."[14] No
amendment to section 76 was proposed, but it was argued that parents
should be given "booklets prepared by the schools to inform them in
their choice of children's schools."[15]

The growing calls for greater parental involvement in the education
system appear to have been only one of the factors which led to the
legislation of 1980. Commentators suggest that one of the major
precipitating factors was the large increase in the number of cases
referred to the Secretary of State under either section 68 or section 37
(the school attendance provision).[16] This "embarrassing problem . . .
gave rise to the Government *perceiving* there to be a demand for parental
choice."[17] There seems to have been a clear link between reorganisation
of secondary schools into comprehensives and the increase in referrals or
complaints to the Secretary of State. The introduction of comprehensive
schools was perceived to have restricted parental choice.[18] The number
of cases received by the Secretary of State increased ten-fold after the
large scale introduction of comprehensives in the 1960s and 70s.[19]
Another factor was the problem of falling rolls, at a time of national
economic difficulty and pressure to restrict public expenditure. LEAs
were said to want their obligations as regards the granting and refusal of
parental choice to be enshrined in statute, hoping that they might
thereby have the authority to limit enrolments and avoid economically
inefficient provision at a time of expenditure restraint.[20] The
Conservatives' commitment to the development of a parents' charter,[21]
involving clearer obligations on LEAs to comply with parental wishes,

---

[14] Plowden, Lady Bridget (chair), *Children and their Primary Schools* Vol. 1. (1967) para.
120.
[15] *Ibid.* para. 130.
[16] See M. Adler *et al., op cit.* p. 32.
[17] A. Stillman *op. cit.* at p. 91.
[18] This point is made in P.S. Taylor and J.B. Saunders, *Law of Education* (8th ed., 1976)
at p. 34.
[19] M. Adler *et al., op cit.,* p. 32.
[20] *Ibid.* p. 33.
[21] See D. Bull, "School admissions: a new appeals procedure" (1985) J.S.W.L. 209 at
p. 212.

increased the pressure on the Labour Government to legislate on parental choice.[22]

In 1977, the Secretary of State for Education, Shirley Williams, issued a circular[23] urging LEAs to provide more information to parents about schools. There was also a consultation paper[24] which was followed, in 1978, with the publication of an Education Bill. The plan was to enable parents to exercise a right to choice of school, but subject to the LEA's right to set a planned admissions limit for the school in the interests of efficiency. Parents would have a right to require the LEA to reconsider admissions decisions and a right to refer the case to the Secretary of State if still dissatisfied. Labour's Bill was not enacted, because of the General Election in 1979, which returned a Conservative government. It was a government that committed itself to extending parental choice of school.

(b) The 1980 Education Act's scheme for parental choice of school

The Conservatives found a way of establishing the primacy of the principle of parental choice while allowing LEAs scope for strategic management of falling rolls. The Secretary of State explained that whilst the aim would be to ensure that parental choice would be maximised, "no choice can ever be absolute. The balance will have to be made between the choice of a parent and the demands on the local education authorities."[25] When the 1980 Act came into effect, parents became entitled to express a preference, which the LEA had to grant[26] unless any one of three conditions applied. These are still in force:

(i) "compliance with the preference would prejudice the provision of efficient education or the efficient use of resources" (section 6(3)(a));

(ii) where the school is aided or special agreement and the admission of the pupil would be incompatible with arrangements made between the governors of the school and the LEA as regards admissions (s.6(3)(b)); or

(iii) if the arrangements for admission to a school are based wholly or partly on selection by reference to ability or aptitude and the admission of the pupil would be incompatible with selection under these arrangements (s.6(3)(c)).

---

[22] M. Adler *et al, op. cit.,* p. 32.

[23] DES Circular 15/77.

[24] *Admission of Children to the School of their Parents' Choice.*

[25] H.C. Debs., Vol. 973, cols. 34–35 (November 5, 1979). Mark Carlisle M.P., Secretary of State for Education and Science.

[26] s.6(2), which is still in force.

In a provision which has spawned a good deal of litigation over the past couple of years, the Act states that the duty to comply with parental preference "shall apply also in relation to. . . any application for admission to a school maintained by a local education authority of a child who is not in the area of the authority" (s.6(5)(*a*)). This provision was said by the Secretary of State to have enabled parents "for the first time to express a wish that their children should be educated in a school in another local education authority area."[27] A question which has arisen, and which has been answered by the courts, is whether LEAs are entitled to give higher priority to applications from within their own area (see below).

The Act has also sought to reduce the scope for individual appeals or complaints about school admission to be referred to the Secretary of State, especially via the school attendance provisions.[28] It has provided a right of appeal to an appeal committee, whose decision is binding on the LEA (or the governors in the case of a voluntary school).[29] Schedule 2 to the Act lays down some basic procedural rules and the Council on Tribunals, under whose supervision the appeals committees operate,[30] has produced a procedural guide. There was much debate during the passage of the Bill about the constitution of these appeal committees. There were calls for the committee to be entirely independent of the LEA. However, as enacted Schedule 2 provided for the committee to consist of three, five or seven members, of whom a majority of one would be LEA-appointed members. The chair of the committee could not, however, be an education committee member. The non-LEA members had to be drawn from persons with experience of education or knowledge of local educational conditions, or parents of pupils (other than pupils whose school was the subject of the appeal).[31] In the case of decisions by the governors of voluntary schools, the appeal committee was to consist of persons appointed by the governing body and, in a minority, those appointed by the LEA.[32]

The rationale for not proposing an independent panel was based on the rather thin argument that "if that appeals procedure is to bind a

---

[27] *Supra* n.25 col. 37.

[28] The number of individual EA 1944 s.68 complaints to the Secretary of State relating to school admissions decisions fell away sharply, from 1,000 in 1979 to 150 in 1984: D. Bull, "Monitoring Education Appeals: Local Ombudsmen Lead the Way" (1985) J.S.W.L. 189 at p. 222. By virtue of ss.10 and 11 of the 1980 Act and the repeal of much of s.37 of the 1944 Act, the parent had either to accept the school named by the LEA in the school attendance order (SAO) or apply to a preferred school in the normal way.

[29] s.7(5).

[30] s.7(6).

[31] Sched. 2 para. 1.

[32] *Ibid.* para. 2.

local authority it must contain members of that authority" because the considerations which had borne upon the LEA in coming to its decision would have to be taken into account.[33] Indeed, it was the Government's view that for this reason an independent committee would only be able to perform an "advisory" role.[34] This view is understandable having regard to the way the legislation, in particular s.6(3)(*a*) (containing the 'efficiency' ground for denying preference), was drafted, but the lack of an independent committee has beeen a major, and justifiable, cause of criticism throughout the period since this part of the Act came into operation in 1982. The EA 1993 has now introduced an independent element (see below).

Finally, the Act (which does not apply to GM schools) requires admissions authorities to publish their admissions arrangements and policies and the number of pupils to be admitted.[35] It also empowers the Secretary of State to prescribe by regulation further categories of information to be published (see below).[36]

3.   THE EDUCATION ACT 1980 IN OPERATION

(a)   Admissions criteria

Even before the 1980 Act it was quite legitimate for an LEA to have an admissions policy and to apply it in the exercise of its discretion on the allocation of school places.[37] The 1980 Act provides that "the policy followed in deciding admissions" must be published by LEAs and governors.[38] Naturally such policies must not be applied too rigidly, for the legitimate exercise of discretion requires consideration of exceptional cases.[39] Any policy which is applied must not only be reasonable in the broad *Wednesbury* sense of being a policy which a reasonable LEA would apply,[40] it must also be consistent with the LEA's statutory obligations.

---

[33] H.C. Deb.., Vol. 973, col. 39 (November 5, 1979). Mark Carlisle M.P., Secretary of State for Education and Science.

[34] *Ibid.*

[35] s.8(1)–(3). GM schools, which are responsible for their own admissions, have similar responsibilities. EA 1993, Sched. 6, paras. 4–6

[36] s.8(5). See below.

[37] *Cumings* v. *Birkenhead Corporation* [1972] Ch. 12, *per* Denning M.R. at p. 37. Here the LEA's policy of allocating to children attending Roman Catholic primary schools places at R.C. secondary schools was considered lawful by the Court of Appeal.

[38] s.8(3)(*c*).

[39] *Cumings* v. *Birkenhead Corporation op. cit.* at p. 38. See also *R.* v. *Canterbury C.C. ex p. Gillespie* (1987) 19 H.L.R. 7, for an analogous ruling in a housing case.

[40] *per* Denning M.R. in *Cumings op. cit.* pp. 37–38; *Associated Provincial Pictures House Ltd* v. *Wednesbury Corporation* [1948] 1 K.B. 223; *Secretary of State for Education and Science* v. *Tameside M.B.C.* [1977] A.C. 1014.

Individual Choice of School

These would include the duties under the SDA 1975[41] and RRA 1976.[42] They would also include the obligations in section 6 itself, for example the duty in section 6(5) to give equal preference to persons living in another district (see below).[43] The 1980 Act does not specify criteria which should be applied or taken into account in prioritising applications,[44] it only provides (in section 6(3)) grounds on which preference may be denied (above).

But that is not to say that the circumstances in which parental preference may be denied under section 6(3) provide the only basis on which the policy may operate. LEAs may generally incorporate within their allocation policy a range of factors, including geographical proximity to the school or the presence of siblings at the school. In the *Greenwich* case,[45] Farquharson L.J. said that:

"Submissions have been made to this court...that any policy for admissions prepared by the local education authority must be confined to the considerations set out in s.6(3): that is to say, priority ... should be governed by whether compliance with parental preference would prejudice the provision of efficient education or the efficient use of resources... I do not consider that the policy of a local education authority should be so restricted. The criteria which have so far been applied of a connection with the school by the presence of a brother or sister already admitted, or geographical proximity, have only a tenuous relationship to the question of efficient education or use of educational resources."[46]

Lloyd L.J. made the same point, holding that "Sibling priority and the proximity rule are sound and lawful policies whether or not they promote efficient education."[47]

The relationship between section 6(3) and admissions policy was most recently considered by the House of Lords in the case of *Choudhury and another* v. *Governors of Bishop Challoner Roman Catholic Comprehensive School*.[48] Here the school in question was a Roman Catholic secondary

[41] s.22.
[42] s.17. In *R.* v. *Cleveland County Council ex p. Commission for Racial Equality* (1992) July 31, the Court of Appeal held that the duty to comply with parental preference in s.6 was outside the scope of s.17 and, because it was not a "function" of the LEA, outside the scope of s.18 as well (see pp. 141–145 below). However, the allocation of school places (*per se*) is specifically referred to in s.17.
[43] *R.* v. *Greenwich L.B.C. Shadow Education Committee ex p. John Ball Primary School* (1990) L.G.R. 589 (C.A.).
[44] *cf.* s.22 of the Housing Act 1985, on council house allocations.
[45] *Supra* (n.43).
[46] *Ibid.* at p. 602.
[47] *Ibid.* at p. 599.
[48] [1992] 3 All E.R. 277 (H.L.).

school for girls. The governing body, as the admissions authority, had refused to admit two girls, one Muslim and the other Hindu. The girls' parents claimed that parental preference, motivated by a desire for single sex schooling for the girls, should prevail. The arrangements concerning admissions were the responsibility of the governors. There was no admissions agreement between the governing body and LEA. Such an agreement might, for example, have provided for preference for Roman Catholics, thereby enabling the governors to invoke section 6(3)(*b*) of the 1980 Act (above) and refuse to admit a child on the ground that such admission would be incompatible with the arrangements contained in the agreement. But because the school was over-subscribed, the governors were entitled under section 6(3)(*a*) to refuse admission on the ground of prejudice to efficient education or the efficient use of resources. Both the Court of Appeal and the House of Lords agreed that the governors could apply their admissions policy under which priority for admission was to be given to Roman Catholic children.

Lord Browne-Wilkinson said that in circumstances in which a school was oversubscribed it necessarily followed that " 'compliance with the performance' of *all* applicants would prejudice proper education at the school through overcrowding." Thus it became "absolutely necessary" in such circumstances for the governing body "to have an admissions policy of some kind in order to select from all those who have expressed such preference which of them are to be accepted and which rejected."[49] That policy was a matter for the governing body to determine: "No doubt the governors' admissions policy has to be reasonable but, apart from the express statutory provisions in section 6 of the 1980 Act, there is no requirement as to the criteria to be adopted."[50] There was nothing unlawful about the application of a religious criterion any more than the proximity or sibling criteria.[51]

If, as Lord Browne-Wilkinson said, the efficiency argument is always satisfied when a school is oversubscribed, parents competing for a school place at an oversubscribed school will always be at the mercy of the admissions policy. Unless it can be argued that an exception should be made, which is always a theoretical possibility in view of the need for policies to provide some flexibility, any cultural imperative on which an application is based (such as a desire for single sex schooling) may well form an insufficient basis for a successful case. Of course, where a school is not oversubscribed the case may be based on a challenge to the efficiency argument itself (see below).

---

[49] *Ibid.* at p. 285.
[50] *Ibid.* at p. 282.
[51] *Ibid.* at pp. 285–286.

In 1988 the DES advised that LEAs and governors could apply "any reasonable criteria they wish for deciding which pupils should have priority of admission," subject to, *inter alia*, the anti-discrimination legislation (above).[52] The introduction of 'open enrolment' under the ERA 1988 (see below), which means that artificial admission limits can no longer apply to keep popular schools less than full in order to ensure that less popular schools have enough pupils to be viable, has not altered the position vis à vis admissions criteria. Nevertheless, there is growing dissatisfaction with the way that some admissions policies are operating, and this has prompted an attempt by the DFE to persuade admissions authorities to tighten up their policies. Although present legislation does not permit the Secretary of State to control admissions policies by regulation, a DFE circular (so far published only in draft), *Admissions to Maintained Schools,* exhorts LEAs and governors to adopt its guidance. The letter accompanying it is expressed in forcible language, and indicates that LEAs will be expected to bring their admissions arrangements into line with the final version of the circular in time for the September 1994 admissions round.

One of the problems for parents which has emerged has been the use, in admissions practice, of an order of preference system. Many LEAs ask parents to prioritise their preferences. If, as is frequently the case, all available places at a school are allocated to those who have named it as a first preference, those who are unsuccessful with their first choice may find that they do not gain a place at their second or other choices, because these schools also fill up with first preference applicants. The Government has announced plans to introduce regulations requiring admissions authorities to publish details of the numbers of applicants to a particular school and the number admitted under each of the admissions criteria.[53] The intention is to enable parents to have a "realistic view of their chance of gaining a place at the school of their first choice" so they can try to avoid wasting their first preference.[54]

The draft circular also advises on the use of what it calls "oversubscription criteria."[55] It suggests that of such criteria, "objective criteria" are the most preferable:

— sibling links, family links or staff links (provided care is taken that there is no indirect racial discrimination against immigrant children who have no historical links in their community);
— distance from home to school

---

[52] DES Circular 11/88 *Admission of Pupils to County and Voluntary Schools* para. 49.
[53] *Admissions to Maintained Schools: Draft Circular* (December 1992) para. 19.
[54] *Ibid.* paras 18 and 19.
[55] *Ibid.* Annex C.

— catchment areas (provided these have a practical or educational justification and do not discriminate against a person who lives near to a school but outside the LEA's area)
— feeder primary schools[56]
— ability (in schools permitted to select in this way).

The DFE is more cautious about, but broadly supports, criteria which involve "an element of judgment":

— medical, social or compassionate grounds;
— educational reasons/contribution to the life of the school/ pastoral benefit
— wish for single sex education[57] ("the admissions arrangements must make quite clear how the relative strength of parental wishes is to be judged")
— religious affiliation.

The DFE condemns "unacceptable criteria." These are criteria which "seem to the Secretary of State to interfere unacceptably with the operation of an open and fair system such as the law requires":

— governors' reserved right
— exclusion of the potentially disruptive[58]
— exclusion of those with special educational needs[59]
— fees[60]
— lots (drawing lots clearly cannot be described as exercising a discretion)

This guidance is unlikely to have much impact on most existing admissions policies (with the possible exception of the paragraphs

---

[56] The links built between the schools via a feeder system are said by the circular to make this practice justifiable on educational grounds; but some LEAs have abandoned such a system in the belief that it overly restricts parental choice and could be unlawful.

[57] In 1982 an unsuccessful application was made to the European Commission on Human Rights by parents who argued that there had been a breach of Article 2 of the First Protocol to the European Convention on Human Rights by denying single-sex selective education: see T. Buck, (1985) J.S.W.L. p. 242 n.61.

[58] There has been evidence that pupils excluded from one school may be rejected by many other schools, with deleterious consequences for their education (see Chap. 7). The DFE says that these children should be given a chance and can always be excluded if they misbehave at their new school. EA 1993, s.13, provides that the governing body or LEA can be "directed" to admit a child who has been excluded permanently from a school.

[59] There is a worry, now that schools' assessment and examination results are published in league tables, that some schools will discriminate against admitting those with special educational needs. However, EA 1993, s.168(5)(*b*), requires statemented children to be admitted to the school named in their statement.

[60] Charging fees for admission to a school and, in general, for the education provided there, are illegal in the state sector: ERA 1988, s.106(1).

dealing with excluded pupils and pupils with special educational needs). Indeed, it seems that the principal goal is to improve the clarity of admissions procedures for the benefit of parents, admissions authorities and appeal bodies. Most LEAs and governing bodies already operate policies which generally conform to the guidance, and the prospects of parents securing the school of their choice will not change. Indeed, these prospects may worsen if schools pursue a policy of limited selection in the interests of specialisation. The draft circular makes reference to the Government's policy of encouraging schools to specialise, which forms part of its wider policy of achieving greater diversity of provision. It suggests that a school might introduce "a strictly limited amount of selection, involving the selection of a total of not more than 10 per cent. of pupils on the basis of ability or aptitude in one or more of music, art, drama and physical education," without this constituting a significant change of character.[61] If the criterion of specialisation applies this will limit choice for parents whose children do not have the special aptitude. Furthermore, the attempt to discourage the rejection of pupils who have been excluded from other schools or who have special educational needs could have a similar impact on parental choice, although this provides no justification for backing down from this socially just approach.

One point addressed by the circular, but only in relation to single sex education, concerns the strength of parental wishes. It would clearly be well-nigh impossible to prioritise competing claims for admission on sucha basis. The courts have recently held that although parental wishes and preference must be considered, there is no legal requirement to take account of the strength of parents' feelings in considering their application for their child's admission to a single sex school.[62] On the other hand, many parents have a very strong preference for single sex education, and the draft circular on admissions acknowledges this. It states that "the admissions arrangements must make clear how the relative strength of parental wishes is to be judged."[63]

(b) Primacy of parental preference over non-discrimination

The SDA 1975 (section 22) and RRA 1976 (section 17) proscribe discrimination by the "responsible body"[64] on the grounds of sex or colour, race, nationality or ethnic or national origins, in, *inter alia*

---

[61] As noted in Chap. 4 if a significant change of character *is* proposed, publication of proposals and approval to implement them would be necessary.

[62] *R.* v. *Governors of the Buss Foundation Camden School for Girls ex p. Lukasiewicz* [1991] C.O.D. 98, *per* Otton J.

[63] *Op. cit.* Annex C para. 9.

[64] This body is defined in these sections as the LEA or the governing body, or, in the case of an independent school, the proprietor.

— the terms on which a pupil is admitted to an educational establishment;

— deciding whether or not to admit a pupil (although single-sex schools may discriminate on the grounds of sex in relation to admissions); and,

— where a person is already a pupil, refusing him or her access to any benefits, facilities or services or excluding the pupil from the establishment.

Thus, in *Mandla* v. *Dowell Lee*,[65] the House of Lords held that when an independent school refused to admit a Sikh boy who, by wearing a turban to school, was adjudged by the head teacher to be in breach of school rules, there had been a breach of section 17 of the RRA by reason of unjustifiable indirect discrimination.

It is also unlawful under both Acts (section 18 of the RRA and section 23 of the SDA) for LEAs to practise race or sex discrimination on the prescribed basis in the exercise of such of their functions as do not fall under section 17/section 22. It was alleged that this duty had been breached in the *Cleveland* case discussed below. A further illegality would arise out of breach by an LEA of its general duty in section 19 of the RRA and section 25 of the SDA "to secure that facilities for education provided by it, and any ancillary benefits or services, are provided without [racial or sexual] discrimination."[66]

The admission of a child is, as we have seen, specifically covered by both Acts. However, it has been argued that the duty in section 6(2) of the EA 1980 to comply with parental preference, may be subject to the "other functions" non-discrimination duty (section 23 of the SDA and section 18 of the RRA (above)). This "other functions" duty only applies to LEAs (and funding authorities), and thus not where the admissions authority is the governing body, as it is in voluntary aided schools. In any event, the Court of Appeal held in *R.* v. *Cleveland County Council ex p. Commission for Racial Equality* that the duty to comply with parental preference under section 6(2) of the 1980 Act was not subject to the non-discrimination duty in section 18 of the RRA.[67]

The *Cleveland* case has implications for the control of racially motivated school choices (although, on the facts, the Court of Appeal found there to have been no racial motive on the part of the parent concerned). A child (K), then aged five, attended a primary school in

---

[65] [1983] 2 A.C. 548.

[66] See above p. 117. On discrimination in the provision of schools, see Chap. 4.

[67] *Supra* (n.42). The discussion here is based on the transcript. Note that in the Divisional Court Macpherson J. doubted whether the duty to comply with parental preference was a "function" for the purposes of s.18. It can, however, be argued that as the LEA was the admissions authority it did have a "function" to which the duty to comply with parental preference related.

Middlesbrough. In December 1987 her mother, Mrs C, wrote to the LEA requesting that the girl be admitted to a different specified school. In her letter, the mother said that she did not think that it was fair that her daughter should have "to go through school with about four white friends and the rest Pakistan (*sic*), which she does not associate with." She stated that although the school was very good, "I don't think it is right when she comes home singing in Pakistan... I don't want her to learn this language." Mrs C wanted her daughter to attend "a school where there will be the majority white children not Pakistani." The LEA acceded to the request, although with reluctance. The Secretary of State refused to intervene under his powers in sections 68 and 99 of the EA 1944.

A similar refusal to intervene had occurred in 1987–1988 when a group of parents in Dewsbury, all of whom were white, collectively opposed the LEA's admissions decisions in respect of their children.[68] Their choice was a school where white children were in the majority. The LEA had allocated places for each of the children at a school where 83 per cent. of the children were said to be of Asian origin, and the parents lodged appeals under section 7 of the 1980 Act which were unsuccessful. The parents refused to send the children to the allocated school and made arrangements for them to receive lessons from a retired teacher in a room above a public house. They argued that this action reflected their concern that the children should be educated in a school with a predominantly Christian ethos. The Secretary of State could find no basis for intervention. Eventually, in the face of legal action alleging illegality in the LEA's admissions procedures, the LEA backed down and found places for the children in two schools where white pupils were in the majority.

Returning to the *Cleveland* case, there were two crucial questions: first whether the duty to comply with parental preference was subject to an overriding requirement not to discriminate on racial grounds by virtue of section 18 of the RRA; and secondly, whether parents' racist motives could be considered relevant to this question. There was also the related point, barely considered by the Court of Appeal but dealt with by Macpherson J. in the Divisional Court, about whether acceding to Mrs C's request resulted in unlawful racial segregation (see below). In response to the Commission for Racial Equality (CRE)'s contention that the section 18 duty had been broken, the LEA argued that although it had a policy of multicultural education for its schools, section 6(2) of the 1980 Act meant that it was obliged to accede to a parent's transfer request unless one of the grounds in section 6(3) applied. The only

---

[68] See A. Bradney, "The Dewsbury Affair and the Education Reform Act 1988" (1989) 1(2) *Education & the Law* 51. This dispute was also referred to, briefly, in Chap. 1.

ground which could have applied was section 6(3)(*a*) (prejudice to efficient education, etc — above); but as the school's admissions limit had not been reached choice could not be denied on this ground. It was further contended that section 18 of the RRA did not constrain the granting of parental preference because the LEA had been acting "in pursuance of [an] enactment" (namely section 6(2) of the 1980 Act). Section 41(1)(*a*) of the RRA permits discrimination in such circumstances, if the action is carried out "in the performance of an express obligation" in a statute or statutory instrument.[69] In the view of the Divisional Court and Court of Appeal in *Cleveland*, the duty to comply with parental preference was a mandatory duty and fell within the scope of section 41, so there had been no illegality in acceding to Mrs C's request. Nevertheless, regardless of the duty to comply with parental preference, LEAs must exercise *discretion* in allocating children to schools, particularly where a school is over-subscribed, and in framing an admissions policy to guide their officers (see above).[70] The Court of Appeal in *Cleveland* was in effect saying that in this context the specific duties concerning preference could be viewed in isolation from the discretion resting with LEAs over school admissions.

The Court also held that because the duty to comply with parental preference was mandatory the reasons for Mrs C's preference were irrelevant. Parker L.J. said that to hold that an LEA need not comply with a request if the reasons were "as a matter of construction" racist, would involve "adding to the three exceptions in section 6(3) a further exception which Parliament [had] not seen fit to put there." He also rejected counsel's argument the LEA had acted on "racial grounds," saying that the authority had merely complied with their duty to uphold the parent's preference[71] and that in any event parents of whatever that race would have received the same treatment.[72]

---

[69] *Hampson* v. *Department of Education and Science* [1991] 1 A.C. 171, *per* Lord Lowry at p. 180.

[70] There was considered to be a distinction between the "mandatory" parental preference duty in s.6(2) of the 1980 Act and the "target" duty in s.8 of the EA 1944 (*per* Woolf L.J. in *R.* v. *I.L.E.A. ex p. Ali and Murshid* (1990) *The Times*, February 21), which *has* been held to be subject to the relevant provisions of the SDA (see Chap. 4 pp. 118–119). It is, however, clear that just as the duty to provide "sufficient schools" is not an absolute duty, so compliance with parental preference may legitimately be denied where a school is full.

[71] Parker L.J. was in effect holding inapplicable to the case Lord Bridge's *dictum* that "the purity of the discriminator's subjective motive, intention or reason for discriminating cannot [prevent] . . . the objective taint of discrimination on the ground of sex [or race]": *James* v. *Eastleigh Borough Council* [1990] 2 A.C. 751, at pp. 765–766.

[72] This "same treatment" test was applied by Lord Goff in *R.* v. *Birmingham C.C. ex p. Equal Opportunities Commission* [1989] A.C. 1155 at 1193–1194 and by Lords Bridge and Goff in *James* v. *Eastleigh B.C. op. cit.* at pp. 765–766 and 774.

It was also argued by the CRE that there was unlawful racial segregation[73] "because the children the transferred child was being kept away from were Asian children, even though there were a few Asian children in the child's new school." In the school the child had been attending, 40 per cent. of the pupils were of Asian origin compared to two per cent. in the new school. Parker L.J. in the Court of Appeal said that "the removal of K from Abingdon Road was the lawful act of her mother" and not the "act" of the LEA, so there could not have been unlawful segregation by the LEA. In the Divisional Court, Macpherson J. had arrived at the same conclusion, but on the basis that "there was no isolation of any race." This view can be challenged on the ground that Parliament did not intend that there would have to be total separation of races for there to be racial segregation. Section 1(2) of the RRA refers to "segregating a *person* from *other persons* on racial grounds" (emphasis added). Macpherson J.'s other argument, that compliance with Mrs C's request could not cause "unfavourable treatment," can also be attacked, on the ground that the Act states (also in section 1(2)) that "segregating a person from other persons on racial grounds *is treating him less favourably than they are treated*" (emphasis added).[74] Moreover, the *Shorter Oxford English Dictionary* defines "segregate" as "To separate (a *person*, a body or class of persons) from the general body or some particular class" (emphasis added). It is possible that it was not so much the fact there there was only one child involved but rather the fact that she was being separated from an entire racial group that influenced Parker L.J.'s thinking on the matter. Even so, section 1(2) of the RRA simply talks of segregation on racial grounds from "other persons." It may be noted that Supreme Court cases in the United States have confirmed that separate schooling as between races is inherently unequal; total separation is not necessary for there to be unlawful racial segregation.[75]

The decision in *Cleveland* indicates that where choice of school is concerned the clear purpose of the RRA 1976 in promoting equal treatment and discouraging racial discrimination may be negated. If a parent's motives in requesting a school transfer form a wholly irrelevant consideration, an LEA which rejects a request for a racially motivated transfer on the grounds of racism is acting in breach of section 6(2) of the EA 1980. Cleveland LEA has said that the ruling has undermined

---

[73] See also Commission for Racial Equality, *Secondary School Allocations in Reading — Report of a Formal Investigation* (1983).

[74] See further Commission for Racial Equality, *Racial Discrimination in Education: Report of a Formal Investigation into Cleveland Education Authority* (1989).

[75] *Brown* v. *Board of Education* 347 U.S. 483 (1954); *Keyes* v. *School District No. 1 Denver Colorado* 413 U.S. 189 (1983).

many equal opportunities and anti-racism policies, and will encourage racially-motivated school choice requests.[76] If one accepts the Court of Appeal's conclusion that the LEA had not practised unlawful segregation by complying with the request, the door is now undoubtedly open to parents to use the parental preference provision in a racist manner. *Cleveland* also demonstrates the individualist focus of the rights in this area,[77] highlighting the inherent difficulty in reconciling two underlying educational policy principles — individual parental choice and racial harmony via a multi-cultural approach to educational provision.

(c) Section 6(3)(a) — balancing parental preference against prejudice to efficient education/use of resources

> "[I]f there were no regard to efficiency, all people would have whatever they wanted, when they wanted it and where they wanted it. People would have exactly the education — or health — provision that they wanted on their doorstep, as they specified it, without let or hindrance. At one extreme lies the sole criterion of efficiency, and at the other lies the wishful criterion of people having what they want by simply passing a law to specify that. Somewhere in between lies reality."[78]

Regarding parental choice of school, the most limiting aspect of the legal regime is contained in section 6(3)(*a*), which, as noted above, has enabled parental preference to be denied where compliance would prejudice the provision of efficient education or the efficient use of resources. However, by virtue of section 26(9) of the ERA 1988, section 6(3)(*a*) does not apply until the school has admitted pupils up to its standard number, which reflects its physical capacity.[79] This change in the law is discussed in the context of "open enrolment" below.

The two stage test developed by Forbes J. in *ex p. Evans*[80] for the application of section 6(3)(*a*) by appeal committees appears still to be

---

[76] See *Daily Telegraph*, October 19, 1991.

[77] See further the discussion of *ex p. Evans* below.

[78] Official Report, House of Commons Standing Committee E, col. 1104, January 26, 1993, Mr E. Forth M.P. (Under Secretary of State (Schools)).

[79] Under ERA 1988, s.27, the standard number is either the 1979–80 intake figure or the 1989–90 figure, whichever is the higher. See N. Harris, *The Law Relating to Schools* (1990) pp. 148–152, which also sets out the circumstances in which the standard number may be reduced.

[80] *R. v. South Glamorgan Appeals Committee ex p. Evans* (1984) Lexis CO/197/84. For analysis, see T. Buck (1985) J.S.W.L. 227 at pp. 240–242 and J. Tweedie [1986] P.L. 407 at p. 420–422.

relevant, although only where a school is admitting pupils beyond its standard number or has allocated more or less up to its physical capacity (if this is greater than the standard number). Although the appeals stage is considered more fully below, it is appropriate to present Forbes J.'s test here, because it clarified the process by which prejudice can be determined (while leaving some uncertainty as to the circumstances in which it might occur).[81] Mr Evans, the applicant, had sought a place for his four year old daughter at a Welsh-medium school at which his son was already a pupil. An admissions limit of 30 was set by the LEA for the class which the boy would have joined, a class which in fact contained 36 pupils at the relevant time. The appeal committee decided that the admission of the child would be "prejudicial to the provision of efficient education at the school" for the purposes of section 6(3)(*a*). A successful application was made to the High Court for an order quashing the decision of the appeal committee. Forbes J. held that the appeal committee had misdirected itself by failing to apply the following two stage test: (i) would the admission of one child prejudice the provision of efficient education at the school (the onus being on the LEA to show that it did)?; if so, then (ii) was the prejudice sufficient to outweigh the "parental factors" (ie the particular arguments or circumstances in support of the parents' case)? Forbes J. found that the appeal committee had failed to apply the second part of the test. (After the High Court's decision the appeal was re-heard by an appeal committee which found that there would be no prejudice.)

The test is applied in considering an individual case, as the appeal committee would have to do, rather than when approaching the matter in a more collectivist way, as the LEA might do when applying its policy to large numbers of children. Tweedie[82] distinguishes between the "substantial justice" approach to school place allocations, which "takes ... account of individual circumstances without significantly displacing the LEA's general policy making authority," and the "individualist rights" approach, which "focuses exclusively on the individual parent's school request, without regard for general policy concerns or the pattern of parents' requests." With the "individualist rights" approach, there would be a strong presumption in favour of the granting of parental choice. There would also be an emphasis solely on the consequences of allowing one particular child to be admitted to the school. On this basis, LEA admissions policies become according to Tweedie "irrelevant to the decision of an appeal" and the LEA can succeed in ensuring rejection of preference under section 6(3)(*a*) "only by

---

[81] See D. Bull, "Monitoring Education Appeals: Local Ombudsmen Lead the Way" (1985) J.S.W.L. 189.

[82] *Supra*, (n.80) pp. 418–419.

marshalling arguments showing why to grant that single request would cause significant harm to education at the school." Tweedie argues that the individualist rights approach was adopted in *ex p. Evans* and suggests that the decision has made it extremely difficult for LEAs to justify a refusal of a place even where a school is full, because of its narrow focus on individual claims.[83] He argues that social welfare programmes need to have a more collectivist focus, although with a requirement that the provider is subjected to a higher burden of justification for its policy.[84]

Forbes J.'s two stage test was broadly supported by the Divisional Court in *R. v. Local Commissioner for Administration ex p. Croydon L.B.C.*[85] In that case, Woolf L.J. accepted that the onus is on the LEA at stage one to show that there would be prejudice. However, it was felt that, at stage two, when the committee has to decide whether the prejudice is sufficient to outweigh the "parental factors," it was inappropriate to talk about "onus"; it was simply a matter of the committee considering, on the basis of the material before them, "where the balance lies."[86] Woolf L.J. did not deal directly with the question of whether the prejudice issue should be determined with reference to proportionality. However, he did approve the practice, adopted by the Croydon L.E.A. in the instant case, of hearing all appeals in relation to admissions to one particular school before deciding on any individual case. By following this practice it becomes difficult for an appeal committee to adopt a wholly individualist rights approach, since cases may be weighed against each other and ranked before the prejudice test is considered.

It might appear in the light of the *Evans* decision that the prejudice test would have to be applied in denying preference in any particular case, whatever the ranking. But the Council on Tribunals' *Code of Practice on Procedure*[87] suggests that when the appeal committee is hearing the entire series of individual appeals before deciding the individual cases, their task at stage one will involve "forming a view as to how many places can be allocated without prejudice." This is clearly not the stage one test enunciated in *Evans* and applied by the Local Ombudsman (D. Yardley) in the complaint which preceded the *Croydon* case,[88] but is an adaptation of it to meet the situation, approved in

[83] *Ibid.* pp. 421–422.
[84] *Ibid.* pp. 434–435.
[85] [1989] 1 All E.R. 1033 at p. 1040.
[86] *Ibid.* at p. 1041.
[87] *Education Appeals: Code of Practice on Procedure* (1992) p. 16.
[88] *Report by the Local Government Ombudsman into Complaint 610/Y/85 against the London Borough of Croydon* (1986) para. 42.

148	*Individual Choice of School*

Croydon, of looking at all appeals before deciding (see above). Even so, the approach may exemplify the continuing difficulty with interpretation of the *Evans* test. Shortly after the case, Buck noted that Forbes J. had set appeal committees quite a difficult task: they had to wrestle with an "amorphous" concept — the degree of prejudice — "and then weigh this against another nebulous concept . . . 'parental factors'."[89] A recent Association of Metropolitan Authorities/Association of County Councils Seminar Report refers to the practical difficulties experienced in applying the test, for example uncertainty as to "how prejudice can be defined and, if prejudice is identified, what, if any, powers the committee has to determine the number of additional pupils the school may take."[90] Indeed, the Report argues that application of the *Evans* test "remains one of the most intractable elements of appeals committee procedure as defined in law."[91] This is confirmed by the findings of the Local Government Ombudsman in several recent cases.[92]

Where a school is over-subscribed, the prejudice argument will be easily satisfied. As Lord Browne-Wilkinson said in the *Bishop Challoner* case (above), "when a school is over-subscribed it necessarily follows that 'compliance with the preference' of *all* applicants would prejudice proper education at the school through over-crowding."[93] It is at this stage that the admissions criteria, the "parental factors," come into play (see above).

(c) Section 6(3)(b) and (6)–(9) — admissions arrangements between LEA and governing body of voluntary aided or special agreement school

Governing bodies of voluntary aided and special agreement schools are permitted by section 6(3)(*b*) to override parental preference by refusing admission of a pupil if the admission would be incompatible with the arrangements agreed with the LEA. This is the case even if the school is left with vacant places as a result.[94] The arrangements are made under section 6(6), which provides that the LEA must make such arrangements with the governing body if requested by the governors to do so; in default of agreement, the terms of the arrangements may be determined by the Secretary of State. The purpose of these provisions is

---

[89] T. Buck *supra*. (n.80), at p. 247.
[90] A.M.A./A.C.C., *Education Appeals Code of Practice — Seminar Report* (March 1992) p. 12.
[91] *Ibid.*
[92] *Report by the Local Ombudsman into Complaints* — 90/A/1467 (L.B. of Havering) (1991); 91/A/0939 (L.B. of Bromley) (1992); and 91/C/0738 (Humberside) (1992).
[93] [1992] 3 All E.R. 277 (see *supra* n.48) at p. 285.
[94] *Ibid.*

essentially to enable the governing body to safeguard the religious character of the school.

The arrangements may also be modified by agreement. In the absence of agreement, the party proposing the changes may refer the matter to the Secretary of State who can approve or reject the proposed changes, direct that they be modified or replace them with proposals of his own.[95]

(d) Section 6(3)(c) — selection partly or wholly by reference to ability or aptitude.

Section 6(3)(c) ensures that where schools are permitted by their articles of government to select by ability or aptitude, selection may prevail over parental preference. In relation to popular schools, other admissions criteria may be applied in addition to ability or aptitude. Such arrangements were considered in *R.* v. *Kingston upon Thames Royal London Borough Council ex p. Emsden.*[96] Here a voluntary controlled secondary school operated a two stage admissions policy. First, a pool of the most academically able children would be established. This invariably contained more children than could be accommodated in the school. Secondly, the available places would be allocated to children within the pool on the basis of proximity of home to school. The children living nearer the school would have priority over those living further away. Schiemann J. said that it was "implicit" in section 6(3)(c) that the admission arrangements would be based partly on the application of a second qualification such as this; the arrangements were not unlawful.

Such arrangements were also in operation in the Wirral district of Merseyside. They were the subject of an application for judicial review by the parents of a girl denied a grammar school place: *R.* v. *Metropolitan Borough of Wirral ex p. Pickard.*[97] For historical reasons Wirral is organised into three areas for schools organisation pruposes: Bebington/Deeside, Birkenhead and Wallasey. All the LEA grammar schools are in the first of these areas. The applicant, who lived in Birkenhead, applied for his daughter to be admitted to Wirral Grammar School for Girls. She was, however, allocated a place at a comprehensive school in Birkenhead. The admissions policy discriminated in favour of those living in Bebington/Deeside: taking all those applicants who reached the required academic standard, preference was given to those living in that area. The same residence-linked preference applied to those considered next (*inter alios*, those gaining within three marks of

---

[95] Subss. (7)–(9) of s.6, added by the EA 1993, s.270.
[96] [1993] 1 FLR 179.
[97] (1991) Lexis CO/1735/91.

the required standard). It was contended for the applicant that the admissions policy was unfair in the way that it was possible for someone living outside Bebington/Deeside to in effect be denied a place by someone living in that area but with a lower mark. However, it was argued by the authority that the reason that the applicant's child was not allocated a grammar school place was that she did not achieve the necessary mark in the 11-plus examination and that the decision would have been the same whichever area she had resided in. Leggatt L.J. said that, in consequence, it could not be said that the girl had been disadvantaged by the policy, and the court would not intervene, "even if the policy of the authority were such as in other circumstances might yield an unfair result." This meant that the legality of the zoning policy affecting admissions in Wirral was not ruled upon.

(e) Section 6(5) and the cross-boundary cases

Parents, especially in urban areas, may be living in a different LEA area to that in which a nearby school, to which they would like to send their child, is located. This is particularly true in London, where educational provision can vary enormously from one area to the next. In the interests of maximising parental choice, section 6(5) provides that the duty to comply with parental preference (under section 6(2)) "shall also apply in relation to . . . any application for admission to a school maintained by a local education authority of a child who is not in the area of the authority . . . and references in subsection (3) . . . to a preference and a preferred school shall be construed accordingly." In including this provision, the Government wanted to make sure that the right to express a preference was "not limited to expressing a preference for a school in an area in which a child lives. Parents will be free for the first time to express a wish that their children should be educated in a school in another local education authority area."[98] The Secretary of State also pointed out that recoupment arrangements would be introduced so that the cost of educating children who attended schools out of their own area would, in effect, be borne by the LEA in whose area the child lived.[99]

Co-operation between authorities has ensured that such arrangements generally operate satisfactorily. But there have been particular difficulties in some areas, especially after the *Greenwich* judgment (below) confirmed that it was unlawful for an LEA to operate a general policy of giving its own residents priority over others when allocating places in its schools.

---

[98] H.C. Debs, Vol. 973, col. 37 (November 5, 1979) Mr Mark Carlisle M.P.
[99] EA 1980, s.31.

The *Greenwich* case (R. v. *Shadow Education Committee of the Greenwich London Borough Council ex p. The Governors of John Ball Primary School*), which reached the Court of Appeal,[1] was the first of three cases concerned with the effect of section 6(5) on particular admissions arrangements. Two neighbouring authorities, Lewisham and Greenwich, had co-operated for a number of years over the practice of enabling children living near to the border between the authorities to attend the nearest school in each other's area. The admissions policy required preference to be given first on the basis of having a sibling at the preferred school and thereafter on the basis of home to school proximity. In July 1989, however, Greeenwich approved a change of policy, under which admissions priority was to be given to Greenwich residents. Among the schools affected was the John Ball Primary School, on the Lewisham side of the border, many of whose pupils had been hoping to attend secondary schools in Greenwich in accordance with the past practice. The admissions policy was revised in October 1989 to take account of various representations made. The effect of this was that pupils attending certain named Lewisham schools, including John Ball School, had higher priority than pupils from other schools in Lewisham and other areas. However, they still ranked after Greenwich residents. In an application for judicial review to quash the education committee's resolution, it was argued for the applicants that while the authority was free to adopt an admissions policy to enable it to discriminate between applicants where a school was over-subscribed, it was unlawful for it to give priority to children from its own area in preference to children from Lewisham. Counsel for Greenwich, however, argued that the duty in section 6(5) did not constrain the operation of an admissions policy in the case of an oversubscribed school, but merely ensured that, where a vacancy at the preferred school existed, a child from a neighbouring authority could not be rejected merely on the grounds of his/her address. The Divisional Court and Court of Appeal rejected this argument and found in favour of the governors of John Ball School. The admissions policy was a matter for the exercise of discretion by the LEA, but "the discretion must be exercised consistently with and so as not to thwart the provisions of section 6(5) . . . [whose] purpose . . . is to ensure that all children from within or without the area rank *pari passu*, that they all come from the starting gate at the same time."[2] Counsel for Greenwich had also pointed to the obligations of the LEA to cater for the needs of pupils in *their area* and to ensure the provision of sufficient schools *for their area*, in sections 7 and 8 of the EA 1944. It

---

[1] (1990) 88 L.G.R. 589 (C.A.).
[2] *per* Lloyd L.J. at 597.

was argued that because these obligations were owed by an LEA only to its own residents, and because an LEA had no obligation to provide education to residents of another area, it would be anomalous if, as was implied by the applicants' (and Divisional Court's) interpretation of section 6(5), such easy access to schooling by those from another area had to be facilitated. But this argument was also rejected. The words of the statute were clear. Farquharson L.J. said: "Neither in the face of these clear words can I see that the duties imposed on the local education authority by the Act of 1944 in relation to the children in their own area affect the provisions of section 6."[3]

Some LEAs had to modify their admissions policy in the light of the *Greenwich* judgment. One such authority was Bromley L.B.C. The authority had been operating a policy under which preference in school admissions was given to Bromley residents. After the *Greenwich* decision Bromley applied the following admissions policy in cases where the preferred school was over-subscribed: priority would be given in the following descending order — children with a brother or sister at the school; proximity of home to school; and accessibility of any alternative school. The policy was subject to the proviso that the authority would depart from the criteria where necessary to comply with its duties under sections 7 and 8 of the 1944 Act (above). The authority had introduced this proviso in order to enable it to preserve the right of its own residents to a school place in Bromley, which was being threatened by the likely influx of children from outside the area. The authority's view was that it would be in breach of sections 7 and 8 of the 1944 Act if it could not guarantee places for Bromley residents at its schools. In addition to several complaints made to the Local Government Ombudsman,[4] there was an application for judicial review of the policy by three parents who, it was accepted by the authority, would have secured a place at a Bromley school but for the proviso. Watkins L.J.[5] accepted that the duties in EA 1980, section 6(5), made it "painfully difficult," when its school places were over-subscribed, for the LEA to comply with its duties under sections 7 and 8 of the 1944 Act to ensure proper educational provision for its residents. However, the Divisional Court was bound by the Court of Appeal's decision in *Greenwich* and granted the applicants a declaration.

Another authority which revised its policy in the light of the *Greenwich* case was the Royal Borough of Kingston upon Thames, entry to whose schools was on the basis of selection by ability. The admissions

---

[3] At p. 603.
[4] *Report by the Local Government Ombudsman into Complaint No. 90/A/0773 and 91/A/039* (L.B. of Bromley) (1992).
[5] *R. v. Bromley London Borough Council ex p. C and Others* [1992] 1 FLR 174.

policy change gave cognisance to the *Greenwich* judgment by providing that under the selection process all applicants, irrespective of area, would be given the same chance. The same argument that had been raised in the *Bromley* case (above), concerning the LEA's duty in respect of its own residents under sections 7 and 8 of the 1944 Act, was presented in a legal challenge to the new policy. One of the principal effects of the policy change had been that Kingston residents who had expressed a preference for single sex education might not be able to obtain it when they would have done in the past. Watkins L.J., giving judgment on the same day as in the *Bromley* case, said that the LEA's policy had been consistent with section 6 of the 1980 Act, as interpreted in *Greenwich*:

> "If primary duty there is in this sphere it is . . . to ensure that there is no discrimination against out-borough residents. Thereafter, the duties to make available efficient education within the area of the [LEA] will remain. Presumably the education would be available in the area of another education authority."[6]

These two cases have illustrated the problems which the *Greenwich* decision has presented to LEAs. LEAs have been expected to plan local provision under the duties in sections 7 and 8 of the 1944 Act. This is extremely difficult if there is a need to respond to consumer demand from a wide geographical area. The scale of that demand, initially at least, must at times be very difficult to gauge. In *Bromley*, Watkins L.J. said that "their Lordships saw great practical difficulty and it does not surprise them to learn that representations have been made to the Secretary of State which seek to bring about a change in the law." Where some schools in the area have acquired GM status the problem may be much worse, not least because the LEA could have joint responsibility with a funding authority for securing sufficient school places in the area (see Chapter 2). Under the 1993 Act it will be possible for the Secretary of State to introduce a scheme for "co-ordinated arrangements for admissions" as between GM schools, the LEA and neighbouring LEAs.[7] This needs to be seen as rather more than a reserve power. For example, in Bromley, where the LEA had sought to resist being caught by the full impact of the *Greenwich* decision, 225 pupils were left without a school place under the initial allocations in April 1992.[8] In addition to cross-border traffic, the authority had the problem of not knowing with any certainty which children each of the 12 GM schools in its area would be admitting.

---

[6] R. v. *Royal Borough of Kingston upon Thames ex p. Kingwell* [1992] 1 FLR 182 at p. 188.
[7] See s.260.
[8] See "A poor choice for some" *The Guardian*, August 4, 1992.

The Government has, however, expressed the hope that GM schools and LEAs in an area can co-operate in voluntary joint admissions arrangements.[9]

Although the case law confirms that section 6(5) has indeed advanced the cause of parental choice of school, it has to be borne in mind that if additional travel costs would be incurred by attending a school further afield than one offering a suitable place, the LEA in whose area the child resides will not be liable to meet these costs, or provide transport, under its duty in section 55 of the EA 1944. This in fact seems to be the case whether or not the school chosen by the parent is inside or beyond the LEA's area.[10]

(f) Section 7 and Schedule 2 — admissions appeals

i. *Introduction*

The appeal committees established under the EA 1980 in respect of school admissions (and also permanent exclusions and special educational needs[11]) are perhaps the most significant mechanism for the enforcement of consumer rights in the context of education, because of the critical importance of school selection to consumers and because the committees are easily the busiest redress of grievance bodies in the sphere of education — with over 15,000 appeals each year in recent years.

Section 7(6) of the EA 1980 put these education appeal committees (EACs), which have to be established by LEAs and governing bodies of voluntary schools, under the supervision of the Council on Tribunals. The Council has played an active role in guiding LEAs and governing bodies in areas such as training, procedure at hearings (with a *Code of Practice on Procedure* developed in consultation with LEAs) and the "prejudice" test in section 6(3)(*a*) (above).

Many LEAs have developed informal procedures for resolving disputes over school allocations. They have to some extent been encouraged in this by the DFE, although as a means of reducing the number of cases needing to proceed to an appeal hearing rather than of attempting to supplant the right of appeal under section 7:

> "Authorities may . . . formulate their appeal arrangements so that the point of appeal is not reached until all other means of

---

[9] *Choice and Diversity*, para. 5.5.

[10] *R.* v. *Essex C.C. ex p. C* (1993) *The Times*, April 29; *R.* v. *Rochdale M.B.C. ex p. Schemet* (1992) *Lexis* CO/211/91. For this purpose, the suitability of the school must now be judged *inter alia*, on the religious preference expressed by the parents: EA 1944, s.55(3) as amended by EA 1993, Sched. 19.

[11] The EA 1993 will transfer the special educational needs appeals jurisdiction to Special Educational Needs Tribunals — see Chap. 7.

settlement have been exhausted. A number of authorities and governors operate an informal review procedure, for example to consider the results of unsuccessful candidates in selection tests. This can be a useful mechanism, but it does not remove the parent's statutory right of appeal."[12]

The Local Government Ombudsman has approved as being in conformity with this guidance the operation of an "admissions panel" by Harrow L.B.C., consisting of three education committee members who are not on the appeals panel plus a head teacher observer.[13]

Information about the right of appeal and the relevant arrangements for exercising it must be sent to each parent with the notification of the school place allocation decision.[14]

Grant-maintained schools Note that similar arrangments operate in the case of admission to GM schools, whose appeals system must be in accordance with the approved instrument and articles of government for the school.[15] The Council on Tribunals has criticised the failure of the model articles of government to make adequate provision for the procedure and other matters relating to the operation of these appeal committees.[16] The Council has been instrumental in the development of a Code of Practice for admissions appeals in respect of GM schools, and it has drawn attention to continuing problems of lack of suitably qualified persons to serve as clerks to appeal committees, unmet need for training of members and under-resourcing of appeals administration.[17]

ii. *Constitution*

The rules governing the constitution of EACs were referred to earlier (p. 134 above). The chief criticism has concerned the lack of independence of the membership, although there has also been concern that a committee of seven members may be difficult to chair successfully and may prove more intimidating to an appellant than a committee of three or five. The Council on Tribunals has referred to both of these problems, recommending against a large committee[18] and proposing a

---

[12] DES Circular 11/88, *op. cit.*, para. 53.
[13] *Report by the Local Government Ombudsman on an Investigation into Complaint No. 89/A/2301 against the London Borough of Harrow* (February 24, 1992).
[14] See the Education (School Information) (England) Regulations 1993 S.I. 1993 No. 1502.
[15] EA 1993, Sched. 6, which also enables governing bodies to make joint appeal arrangements with other schools. The Council on Tribunals has supervisory jurisdiction over GM schools' appeal committees: ERA 1988, Sched. 12 para. 12.
[16] Council on Tribunals, *Annual Report 1989–90* (1990) para. 2.85.
[17] Council on Tribunals, *Annual Report 1991–92* (1992) para. 1.36.
[18] Council on Tribunals, *Annual Report 1987–88* (1988) para. 2.35.

change in the legislation to achieve a more evenly balanced constitution.[19] As noted above, the Government's case for the LEA dominated membership established under the Act was that there would be a benefit from the fact that LEA members would have an appreciation of the broad considerations affecting admissions decisions within the authority. The counter-argument from the Council on Tribunals was that although the appeal committee members would not have been involved in the decision being appealed against, there might be "a suspicion (particularly among parents whose appeals have been unsuccessful) that an Appeal Committee will tend to defend decisions rather than approach them with an open mind if most of its members have a direct connection with the original decision maker."[20] The Council on Tribunals reported a lack of impartiality in some hearings. The Local Government Ombudsman has found similar evidence in a number of cases — for example, a failure to test the LEA's case regarding "prejudice" fully[21] and discussions between the EAC and the LEA's appeal officer prior to the opening of a hearing.[22]

The Government finally responded to the problem of potential or perceived partiality by including provisions amending the constitution of EACs in the Education Bill published in 1992. The EA 1993 now provides for a lay element in EACs by requiring one of the members nominated by the LEA (or governing body, in the case of aided or special agreement schools) to be "from among persons eligible to be lay members."[23] Persons are eligible to be lay members only if they have no experience in the management of a school and (in the case of voluntary aided and special agreement schools) no connection with the school or

---

[19] *Ibid.* para. 2.34.

[20] *Ibid.*

[21] *Report by the Local Government Ombudsman of an Investigation into Complaint* — No. 90/A/1462 (Havering L.B.C.) (26/9/91) and No. 91/A/0939 (Bromley L.B.C.) (August 27, 1992).

[22] *Report by the Local Government Ombudsman of an Investigation into Complaint No. 91/C/1595 against Bolton Metropolitan Borough Council* (November 11, 1992). For references to some of the investigations concerning bias in the early years of the EACs, see D. Bull (1985) J.S.W.L. *op. cit.* p. 194. In one case the Local Government Ombudsman found there to have been maladministration, but no injustice, when one of the members of the appeal committee was a governor at school A, at which the appellants had been offered a place but turned it down. The governor had extolled the virtues of school A during the hearing of the appeal in respect of school B. The Ombudsman accepted that the appellants had been entitled to feel that this committee member might not act impartially in determining the appeal: *Report by the Local Govt. Ombudsman of an Investigation into Complaint No. 90/A/0773 against Bromley L.B.C.* (August 28 1991).

[23] EA 1993, s.266 and Sched. 16 para. 2(1), 3(1) and 4, substituting new paras 1(2) and 2(2) of Sched. 2 to the EA 1980. The Secretary of State may now make regulations requiring LEAs (or governing bodies of aided and special agreement schools) to advertise for lay members of appeal committees: EA 1993, s.267.

its employees or governors, or (in the case of other LEA-maintained schools) no connection with the LEA or any employee or member of it.[24] The 1993 Act has also removed the need for LEA members to outnumber the other member(s) by one.[25] Chairmanship of EACs established by LEAs was barred to EAC members who were also members of the education committee; the 1993 Act has removed this prohibition but has barred from chairmanship LEA members and employees of the authority.[26]

The changes introduced under the 1993 Act seek to achieve a balance between the aim of ensuring that appeals are heard by persons who can make informed decisions which take proper account of local administrative factors and policy arrangements, and the need for an objective and impartial evaluation of individual and competing claims. Attempts are being made to remedy basic deficiencies in the conduct of hearings and in the recording of reasoned decisions,[27] through the development and continuing refinement of a suitable guide to procedure and the institution of local training. But the time may now have come for the introduction of an entirely new, nationally/regionally co-ordinated and independent structure, as is being introduced in special educational needs cases (see Chapter 7).

iii. *Procedure*

Unlike the appeal committees dealing with admissions appeals in Scotland, the EACs are not subject to comprehensive and detailed procedural rules. The Council on Tribunals has suggested that this has given rise to some of the problems experienced with the work of the committees (see above).[28] The 1980 Act lays down only a small number of procedural rules, and this has contributed to the diversity of practice observed by the Council.[29] Among the rules laid down in the Act are those stating that written notice of the appeal, setting out the grounds, must be given; the appellant must be allowed to present a case and be accompanied or represented; the committee's decision may be by majority; the decision must be communicated in writing to the appellant and must state the grounds for the decision; and the hearing

---

[24] New para. 4A of Sched. 2 to the EA 1980. For such a "connection" to apply it must be "of a kind which might reasonably be taken to raise doubts about his ability to act impartially in relation to the [authority/school]."

[25] Paragraph 1(4) of Sched. 2 to the 1980 Act has been amended by Sched. 16 para. 2(3) of Sched. 16 to the EA 1993.

[26] New para. 1(5) of Sched. 2 to the EA 1980, substituted by Sched. 16 para. 2(4) to the EA 1993.

[27] See Council on Tribunals, *Annual Report 1987/88* (1988) para. 2.41.

[28] *Ibid.* para. 2.30.

[29] *Ibid.* para. 2.31.

should be in private except where the governors or LEA direct otherwise.[30] In addition, the committee must take account of the following matters in reaching their decision:

    (a)   any preference expressed by the appellant(s) under section 6 of the 1980 Act; and

    (b)   the arrangements for admission (which would include the admissions criteria) published in accordance with section 8 of the Act.[31]

The published *Code of Practice on Appeals* offers guidance on the running order of proceedings, provision of interpreters, adducing evidence, calling witnesses and the role of the clerk. It also explains how the stated duties (such as the duty to give reasons for the decision) can best be complied with.

In cases where a school is over-subscribed, and where there are multiple appeals in respect of one school, the EAC faces "a daunting task."[32] The problem is one of "indivisibility," a problem which rarely confronts an administrative tribunal, in that the number of meritorious claims may exceed the number of school places which are available to meet them.[33] The recommended procedure has been to hear each case individually (as opposed to hearing appeals jointly),[34] but not to decide between the competing claims until all the appeals have been heard, a practice sanctioned by Woolf L.J. in the *Croydon* case.[35] Woolf L.J. said that the advantage of this practice is avoidance of the problem that "children whose appeals are heard last ... be prejudiced because of decisions which had been reached already by an appeal committee to send children to a particular school."[36] However, the Council on Tribunals has recently concluded that the arguments for and against individual or grouped hearings are evenly balanced, and it is now recommending that whichever system is considered more appropriate in the particular circumstances be operated.[37]

In one case the three-member EAC had adjourned after hearing a number of individual appeals but before all the appeals in respect of the school in question had been heard. When the committee was due to reconvene on another day, one of the members was unable to attend and was replaced for these remaining hearings. When a legal challenge was

---

[30] EA 1980, Sched. 2 paras. 5, 6 and 8–10.

[31] *Ibid*. para. 7.

[32] Council on Tribunals, *Annual Report 1986/87* para. 3.21.

[33] See D. Bull (1985) J.S.W.L. *op. cit.* pp. 195–196.

[34] *Supra* (n.27) para. 2.39.

[35] Page 147, (n.85), *supra*.

[36] *Ibid.* at p. 1041.

[37] Council on Tribunals, *Annual Report 1991–92* (1992) para. 1.24.

brought by an unsuccessful appellant, Nolan J. said that even though the law permitted decisions to be made by majority, the committee should consist of the same members throughout if the *Croydon* method was being employed.[38]

(g) Section 8 — the publication of information

The requirements in section 8 of the 1980 Act concerning the publication of information about schools and schooling are considered below in the context of the information regime in a whole, which includes changes introduced under the ERA 1988 and the Education (Schools) Act 1992.

4. 'OPEN ENROLMENT'

The principle of parental choice embodied in several key parts of the EA 1980 was to some extent undermined by the Act's provisions on standard numbers. This was because LEAs had the power to fix an admissions limit which kept the intake up to 20 per cent. below the school's "standard number," which was determined generally with reference to the school's intake in 1979–80 (a peak year).[39] Moreover, as we have seen, adherence to an artificially low admissions limit could be justified in individual cases with reference to the efficient use of resources. As a result, the 1980 Act is said to have "put parental rights of choice at the forefront, but in reality was a way of curbing them more effectively."[40]

In the early 1980s, some within the Conservative Party continued to advocate a system of education vouchers as a means to creating a free market for schooling and greater choice. That it never found its way into legislation during the period of radical privatisation that marked the Thatcher premiership owed much to doubts about its feasibility and the emergence of a more pragmatic and subtle solution to the problem of how to put the consumer into a more dominant position. The Conservatives' General Election manifesto in 1987 promised that LEAs would be required to admit pupils up to the limit of each school's physical capacity and would no longer be permitted to place artificial restrictions on pupil numbers. The allocation of school places would become ever more firmly based on the exercise of consumer choice, and popular schools would be allowed to expand in response to parental demand. In this way, consumer power would force producers to strive

---

[38] *R. v. Camden Borough Council ex p. S* (1990) *The Times,* November 7.
[39] The standard number is defined in n.79 above (p. 145).
[40] S. Maclure, *Education Re-formed* (3rd ed., 1992) p.35.

for better standards. According to Maclure "there was the ideological belief that education could get some of the benefits of a competitive market if consumers had more power to influence the producers by showing, actively, their preference for one school and one kind of education over another."[41] Competition between schools would be intensified by the way that formula funding under LMS (see Chapter 3) made the major determinant of a school's budget share the number of pupils on roll. The Government has since argued that this has "ensured that parental choice directly influences individual schools — the more pupils a school attracts, the larger its budget."[42] But the converse is also true; the fewer pupils a school is able to attract, the more difficult it becomes on resource grounds alone for the school to survive. A poorly resourced school can offer only inferior facilities and will thus prove less attractive to parents, thereby sinking into possibly terminal decline.

Open enrolment was introduced under sections 26–32 of the ERA 1988 and now applies to all LEA-maintained schools.[43] An LEA can no longer refuse admission of a child to a school on the ground that the admission would prejudice efficient education or use of resources, where the total number of admissions in the year would be less than the school's "standard number."[44] The open enrolment provisions also enable a school to admit beyond the standard number provided, *inter alia*, the school buildings can accommodate all the school's pupils. Critics have suggested that LEAs' ability to carry out rational planning, often with a view to ensuring efficient provision, has been seriously hindered by "the unpredictability of parental demand."[45] Indeed, in combination with opting out, open enrolment must have had a de-stabilising effect on local schools provision. It has also been argued that, by extending parental choice, open enrolment may lead to greater social division. For example, one commentator predicts that "racial stratification in schools is also likely to increase. Many white parents are likely to embrace enthusiastically the opportunity to remove their children from schools where there are significant black populations."[46] (This issue was also considered earlier in the context of the *Cleveland* case and Dewsbury dispute.) It has also been suggested that as the more successful schools become increasingly popular a system of covert

---

[41] *Ibid.* p. 33.

[42] *Choice and Diversity*, para. 1.17.

[43] In GM schools, there is an "approved admission number." The governing body must not restrict the size of the intake below this: EA 1993, s. 149(1).

[44] ERA 1988, s. 26(1).

[45] P. Meredith, "Educational Reform" (1989) 52 M.L.R. 215 at pp. 221–222.

[46] D. Coulby, "Ideological Contradicitions," in L. Bash and D. Coulby, *The Education Reform Act: Competition and Control* at p. 115.

selection may emerge.[47] In this way open enrolment may ultimately result in *less* parental choice for some and in schools choosing parents and pupils rather than the other way round.

5. PUBLICATION OF INFORMATION ABOUT SCHOOLS AND SCHOOLING

(a) Introduction

Over a decade before the enactment of the 1980 Act, the Plowden Report had recognised the value of the provision of information about schools in aiding the exercise of parental choice and the development of an effective partnership between home and school:

> "The local education authority might suggest that schools prepare a booklet, giving parents the basic facts about their organisation, the size of classes, whether they are streamed,... the school's educational objectives and methods... Parents would in effect receive a prospectus, as in an independent school. It would help them both to choose a school for their children and to work with the school once the choice was made."[48]

But it was not until 1977 that any government action was taken to encourage the provision of written information about educational provision to parents.[49]

When the provision of information about schools and schooling finally became a statutory duty, with effect from September 1982, the categories of information which had to be published were in fact very similar to those set out in the 1977 circular (see below). However, they differed in one significant respect. LEAs were required to publish information about school examination results. Seen in the context of the rest of the regime in section 8 of the EA 1980, which referred to information about admissions arrangements, it was clear that this part of the legislation was designed first and foremost to facilitate choice in education.

There was controversy over the publication of examination results right from the start. The National Association of Head Teachers came out firmly against the practice[50] and the Shadow Education

---

[47] N. Clough *et al.*, "Restructuring the Education System?," in L. Bash and D. Coulby *op. cit.* at p. 33.

[48] Plowden, Lady Bridget (chair), *Children and their Primary Schools* Vol. 1. (1967) para. 42.

[49] DES Circular 15/77, *Information for Parents* (1977).

[50] The Association said that it would lead to "false judgements" about schools: *The Times*, December 8, 1980.

Secretary, Neil Kinnock M.P., condemned published school examination results as "a highly suspect means of assessing the performance of a school."[51] The debate was later re-kindled during the passage of the ESA 1992, which facilitated the publication of comparative tables of school examination results — the "league tables."

The publication of information regime has been built up in stages.

(b)   The publication of information regime, including the "league tables"

The first stage involved section 8 of the 1980 Act. As noted earlier, this section requires LEAs to publish details of their school admissions arrangements and numbers of pupils to be admitted, together with other information prescribed by regulation. The Education (School Information) Regulations 1981 provided for information to be published both in respect of LEAs' policy and arrangements concerning primary and secondary education and in respect of provision at individual schools; these provisions are now contained, in amended form, in the 1993 Regulations.[52] The information about individual schools must be published by the governing body in a school "prospectus," as recommended by the Plowden Report (above).

The information relating to LEAs' policy and arrangements must include lists of school names and addresses, the numbers on roll and the religious affiliation of each school. It must also include details of LEA policy on such matters as educational grants for pupils and students, special educational needs, charging for services and examination entry. This information must be published and (where it covers secondary education) sent to parents of prospective pupils at least six weeks before they may express a preference for a school under the admissions arrangements.[53] Copies must also be made available at schools, public libraries and LEA offices.

Each school prospectus must be published by the LEA or by or on behalf of the governors of an aided or special agreement school. Any changes to the prospectus from one year to the next must be notified to the parents in the governors' annual report to them.[54] The prospectus must contain a wide range of prescribed categories of information

---

[51] H.C. Debs., Vol. 973, col. 37 (November 5, 1979).

[52] SI 1981 No. 630, replaced by the Education (School Information) (England) Regulations 1993 (SI 1993 No. 1502). (There were no new regulations covering Wales at the time of going to press.)

[53] *Ibid*. reg. 5.

[54] Education (School Curriculum and Related Information) Regulations 1989 SI 1989 No. 954, reg. 4(1). Publication of the governors' annual report is required by s.30 of the E(No. 2)A 1986.

relating to educational provision at the school, including special education, Welsh language and Welsh teaching (in Welsh schools), sex education, extra-curricular activities, discipline, and school uniform and dress. The intention clearly is to facilitate the exercise of parental choice, and with this in mind the regulations also provide for the inclusion of information about both the arrangements for visits by parents of prospective pupils and, more significantly, the school's public examination results by year groups.[55] As noted above, the publication of examination results was a highly contentious issue when first proposed by the Government over ten years ago, and it is still controversial today (see below).

Following amendments in 1989–90, the regulations now, in addition, require the inclusion of information regarding curriculum policy and content, organisation of National Curriculum, policy on charging and curriculum complaints procedures.[56] However, in one survey of school prospectuses it was found that only one in five contained the required information on complaints procedures.[57] Further changes were introduced in 1991, including provision for publication of statistics on pupil absences.[58] Subsequent changes[59] laid down a more complex regime for the compilation and publication of statistics relating to public examination results, paving the way for the changes introduced under the ESA 1992.

The second major stage in the development of the information regime resulted from section 22 of the ERA 1988, which extended the powers of the Secretary of State to require schools and LEAs to publish information "in such form and manner and at such times as may be prescribed".[60] The publication of information relating to National Curriculum assessments could now be required, and GM schools were brought within the scope of some of the requirements. Various documents now have to be available to the public for inspection at schools,[61] including statutory instruments, departmental circulars,

---

[55] 1981 Regs. *op. cit.* Sched. 2 para. 15.

[56] Amendments made to Sched. 2 by the Education (School Curriculum and Related Information) Regulations 1989 SI 1989 No. 954.

[57] N. Harris, *Complaints About Schooling: The Role of Section 23 of the Education Reform Act 1988* (1992) p. 121.

[58] Education (School Hours and Policies) (Information) Regulations 1989 SI 1989 No. 398 and the Education (Pupils' Attendance Records) Regulations 1991 SI 1991 No. 1582.

[59] SI 1991 No. 1265, revoked and replaced by the Education (School Performance Information) (England) Regs 1992 SI 1992 No. 1385 and (Wales) Regs. 1992 SI 1992 No. 2274.

[60] ERA 1988, s.22(1).

[61] *Ibid.* s.22(2) and (3) and the Education (School Curriculum and Related Information) Regulations 1989 SI 1989 No. 954., as amended.

published school HMI reports, schemes of work in current use and syllabuses and other documents.

The ESA 1992 has taken the powers to require the provision of information an important stage further. Information relating to the educational standards achieved by groups of pupils, as reflected in National Curriculum assessments, public examination results, truancy rates and 'school leaver destinations,' can form the basis of comparison between schools (including maintained and independent schools and city technology colleges[62]), thereby facilitating the exercise of consumer choice. (There are also requirements on providing parents with reports on the performance their own children.[63]) The Secretary of State must regulate with a view to ensuring that the information to be made available is likely to "assist parents in choosing schools for their children" in addition to increasing public awareness of standards of education in the schools and aiding judgment of the efficiency with which financial resources are being managed.[64]

The Regulations[65] require governing bodies to compile statistical information on examination entries and results in the prescribed form. Comparative tables are produced by the DFE, and governors must make them available at schools for reference by parents and others. The comparative nature of the tables is emphasised by the requirement that LEA and national averages be shown.[66] The Government originally planned that from September 1993 the tables would relate not only to aggregated GCSE and A/AS level results but also vocational qualifications obtained, National Curriculum assessment results at key stages 1 and 3; in due course they will also cover truancy rates and pupil destinations.[67] However, publication of these National Curriculum test results has been temporarily abandoned. Local tables have to be published at least two weeks before the closing date for expressions of preference by parents, and much of the content must be contained in school prospectuses.[68] All local

---

[62] ESA 1992, s.16, as amended by EA 1993 s.263.

[63] See the Education (Individual Pupils' Achievements) (Information) Regulations 1992 and (Same) (Wales) Regulations 1993 SIs 1992 No. 3168 and 1993 No. 835. Pupils aged 18 or over are entitled to a report in their own right.

[64] ESA 1992, s.16(3).

[65] Education (School Performance Information) (England) Regs 1993 (SI 1993 No. 1503) and (Wales) 1992 (SI 1992 No. 2274).

[66] The national averages shown will be those relating to the previous year.

[67] Pupil destinations shown in tables will be based on "intended — not actual — destinations," because it is felt to be difficult for LEAs to determine the latter by tracing pupils who have left school: Official Report, House of Commons Standing Committee F, col. 393 January 14, 1992. Schools will, however, be urged to base the information on "reasonably firm evidence of pupils' actual destinations wherever possible": DES, *Implementing Parent's Charter Requirements in 1992 — Document 3: Publication of Destinations of School Leavers* (1992) para. 3.

[68] See the Education (School Information) (England) Regulations 1993 SI 1993 No. 1502 Reg. 11 and Sched. 2.

maintained schools and independent schools have to be covered by the tables. Although portrayed by the media and the Opposition as "league tables" (and in some cases referred to by ministers as such), it was the press that decided that the first set of tables, in 1992, should show schools in descending order of GCSE and A level attainment by pupils. The Government had all along insisted that the official LEA list would show schools in alphabetical order.[69]

The Government has said that "the intention is that these tables should be useful, informative and uncomplicated."[70] But critics have suggested that the raw data shown presents an over-simplified picture, creating a distorted impression of the worth of a particular school.[71] They also note the absence of any requirement for the published information to make any reference to surrounding social and environmental factors affecting pupil performance. The Government's view is that reference to these factors would stigmatise schools in certain districts,[72] but HMI has argued that they should be referred to.[73] Critics also emphasise that the tables will not show the "value added" by the school to each child's level of achievement.[74] The "raw data" versus "value added" controversy was further fuelled by published research findings which showed that a different ranking of schools would occur when the value added factor was used and that correlating GCSE and A level results offered a sound basis for measuring value added by sixth form teaching.[75]

By the time that the Secretary of State was summoned to give evidence to the House of Commons Education Committee in November 1992 (to explain why the published examination league tables had contained errors[76] and why special schools were included in the tables) the Government had decided after all to include information about value

---

[69] DES, *supra* (n.67) para. 15(c).
[70] *Ibid.* para. 13.
[71] See "Limits of the league table" *The Independent*, September 19, 1991; "League table proposal still creating divisions" *T.E.S.*, October 10, 1991; "School heads vote to reject exam leagues" *The Times*, May 28, 1992; "Heads fear exam tables misleading to parents" *The Independent*, October 17, 1992.
[72] House of Commons Education Committee, Session 1992–93 *Publication of School Examination Results: Minutes of Evidence* Wednesday Nov. 25, 1992, Q. 17, *per* John Patten M.P., Secretary of State for Education.
[73] See H.M.I., *Aspects of Education in the U.S.A: Indicators in Educational Monitoring* (1991).
[74] See H.C. Debs., Vol. 199, cols. 194, 204, 211, 223 and 230, (November 19, 1991) and H.L. Debs., Vol. 536, cols. 587–616 (March 2, 1992).
[75] See "Town halls to offer rival league tables for schools" *The Times*, Feb. 6, 1992; Audit Commission, *Two Bs or Not. . .? Schools and Colleges' A-level Performance* (1991).
[76] Manchester High School for Girls was reported to be threatening legal action after its 100 per cent. record for pupils achieving five or more GCSE passes at grades A-C was shown in the tables as 16 per cent: "Major denies exam survey was botched" *The Times*, November 20, 1992.

added performance in future tables.[77] The Secretary of State indicated that, from 1995, the comparative tables would show "enhancement" between ages 7 and 11 and ages 14 and 16, and in due course between ages 11 and 14 (from 1997) and 11 and 16 (from 1999).[78] Thus the Government has begun to bow to the weight of considerable pressure to produce a more appropriate basis on which a school's effectiveness may be assessed by consumers.

5. CONCLUSION

The rhetoric of parental choice has featured prominently in Government education policy statements since 1979. The ideal has been translated into a number of consumer rights and corresponding obligations on the part of LEAs concerning school admissions. Recent emphasis has been on extension of choice through diversity on the supply side. This may be as much an attempt to mask the serious limitations to consumer rights in respect of individual choice of school as an indication of the Government's continuing commitment to the overall subjection of education to the forces of consumerism. Although the open enrolment provisions of the ERA 1988 were intended to give a major boost to the choice of school policy, and despite Government claims that they have "secured more choice for parents,"[79] in reality what has emerged is more choice for *some* and less choice for others. Popular schools may become more successful and soon fill up, while less popular schools may go into decline and present an unacceptable choice, which some parents will inevitably be forced to accept.

It is claimed that even before open enrolment around 95 per cent. of parents were securing a place for their child at the school of their choice.[80] This figure is a little difficult to accept, when one takes account of the limits to parental choice resulting from local admissions criteria such as geographical area or feeder primary school. But in any event, it is probably true to say that the choice of school legislation has made a difference, if only at the margins. The right of appeal, for example, has helped some parents (about 5,000 per year) to have their preference upheld.

Although its impact on individual choice may have been limited, the law on parental preference has rightly made LEAs and governors more accountable for the way that allocations are made; and although the

---

[77] *Supra* (n.72) Q.1.
[78] *Ibid.* Annex A to Minutes November 25 1992. See also *The Independent*, August 3, 1993.
[79] *Ibid.*
[80] N. Clough *et al.*, *supra* (n.47).

appeals system is only providing redress to a minority of dissatisfied parents, it has caused LEAs to tighten up their procedures. The recent introduction under the EA 1993 of a more independent element into the appeal committees, whose role is certain to remain important, is to be welcomed.

The exercise of parental choice is said to have been facilitated by the publication of wide-ranging information about schools and schooling. Much of the information, especially that relating to "performance," such as the controversial league tables, serves twin aims of aiding school selection whilst contributing to quality assurance and accountability for standards (see Chapter 6). The Secretary of State has said that the league tables published in 1992 marked "the start of an information revolution that will bring an end to a system that has too often denied parents the right to know how schools are performing and prevented them from making informed choices about where they want their children educated."[81] But the performance-related data can create a false impression not only of the worth of a particular school but also of the degree of choice available to parents. The latter may be illustrated with regard to the 1992 league table results in respect of secondary schools in Liverpool. Of the "top" 12 schools in the table, not one was a county school. There were three independent schools, one GM Roman Catholic school and eight voluntary schools (Roman Catholic, Church of England and Jewish). The provisions of the 1980 Act enabling denominational or selective schools to restrict entry on religious or ability grounds have not been made subject to the open enrolment provisions.[82] Thus many children would have been excluded from these academically successful schools in Liverpool on religious or (in the case of the independent schools) ability grounds. The thirteenth school is a community comprehensive school for which there is a defined admissions area. It is over-subscribed, and those living outside the admissions area have only a slim chance of securing a place at the school unless they have a child there already. On this basis, the published information will merely confirm for some parents that choice will be restricted to schools which are well down the league table.

For schools which are known to be successful, the publication of league tables is particularly meaningless. As a teacher at one of the top schools in the country under the 1992 table was reported as saying:

---

[81] John Patten M.P., in the *The Times School Report* (November 19, 1992), which set out the first national examination league tables.
[82] S. Maclure, *Education Re-formed* (3rd ed. 1992) at p. 38, says that the bishops expressed considerable concern that the character of Roman Catholic schools might change if they were compelled to admit non-Catholic children up to their physical capacity. Section 30 of the ERA 1988 makes provision for the character of such schools to be preserved under an agreement between the LEA and the governors.

"The whole exercise appears to ignore the fact that this school is full to bursting. If as a result of this table the parents of 200 children demand they come here, where would we put them — on the roof?"[83] For schools near the bottom, who tend to serve socially and economically deprived areas, the league table merely confirms their apparent academic inferiority (in terms of pupils' attainment) and may undermine teacher morale. It will also lead to the schools' increasing unpopularity with parents, exacerbating the difficulties facing them. The range of information available to parents will increase when the first sets of school inspectors' reports are published. It is expected that each school will be inspected at least once every four years (see Chapter 6), and these reports will give parents a broader view of the school's performance. Research has shown that parents will tend to look for a school where educational standards and the academic record appear to be sufficiently good,[84] but that the final choice may be swayed by other factors.[85] These factors may include a school's equipment levels, state of decor, standard of discipline, attitude of staff or simply the general atmosphere experienced by parents during a visit to the school.[86]

The content of the prospectus may also be quite influential in school selection,[87] so it is appropriate that schools are required to include particular types of information in it. In practice the assistance provided by school prospectuses tends to be variable: some are informative and easily intelligible whilst others are overly legalistic or minimalistic.[88] Choice of school also tends to be quite strongly influenced by the views of the child concerned.[89] It has been argued that the legislation on provision of information ought to take this fact into account by requiring the information to be addressed to children as well.[90]

---

[83] *The Times*, November 20, 1992.

[84] F. Echols *et al.*, "Choice Among State and Private schools in Scotland" (1990) 5 *Journal of Educational Policy* 207; J.D. Willms and F. Echols, "Alert and Inert Clients: The Scottish Experience of Parental Choice of Schools" (1992) *Economics of Education Review* 339.

[85] A. Stillman, "Legislating for Choice," in M. Flude and M. Hammer (eds.), *The Education Reform Act 1988 — Its Origins and Implications* (1990) p. 100.

[86] See J. Elliott, "How do parents choose and judge secondary schools?" in R. Macormick (ed) *Calling Education into Account* (1982); A Stillman and K. Maychell, *Choosing Schools: Parents, LEAs and the 1980 Education Act* (1986); A. West and A. Varlaam, "Choosing a Secondary School" (1991) 33:1 *Educational Research* 22; J. Hunter, "Which School? A study of parental choice of secondary school" (1991) 33:1 *Educational Research* 31; J. Coldron and P. Boulton, "Happiness as a Criterion of Parents' Choice of School" (1991) 6 *Journal of Educational Policy* 169; A. West *et al.*, *Choosing a Secondary School: The parents' and pupils' stories* (1993) pp. 33–38.

[87] J. Elliott *op. cit.* p. 38.

[88] N. Harris, "Choice of school" (1983) 13 Fam Law 156; A. Stillman *op. cit.* p. 98.

[89] A. West *et al.*, *op. cit.* pp. 35–36.

[90] A. Stillman *op. cit.* p. 101.

Any notion of a right to individual choice of school has been shown to be more myth than reality. This is attributable only to a small extent to the reduction in spare capacity in schools, which the Government has been keen to foster but which can be assumed not to have affected the most popular schools. More significantly, LEAs, and governing bodies have, in relation to school admissions, continued to enjoy a relatively wide discretion, despite the parental preference and open enrolment provisions, and the cases have reinforced this. The elaborate requirements on the publication of information about schools and schooling, on which parents are being invited to base their choice of school, cannot mask this basic reality.

6

QUALITY ASSURANCE

1. INTRODUCTION

"All the mechanisms and procedures that we have put in place are designed to ensure the highest quality in our education system."[1]

The Government has argued that "choice, wherever possible between competing providers, is the best spur to quality improvement."[2] This principle has been incorporated with increasing vigour into the Government's education reforms, as previous chapters have shown. However, consumer choice is inevitably more constrained in the context of largely public sector provision than it is in a free market. Thus there is perceived also to be a need "to develop other ways of ensuring good standards of service."[3] The Government has claimed that "regulation protects the consumer."[4] As noted in Chapter 1, an increasingly tight regulatory regime in education has been introduced to control standards of provision and secure value for money — for example through agency regulation, the use of performance indicators and targets and central monitoring (as with the Annual Curriculum Returns collated by LEAs and sent to the Secretary of State each year[5]).

One of the key quality assurance mechanisms in the schools sector is the new schools inspection system established under the ESA 1992, which is controlled centrally through the new (non-statutory) Office for Standards in Education (OFSTED). Much of the inspection service has in fact been privatised; thus consideration needs to be given to the way in which the public interest is safeguarded. There is an element of public accountability inherent in the planned publication of inspectors' reports

---

[1] Official Report, House of Commons Standing Committee E, col. 954, January 19, 1993, Mr Eric Forth M.P., Under Secretary of State for Education.

[2] *The Citizen's Charter* Cm 1599 (1991) p. 4.

[3] *Ibid.*

[4] *Ibid.* p. 4.

[5] See the Eudcation (School Curriculum and Related Information) Regulations 1989 SI 1989 No. 954, as amended, regs. 8–11 and Scheds. 1 and 2. The returns prepared by GM schools are sent direct to the Department for Education.

and governing bodies' "action plans" drawn up in response to specific criticisms and recommendations. Furthermore, there is also provision for consumer involvement in the inspection process itself. The central powers available where schools are found to be performing badly, considered briefly in Chapter 2, are also highly important. These mechanisms are intended to provide some safeguards at a time of increasing independence for schools and much reliance on internal regulation.

In the chartered universities, there has traditionally been a significant element of internal regulation. But, in recent years, the Government's drive for greater efficiency and value for money has led to the institution of significantly more central control, including quality control. Under the changes introduced progressively, via the ERA 1988 and FHEA 1992, the new university sector as a whole is, as noted in Chapter 3, being subjected to a strict quality assurance regime. Assessment of quality is set to play a key role in the determination of levels of funding, complementing the value for money and efficiency measures which have also been introduced.

If it is accepted that achieving the best possible educational provision for all should be the overriding educational policy aim, it is easy to justify a rigorous system of quality assurance. In addition to the need to safeguard standards, it is important to ensure that resources are used in the most effective manner. But quality assurance may also perform a political function in providing an opportunity for the exertion of greater control over the allocation and disposition of resources. A quality assurance regime may help ministers to target resources and justify, or to some extent conceal, the reining-in of particular heads of public expenditure. Under such a regime, the definition of quality used by government, and employed by those allocated a statutory responsibility for monitoring standards of provision, becomes of critical importance.

In this Chapter, key aspects of the new quality assurance regimes in the schools and higher education sectors will be considered. Discussion of the further education sector regime is omitted partly because of lack of space, but also because it is still in a considerable state of flux. It may be noted that under the FHEA 1992,[6] the FE Funding Councils have similar responsibilities, as regards quality assurance, to those of the Higher Education Funding Councils (discussed below).

2. QUALITY ASSURANCE AND THE SCHOOLS SECTOR

(a) Introduction

The introduction of more rigorous quality control mechanisms in the schools sector was seen as necessary for the success of the curriculum

---

[6] s.9.

reforms introduced under the ERA 1988. Existing mechanisms, including the LEA inspection and advisory services and Her Majesty's Inspectorate (HMI), were considered inadequate to provide proper monitoring both of standards of provision in general and the implementation of the National Curriculum in particular.

The Government's *Parent's Charter* (1991) contained plans not only for what have become known as the performance "league tables" (discussed in the previous chapter), but also for an entirely new, and controversial, system for the inspection of schools. When the Education (Schools) Bill (the "Parent's Charter Bill"[7]) was published, it was clear that the Government was contemplating a drastically pared-down HMI, a largely privatised schools inspection service and a new power for schools to select inspectors. Labour's education spokeswoman in the House of Lords, Lady Blackstone, described the Bill "as the worst piece of education legislation I have seen in nearly 30 years."[8] LEAs condemned the inspection proposals, which they said threatened to undermine their powers of inspection of schools. Disbelief was expressed at the plans to enable school governors to select the inspectors who would assess the performance of their school and for it to become compulsory for a school inspection team to contain a person who possessed *no* knowledge or professional experience of the education system. There was deeply felt concern in education circles about the reduced role for, and size of, HMI. Furthermore, there were claims that the Secretary of State had suppressed a report which allegedly showed that the numbers of HMIs needed to run the new inspection system was much higher than had been stated by the Government.[9] (The criticism made of the provision for examination "league tables" was discussed in the previous chapter).

Although the methods of achieving quality assurance in the schools sector under the ESA 1992 have been criticised by the opposition parties, there is general consensus on the importance of quality control and accountability in respect of performance. The month before the publication of the *Parent's Charter* came *Raising the Standard*, containing the Labour Party's proposals for an "Education Standards Commission," whose creation would be aimed at improving education participation rates and increasing quality and accountability. The Government placed a renewed emphasis on quality assurance in its

---

[7] H.L. Debs., Vol. 536, col. 1451 (March 12, 1992), *per* Baroness Blatch.

[8] H.L. Debs., Vol. 535, col. 598 (February 11, 1992).

[9] See *The Independent*, November 14, 1991. This is borne out by the appointment in 1992 of nearly 300 HMIs as opposed to the 175 the Government said were needed (see below).

White Paper, *Choice and Diversity*, published in July 1992.[10] There was reference not only to the teacher appraisal schemes introduced under the E(No.2)A 1986[11] and the school inspection and performance indication measures in the ESA 1992, but also to planned further measures to tackle "failing schools" — schools which are "at risk of failing to give their pupils an acceptable education" (see below).[12]

(b) Inspection of schools: HMI and 'registered' inspectors

i. *HMI and the Chief Inspectors*
In the past, HMI, established in 1839,[13] was responsible for all formal school inspections, in addition to giving advice to the Government on educational matters.[14] In recent years, a number of HMI reports, including the reports of the Senior Chief Inspector, have drawn attention to falling standards in areas such as reading and the state of school premises.[15] But with an inspectorate of 480, it had not been possible for HMI to carry out regular inspections of all 24,000 or so schools in England and Wales. Only around 150 schools were inspected each year. Thus, as Government pointed out, it would have taken around 200 years before each primary school in England and Wales had received an HMI inspection.[16]

One of the Government's principal aims, therefore, was to secure more regular and frequent inspections of schools. Greater frequency of inspection has also been urged by the Labour Party.[17] One way of achieving this might have been through an increase in the size of HMI. But the Government, who plan to secure that each school is inspected at least once every four years,[18] rejected this on the grounds of cost as well

---

[10] Cm 2021.

[11] Teacher appraisal is carried out under arrangements made under s.49 of the E(No. 2)A 1986.

[12] *Choice and Diversity*, p. 48.

[13] See R. F. Goddings and J. E. Dunford, "Her Majesty's Inspectorate of Schools, 1839–1989: The Question of Independence" (1990) XXII(1) *Journal of Education Administration and History* 1, for a review of the historical and legal background to the independence of HMI.

[14] EA 1944, s.77(2). See now ESA 1992 s.1(2).

[15] See for example HMI, *Secondary Schools. An appraisal by HMI* (1988); *Education in England 1990–91: The Annual Report of HM Senior Chief Inspector of Schools* (1992).

[16] H.C. Debs., Vol. 199, col. 157 (November 19, 1991), *per* Kenneth Clarke M.P., Secretary of State.

[17] J. Straw, M.P., *Raising the Standard — Labour's Plans for an Education Standards Commission* (1991) para. 36.

[18] Official Report, House of Commons Standing Committee F, col. 194, December 10, 1991. The ESA 1992 empowers the Secretary of State to prescribe the period between inspections: s.9(1), (2) and (5).

as barely concealed misgivings about HMI's traditional methods of investigation and report. The Labour Party favoured giving the inspection work of HMI to their proposed "Education Standards Commission" and separating the policy/advisory and monitoring functions of the Inspectorate to give it greater independence from government.[19] Greater independence for HMI was also promised by the Government. But the only measure in the ESA 1992 which enhances it is the creation of a new statutory office of Chief Inspector, one for England[20] and one for Wales;[21] formerly the office of Her Majesty's Chief Inspector was non-statutory. Various amendments to prevent the Secretary of State playing a role in the appointment of each Chief Inspector (C.I.) (formally appointed by Her Majesty by Order in Council[22]) were defeated. Moreover, Opposition attempts to remove what many M.P.s and peers considered to pose a particularly dangerous threat to a C.I.'s independence, namely his or her duty "to have regard to such aspects of Government policy as the Secretary of State may direct" when exercising any of his/her functions,[23] also failed. A further point is that the Secretary of State is also empowered to assign supplementary functions to a C.I., to add to the advisory, information provision, monitoring and review functions set out in the Act.[24]

The C.I.'s general duty as regards the provision of information relates to information concerning "the quality of education provided by schools," "educational standards achieved in ... schools," "whether financial resources made available to schools are managed efficiently" and "the spiritual, moral, social and cultural development of pupils" at school.[25] Each C.I. may be appointed for up to five years at a time.[26] The two most recent Chiefs of HMI each held office for eight years. The Act permits a C.I. to be reappointed after the expiry of his/her term of office.[27] The first C.I. for England (and head of the Office for Standards in Education — OFSTED) is Professor Stewart Sutherland, vice-chancellor of the University of London.[28]

---

[19] J. Straw, *op. cit.*, paras. 19–36, 58 and 59.

[20] s. 1.

[21] s.4.

[22] ESA 1992, ss. 1(1) and 4(1).

[23] *Ibid.* ss. 1(6) and 4(6).

[24] *Ibid.* ss.2 and 5.

[25] ss.2(1) and 5(1). "Cultural" development was added for consistency with s. 1 of the ERA 1988: see p. 202 above. "Social" was added "to ensure that matters of discipline and behaviour, and relationships between pupils and staff are fully covered": H.L. Debs., Vol. 536, col. 1224 (March 10, 1992), *per* Baroness Blatch.

[26] ss. 1(1) and 5(1).

[27] s. 1(5) and 5(5).

[28] Education (Chief Inspector of Schools in England) Order 1992 SI 1192 No. 1295.

As noted above, despite its plans to increase school inspections, the Government did not contemplete an expansion of HMI. Instead, a scheme was drawn up whereby registered inspectors would lead inspection terms who would carry out the inspections. There would be a reduction in the size of HMI from 480 to 175 (in fact, 298 HMIs were appointed in 1992 under section 1(2) of the Act[29]), with 40 HMIs responsible for monitoring inspections.[30] HMI would also have responsibility for registration of inspectors and setting of standards for inspections.[31] There were claims that this would lead to fragmentation of HMI, with loss of many of its specialist skills.[32] However, the Government's plans were incorporated into the 1992 Act (see below).

Under the Bill as originally drafted, it would, in most schools, have been the governing body's responsibility to arrange for the school to be inspected. There was considerable opposition to this proposal. It was suggested that governors would tend to choose inspection terms that they "knew would give a good report of the school."[33] Lord Ritchie remarked that "If schools can pick and choose their own inspection teams . . . will we not next have hotel and catering establishments doing the same, theatre impresarios picking and paying their own critics and criminals choosing their own judges?"[34] Some critics referred to the possibility of a "cosy relationship" emerging over time between schools and favoured registered inspectors. An amendment, successfully moved at the Committee stage in the House of Lords by Lord Peston,[35] left the responsibility for arranging an inspection with the C.I., under section 9. The C.I. has to invite tenders from at least two registered inspectors (at "arm's length" from each other).[36] There has to be consultation with the governing body or proprietor over the tender specification.

It should perhaps be noted that the C.I.s for England and Wales respectively have retained the power to order an inspection of schools by HMI.[37] This power extends not only to maintained schools but also to independent schools. In fact, the majority of independent schools are

[29] Education (Inspectors of Schools in England) Order 1992 SI 1992 No. 1713.

[30] Official Report, House of Commons Standing Committee F, cols. 41–43, November 28, 1991. Her Majesty's Inspectors are now appointed under s. 1(2) of the ESA 1992 by Order in Council.

[31] See Her Majesty's Chief Inspector of Schools in England, *Framework for the Inspection of Schools* (1992).

[32] See, *e.g.* H.C. Debs., Vol. 199, col. 192 (November 19, 1991).

[33] *Ibid.* col. 176, Mr G. Steinberg M.P.

[34] H.L. Debs., Vol. 535, col. 609 (February 11, 1992).

[35] *Ibid.* Vol. 536, cols. 658–665 March 2 1992.

[36] ESA 1992, Sched. 2 para. 2.

[37] *Ibid.* ss. 3 and 7. There is a new offence of wilfully obstructing a member of HMI when s/he is carrying out such an inspection: s. 7(4).

not covered by the main inspection arrangements laid down in section 9 (set out below). The Opposition were keen to point out what they perceived to be an apparent contradiction in Government policy. It was clear that, as with state schools, independent schools' examination results and other performance data would be published, so that parents could compare *all* schools. But the Government was accused of displaying a double standard in excluding most independent schools from the inspection arrangements: "they want some information about private schools to be made available, but they are not willing to subject private schools to the same scrutiny of the effectiveness of education that is required of state schools."[38] In reply, the Minister seemed to be suggesting that legislation was unnecessary because it was "likely that parental pressure, as well as professional pride, will ensure that parallel arrangements will emerge in the private sector."[39] But there are so far no signs of such a "parallel" system emerging.

ii. *Registration and de-registration of inspectors*

Inspections under section 9 must be carried out by "registered" inspectors, although where the C.I. considers that this is not practicable s/he can arrange for inspection by HMI.[40] The Act provides that no one (other than an HMI inspector) shall conduct an inspection of a school in England/Wales unless s/he is registered as an inspector in the register kept for this purpose by the C.I. for England/Wales.[41] But these provisions are somewhat misleading in this respect, for the Act provides that the inspection "shall be conducted by a registered inspector with the assistance of a team (an 'inspection team') consisting of persons who are fit and proper persons for carrying out the inspection."[42] What this means is that of those persons carrying out the inspection only *one* needs to be registered as an inspector.

It is for the registered inspector leading the team to determine its composition,[43] but this discretion is constrained in several respects. First, there is the rather bizarre requirement that at least one member of the team must be a person "without personal experience in the management of any school or the provision of education in any school (otherwise than as a governor or in any voluntary capacity)."[44]

---

[38] Official Report, House of Commons Standing Committee F, col. 215, December 10, 1991.

[39] *Ibid.* col. 219.

[40] ESA 1992, Sched. 2 para 12; EA 1993, s.205(1).

[41] s.10(1). A person may be registered for inspections in England *and/or* Wales.

[42] Sched. 2 para 3(1).

[43] *Ibid.* para 3(3).

[44] *Ibid.* para 3(2). Note that the registered inspector may ignore any experience which s/he regards as "insignificant": Sched. 2 para. 3(4).

This member's primary function on the team must not be that of providing financial or business expertise. The idea is that the inclusion of such a member (or those members, for there is nothing to prevent two or more 'lay' team members being selected), will enable the team to benefit from an "outside view."[45] Secondly, the registered inspector must ensure that no team member has, or has at any other time had,

> "any connection with—
> (a) the school in question;
> (b) any person who is employed at the school;
> (c) any person who is a member of the school's governing body;
> (d) The proprietor of the school;
> of a kind which might reasonably be taken to raise doubts about his ability to act impartially in relation to that school."[46]

Thirdly, a person cannot be engaged to carry out inspection work in conflict with any conditions imposed on the registration of a registered inspector.[47]

There are legitimate fears that appropriate specialist expertise will not always be available to registered inspectors. For example, Baroness Warnock proposed that the law should require each inspection team to contain at least one member with experience and expertise in special educational needs and provision. She also proposed that there should be a requirement that where an inspection of a special school or a specialist unit in a school was undertaken, the inspection team should have expertise in the specialist area concerned. Baroness Warnock's proposed amendments[48] were not supported by the Government although assurances were offered that the C.I.s for England and Wales would be urged to include recommendations to this effect in their guidance to registered inspectors assembling inspection teams.[49]

Registration is a critical element of the new system, especially in view of the disquiet which has been expressed about the transfer of the role of schools inspection from the highly qualified HM inspectors to others. But the statutory conditions which must be satisfied by an applicant for registration are vague. It must appear to the C.I. that the applicant is "a fit and proper person for discharging the functions of a

---

[45] *The Parent's Charter* (1991), p. 4.
[46] Sched. 2 para 5.
[47] *Ibid.* para 3. Such conditions may be imposed under s. 10(2)(c).
[48] House of Lords Committee stage amendments nos. 128 and 129A.
[49] H.L. Debs., Vol. 536, col. 702–3 (March 2, 1992), *per* Baroness Blatch. See further *supra* n.31.

registered inspector" and that he or she "will be capable of conducting inspections . . . competently and efficiently."[50] At the Committee stage of the Education (Schools) Bill in the House of Commons, several M.P.s referred to the uncertainty which it was believed would be produced by these imprecise general requirements. As drafted, they would, it was argued, undermine the credibility of the new scheme. An amendment was proposed, to make qualified teacher status a necessary condition, but it was rejected. The Minister argued that such a condition "would exclude many people with experience of education but who do not happen to be qualified teachers, including those who work in education administration, higher education or research."[51] But it was accepted later that, in practice, "most registered inspectors are highly likely to have been teachers."[52]

The C.I. has the option of imposing conditions as to registration and the period of registration.[53] One of the conditions which has been laid down is that an inspector must adhere to the C.I.'s *Framework for School Inspections*. This sets out "the principles on which inspections are to be based and the criteria against which their quality is assessed." It also lays down an inspection schedule, which specifies, under separate headings, the factors to be examined in the course of an inspection.

There is no right of appeal against a straightforward refusal of registration. But an unsuccessful applicant for a renewal of registration, or an applicant who wishes to challenge the imposition or variation of a condition of his registration, may appeal to a tribunal.[54] The tribunal consists of a chairman (a lawyer of at least seven years' standing) and two other members (for whom there are no prescribed qualifications), appointed by the Secretary of State. A similar right of appeal exists in the case of a person whose name is to be removed from the register under section 11.[55] The C.I. may remove the name of an inspector from the register if he or she is satisfied that the inspector "is no longer a fit and proper person for discharging the functions of a registered inspector" or "is no longer capable of conducting inspections . . . competently and effectively . . ."; or that there has been a significant failure on the part of the registered inspector to comply with any condition subject to which his registration has effect;[56] or that the

---

[50] ESA 1992, s.10(3).
[51] Official Report, House of Commons Standing F, col. 326, December 17, 1991, Mr Fallon M.P.
[52] *Ibid*. col. 332.
[53] s.10(5)(c) and (8).
[54] s.12(1).
[55] *Ibid*.
[56] Such conditions may be imposed under s.10(5)(c).

registered inspector "has knowlingly or recklessly produced a report of
an inspection which is, in whole or in part, seriously misleading."[57]

The control which may be exerted by the C.I. over registration has
been presented by the Government in defence of claims that the new
system will reduce the effectiveness of school inspections. A further
defence, made in particular in response to claims that the new
inspection system is amateuristic, has been that all registered inspectors
and members of inspection teams must, unless exempted by the C.I.,
undergo approved training.[58]

iii. *What kind of inspection?*

"Inspection" is nowhere defined in the Act. All that the law requires is
that the C.I. shall issue guidance to inspectors (above) and that an
inspection must be completed by the date specified by the C.I. and
during a prescribed period.[59] However, as adherence to the C.I.'s guidance on inspections is a condition of registration (above), and failure
to adhere to it a ground for removal from the register, modes of inspection of schools are in effect closely regulated. The guidance spells
out evaluation criteria, the kind of evidence which should be gathered
and the matters which should be covered by the inspector's report.
The guidance also specifies the minimum number of days each inspection should last, which varies according to the size and category
of school, (i.e. primary, secondary, special, etc). These various require-
quirements are aimed at standardising schools inspection. However,
the fact that 6,000 schools will be inspected each year may make
effective monitoring of adherence to the guidance difficult.

The 1992 Act itself does prescribe one feature of all inspections: a
meeting between the inspector and parents.[60] According to the *Parent's
Charter*, this is to be "an open meeting for parents to talk about the
school." In a survey carried out by the author, parental interest in
participation in school inspection visits was found to be widespread.[61]
Of 434 parents questioned, 269 said that they would be interested in
participating and only 80 (around 18 per cent.) said they definitely
would not. The Chief Inspector's *Framework* criteria also prescribe

---

[57] ESA 1992, s.11(2).

[58] ESA 1992, Sched. 2 paras. 4(1) and (2) and 5(1) and (2). Approval for training is given
by the C.I.

[59] ESA 1993, s.208 and ESA 1992 Sched. 2, para. 9B. The period may be extended but
must not exceed three months. At the time of writing the Education (School)
Inspections Regulations 1993 (SI 1993 No. 1492) were applicable, but these may be
replaced following the commencement of the 1993 Act.

[60] ESA 1992, Sched. 2, para 6.

[61] N. Harris, *Complaints About Schooling: The Role of Section 23 of the Education Reform Act
1988* (1992), p. 125.

discussion with pupils, on matters such as the curriculum and the incidence of bullying at the school.

iv *After an inspection*

If the inspection is to produce improvements in, and greater accountability for, standards of provision, it is necessary to ensure that the school is aware of its strengths and weaknesses, as independently assessed, and that parents are able to see firm evidence of plans to rectify any problems which have been identified. The inspector must prepare a report, plus a summary, within a prescibed period and ensure that copies are sent to prescribed persons (usually the governing body, as the "appropriate authority," and the C.I.).[62] The appropriate authority must in turn distribute copies of the summary to parents of registered pupils and make copies of the report and summary available to the public. It is clear that the appropriate authority cannot simply sit on the inspector's findings and recommendations. Within a prescribed period they must prepare an action plan — a written statement of the action they propose to take in the light of the inspector's report and the period of time in which they will be taking it.[63] The plan must be distributed widely, to parents and others.[64]

There is provision for special monitoring of the implementation of an action plan where a particularly damning report is issued by the inspector[65] — that is, where a school is, in the opinion of the registered inspector, "failing, or . . . likely to fail, to give its pupils an acceptable standard of education."[66] The task of monitoring in these cases has been placed on the C.I. by the EA 1993, which also provides for action to be taken where the problems identified by the inspection have not been rectified (see below).

(c) Further measures in respect of "at risk" schools: Education Act 1993

The first round of school inspections under the ESA 1992, beginning in September 1993, is expected to target schools likely to be "at risk."[67] The 1993 Act provides a number of important measures to deal with such schools, which could lead ultimately to an LEA-maintained school

---

[62] EA 1993, ss.206, 208 and 209; ESA 1982 Sched. 2 paras. 9B and 9C. Extension of the period for preparation of the report by up to three months has been provided for under amendments made by the EA 1993.

[63] EA 1993, s.210; ESA 1992, Sched. 2 para. 10.

[64] *Ibid.*

[65] EA 1993, s.212; ESA 1992, Sched. 2, para. 11.

[66] EA 1993, s.204(3); ESA 1992, Sched. 2 para 1.

[67] *Choice and Diversity*, para. 11.4.

being given GM status or closed. Some of these additional measures apply only to county and voluntary schools.[68]

The procedures in the 1993 Act commence with an inspector's conclusion, following an inspection of a school, that "special measures are required to be taken."[69] Where the inspector is of the opinion, s/he must send a draft of his or her report to the C.I. The C.I. must then inform the inspector of his or her view, which must be incorporated into the inspector's final report.[70] In the case of inspections carried out by members of HMI, such reference to the C.I. is not required.[71] Copies of all reports indicating that special measures are needed must be sent to the Secretary of State or the C.I.[72] Generally, the governing body must send a written statement of the action they propose to take, in the light of the report, to the C.I., LEA and others. In the case of GM schools a copy must be sent to the Secretary of State. In the case of LEA-maintained schools only, if the report was made by HMI or endorsed by the C.I., the governors' statement must also be sent to the Secretary of State,[73] and the LEA must inform the C.I. and Secretary of State of the action *it* proposes to take.[74]

This regime is given considerably more teeth in the case of LEA-maintained schools by the prohibition on opting out,[75] and, more particularly, the inclusion of quite far-reaching powers which may be exercised in respect of these "at risk" schools. These powers apply where a subsequent follow-up inspection fails to give the school the all-clear.[76] Under almost the only provisions in the 1993 Act which extend their powers, LEAs may, if certain conditions are satisfied, appoint additional governors ("such number . . . as they think fit") and/or may use their power under section 37 of the ERA 1988 to suspend the governing body's right to a delegated budget.[77] If these measures fail, the Secretary of State has a number of further powers. First, he may de-group the school (de-group the school from another school or schools

---

[68] See EA 1993, ss.213–216, which cover, *inter alia*, suspension of the right to a delegated budget.

[69] See *ibid.*, s.204(3).

[70] EA 1993 s.206.

[71] *Ibid.* s.207.

[72] s.209. The report must go to the Secretary of State if made by HMI or if the C.I. has endorsed a registered inspector's recommendations that special measures are needed.

[73] s.210.

[74] s.211.

[75] s.217.

[76] See s.213.

[77] ss.214 and 215. Note that in aided and special agreement schools the appropriate appointing authority can appoint additional foundation governors. The LEA has no power under these sections to appoint additional governors or suspend the right to a delegated budget in relation to these schools.

with which the school in question has been permitted to be grouped under one governing body under section 9 of the E(No. 2)A 1986).[78] Secondly, he can establish a body corporate, described as an "educational association," which, under his direction, is to take over all the functions of the governing body of the school.[79]

Once an education association is involved, the school will cease to be maintained by the LEA. It would appear that unless the Secretary of State is not satisfied that the measures planned by the LEA and/or governing body are likely to be successful, the LEA and governors would normally be permitted up to twelve months to improve the quality of provision at the school before the power to involve an education association would be exercised.[80] An education association would be expected to serve all failing schools in their area. It would operate in a similar way to the governing body of a GM school, under special articles of association.[81] The Minister expects education associations to include "local businessmen, professionals and possibly parents"; an accountant may be included if the problem is one involving poor financial management.[82] However, it will contain no elected members; indeed there are no statutory requirements on qualification for membership. The Act provides that it shall have not less than five members appointed by the Secretary of State, one of whom shall be appointed to chair the association.[83] It would appear that most, if not all, of the members of this "small and cohesive body" will carry out their functions on a part-time basis.[84] The Government expects education associations to take active and, where necessary, drastic steps to improve the school. These steps might include staffing changes at senior management levels and within the teaching force.[85] These are far reaching powers for a body with seemingly no real accountability to parents or the wider public.

Once the school has been declared by HMI to be no longer in need of special measures, the Secretary of State may order that the school becomes GM.[86] If, however, the school is still in difficulty, the Secretary of State may order the discontinuance of the school.[87]

---

[78] s.216.
[79] ss.218–223.
[80] *Choice and Diversity*, para. 11.8.
[81] EA 1993, s.223. Supplementary powers of education associations are laid down in Sched. 12.
[82] Official Report, House of Commons Standing Committee E, col. 1245, Feb. 2, 1993, Mr T. Boswell M.P.
[83] s.218(3).
[84] *Choice and Diversity*, para. 11.9.
[85] *Ibid.* para. 11.11.
[86] s.224.
[87] s.225.

(d)   Inspections of denominational education

Inspections of denominational education are dealt with separately, in section 13 of the ESA 1992.[88] For the purpose of the Act, denominational education is defined as "religious education which is required . . . to be included in the school's basic curriculum, but is not required to be given in accordance with an agreed syllabus."[89] Religious education (RE) which *is* provided under the "agreed syllabus" will be covered by the inspection arrangements made under section 9 (above). As RE in all county schools must be in accordance with such an "agreed syllabus," inspections under section 13 will take place in voluntary schools only (and in former voluntary schools which are now GM schools). Not surprisingly the Churches have exercised a major influence over the shaping of these new inspection arrangements and were instrumental in the extensions to their scope made by the EA 1993 (section 259). Section 13 now extends to collective worship and empowers inspectors to report also on the "spiritual, moral, social and cultural development of pupils."

Unlike section 9 inspections, the governing body will select the inspector.[90] By agreement between Church and State, RE in Church schools has been subject to different arrangements for over 150 years, and according to the Minister "it would have been a very great break with that long-standing agreement to have required Church schools to use secular registered inspectors for the inspection of their own denominational provision."[91]

Among the important changes made by the ESA 1992 to the previous arrangements[92] are stipulations that inspections of a school's denominational education must be carried out at prescribed intervals and that strict requirements as to the preparation, dispatch and dissemination of the inspector's report plus summary must be adhered to.[93] The governors must make the inspection report plus summary available to the public and supply a copy of the summary to the parents of each registered pupil. Furthermore, they must prepare and distribute a written statement (called "the additional action plan") setting out the action they propose to take in the light of the report. Also, when the governors prepare their annual report for parents, they must include in it a statement of the extent which the plan has been carried into effect.

---

[88] Inspections under s.9 may not extend to denominational education or the content of collective worship to be inspected under s.13: s.9(6), as amended.

[89] ESA 1992, s.13(3A). The requirement to provide RE as part of the basic curriculum is in ERA 1988, s.2(1): see Chap. 7.

[90] In a voluntary controlled school, only the foundation governors select the inspector.

[91] H.L. Debs., Vol. 536, col. 684 (March 2, 1992), *per* Baroness Blatch.

[92] EA 1944, s.77(5), repealed by the 1992 Act.

[93] ESA 1992, Sched. 2, Part II.

(e) Inspections by LEA inspectors

In a 1989 report, the Audit Commission stated that while a result of recent reforms (in particular the ERA 1988) was that school governors and head teachers now carried "first-line responsibility for quality assurance," the legislation had left LEAs with their previous responsibility for ensuring the provision of an effective education service.[94] In particular, it had been made clear by the DES that LEAs had a responsibility for monitoring the implementation of the National Curriculum.[95] The Audit Commission noted that even with the establishment of performance indicators for schools, based on the reporting of examination and formal test results, "LEAs will still need their own direct observations of teaching and learning . . . to satisfy themselves that the national curriculum is being taught and . . . to serve as a foundation for steps to secure improvement."[96] It was, therefore, difficult to accept the case presented by the Government for removing from LEAs their right to inspect, under EA 1944, section 77(3), especially in the light of the Audit Commission's proposals for strengthening the role of LEA inspection and advisory services. As Opposition peer Lord Ritchie said, "In proposing to repeal section 77(3) of the 1944 Act Her Majesty's Government would remove from LEAs the right to inspect the very schools for which they are responsible."[97] But the Minister said that it was undesirable that "At any time . . . the LEA could enter a school against the wishes of the governors."[98] Nevertheless, the Government suffered a defeat. Section 77(3) of the 1944 Act has not been repealed, but the scope of the LEA's right to inspect has been defined. LEA inspectors may enter and inspect schools maintained by them if they wish to obtain information "about any matter in connection with a school . . . for the purpose of enabling them to exercise any function of theirs" provided it is "not reasonably practicable for them to obtain it in any other manner."[99]

LEAs may also provide inspection services for the purposes of sections 9 and 13 (general and denominational education inspection respectively) on a full cost basis and subject to, *inter alia*, the keeping of accounts, requirements imposed by the C.I. and regulations governing competitive tendering.[1] These services may be offered to schools in their area, whether or not maintained by the LEA.

---

[94] *Assuring Quality in Education: the role of local education authority advisers and inspectors*, paras 1 and 2.
[95] *Ibid.* para. 16.
[96] *Ibid.* para. 20.
[97] H.L. Debs., Vol. 535, col. 608 (February 11, 1992).
[98] *Ibid.* col. 670, *per* Lady Blatch.
[99] ESA 1992, s.15(1).
[1] *Ibid.* s.14.

3.   QUALITY ASSURANCE IN HIGHER EDUCATION

(a)   Introduction

Quality assurance has become a central element in the new regime for
the provision of higher education created by FHEA 1992. Both the
former polytechnics and the chartered universities are subject to the
quality assurance jurisdiction of the Higher Education Funding Councils
(HEFCs),[2] which have replaced the Polytechnic and Colleges Funding
Council (PCFC) and Universities Funding Council (UFC) (see Chapter
3). Similarly, in the FE sector, which broadly consists of the colleges
providing sub-degree academic and vocational courses, the Further
Education Funding Council (FEFC) has a statutory responsibility for
ensuring that provision is made for the assessment of the quality of
education provided (including provision in sixth form colleges).[3] In
relation to further education provision for which LEAs remain
responsible, which is somewhat limited in scope in view of the transfer
of much of their reponsibility to the FEFC,[4] HMI and LEAs have
continued to have a general inspectorial jurisdiction but also have some
new, specific responsibilities in monitoring the quality of provision.[5]

The structural changes to further and higher education were discussed
in Chapter 3. Noted in particular were: the progressive reduction in
LEA involvement and the creation of further education corporations and
higher education corporations to manage certain categories of institution; increased central regulation and control of chartered universities;
the removal of any binary line and conferment of university status on
polytechnics and certain colleges; and the increasingly competitive basis
to the funding of higher education. The quality assurance regime
resulting from the 1992 Act is discussed below.

(b)   Quality of Education

One of the principal concerns about the Government's plans for an
expansion of higher education into the next century, which contemplate
a near-doubling of the numbers of full-time equivalent students between

---

[2] As discussed in Chap. 3, there are two councils, one for England and one for Wales:
FHEA 1992 s.62(1).

[3] FHEA 1992 s.9. The FEFC must establish a Quality Assessment Committee to give
advice to it on assessment of quality: s.9(1)(b).

[4] LEAs have a *power* to provide full-time further education to persons over the age of 18
and part-time education, but this does not apply to education which is the
responsibility of the FEFC under ss.2 and 3 of the Act: EA 1944, s.41(1) and (2), as
substituted by s.11 of the FHEA 1992. Duties to secure the provision of sufficient
facilities for full-time education for persons aged 16–18 and adequate facilities for full-
time education for persons over 18 and part-time education for those above compulsory
school age rest with the FEFC under ss.2 and 3.

[5] FHEA 1992, s.55.

1987 and 2000,[6] is the potential impact on the quality of educational provision. This concern arises out of the Government's commitment to achieve the required expansion within tight financial constraints: "greater efficiency ... cost effective expansion."[7] While the Government plans to make student demand a major determinant of funding, it also expects quality to be taken into account.[8] The question of how to achieve two of the objectives espoused by the Robbins Report in 1963, but difficult to reconcile under a policy of strict public expenditure restraint, namely expansion and continued high quality of provision, has been addressed with reference to the concept of quality assurance.

The 1991 White Paper spelled out various aspects of quality assurance in higher education.[9] "Quality control" was exercised via the mechanisms within institutions for enhancing the quality of provision. Although the power to award degrees was the only context to quality control that was discussed, the Government clearly had in mind academic boards and other parts of the internal committee structures within institutions. "Quality audit" consisted of external scrutiny aimed at providing guarantees that institutions have suitable quality assurance mechanisms in place. Within the university sector, this role was performed on a non-statutory basis by the Academic Audit Unit established under the aegis of the Committee of Vice Chancellors and Principals (CVCP). The quality audit role in the polytechnic and colleges sector was performed by the Council for National Academic Awards (CNAA), which validated courses. With the Government keen to establish a single quality audit mechanism following the removal of the binary line,[10] and with former polytechnics gaining degree awarding powers[11] on condition that they operated effective internal validation and review processes (as recommended by the Lindop Report[12]), discontinuation of the CNAA was considered possible.[13] The CNAA had already accredited certain of the larger institutions for validation and monitoring of their own courses.[14]

---

[6] Secretary of State for Education and Science and others, *Higher Education: A New Framework* (1991) Cm 1541, pp. 10–11.

[7] *Ibid.* paras. 15–17.

[8] *Ibid.* para. 24.

[9] *Ibid.* para. 60.

[10] *Ibid.* para. 68.

[11] FHEA 1992, s.76. The section gives the Privy Council the power to specify by order an institution as competent to grant certain awards, including degrees, diplomas and certificates.

[12] *Report of the Committee of Enquiry into the Academic Validation of Degree Courses in Public Sector Higher Education* (1985).

[13] CM 1541 *supra* (n.6) paras. 73 and 74. CNAA had been established in 1965. It was abolished under s.80 of the FHEA 1992 and the Education (Dissolution of the Council for National Academic Awards) Order 1993 SI 1993 No. 924.

[14] See D. Coulby, "Higher Education and the Enterprise Culture," in L. Bash and D. Coulby *The Education Reform Act: Competition and Control* (1989) p. 102.

The final area of quality assurance, and one in respect of which the new HEFCs have specific statutory responsibility, is "quality assessment." In the 1991 White Paper, the Government argued that arrangements for the assessment of the quality of provision were needed to complement the quality control and audit arrangements that were being proposed. They explained that while the precise arrangements should be a matter for the Funding Councils, quality assessment should have two central elements. The first would involve looking at "quantifiable outcomes"; performance indication and calculations of value added could be involved.[15] The second would comprise "external judgments on the basis of direct observation of what is provided."[16] The assessment of quality would be carried out by a quality assessment unit established by the Funding Councils, which would be staffed, initially, by a complement of HMI with responsibility for higher education and by academics.

Section 70(1) of the FHEA 1992 has given the HEFCs a specific duty to "secure that provision is made for assessing the quality of education provided in institutions for whose activities they provide, or are considering providing, financial support ..." It has also required the HEFCs to establish a "Quality Assessment Committee" (QAC), the majority of whose members cannot be members of a HEFC and all of whose members must have "experience of, and (proven) capacity in, the provision of higher education."[17] The role of the QAC is to give advice to the HEFCs on the assessment of quality and carry out such other functions as the Council may determine.[18] The HEFCs are not required to carry out assessments themselves; as section 70(1) indicates (above), the Councils' role is to ensure that assessment is *carried out*. Under the arrangements set out by the HEFC for England (HEFCE) in its Circular (3/93) issued in February 1993,[19] institutions will be expected to carry out self-assessment, in accordance with the specified arrangements, and report on this self-assessment (with supporting statistical indicators). This information will be examined by assessors working in a newly-established Quality Assessment Division of the HEFCE. Judgment will be based on the content of the documentation and, in some cases, visits to institutions by teams of assessors.

---

[15] Cm 1541 *supra* (n.6) para. 80. According to Maclure (*Education Re-formed* (3rd edn., 1992) p. 96), "accountability will demand more and more attention to prescribed performance indicators and the monitoring of output information."

[16] *Op. cit.* para. 81.

[17] s.70(2) and (3).

[18] See the HEFC for England's Circular on *Assessment of the Quality of Education* (Circular 3/93), February 1993, Section B para. 6.

[19] *Ibid.*

Some of the assessors will comprise a permanent core of HEFCE staff; others, who may be academics, but may also be drawn from the professions and industry, will be seconded to the Council on a contract basis for one to three years, or will be engaged as subject specialist assessors. All the assessors will take part in an induction and training programme. The first assessment period runs from February 1993 to September 1994 and will involve assessments in eight subject areas.[20] The Circular sets out the kinds of matters on which assessment will be based and examples of what would be regarded as good practice.[21] The purposes of quality assessment are stated as: to ensure that education is of a satisfactory standard or better; to encourage improvements in quality (through publication of assessment reports and an annual report); and to inform funding and reward excellence.[22]

Perhaps the crucial question arising out of the initial arrangements themselves concerns the likely impact of an assessment on the funding of an institution and its academic programmes. The Circular is not specific as to the way that assessment will inform funding; but it does indicate the general approach. Provision will be ranked as excellent, satisfactory or unsatisfactory. A satisfactory rating would be expected to enable funding to provide for planned expansion; but if an unsatisfactory rating is given:

"the institution will be ineligible in the first year after the assessment for any funding allocated by the Council for growth. It will also be informed that if the quality does not improve, core funding and places will be successively or immediately withdrawn."[23]

There is no precise indication as to how excellence would be rewarded. However, it seems that a substantial increase in funding should not be expected to result from the first year's assessments: the Council says it will be "particularly cautious about the impact of the link between funding and an excellent grade,"[24] although no explanation is offered.

A further and broader question concerns the kind of trade-off between quality and efficiency which will occur in the allocation of funding. For

---

[20] *Ibid.* Section B paras. 55 and 56. The first four areas are chemistry, history, law and mechanical engineering; the assessments will "inform funding for 1994–95." The subsequent four areas will be architecture, business and management, computer science and social work; assessment will inform funding for the following year.

[21] *Ibid.* paras. 46–49.

[22] *Ibid.* Section A para. 5.

[23] Section A para. 27.

[24] *Ibid.* para. 26.

example, what would happen to funding if it were to be discovered that an institution provided an excellent course at what was considered to be a disproportionately high cost? Furthermore, when institutions are competing for student funding, what advantage (if any) would those offering satisfactory provision at a relative low unit cost have over those offering excellent provision at a higher cost? If information about the quality of provision at institutions is expected to foster competition for students (and employer support) in a market for higher education,[25] institutions need to know how the quality of their provision will be translated into resources to fund the additional places which may be demanded by consumers.

(c) Research

The Government decided against creating separate channels for the distribution of central government funds for teaching and general research.[26] Thus the HEFCs have responsibility for the allocation of general research funds as well as teaching funds.[27] Additionalresearch monies are allocated as in the past by the Research Councils.

Allocation of research monies by funding councils has become increasingly dependent upon assessment of the quality of research — funds being distributed selectively on the basis of this assessment. The University Grants Committee, the non-statutory funding allocation body which was the predecessor of the Universities Funding Council and HEFC, first introduced some selectively in its funding of research in 1984, and the Croham Committee in 1987 recommended continuation of this practice.[28] The results of the first research selectively exercise after the removal of binary divide were published towards the end of 1992. It is not surprising that the former polytechnics for the most part fared badly in comparison with the chartered universities. They had never received any direct government financial support for basic research, and when an opportunity to depart from previous practice had arisen, with the creation of the PCFC under the 1988 Act, it had not been taken by the Government. A letter to directors of polytechnics and colleges from the Secretary of State had indicated that research funds would not be allocated to the PCFC sector.[29]

---

[25] See White Paper *supra* (n.6) para. 58.

[26] *Ibid.* paras. 41–44.

[27] FHEA 1992, s.65(2)(*a*). Prior to the establishment of the HEFCs, the Universities Funding Council and Polytechnics and Colleges Funding Council administered general research funds, under, respectively, ss. 131(5) of the ERA 1988.

[28] *Review of the University Grants Committee* Cm 81 (1987).

[29] See G. Williams, "Higher Education," in M. Flude and M. Hammer, *The Education Reform Act 1988: its Origins and Implications* (1990) p. 265.

The extent of the funds available for distribution by the HEFCs is a matter for the Secretary of State; the degree of control over both the payment of funds to the HEFCs and the disposition of those funds by the Councils was considered in Chapter 3.

4 CONCLUSION

Various elaborate quality assurance mechanisms have been developed in the schools and higher education sectors. Quality assurance has become an area of intense regulation, although there are considerable differences in the statutory framework (which is relatively bare in the case of higher education and intricate in the case of schools) and in the systems in operation in each sector. There may, however, be a common underlying policy to each. The exposure of unsatisfactory provision can lead to blame for deficiency being placed on LEAs and higher education institutions themselves and can justify strict government controls. Also, quality assurance regimes may, by suggesting that the Government is taking firm steps to improve the quality of provision, deflect criticism away from inadequacy in overall funding levels for education at a time of planned expansion in student numbers.

The quality assurance reforms in the schools sector have an experimental character about them. As a result, a number of questions have to be asked — questions as to, for example, the future role of HMI, the degree of independence of the office of C.I. from government and, in particular, the likely standard of school inspections by registered inspectors. One question is whether the increased number of inspections will be as beneficial as the Government has led us to believe. Undoubtedly some education consumers would regard the availability of a reasonably up to date inspection report as advantageous, especially those about to select a school for their child. But what about those whose children are happily settled into a school and doing GCSE courses and who suddenly discover, as a result of a published inspector's report, that the school is performing badly in several areas of activity? Arguably they will at least have the reassurance of the governors' action plan to put matters right. But from the school's point of view, remedial action may in part be dependent on resources whose availability is in doubt. Moreover, regardless of the efforts being made to improve matters, and a commitment to strive for better performance, a poor report could leave a school's reputation irreparably damaged. The result may be less consumer interest (resulting in reduced funding), stigmatisation of pupils making the transition to work or further or higher education, and erosion of staff morale.

A further question has concerned the more practical issue of who will carry out the inspections. LEAs will tender for it; but what about private organisations or individuals? It was reported in the press in 1991 that consultancy firms such as Coopers & Lybrand Deloitte and Price Waterhouse considered that the work would be uneconomic, and it was suggested that the Treasury would need to allocate a considerable amount of additional money to increase the profitability of inspections to private firms.[30] Nevertheless, a massive recruitment campaign and the promise of free training by the Government are claimed to have generated sufficient interest to ensure that there will be enough registered inspectors to complement an HMI less reduced in size than originally proposed.

The quality assurance arrangements in higher education also have an experimental character about them, especially as regards self-assessment of quality, although many other aspects are based around previous practice adopted by HMI (some of whose inspectors have joined the HEFCE's Quality Assurance Division) and the CVCP's Academic Audit Unit. The HEFC has indicated that the method of quality assessment will be reviewed at the end of 1993.[31] At present, there is considerable uncertainty about the actual impact that quality assessment will have on funding.

---

[30] See the editorial in the *The Independent*, March 4, 1992.
[31] Circular 3/93 *op. cit.*, Section A para. 28.

7

THE SCHOOL CURRICULUM: CONTROL, CHOICE AND INVOLVEMENT

1. INTRODUCTION: FUNDAMENTAL PRINCIPLES

There are a number of fundamental principles on which state education is based in most democratic states: that education should be available to all; that it should be available free of charge (but private schools may be permitted to operate); that it should be compulsory up to a certain age; and that it should uphold religious freedom and recognise parents' philosophical convictions. English education law for the most part reflects these basic tenets, although there are important exceptions, for example in the absence of a specific "right" to education[1] and the limited nature of the requirement that "children should be educated in accordance with the wishes of their parents."[2]

Outside the United Kingdom, the principles identified above are often enshrined in states' written constitutions. Thus the U.S. Supreme Court has, for example, held as unconstitutional: the denial to parents of a right to send their children to private schools;[3] the provision of racially-segregated schooling;[4] a state law that required schools to post the Ten Commandments on classroom walls;[5] and, in an exceptional case, compulsory schooling, beyond eighth grade, of Amish children.[6] The last of these cases contrasts with a decision of the Supreme Court of Canada which held that the compulsory attendance legislation in Alberta

---

[1] But see p. 12 *supra* and p. 208 *infra*.

[2] EA 1944, s.76, discussed at pp. 120–122 and 130–131 *supra*.

[3] *Pierce* v. *Society of Sisters* 268 U.S. 510 (1925). Despite this right to select religious schooling, the Constitution prohibits state funding of religious schools: *Lemon* v. *Kurtzman* 403 U.S. 602 (1971). See T. McConnell, "The Selective Funding Problem: Abortions and Religious Schools" (1991) 104 *Harvard Law Review* 989.

[4] *Brown* v. *Board of Education* 347 U.S. 483 (1954); *Keyes* v. *Denver School District* 413 U.S. 189 (1983).

[5] *Stone* v. *Graham* 101 S Ct. 192 (1981). This is one of several cases where there was an alleged violation of the Establishment Clause of the First Amendment, which aims to guarantee religious neutrality in state provision: see B. Levin, "The United States of America," in I. K. Birch and I. Richter (eds.) *School Law* (1990) pp. 23–25.

[6] *Wisconsin* v. *Yoder* 406 U.S. 205 (1972).

was not unconstitutional even though it meant that a child from a fundamentalist Christian family would have to attend school despite his parents' religious objections to state education.[7] Nevertheless, the Canadian Charter upholds freedom of religion,[8] and in one case the Court of Appeal of Ontario held that the school prayer at the start of the day was in violation of the Charter.[9] The Dutch Constitution similarly requires education provided by public authorities to show "due respect to everyone's religion or belief."[10]

These fundamental principles are also recognised in international human rights instruments[11] — most notably the European Convention on Human Rights,[12] the International Covenant on Economic, Social and Cultural Rights and the U.N. Convention on the Rights of the Child. For example, the European Convention provides that "no person shall be denied the right to education."[13] This article of the Convention requires state provision of education and teaching to be in conformity with parents' religious and philosophical convictions.[14] Yet in *Kjeldsen, Busk Masden and Pedersen*,[15] the European Court of Human Rights held that the compulsory sex education in Danish state primary schools did not amount to a breach of the Convention. It was said that the state had an overriding duty to present information and knowledge objectively, pluralistically and critically. In another case, *Campbell and Cosans* v. *United Kingdom*, which led to the removal by Parliament of the defence (in civil proceedings) of lawful chastisement of pupils by teachers in state schools in England and Wales, the Court held that the exclusion of pupils from school because their parents refused to permit them to be subjected to corporal punishment infringed the right to education in conformity with parents' philosophical convictions.[16]

---

[7] *R* v. *Jones* [1986] 2 S.C.R. 286.

[8] s.2.

[9] *Zylberberg et al.* v. *Sudbury Board of Education et al.* (1988) 65 O.R. (2d) 641.

[10] Article 23(3).

[11] Freeman comments on the vagueness of the language that tends to be used in such treaties, while at the same time emphasising the importance of the protections offered: M. D. A. Freeman, *The Rights and Wrongs of Children* (1986), at pp. 42–43.

[12] See G. Douglas, "The Family and the State under the European Convention on Human Rights" (1988) 2 *International Journal of Law and the Family* 76 at pp. 90–93.

[13] Article 2, First Protocol to the Convention. But in the '*Belgian Linguistics*' case French-speaking parents who complained that schools in the locality did not offer French language education failed in their attempt to establish a denial of a right to education (Judgment, Series A, Vol. 6.).

[14] Thus where religious education is presented as compulsory, there may be a breach of the Convention where a child's family is of different religion: *Karnell and Hardt* v. *Sweden* 39 Coll. 81, cited in Douglas (*supra* n.12) at p. 92.

[15] (1976) 1 E.H.R.R. 711.

[16] (1982) 4 E.H.R.R. 293. Convictions for this purpose were described by the court (at p. 305) as "such convictions as are worthy of respect in a democratic society and are not incompatible with human dignity."

The UN Convention on the Rights of the Child contains similar general provisions,[17] but embodies more specific requirements on educational provision. Article 28 requires states to offer a right to education. The Convention aims to secure the progressive and equal acquisition of this right by requiring that primary education be compulsory and free and that secondary education is offered in different forms, including general and vocational. The article also requires measures to be taken to secure regular school attendance, and requires discipline to be administered in a manner that is, *inter alia*, consistent with human dignity. Article 29 sets underlying objectives for the education of children, including the development of respect for: parents; persons of a different nationality or cultural identity; human rights and fundamental freedoms in general; and the environment. It also requires states to ensure that education encourages respect for the child's own cultural identity, language and values and also for national identity and values.[18] As noted in Chapter 1, there is also explicit recognition in the Convention of the child's right to think and act independently, which increases progressively with age,[19] and this would suggest that, in relation to the elements of schooling over which there is some choice or right of appeal, older children's views should be taken into account. Yet, as also noted, English education law has been slow to adopt this approach.

An important issue, which shall be addressed in this chapter, concerns the degree to which "consumer" rights extend over the content of education in England and Wales. In higher education, prospective students have for many years been able to select from a wide range of courses. Furthermore, in recent years the development of modular courses or programmes which maximise consumer choice and widen access has been encouraged by the Government. The Government has also required institutions to seek a greater proportion of their funding in the form of student fees, which has been designed in part to make them more responsive to the needs and wishes of students.[20] In relation to the schools system, there is a curious inconsistency. On the one hand the

---

[17] See B. Walsh, "The United Nations Convention on the Rights of the Child: A British Perspective," 5(2) (1991) *International Journal of Law and the Family* 170; D. McGoldrick, "The United Nations Convention on the Rights of the Child" (1991) 5(2) *International Journal of Law and the Family* 132. See also the Council of Europe's European Social Charter (1961) Art. 10.

[18] However, as McGoldrick (*op. cit.* p. 148) comments, multi-cultural societies find it increasingly difficult to achieve a satisfactory balance between the promotion of cultural and national identity.

[19] Articles 5, 12 and 14.

[20] G. Williams, "Higher Education," in M. Flude and M. Hammer (eds.), *The Education Reform Act 1988: Its Origins and Implications* (1990) at p. 267.

Government is keen to foster competition between schools with a view to driving up standards, through the operation of market forces. The introduction of open enrolment, formula based funding and published tables of performance related information, all of which were discussed in previous chapters, demonstrate this clear and explicit policy. Moreover, greater diversity of provision, through the addition of GM schools and city technology colleges to the existing public sector and local specialisation, will also increase choice. Yet there may be little choice about what is provided *within* state schools. The co-existence of policies of choice and central determination of the curriculum constitutes one of the major ideological contradictions inherent in current educational policy,[21] as noted in the introduction. But in any event, parents do have some important rights over the content of education. These rights are considered in this chapter, which also explains the role played by the law in the control of the school curriculum.

2.   THE CURRICULUM

It is necessary, at this point, to define what is meant by 'the curriculum.' It is clear that it extends beyond the formal programme of lessons and subject content. Schooling is expected to play a socialising role, instilling moral, cultural and social norms and values in each generation of young people. This role is fulfilled, in particular, through the hidden or 'affective' curriculum in which certain intrinsic values, reflected in the broad educational philosophy employed at a school, influence patterns of behaviour and attitudes of pupils — values such as racial tolerance, consideration of others, hard-work and perseverance, trustworthiness, patience, and so on. The hidden curriculum may also affect perceptions of gender roles; it can do this in, for example, the way that subjects are taught (such as referring to doctors as "he" and nurses as "she"), in the way that careers advice is given, in the way subject choices are presented to pupils and, more generally, in the extent to which gender identification is unnecessarily emphasised (for example in boys versus girls quizzes).[22] The hidden curriculum plays a similar role in relation to ethnicity and cultural differences.

---

[21] Coulby argues that "the proffered choice of school is largely illusory: parents are free to choose which institution will slavishly teach the Secretary of State's curriculum to their children": D. Coulby, "The Ideological Contradictions of Educational Reform," in L. Bash and D. Coulby, *The Education Reform Act: Competition and Control* (1989) at p. 114.

[22] The extensive literature includes J. Whyte, *Beyond the Wendy House: Sex Role Stereotyping in Primary schools* (1983); M. Marland (ed.), *Sex Differentiation and Schooling* (1983); B. Anderson, "The Gender Dimensions of Home-School Relations," in F. Macleod (ed.) *Parents and Schools: The Contemporary Challenge* (1989).

The law plays an important role in regulating many of these aspects of the curriculum. Of course, it is principally concerned with subject content, as exemplified by the prescriptive nature of the National Curriculum foundation subjects, programmes of study, attainment targets and assessment arrangements. But it also seeks to influence moral attitudes (as for example in the case of sex education) and promote good behaviour (as in the provisions governing maintenance of discipline). In this way the law seeks to impose a set of values on the education system, some of which are liberal in character (such as racial and gender equality, in the case of anti-discrimination legislation), others of which are more conservative (such as proscribing the promotion of homosexuality and enabling schools to be prescriptive as to school uniform). There has been a shift towards formalising some of the aims of the hidden curriculum by establishing them as part of the formal curriculum, for example by establishing Citizenship as one of the cross-curricular themes in the National Curriculum[23] and, more particularly, by calling on schools to promote particular moral values and asking teachers to lead by example in matters of dress and language.[24]

Sutherland suggests that "where it is believed that education must make children into good members of society, greater emphasis will be given to the right of society to make decisions and such decisions may involve over-riding parents' preference and wishes."[25] This, as we shall see, is broadly the case under the law in England and Wales. Even though the development of the law has also been greatly influenced by the general recognition of the value of parental involvement in children's education,[26] the scope for parental wishes to be upheld has on the whole been limited.

3. TOWARDS GREATER CENTRAL CONTROL

"What we do not want is lessons laid down by law."[27]

So wrote H.C. Dent, the leading educationalist, when the Education Bill was before Parliament in 1944. When enacted some months later,

---

[23] See National Curriculum Council, *Circular No. 6* (1989) paras. 6–16, and The Children's Society, *Education for Citizenship* (1992).

[24] National Curriculum Council, *Spiritual and Moral Development — A Discussion Paper* (1993).

[25] M. Sutherland, *Theory of Education* (1988) p. 166.

[26] See, *e.g.* Plowden Report *Children and Their Primary Schools* (1967) Vol. 1., Chap. 4; John Newsom (Chairman), *Half Our Future — A Report on the Central Advisory Council for Education (England)* (1963) para. 204; Warnock Committee, *Special Educational Needs* (1978).

[27] H. C. Dent, *The New Education Bill* (1944) p. 30.

the EA 1944 imposed a broad duty on central government to promote educational provision in accordance with national policy, and required LEAs to "contribute towards the spiritual, moral, mental and physical development of the community."[28] But the Act was silent on curriculum content, merely giving LEAs the power to determine the secular curriculum for schools in their area and establishing arrangements for the local determination of RE syllabuses (see below). As noted in Chapter 2, sufficient schools had to be available to ensure that all pupils might be suitably educated according to their "age, ability and aptitude."[29] These provisions were largely uncontroversial. At a time of general political consensus and national unity there was a willingness to co-operate between teachers, local authorities and the Ministry of Education, on which the 'partnership' between these various parties, discussed in Chapter 2, was built. Seen against this background, the lack of any centrally regulated curriculum for schools in England and Wales until very recently seems unsurprising.

The idea of a central curriculum in Britain was for many years associated with the kind of threat to democracy posed by totalitarian states. Dent, for example, commented that "stereotyped curricula would mean the end of democratic education."[30] Yet many democratic states other than the U.K. have a long history of curriculum regulation, via either a national curriculum, such as in France, or a federal state-directed curriculum, such as in Switzerland and the former West Germany.[31] In the United States, the content of education is regulated by federal and state legislation. The former is used to direct federal funds into areas of national priority or concern — for example the Metric Education Act 1978, which aimed to promote metric education programmes in schools — whilst state legislation may control textbook selection and educational content.[32]

The reforms in England and Wales have resulted in a more centralised curriculum than is found in any of these nations. In the space of a few years there has been a complete transformation. If we examine the history of curriculum regulation, we see that there was but a small element of prescription in England and Wales prior to 1944,

---

[28] EA 1944, s.7.

[29] *Ibid.* s.8.

[30] H. C. Dent, *op. cit.*

[31] I. Richter, "West Germany, Switzerland and Austria," in I. K. Birch and I. Richter *Comparative School Law* (1990) at pp. 125–126.

[32] See M. G. Yudof *et al.*, *Educational Policy and the Law* (2nd edn. 1982) p. 381, and B. Levin, *supra* (n.5) pp. 5, 11–12.

but it was in decline. From 1898, when the system of paying teachers by results (namely the results of pupils entered for examinations set by HMI) was abolished, the teaching profession acquired increasing freedom over the curriculum. The Board of Education issued a *Handbook of Suggestions for the Consideration of Teachers* and an Elementary Code, which laid down a very basic framework but left a degree of choice over curriculum content to individual schools. The Code, which had become increasingly permissive,[33] was scrapped in 1944. From the 1950s, there was a growing acceptance that some kind of set structure would prove advantageous, especially for the less able pupils whose poor literacy and numeracy skills were the subject of concern. In 1963 the Newsom Report recommended that all secondary school pupils should study mathematics, science and the humanities.[34] However, the Report came out against prescribed subject content, and against a national curriculum (apart from the above subjects), not so much on ideological grounds (these might have included the progressive/liberal ideas of child-centred and largely unstructured education developed by Rousseau and Dewey, *inter alios*[35]), but rather the practical difficulty of ensuring that the curriculum would meet the needs of *all* pupils given their diverse abilities and interests.[36] Nevertheless, the widening diversity of approach among teachers and LEAs towards curriculum content suggested that the co-ordination and guidance of a national body was needed, and in 1964 the Schools Council for the Curriculum and Examinations was established, comprising representatives of teachers' organisations, the DES, LEAs, colleges and universities. From the 1970s there was also a growing interest on the part of the DES in the operation of the curriculum at local level,[37] but also a general belief that existing legislation rightly gave little power to central government to dictate to LEAs on the subject of curricular provision.[38] It is said that the Schools Council's work had checked the DES's involvement temporarily;[39] when the Council was abolished in 1984 by the

---

[33] White comments that before 1926 "there was a fairly strict centralized surveillance of the content of elementary education," but from 1926 "individualism . . . was given free rein": J. P. White, *Towards a Compulsory Curriculum* (1973) p. 3.

[34] John Newsom, *supra* (n.26), para. 349.

[35] On the contrasting approaches advocated by progressives and authoritarians, see P. H. Hirst and R. S. Peters, *The Logic of Education* (1970) pp. 28–32.

[36] J. Newsom, *op. cit.* para. 350.

[37] See, *e.g.*, DES/Welsh Office, *Local Arrangements for the School Curriculum* (1979).

[38] See *Ibid.* pp. 6–7, and House of Commons Select Committee on Education Science and the Arts, *Second Report 1981–82, The Secondary School Curriculum and Examinations* (1982) HC 116–1, Chap. 9, and reply by Secretary of State, Mr Mark Carlisle M.P.

[39] T. Becher and S. Maclure, *The Politics of Curriculum Change* (1978).

Education Secretary, Sir Keith Joseph, there were fears that consensus would give way to "prescription through authority."[40] The implication was that "the voice of the (teaching) profession was no longer to be heeded in curricular and examination policy at national level."[41]

The vacuum left by the Schools Council was increasingly filled by the DES, which issued a series of curriculum policy documents.[42] This process was to continue up to and beyond the passage of the ERA 1988. There was a growing interest on the part of the Government in asserting greater authority in the light of perceived shortcomings among the teaching profession and some of the more left-wing LEAs. This political background was discussed in Chapter 2. A new structure was proposed in the *Better Schools* White Paper in 1985[43] and brought into effect under the E(No. 2)A 1986. This Act also regulated specific areas of the curriculum, such as sex education and the treatment of political issues in the classroom (see below); it also provided for freedom of speech in the universities.[44] Together, the 1986 Act and, more especially, the ERA 1988 have instituted a strict legal regime for the content of education in maintained schools in England and Wales (see below).

4.   PRESENT LEGAL STRUCTURE OF CONTROL

(a)   General control of the secular curriculum and discipline

In Chapter 2 we saw how, under the EA 1944, responsibility for the secular curriculum was placed with LEAs and how central government viewed its powers to intervene in respect of deficiencies in curricular provision by LEAs to be dangerously punitive and a matter of last resort.[45] Since the mid-1980s, LEAs have lost virtually all influence over curriculum content to the Secretary of State and, in the case of

---

[40] M. Plaskow, "A long view from the inside," in M. Plaskow (ed.), *Life and Death of the Schools Council* p. 1.
[41] D. Coulby, "From Educational Partnership to Central Control," in L. Bash and D. Coulby (eds.) *supra* (n.21) p. 9.
[42] *e.g.*, *Organisation and Content of the 5–16 Curriculum* (1984); *Science 5–16: A Statement of Policy* (1985); and *Modern Languages in the School Curriculum* (1988).
[43] Cmnd 9469.
[44] See E(No. 2)A 1986, s.43. In *R v. University of Liverpool ex p. Caesar-Gordon* [1990] 3 All E.R. 821 (Q.B.D.) the court held that by virtue of s.43, a ban by the University on speeches there by members of the South African London embassy, on the ground that there might be unrest and disturbance outside the University precincts, was unlawful.
[45] *Supra*, p. 32.

local curriculum policy, to school governing bodies. In the face of concern about standards in schools and the policies and practices of some LEAs (for example in the introduction of peace studies[46] or the use of texts allegedly promoting homosexuality[47]), the Conservatives have pursued a policy of tight central government control — a policy which for a time also threatened academic freedom in the universities.[48] The National Curriculum constitutes the key area of control (see below). Among the other areas which are centrally controlled is the public examinations system: no examination course may be provided to pupils aged 5–16 in schools unless the qualification has been approved by the Secretary of State or a designated body.[49] Despite the greater centralisation of authority over the curriculum, the general policy of promoting increased school autonomy has led to specific powers and duties also being placed on head teachers and governing bodies.

As noted earlier, LEAs' control over the secular curriculum has disappeared as a result of the repeal of section 23 of the 1944 Act.[50] However, they do still have several important duties and powers. They retain a general duty to "contribute towards the spiritual, moral, mental and physical development of the community."[51] Under the EA 1993 they have duties in respect of pupils special educational needs. They also retain responsibility for the enforcement of school attendance and for the operation of a curriculum complaints procedure (see below). LEAs also have non-discrimination duties under the SDA 1975 and RRA 1976 in respect of both admission to schools and the provision of facilities for education (see below).[52] However, governing bodies will also be responsible for ensuring that unlawful discrimination does not occur under the curriculum.[53] LEAs share with the Secretary of State,

---

[46] See N. Harris, "Law and Peace Studies" (1987) 137 *Education Today* 30.

[47] See M. R. T. Macnair, "Homosexuality in Schools — Section 28 Local Government Act 1988" (1989) 1(2) *Education and the Law* 35.

[48] The University Commission (consisting of five commissioners) was charged with the responsibility of reviewing and amending each university's charter so that staff could be dismissed for redundancy or good cause (see ERA 1988, ss.202–208 and Sched. 11; and *Page* v. *Hull University Visitor* [1993] 1 All E.R. 97). A House of Lords amendment proposed by Lord Jenkins of Hillhead ensured that the Commissioners would have to have regard, *inter alia*, to the need "to ensure that academic staff have freedom within the law to question and test received wisdom, and put forward new ideas and controversial and unpopular opinions, without placing themselves in jeopardy of losing their jobs or privileges they may have": ERA 1988 s.202(2)(a).

[49] ERA 1988, s.5(1). The School Examinations and Assessment Council was the designated body until replaced by the School Curriculum and Assessment Authority — see below.

[50] By Sched. 6 to the E(No. 2)A 1986.

[51] EA 1944, s.7.

[52] SDA 1975, ss.22, 23 and 25; and RRA 1976, ss.17–19.

[53] See SDA 1975, s.22 and RRA 1976, s.17, discussed below.

governing bodies and head teachers, a duty to ensure that the curriculum of a school is "balanced and broadly based," "promotes the spiritual, moral, cultural, mental and physical development of pupils at the school and of society" and "prepares such pupils for the opportunities, responsibilities and experiences of adult life."[54] They also share with governors and head teachers (but not, it seems, teachers[55]) responsibility for ensuring that the National Curriculum is provided in county and voluntary schools.[56]

In schools other than voluntary aided schools, responsibility for the "determination and organisation of the school curriculum" rests with the head teacher.[57] He or she has a specific duty to ensure that the curriculum is not in conflict with any enactments relating to education[58] (these include provisions on the treatment of political issues and charging for educational provision — see below) and that it is compatible with the LEA's curriculum policy as modified by the governing body's statement of curriculum aims for the school.[59] In voluntary aided schools the secular curriculum is under exclusive control of the governing body.[60]

The way in which discipline is enforced in schools is essentially a matter for the head teacher: s/he has a duty to determine the measures (which may include rules) needed to achieve, among pupils, "self-discipline," "proper regard for authority", "good" or "acceptable" behaviour and "respect for others."[61] Furthermore, the head teacher alone has power to exclude a child from school,[62] but must act within the legally prescribed framework (see below).[63] Nevertheless, as noted in Chapter 3, the general conduct of the school must be under the direction of the governing body, and the head teacher's disciplinary regime must be in accordance with any written statement of principles prepared by the governors; the head teacher must also have regard to any guidance offered by the governors in relation to particular matters in this context.[64]

---

[54] ERA 1988, s.1(1) and (2).

[55] *Wandsworth L.B.C.* v. *N.A.S./U.W.T.* (1993) *The Times*, April 19. In this case the Court of Appeal rejected the London Borough of Wandsworth's argument that a boycott of National Curriculum testing of 14 year olds by members of a teaching union would amount to a breach of the ERA 1988.

[56] ERA 1988, s.10(2).

[57] *Ibid.* s. 18(5).

[58] E.(No. 2)A 1986, s.18(6).

[59] *Ibid.*

[60] *Ibid.* s.19(1). The governors must have regard to LEA policy (s.19(2)).

[61] E(No. 2)A 1986, s.22(*a*). The reference "respect for others" is the result of an amendment made by the EA 1993.

[62] *Ibid.* s.22(*f*).

[63] *Ibid.* ss.23–26.

[64] *Ibid.* s.22(*b*).

(b) Central control under the National Curriculum

It was realised right from the start that the proposed legal structure of the National Curriculum would result in unprecedented central government power over the content of children's education in state-maintained schools. The Government was not only proposing a core curriculum, it was prescribing the entire curriculum up to the age of 16, including arrangements for testing pupils, and was proposing that the Secretary of State would be able to stipulate the proportion of available teaching time to be allocated to individual subjects.[65] These reforms were considered necessary in order to raise standards and levels of accountability. Pupils would receive a balanced and broadly based curriculum that would prepare them for adult life and which would be based on prescribed objectives covering the full range of abilities and backed up with regular assessment. Schools could be measured against each other following publication of pupils' assessment results. The National Curriculum would present teachers with "a framework not a straightjacket."[66] But it was argued that "to be effective (it) must be backed by law."[67]

The omission of independent schools from the National Curriculum appears to have been based partly on the view that these schools have to be responsive to market forces and will therefore teach the National Curriculum if that is what parents want. Yet this argument could equally be applied to state schools, in the new era of competition and choice. Another argument is that independent schools are not in receipt of public funds and so should not be tied to a state-directed curriculum. Whitty suggests that this argument is spurious not only because some public funding supports a good number of these schools, via the assisted places scheme (see Chapter 1), but, more particularly, because lack of public funding has not provided a basis for relieving privatised industries from regulation.[68]

The broad structure of the National Curriculum, based around 10 foundation subjects (three of which, English, mathematics and science, are "core subjects"[69]), is laid down in the ERA 1988. But the Secretary of State has the power to prescribe the content of and assessment arrangements for each subject,[70] change any or all of the foundation

---

[65] DES/Welsh Office, *The National Curriculum 5–16 — A Consultation Document* (1987).
[66] *Ibid.* p. 5.
[67] *Ibid.*
[68] G. Whitty, "The New Right and the National Curriculum," in M. Flude and M. Hammer *supra* (n.20) p. 28.
[69] ERA 1988, s.3(1) and (2). There is an additional foundation subject and fourth core subject, Welsh, in Welsh-medium schools in Wales: s.3(1)(*a*).
[70] ERA 1988, s.4(2). Under s.2(2), the content is based on "attainment targets" (the knowledge, skills and understanding expected of pupils) and "programmes of study"
—continued on next page

subjects,[71] and alter, within limits, the age at which subjects will be taught.[72] A power to prescribe the proportion of time to be allocated to each subject was omitted from the Education Reform Bill. But to remove any doubt, the Bill was in any event amended to prohibit the Secretary of State from apportioning curricular time when using his power to prescribe attainment targets, programmes of study and assessment arrangements.[73]

The power of the Secretary of State seems on the face of it to be limited only by the need to lay the various orders specifying the programmes of study, etc, for each subject before Parliament. It is true that the Secretary of State must refer proposed orders to the Curriculum Councils (soon to be in effect merged with the School Examinations and Assessment Council under the EA 1993, to form the School Curriculum and Assessment Authority (SCAA[74])), who must in turn put them out to consultation and report back to the minister.[75] But their 10–15 members[76] are appointed by the Secretary of State,[77] and more importantly the Secretary of State has the final say on the content of the orders; he merely has to offer reasons for failing to follow the recommendations of the Curriculum Councils (and in due course those of the SCAA).[78] In fact, their recommendations have been followed on a

---

[70]—*continued from previous page*
(the "matters, skills and processes" to be taught); the "assessment arrangements" involve formal testing at or near the end of each key stage. The provisions specifying which of the attainment targets, etc., have to be aimed for at each key stage in relation to each subject are contained in orders made by the Secretary of State. The actual attainment targets, etc, are set out in separate documents, published by HMSO, to which reference will be made in the order and which, by virtue of the enabling power in the 1988 Act (s.4(4)), have legal force. The EA 1993 (s.241(4)) has introduced a controversial requirement that the Secretary of State must revise the National Curriculum to eliminate the study of HIV/AIDS, sexually transmitted diseases and "aspects of human sexual behaviour, other than biological aspects." Sex education will in effect be taken out of the National Curriculum.

[71] ERA 1988, s.3(4)(*a*).

[72] ERA 1988, s.3(4)(*b*). The National Curriculum programmes are based around the four progressive "key stages ": KS1 — ages 5–7; KS2 — ages 7–11; KS3 — ages 11–14; and KS4 — ages 14–16: s.3(3).

[73] ERA 1988, s.4(3).

[74] See EA 1993 ss.244–248 and Sched. 14.

[75] ERA 1988, ss.20 and 21. The two Curriculum Councils are the National Curriculum Council and the Curriculum Council for Wales: *ibid.* s.14.

[76] Membership of the Councils must "include persons having relevant knowledge or experience in education": s.14(2). Members are appointed "in a personal rather than a representative capacity": DES/Welsh Office *supra* (n.65), p. 16. The SCAA will be similarly constituted and appointed: EA 1993, s.244.

[77] Following the resignation of Duncan Graham as chair of the National Curriculum Council in 1991 (see below), David Pascall, a former member of Mrs Thatcher's No. 10 Policy Unit and a senior executive with B.P., was appointed as replacement. The head of the SCAA is to be Sir Ron Dearing, formerly head of the Higher Education Funding Council for England.

[78] ERA 1988, ss.20(5) and (6) and 21(3) and (4). The EA 1993 is amending these provisions so that they refer to the SCAA.

number of occasions: for example, the Secretary of State from 1992, Mr Patten, accepted the National Curriculum Council's recommendations on the revised English Order and the SEAC's advice that English tests for 14 year olds should include questions on three specified Shakespeare plays.[79] Nevertheless, all Secretaries of State since the introduction of the National Curriculum in 1989 have used their authority to override the Curriculum Councils on a number of occasions — in particular over the history and geography specifications. One Secretary of State, Mr MacGregor, demanded more emphasis on knowledge in the attainment targets for history, whilst another, Mr Clarke, insisted that history "should run from the turn of the century to a time 20 years before the present."[80] Duncan Graham, a former chairman of the National Curriculum Council, has said that this "raises the serious question of the role of ministers in the curriculum and the dilemmas caused when politics clash with educational needs."[81] Although over-subscription and a lack of flexibility remain two of the principal criticisms of the National Curriculum,[82] it is the almost unbridled power of the Secretary of State that has the most long-term significance. Graham warns of "improper political prescription of content" and of enforced teaching methods based on "prejudice"; he writes that "everybody concerned about education should be alert to the dangers."[83] Coulby comments that while central control of the curriculum may not in itself be undemocratic, since the government is accountable to the electorate, "dramatic curricular shifts with each change of government and significant curricular change with each Secretary of State are now a likelihood."[84]

Resistance by some head teachers to the tests for seven year olds in 1991 almost resulted in legal action, before the Secretary of State agreed to modifications. The 1993 boycott of tests for 14 year olds by classroom teachers precipitated one major court case (above) and may presage further legal battles over the school curriculum. The disputes to date are not merely a symptom of teething troubles, but seem to

---

[79] See *T.E.S.* September 11, 1992. The SEAC recommendations were leaked to the press by a "mole" (see "Council unearths English tests 'mole'" *T.E.S.*, January 29, 1993), a fact which emphasises the politically controversial nature of National Curriculum developments.

[80] D. Graham with D. Tytler, *A Lesson for Us All — The Making of the National Curriculum* (1992) p. 74.

[81] *Ibid.* pp. 68–70.

[82] For a general review, see P. Francis, *What's Wrong with the National Curriculum?* (1992).

[83] *Op. cit.*, p. 148.

[84] D. Coulby, "The National Curriculum" in L. Bash and D. Coulby, *The Education Reform Act: Competition and Control* (1989) p. 60.

represent a more deep-seated resistance to the Secretary of State's powers over the curriculum. The Government's acceptance of the main recommendations of the recent interim report of the Dearing review of the National Curriculum, which include reducing the prescribed content of the core subjects to give teachers greater flexibility and streamlining the rest of the compulsory curriculum to allow other subjects to be introduced by teachers, may, however, presage a partial relinquishment of control.[85]

(c)　Control of religious education and collective worship

Under the ERA 1988, provision for religious education and a daily act of collective worship is compulsory in all maintained schools.[86] Responsibility for making the arrangements for collective worship rests with the head teacher in a county school and with the governing body in a voluntary school or GM school.[87] Normally, collective worship must be held on the school premises and may take place in age or class groups.[88] Most acts of collective worship must be "wholly or mainly of a broadly Christian character" (see below), but the standing advisory council on religious education (SACRE) for the area may direct otherwise in the case of individual county schools and certain GM schools.[89] The SACRE may also advise on religious education under the "agreed syllabus" for the area.[90] Its advice can include guidance on teaching methods, the choice of materials and the provision of training for teachers.[91]

The LEA is responsible for constituting the SACRE. The Act requires it to comprise a collection of representative groups: one is to represent "such Christian and other religious denominations as, in the opinion of

---

[85] See "New school tests mark death of Baker system" *The Independent* and "Ministers backpedal to save education policy" *The Guardian*, both August 3, 1993.

[86] ss.2(1)(*a*) (religious education) and 6(1) (collective worship). On the background to the inclusion of these provisions in the 1988 Act, see S. Maclure, *Education Re-formed* (3rd edn., 1992) pp. 18–21. The requirement that each school day should *begin* with an act of collective worship, contained in the Education Act 1944, has been dropped. Poulter has examined the case for reform of the law on collective worship: S. Poulter, *English Law and Ethnic Minority Customs* (1986) p. 169 and "The religious education provisions of the Education Reform Act 1988" (1990) 2(1) *Education and the Law* 1 at p. 8.

[87] ERA 1988, s.6(3).

[88] s.6(2)–(6).

[89] ss.7(6) and 12(1). Directions under s.12(1) may also now be made at the request of the head teacher of a GM school which is a former county school or which has been established as a new school: EA 1993, s.138. The SACRE has to review its decision when requested by the head teacher (after consultation with the governing body) or, in any event, within five years: ERA 1988, s.12(5).

[90] ERA 1988, s.11(1).

[91] s.11(2).

the authority, will properly reflect the principal religious traditions of the area"; the others must represent the Church of England (apart from in Wales), the LEA and teachers' associations.[92] Poulter has commented that it is "far from satisfactory" that "in a particularly cosmopolitan area one group (with a single vote) might have to represent, for example, Muslims, Hindus, Sikhs and Jews as well as Roman Catholics, Methodists and Baptists."[93] The EA 1993 now requires the number of members appointed to any representative group to "reflect broadly the proportionate strength of that denomination or religion in the area."[94] The SACRE must also contain a representative of the governing bodies of GM schools which were formerly county or voluntary controlled schools, and it may also have co-opted members. Each of the representative groups is to have but one vote when decisions are being taken,[95] for example on the question of whether to require a review of the agreed syllabus for religious education.[96]

Religious education in a county school must be in accordance with an "agreed syllabus"; this must be drawn up by a local "conference" under a procedure laid down in Schedule 5 to the EA 1944.[97] The conference consists of the same representative groups as the SACRE. In the event of a failure to agree a syllabus, the Secretary of State may use a reserve power in the Schedule to appoint a body to prepare a syllabus for the authority. However, he has no power to compel LEAs to update the agreed syllabus. There is evidence that even after the 1988 Act and DES and National Curriculum Council guidance[98] a substantial number of LEAs (80 out of 109, according to a recent survey[99]) have still not sought a revision of the agreed syllabus, which in some cases is 10 or 15 years old. However, the EA 1993 has amended Schedule 5 to require that all syllabuses not reviewed since the ERA 1988 be re-examined by a conference within one year of the commencement of the section.[1]

---

[92] s.11(3) and (4).
[93] S. Poulter (1990) *op. cit.*, at p. 2.
[94] EA 1993, s.255, which also requires the SACRE to be reconstituted within six months of the commencement of the section.
[95] s.11(6).
[96] s.11(7).
[97] EA 1944, s.26(1). The National Curriculum Council has reported that some of the older agreed syllabuses, still in operation, give very little detail about what children should be taught and may be in breach of the ERA 1988: *The Independent*, March 11, 1993.
[98] DES Circular 3/89 *The Education Reform Act 1988 — Religious Education and Collective Worship*; National Curriculum Council, *Religious Education: A Local Curriculum Framework* (1991).
[99] *The Independent*, March 11, 1993.
[1] s.256. The agreed syllabus will have to be reconsidered at least every five years thereafter: *ibid.*

In voluntary schools, RE must be in accordance with either the agreed syllabus or the trust deed for the school or the practice which applied before the school acquired its voluntary status.[2] If a school acquires GM status, the arrangements for RE which were in operation under its previous status would generally continue.[3]

Important changes have been made by the EA 1993 to provide for an element of accountability in respect of SACREs and Schedule 5 conferences. The Act provides for a right of public access to their meetings and documents (section 258) and enables certain complaints about a SACRE to be investigated by the Secretary of State (who can issue directions if the complaint is upheld) (section 257).

4. CONSUMER CHOICE, PARTICIPATION AND REDRESS

(a) Compulsory schooling

Children's notional 'right' under domestic law to an education derives partly from a parent's legal obligation to ensure that a child is educated between ages 5–16.[4] Although some aspects of the recent education reforms have sought to promote the private over the public interest, most particularly in the area of school choice, the public interest in ensuring that children receive an education and are aided to become fit members of society has not diminished. A range of philosophies has over time been applied to justify intervention in cases of non-attendance, from Blackstone's natural-law based ideas, centring on the moral obligation of parenthood to educate one's child,[5] to Benthamite utilitarian ideas,[6] and on to recent political emphasis on the links between truancy and criminality.[7]

At present, tough approaches to the legal enforcement of school attendance are being encouraged, in the face of increasing concern about

---

[2] EA 1944, ss.27(1) and (6) and 28(1).

[3] See EA 1993 ss.139–141.

[4] EA 1944, s.36 — see below. The date on which compulsory schooling ends is defined in s.277 of the EA 1993. There is no duty on LEAs to provide nursery education (education for children aged between two and four inclusive), but there is a power to do so: EA 1944, s.9(2); EA 1980 24(2). On the duties in respect of education for children under five with special educational needs, see below. On day care provision for the under fives, under the Children Act 1989, see N. S. Harris, "The Children Act 1989: the Education Provisions" (1992) 4(2) *Education and the Law* 61.

[5] Blackstone wrote "It is not easy to imagine or allow that a parent has conferred any considerable benefit on his child by bringing him into the world, if he afterwards entirely neglects his culture and education, and suffers him to grow up like a mere beast, to lead a life useless to others and shameful to himself": *Commentaries on the Laws of England* (1830) Vol. 1, p. 446.

[6] See P. Carlen *et al.*, *Truancy: The Politics of Compulsory Schooling* (1992) Chap. 1.

[7] "Truancy . . . can be the first step towards a life of crime": Eric Forth M.P., Schools Minister, DFE Press Release 253/92, July 20, 1992.

the scale of the truancy problem (an estimated 200,000 children play truant during each school day[8]). Improvement in school attendance rates is being sought through a variety of local and national initiatives — from strict enforcement measures, such as truancy patrols,[9] to attemps to make schools less alienating. But there is still considerable debate about whether sufficient attention is given to the causes of truancy and about the effectiveness of the legal procedures.[10]

Schools are currently being encouraged to give more attention to the problem of truancy: by having to publish their truancy rates; through changes to school registration regulations so that "hidden truancy" (truanting occurring during only part of the school day[11]) is monitored more effectively;[12] by the application, by school inspectors, of evaluation criteria on attendance[13]; and by the Reducing Truancy programme funded by government grants.[14]

The basic legal duty on a parent to ensure that his or her child receives an efficient full-time education suitable to his or her age, ability and aptitude, either "by regular attendance at school or otherwise," has not changed since the EA 1944.[15] Although the words "or otherwise" imply a degree of choice,[16] in practice it has proved extremely difficult to satisfy LEA education officers that suitable education can be provided outside the school setting, and well-nigh impossible since the introduction of the National Curriculum. There are circumstances when children would be better off educated outside school, for example in a special unit for pregnant schoolgirls or schoolgirl mothers,[17] or via home tutors, and LEAs are being given a legal duty to make such provision where appropriate (in place of the discretion provided by section 56 of the EA 1944).[18]

---

[8] *The Guardian*, October 16, 1990.

[9] See M. Grenville, "Police truancy patrols" (1989) 1(2) *Education and the Law* 65.

[10] For discussion, see N. Harris *et al.*, *The Legal Context of Teaching* (1992) pp. 75–81, citing work by Galloway, Pratt and Grimshaw, Reid and others. Carlen *et al.* (*op. cit.*, at p. 48) could find "no strong evidence that compulsion or legal threats have significantly influenced school atttendance one way or the other" — but see J. Ruddick and T. Wood, "In search of the holy grail — an alternative view" (1990) 2(1) *Education and the Law* 13–16.

[11] See D. C. Pack (Chair), *Truancy and Indiscipline in Schools in Scotland* (1977).

[12] See the Education (Pupils' Attendance Records) Regulations 1991 SI 1991 No. 1582.

[13] See H.M. Chief Inspector of Schools in England, *Framework for the Inspection of Schools* (1992) pp. 18–19.

[14] DFE, Press Release 6/93, January 8, 1993. £10m was allocated for 1993–94; 64 LEAs received grants, on a bidding basis.

[15] EA 1944, s.36.

[16] See *R* v. *West Riding of Yorkshire Justices ex p. Broadbent* [1910] 2 K.B. 192.

[17] See M. D. A. Freeman, "Children's education and the law" (1980) L.A.G. Bulletin 62.

[18] EA 1993, s.298(1). (EA 1944, s.56 has been revoked.) A school which is specially established for such purposes is to be known as a "pupil referral unit" (see EA 1993, Sched. 18.).

Parents can be prosecuted for a failure to comply with a school attendance order or to prevent the child's non-excused absence from school,[19] both of which appear to be strict liability offences.[20] The law lays down a list of excuses which has been held to be exhaustive.[21] The first excuse relates to leave of the school. The second concerns the child's sickness or other avoidable cause relating to the child. In *Jenkins* v. *Howells*[22] it was held that the parent's illness, which meant that the child was needed at home to do housework, was not an unavoidable cause relating to the child. In *Jarman* v. *Mid-Glamorgan Education Authority*,[23] May L.J. held that absence from school because of parental opposition to corporal punishment was not due to unavoidable cause; he also said that "the words 'unavoidable cause' . . . should in no way be equated with 'reasonable grounds'." The third excuse relates to a day of religious observance. The final excuse is that the school is not within walking distance (two miles for a child aged under eight, and three miles for an older child) and no suitable arrangements have been made by the LEA for transport, board or the transfer of the child to a school nearer his or her home.[24] In assessing whether a route is "available," account now has to be taken of the nature of the route and the age of the child.[25] The LEA is entitled to expect children living within walking distance to be accompanied to school by parents when necessary.[26]

The Department continues to recommend that, in the enforcement of school attendance, early prosecution of parents and a firm approach "may bring a prompt and sustained improvement."[27] The Children Act 1989 has not removed the power to prosecute but has made a number of changes, including the removal of the court's (rarely used) power to imprison a parent in a non-attendance case. (A power to fine on level three is available under section 202 of EA 1993, but recently it was reported that on average one-third of parents receive a conditional discharge.[28]) More importantly, the Children Act has established an

---

[19] EA 1993, ss.198 and 199.

[20] *Crump* v. *Gilmore* (1970) 68 L.G.R. 56.

[21] EA 1993, s.199(3) and (4), formerly in EA 1944, s.39(2); see *Spiers* v. *Warrington Corporation* [1954] 1 Q.B. 61.

[22] [1944] 1 All E.R. 942.

[23] (1985) *The Times* February 11 (C.A.). See also *Happe* v. *Lay* (1977) 76 L.G.R. 313.

[24] EA 1993, s.199(4).

[25] EA 1944, s.55(3), amended following the decision in *Rogers* v. *Essex County Council* [1986] 3 All E.R. 321 (H.L.).

[26] *George* v. *Devon County Council* [1988] 3 All E.R. 1002.

[27] DES, *Education Supervision Orders — Guidance* (1991).

[28] *The Times*, July 12, 1993, reporting the findings of a survey of 61 LEAs by the National Association of Social Workers in Education.

entirely new system for the enforcement of school attendance, as recommended by the DHSS *Review of Child Care Law* (1985), to replace the use of care proceedings in truancy cases. The new system involves education supervision orders (ESOs). An ESO may be made where a child "is of compulsory school age and is not being properly educated."[29] The ESO will require a person (generally an education welfare officer) to advise, assist and befriend a child and empower this supervisor to give directions to the family as to the resumption of schooling.[30] The Department's guidance states that such directions should be given in writing and used "only where necessary," for example to require a pupil and parents to attend a meeting with the supervisor or teachers at the school to discuss the child's progress.[31] Non-compliance with directions amounts to a criminal offence.[32] In ESO proceedings the court must apply the paramountcy principle (the child's welfare shall be the paramount consideration) and have regard to the various factors set out in the so-called "statutory checklist."[33] Where there is a prosecution for non-excused absence, the court can direct the LEA to apply for an ESO. Before bringing the prosecution in the first place the LEA must decide on the appropriateness or otherwise of applying for an ESO.[34]

In the past, non-attendance at school was, in essence, a ground for ordering that a child be taken into care.[35] During the Committee stage of the Children Bill, the minister commented that continuing with this would "not meet the spirit of the times."[36] However, where non-attendance is a symptom of deeper difficulties, for example parental indifference or neglect, it is possible that the local authority social services department will become involved and that care proceedings may be warranted, on the ground that the child is suffering or is likely to suffer significant harm.[37]

There is not the space here for lengthy evaluation of the legal regime governing the enforcement of school attendance. What can be suggested

---

[29] Children Act 1989, s.36(3). A child is being "properly educated" "only if he is receiving efficient full-time education suitable to his age, ability and aptitude and any special educational needs he may have": s.36(2).

[30] Children Act 1989, Sched. 3, para. 12(1).

[31] *Op. cit.*

[32] Children Act 1989, Sched. 3, paras. 18 and 19.

[33] s.1(1) and (3).

[34] EA 1993, s.202(1) and (2).

[35] Children and Young Persons Act 1969, s.1(2)(e). See *Re DJMS* [1977] 3 All E.R. 582.

[36] Official Report, House of Commons Standing Committee B, col. 248, May 23, 1989, Mr D. Mellor M.P.

[37] s.31(2). This was the view of Brenda Hoggett before the Children Act (*Parents and Children: the Law of Parental Responsibility* (2nd edn., 1987) p. 13), vindicated as a result of the decision in *Re O (a minor) (care proceedings: education)* [1992] 4 All E.R. 905.

is that the Children Act 1989 provisions represent a significant improvement by placing far greater emphasis on the individual child's welfare than on punitive measures. Through Education Welfare Officer (EWO) involvement, they may, in particular, also result in greater emphasis on the causes of truancy and in working out a suitable regime for resumed schooling.[38] Since bullying and indiscipline are sometimes casual factors in truancy, the Elton Report was right to recommend that schools maintain adequate EWO numbers,[39] although LEAs are currently finding this difficult in the face of considerable financial pressures.

Despite these changes, the law continues to provide for compulsory education to the age of 16. Indeed, at various times since the early 1980s there has been discussion about whether the school leaving age should be raised, in the face of poor staying-on rates (relative to other western states) and the high rate of unemployment. Grenville has suggested that the older child, perhaps one aged 14 plus, should be empowered to exercise a choice over whether to remain at school.[40] This would recognise the principle (embodied Children Act 1989) of the views of older children being taken into account, but would undermine the pre-eminence of the public interest in the matter of compulsory schooling. It has been suggested that in the matter of school attendance the "element of compulsion is difficult to reconcile with the government's putative freely choosing consumer."[41] But amongst a society which almost universally accepts education as a necessity, there would be little interest or perceived value in extending choice to the extent that education becomes entirely optional.

(b) Discipline

Traditionally the teacher's legal authority to enforce discipline through sanctions such as corporal punishment, confiscation of property, detention or exclusion, was considered to derive from the *in loco parentis* principle.[42] For example, in *Cleary* v. *Booth* Collins J. stated:

---

[38] See N. Harris, "Supervision of Truants: Whose Role?" (1989) 19 *Fam Law* 404.

[39] Lord Elton (Chair), *Discipline in Schools. Report of the Committee of Enquiry chaired by Lord Elton* (1989), R. 104.

[40] M. P. Grenville, "Compulsory school attendance and the child's wishes" (1988) *Journal of Social Welfare Law* 4.

[41] P. Carlen *et al.*, *op. cit.*, p. 59.

[42] Under this principle the teacher is said to act "in place of the parent." A parent has disciplinary authority in respect of a child for whom s/he has parental responsibility: see Children Act 1989, s.3(1) and S. M. Cretney and J. M. Masson, *Principles of Family Law* (1990) pp. 488–489.

"It is clear law that a father has the right to inflict reasonable personal chastisement on his son. It is equally the law, and it is in accordance with very ancient practice, that he may delegate this right to the schoolmaster. Such a right has always commended itself to the common sense of mankind."[43]

Similarly, in *Ryan* v. *Fildes* Tucker J. said that:

"when a parent sends a child to school, he delegates to the teachers at the school the power to inflict reasonable and moderate punishment as required . . . in the same way as he, as a parent, would have the power . . . and . . . the taking of such steps as are necessary to maintain discipline with regard to the child committed to the teacher's care."[44]

Indeed, the courts accepted that the teacher's delegated authority extended to acts outside the school, such as in *Cleary* v. *Booth* itself, when the child was punished for fighting in the street on the way to school, and in *R* v. *Newport (Salop) JJ ex p. Wright*,[45] when a child was caned for smoking in a public street contrary to a school rule banning smoking during term time in school or elsewhere. In *ex p. Wright*, the court, in upholding the right of the teacher to discipline the child in these circumstances, said that by sending the boy to the school the parent had impliedly delegated to the teacher the right to punish his son for breach of a school rule.

Today, the prevalent view is that the teacher's authority is probably independent of parental delegation, although the Elton Committee recommended that to avoid any uncertainty on the subject the matter should be resolved via legislation.[46] The independent nature of a teacher's authority to discipline a child, within the limits the law allows (note the absence since 1987 of the option of corporal punishment in the state sector[47]), is reinforced by section 1(7) of the Children and

---

[43] [1893] 1 Q.B. 465 at p. 468.

[44] [1938] 3 All E.R. 517 at p. 521.

[45] [1929] 2 K.B. 416.

[46] Lord Elton *op. cit.* para. 72. See also M. Brazier *Street on Torts* (1988) p. 87 and A. K. Scutter, "Schoolteachers' Position as to Corporal Punishment — 1" (1978) 122 *Solicitor's Journal* 671. An implication of the teacher's enjoyment of an independent right to discipline a child is that there would be no need for a teacher to have been delegated "parental responsibility" by a parent under s.2(9) of the Children Act 1989.

[47] s.47 of the E(No. 2)A 1986 removed from teachers the defence of lawful chastisement in civil proceedings, in respect of corporal punishment inflicted on children in state schools or whose education in the private sector is supported by public funds (see also Education (Abolition of Corporal Punishment) (Independent Schools) Regulations 1987 SI 1987 No. 1183, as amended, and the Education (Abolition (Etc.)) (Prescribed Categories of Persons) Regulations SI 1989 No. 1825. Note the European Court of Human Rights' narrow (5–4) rejection, on its facts, of the claim in *Costello-Roberts* v.

—*cont. on next page*

Young Persons Act 1933. This states that "nothing in this section (prescribing offences of cruelty) shall be construed as affecting the right of any parent, teacher, or other person having lawful control or charge of a young person to administer punishment to him." Furthermore, the establishment of the head teacher's role under section 22 of the E(No. 2)A 1986 with regard to, *inter alia*, "regulating the conduct of pupils" and exercising "the power to exclude a pupil," offers pretty conclusive additional evidence of teachers' independent authority. This means that parents would appear to have little choice over the way their child is disciplined at school, although they may be able to assert their rights under the European Convention on Human Rights, as in the *Campbell and Cosans* case (see above). It is also unlikely that section 76 of the EA 1944 ("children are to be educated in accordance with the wishes of their parents") would be applicable, since the general principle laid down could be subjugated to broader disciplinary concerns. However, parental wishes may be factor in determining whether a punishment act was reasonable.[48]

Parents' private interest receives some, albeit limited, recognition in the opportunities for redress provided by the law. These include action under anti-discrimination legislation on the ground that there has been racial or sexual discrimination in exclusion "or other detriment"[49] or in withdrawal of privileges.[50] There is considerable evidence of differential treatment of pupils based on gender. But although fewer girls than boys are excluded from school (four boys for every girl[51]), this may be attributable to differences in the kind of deviant behaviour displayed

---

[47]—*cont. from previous page*

U.K. (*The Times*, March 26, 1993) that the slippering of a child in a boarding school constituted inhuman and degrading treatment under Art. 3 of the European Convention on Human Rights. The Court said that, following *Tyrer* v. *U.K.* (1978, April 25, Series A, No. 26), illegality was dependent upon reaching a particular level of severity of punishment. The EA 1993 (s.293, adding subss.(1A) and (1B) to E(No. 2)A 1986, s.47) has sought to incorporate parallel provisions to Art. 3 into domestic law in a way that reflects the ECHR rulings. For discussion of the law on detention and other disciplinary measures, see N. Harris, "Discipline in Schools: The Elton Report" (1991) *Journal of Social Welfare and Family Law* 110.

[48] *R.* v. *Hopley* (1860) 2 F & F 202. See Brazier *op. cit.* Note the relevance given to parental wishes in assessing the reasonableness of detention of a whole class in *Terrington* v. *Lancashire County Council* (1986) Blackpool County Court, June 26 (unreported), discussed in M. Rosenbaum, "The Children's Legal Centre: Evidence to the Elton Committee," in N. Jones (ed.), *School Management and Pupil Behaviour* (1989).

[49] If these general words are subjected to the *ejusdem generis* canon of statutory interpretation, as in the employment case *De Souza* v. *Automobile Association* ([1986] IRLR 103 (C.A.)), the result would probably be that only detriment equivalent to exclusion would be covered by this definition, found in s.22(c) of the SDA 1975 and s.17(c)(ii) of the RRA 1976.

[50] Withdrawal of privileges is assumed to be covered by the "benefits, facilities or services" ground in s.22(c) and s.17(c) respectively.

[51] DFE, *Exclusions: A Discussion Paper* (1992) para. 16.

by boys and girls at school, the former tending to be more *overtly* disobedient and disruptive.[52] There is also evidence of race discrimination by schools,[53] and the Elton Report warned against racial stereotyping of pupils from ethnic minorities as troublemakers.[54]

Exclusions from school are regulated under the E(No. 2)A 1986 and EA 1993. The parents (or the pupil him or herself, if aged 18 or over) must be informed, "without delay," of any decision to exclude, together with the reasons for, and period of, exclusion and the right to make representations.[55] Exclusions may be for a fixed period or permanent; indefinite exclusion has been abolished under the EA 1993, which has also restricted the total number of days for which a pupil can be subjected to a fixed period, or fixed periods, of exclusion in any one term.[56] There is a general duty to consider reinstatement of a pupil and to inform the parent (or pupil if aged 18 or over) of a decision not to reinstate.[57] The parent, or pupil aged 18 or over, has a right of appeal under section 26 (E (No. 2) A 1986) in respect of permanent exclusion. Appeal lies to the same committee that has jurisdiction over school admissions appeals (see p. 134 above). But complaints about the conduct of hearings (in particular, the absence of a judicial approach) have led the Council on Tribunals to consider the case for a legally qualified chairperson.[58] The committee, whose decision is binding,[59] is expected to conduct a complete rehearing of the issues.[60]

These limited rights are important given the massive increase in the number of exclusions over the past few years. A National Union of Teachers survey in 1992 revealed a 20 per cent. increase in a single year,[61] and a survey for the BBC *Panorama* programme in early 1993

---

[52] See M. McManus, *Troublesome Behaviour in the Classroom* (1989) pp. 11–12.
[53] "Afro-Caribbean pupils appeared to be disproportionately represented within the excluded pupil population (8.1 per cent. of the overall total)": DFE, *supra* (n.51). The Commission for Racial Equality considered the exclusion of four times more black children than whites in Birmingham between 1974–80 to have been in part as least the result of racial discrimination: *Birmingham Local Education Authority and Schools' Referral and Suspension of Pupils, Report of a Formal Investigation* (1985). On discrimination in the classroom, see J. Murphy, "Race, Education and Intellectual Prejudice," in F. Macleod (ed.) *Parents and Schools: the Contemporary Challenge* (1989) 31.
[54] Lord Elton *op. cit.*, and at R. 91 p. 159.
[55] E(No. 2)A 1986, s.23. See DES Circular 7/87 paras. 5.12.6–5.12.18.
[56] EA 1993, s.261 and Sched. 19, para. 96. Regarding the former power of indefinite exclusion, the Minister said that it had led to some pupils ending up in "educational limbo": H.L., Debs, Vol. 547, col. 173 (June 21, 1993) *per* Baroness Blatch.
[57] See E(No. 2)A 1986, ss.24 and 25. Reinstatement can, depending on the circumstances, be ordered by the governing body or LEA. Time limits may be prescribed for the procedural stages: EA 1993, Sched. 19, para. 99.
[58] Council on Tribunals, *Annual Report 1991–92* (1992) para. 1.28.
[59] E(No. 2)A 1986, s.27(5).
[60] Council on Tribunals, *Education Appeals Code of Practice on Procedure* (1992) para. 19(b).
[61] See *The Times*, December 1, 1992.

found a 60 per cent. increase over the previous two years, which was attributed largely to the competitive pressures on schools;[62] these were leading to extra sensitivity about truancy and misbehaviour and increasing resort to exclusion as a means of removing disruptive children, who take up a good deal of staff time.[63] Violence by pupils is reported to have grown significantly in scale and severity of late,[64] and the increased resort to exclusion may also be a response to that.

OFSTED regards the number of exclusions at present as excessive and recommends financial disincentives for schools which exclude too readily.[65] A large increase in the number of permanent exclusions, from 2,910 in 1990–91 to 3,833 in 1991–92, has prompted the Government to back OFSTED's recommendation.[66] Another problem has been delay in finding places for excluded children at other schools. The DFE has argued that "where pupils are excluded . . . the aim should be to return them to mainstream education at the earliest opportunity";[67] the EA 1993 aims to tackle this problem by enabling schools to be ordered to admit excluded pupils and by requiring that LEAs make alternative provision at school or otherwise for excluded pupils.[68]

The right of appeal in exclusions cases has had little impact on the rising tide of exclusions. The National Exclusion Reporting System, introduced after the Elton Report, found that in 1990–91 there were only 205 cases (out of nearly 3,000 (see above)) where a permanently excluded pupil had been reinstated and only 14 successful appeals out of 92 appeals in all.[69]

So far as other remedies are concerned, in cases of unlawful chastisement giving rise to trespass to the person, damages may be recoverable in tort. But the cases show that it can be difficult to establish that punishment was excessive and thus unlawful.[70] Moreover,

---

[62] As noted in Chap. 5, research has shown that a school's disciplinary record can be a factor in parental choice of school.

[63] *Panorama*, March 15, 1993.

[64] See *The Times* January 9, 1993. Violence towards staff is part of the problem. In one study there were found to be over 500 physical attacks on teachers in London in one year: B. Poyner and C. Warne, *Preventing Violence to Staff* (1988). In March 1993 it was reported that an attempted rape of a teacher by a 13 year pupil had occurred at school: *The Times*, March 25, 1993.

[65] See OFSTED, *Exclusions: a response to the DFE discussion paper* (1993) p. 3.

[66] "Schools to be fined £2,000 for every pupil they expel," *The Times*, April 24, 1993. What the EA 1993 in fact provides is that of the annual resources provided to a school for the education of a child, the remaining amount as at the date the child is permanently excluded shall in effect be transferred to the new provider: s.262.

[67] *Supra* (n.51), para. 44.

[68] EA 1993, ss.13 and 298.

[69] *Ibid.*

[70] See, *e.g.*, *Ryan* v. *Fildes* (*supra*, n.44). In *Warwick* v. *U.K.* ((1986) A9471/81) the European Commission on Human Rights considered a claim for breach of Article 3 of

—*cont. on next page*

unjust exclusion from school gives rise neither to tortious liability, nor public law liability, in the case of an independent school.[71] In the case of a state school, public law remedies may be available, for example for breach of natural justice by a governing body when confirming the exclusion of a pupil.[72] In *R* v. *Board of Governors of Stoke Newington School ex p. M*[73] the Divisional Court held that there had been a breach of natural justice in a case where the governing body's panel, which decided not to reinstate a pupil, included, as a teacher governor, the pupil's head of year. In that capacity, the teacher had had responsibility for the girl concerned. Damages have been recommended or paid via settlement in cases before the European Court of Human Rights concerning corporal punishment.[74] Damages have also been awarded in respect of maladministration in the conduct of an exclusion appeal[75] and arising out of undue delay in securing the admission of an excluded child to another school.[76]

---

[70]—cont. *from previous page*

the European Convention on Human Rights by a girl who, at the age of 16, had been caned on one hand and badly bruised as a result. She had failed in a civil action for assault in England. In *Costello-Roberts* v. *U.K.* (1993) *The Times*, March 26, the Court of Human Rights rejected an argument that such difficulty before the English courts meant that the applicant was without an effective remedy under domestic law, contrary to Article 13 of the Convention. (See also *Y.* v. *U.K.* (1992) Series A No. 247–A.)

[71] *R* v. *Headmaster of Fernhill Manor School and Another ex p. Angela S. Brown* (1992) *The Times*, June 5, 1992. Brooke J. said *obiter* that the only remedy available to the parents would lie in private law for a breach of private law rights under the parent's contract with the school. Brooke J. drew analogy with the post-*Roffey* (*R* v. *Aston University Senate ex parte Roffey* [1969] 2 W.L.R. 1418) university cases which suggest that the contractual basis to the relationship between student and university generally renders inapplicable the court's public law jurisdiction. However, His Honour may have over-simplified the position vis à vis the universities: see M. H. Whincup, "The exercise of university disciplinary powers" (1993) 5(1) *Education and the Law* 19.

[72] *R* v. *Board of Governors of London Oratory School ex p. R* (1988) *The Times*, February 17, *per* McCullough J.

[73] (1992) Lexis CO/1753/91.

[74] The families bringing the *Campbell and Cosans* case (*op. cit.*) were awarded a combined total of £12,000 damages. In another settlement (in 1982), the European Commission on Human Rights agreed that a caned 14 year old should receive £1,200 plus £1,000 legal costs: *The Times*, February 27, 1982. Recently, in a similar case, the Government agreed to an £8,000 settlement, plus £12,000 legal costs, in a case before the Eurpean Court of Human Rights: *The Times*, November 14, 1992. This was despite the applicant's failure in a county court action against the head teacher of the private school in question in 1984.

[75] *Report of an Investigation by the Local Government Ombudsman into Complaint 90/C/2287 Against Rotherham Metropolitan Borough Council* (1992); the award was of £250 in respect of the failure by the LEA to specify the reasons for the exclusion in sufficient detail.

[76] *Report of an Investigation by the Local Government Ombudsman into Complaint No. 88/A/0709* (1990) (I.L.E.A.); see also *Reports ... 89/C/1507* (1991) (Sheffield City Council), *89/A/2176* (1992) (I.L.E.A.) and *90/A/2257* (Kent C.C.), where the complaint concerned the inadequate arrangements made for the education of an excluded child.

(c)　Choice within the secular curriculum

i.　*Choice and the National Curriculum*

The National Curriculum imposes severe constraints on teachers' scope for coverage of subjects outside it;[77] and the degree of regulation surrounding it also results in little scope to respond to parental choice. As discussed above, there is a stark contrast between the general policy of parental choice in education, which is centred on school selection, and choice of what is studied at school. Apart from the choices that exist at key stage 4, when GCSE subjects are selected (and even here there is less choice as a result of the integrated science and humanities syllabuses taught in some schools), the secular curriculum is tied to the National Curriculum attainment targets.

There are, at present, moves towards greater flexibility,[78] which will give more choice to teachers but not necessarily to parents. Individual parents have traditionally had little scope for insisting on replacement lessons in respect of the secular curriculum.[79] Naturally, the logistics of curriculum organisation and the duty to fulfil the requirements of the National Curriculum have made it even more difficult for schools to accommodate parental choice in this way. For example, members of some religious sects will not permit their children to use computers; schools are asked to make alternative provision. But the use of computers is a legal requirement under the National Curriculum. In cases such as this, the European Convention on Human Rights warrants consideration. As discussed earlier, parents' religious and philosophical convictions have to be recognised in the educational context. Nevertheless, in the light of the *Kjeldsen* case[80] the Court might take the view that computing skills are essential to modern society

---

[77] For example, a survey by the Joint Association of Classical Teachers has revealed that teaching of classics in state schools has been squeezed by the National Curriculum and that many schools regard the classics as having little future in the state sector: *The Times*, March 20, 1993.

[78] See "Advisers admit curriculum fails to provide broad education" *The Times*, January 19, 1993, and "Curriculum rethink puts brake on the pace of changes" *The Times*, August 3, 1993, reporting on the interim recommendations of the Dearing review, which include a reduction in compulsory content especially at ages 14–16. The 1987 Consultation Document promised teachers "sufficient flexibility in the choice of content to adapt what they teach to the needs of the individual pupil": DES/Welsh Office, *The National Curriculum 5–16* (1987) para. 27. But the DES' guidance on the school curriculum post-ERA 1988 emphasised that "teachers and schools will not be free to pick and choose ... teachers should know what is expected of them": DES, *National Curriculum: From Policy to Practice* (1989), para. 10.2.

[79] *Cf* M. M. Wells and P.S. Taylor, *The New Law of Education* (4th edn. 1954) p. 197, who suggest that s.76 of the EA 1944 (children to be educated "in accordance with the wishes of their parents") has "special significance" as regards the secular curriculum. But in relation to requests by parents that their children be withdrawn from National Curriculum tests, the DFE's policy guidance correctly states that s.76 "does not impose an absolute duty to educate children exclusively according to the wishes of parents" — see p. 222 below.

[80] (1976) 1 EHRR 711, see p. 194 *supra*.

and that teaching them in schools is necessary in the national interest. There is, however, some limited scope for excepting a child from all or part of the National Curriculum, in which case alternative provision would be made. But such exception is intended to be almost exclusively at the instigation of the teacher or head teacher rather than the parent.[81]

If alternative provision is not feasible, parents may simply wish to exclude their child from a lesson or a subject as a whole. As we saw earlier, similar issues have arisen in other states. In one case in the Netherlands, parents with fundamentalist Christian views wanted their daughter excepted from swimming and gym lessons because they did not want her to be seen in a swimming costume by others.[82]

ii. *Sex education*

One of the most controversial areas of the school curriculum in England and Wales has been sex education. Until the EA 1993 it was not altogether clear whether schools were legally obliged to offer sex education. The fact that the governors were given a power to decide whether sex education should form part of the secular curriculum[83] suggested not. But on the other hand, under the ERA 1988 the curriculum must, as noted earlier, prepare pupils for the "experiences of adult life."[84] Moreover, the National Curriculum attainment targets for science have referred specifically to human reproduction.[85] The need to

---

[81] ERA 1988, ss.17–19. Section 17 permits the Secretary of State to prescribe cases or circumstances where the National Curriculum shall not apply. This power has been used as follows: in the case of Welsh and English teaching in Wales (Education (National Curriculum) (Exceptions) (Wales) Regulations 1989 SI No. 1308 and 1990 SI 1990 No. 2187); to permit departure by schools from offering separate humanities and science subjects for GCSE (Education (National Curriculum) (Exceptions in . . . at Key Stage 4) Regulations 1992 SI 1992 No. 156 (history and geography) and No. 157 (science)); and to disapply a National Curriculum subject where a pupil has taken the examination a year early (the Education (National Curriculum) (Exceptions) Regulations 1992 SI 1992 No. 155). Section 18 permits exception in the case of a pupil for whom a statement of special educational needs has been issued. Section 19 empowers regulations to specify further exceptions. The Education (National Curriculum) (Temporary Exceptions for Individual Pupils) Regulations 1989 SI 1989 No. 1181 enable the head to direct that a child should be excepted from all or part of the National Curriculum if it would be inappropriate for him or her to follow it over the next six months or where the child's special educational needs are being assessed. A new section (ERA 1988, s.17A) added by the EA 1993, s.241(3), provides parents with a right to withdraw their child from most sex education at the school.

[82] But the court said that the school's decision to exclude the child from the private school in question was lawful: Case *Hof Den Bosch* September 5, 1989, KG 1989, 394.

[83] E(No. 2)A 1986, s.18(2) which, following the EA 1993, now applies only to primary schools.

[84] ERA 1988, s.1(2)(*b*).

[85] Science attainment target 3: Processes of Life — level 6: "Pupils should . . . know about the physical and emotional changes that take place during adolescence, and understand the need to have a responsible attitude to sexual behaviour . . . understand the processes of conception in human beings."

warn pupils of the dangers of sexually-transmitted diseases has obviously
been too great for schools to ignore. Given the fact that many schools
have been failing to provide proper sex education,[86] further legislation
on this subject was desirable. The EA 1993 (section 241) has made sex
education part of the "basic curriculum" that maintained secondary
schools must provide and has for the first time provided a definition of
it in law ("sex education" includes education about (a) [AIDS] and
[HIV], and (b) any other sexually transmitted disease"). At the same
time, sex education (other than "biological aspects" of human sexual
behaviour) will be removed from the National Curriculum, as noted
earlier (above p. 204 note 70).

Although the law now requires that sex education be given "with due
regard to moral considerations and the value of family life,"[87] there are
still some parents who prefer that their children should not receive sex
education at school, usually on religious grounds. In one case, parents
who were members of a religious sect brought a formal complaint under
section 23 of the ERA 1988 (see below) against a governing body's
policy of compulsory sex education. The governing body was
recommended (by the LEA's complaints panel), and agreed, to show a
little more flexibility and permit withdrawal from any specific aspects of
sex education that were of particular concern to parents.[88]

But the Government's guidance that schools should be sensitive to
parents' wishes and acknowledge that parents may have reservations
about sex education because of their religious or philosophical views,
may conflict with the boarder principle of the paramountcy of the
welfare of the child, reflected in the Children Act 1989 and the U.N.
Convention on the Rights of the Child (above). Furthermore, under this
principle, the views of the child concerned should be taken into
account,[89] although the danger of damaging parent-child relationships
in the process would have to be considered. In the complaint about sex
education referred to above, the girl concerned was aged 14, but there
had been no attempt to elicit her view. The courts have recently
emphasised the importance which should be attached to the views of
children in the 11–14 age group on matters of choice of school and
religion,[90] and this principle surely extends to sex education as well. It

---

[86] Sex Education Forum, *A Inquiry into Sex Education* (1992).

[87] E(No. 2)A 1986, s.46.

[88] Reported in N. Harris, *Complaints About Schooling: The role of section 23 of the Education Reform Act 1988* (1992) National Consumer Council pp. 87–91. A similar complaint is referred to in J. Robinson, "Back to School and a White Paper" (1992) N.L.J. 1190 at 1191.

[89] As provided for by s.1(3) of the Children Act 1989 and Article 12 of the UN Convention on the Rights of the Child.

[90] *Re P (A Minor) (Education)* [1992] 1 F.L.R. 316, *Re S* [1992] 2 F.L.R. 313 and *M v. M (Minors) (Jurisdiction)* (1993) Fam.Law. 396, see p. 22 *supra*.

is clear that young people often have strong views on sex education. Evidence suggests that they are generally dissatisfied with the quality of sex education given at school.[91]

The Government's 1987 circular on sex education links that subject to homosexuality, by advising that "there is no place in any school in any circumstances for teaching which advocates homosexual behaviour as the 'norm', or which encourages homosexual experimentation by pupils." The notorious clause 28 (now s.2A of the Local Government Act 1986) prohibits *inter alia*, the promotion by local authorities of the teaching, in any school, of homosexuality as a "pretended family relationship." This is one of the most value-laden provisions to be passed into law in recent years; for one thing, it implies that a homosexual person is not capable of sustaining a true familial relationship. It has been suggested that this provision was introduced to prevent the use of books like *Jenny Lives with Eric and Martin*, which portrays a girl living with her father and his male sexual partner;[92] its adoption by the ILEA was highly controversial.

iii. *Testing*

Another controversial area has been the testing of pupils under the SATs — the "standard assessment tasks" — which take place at or near the end of each key stage. As indicated above, the Secretary of State prescribes assessment arrangements by order. In some cases parental and teacher pressure has resulted in modification of the tests: for example, testing at the end of key stage 2 was restricted to the three core subjects, and the tests at the end of key stage 1 were simplified.[93] Legal action arising out of parental dissatisfaction with the tests for seven year olds was only narrowly averted. (There was, however, also a report that over 20 per cent. of parents wrongly thought that their child had not been tested or were unsure whether s/he had been.[94]) In one case in Leeds, a child had been kept away from school by his parents who refused to allow him to participate in the tests. The parents, who said that it was "an issue of parental choice,"[95] objected to the tests because they regarded them a taking up a disproportionate amount of time (some five weeks) and displacing other, more beneficial, classroom activities. After the child's exclusion, a petition was signed by a large number of parents at the school calling for the tests to be suspended. At

---

[91] See "A sexual timebomb" *The Guardian*, June 9, 1992.

[92] M. R. T. Macnair, "Homosexuality in schools — Section 28 Local Government Act 1988" (1989) 1(1) *Education and the Law* 35–39.

[93] One recent criticism of the key stage 1 tests for seven year olds is that they have proved unfair to bilingual children because of the complex language used and the particular cultural context to some of the questions: see *T.E.S.*, May 29, 1992.

[94] *The Independent*, August 14, 1991, reporting research by the University of Exeter.

[95] *The Independent*, April 19, 1991.

the same time, a mother in Devon managed to persuade her LEA that the school could exempt her son from the tests under the Temporary Exceptions regulations.[96] At another school, in Cardiff, the head teacher suspended the tests due to fears that substantial numbers of parents would keep their children away from school.[97] The head teacher's view was that the law was ambiguous, because the EA 1944 (section 76) required parental wishes to be taken into account. These cases prompted the DES (as it then was) to issue guidance.[98] The Department's view, which appears correct, was that the section 76 duty is overridden by the requirement in section 10 of the ERA 1988 to apply to National Curriculum in full, save in the specific circumstances were exception is possible.[99] The guidance suggests that the wishes of a parent seeking exemption for a child for whom the tests might prove unduly stressful should only be granted it where the child might suffer harm. This is consistent with the Department's circular on National Curriculum assessment, which emphasises that temporary exception should be considered only in rare exceptional cases, such as where a child has been suffering severe emotional problems.[1] However, the legislation gives so much discretion to the head teacher that unless or until this matter is tested in the courts the appropriateness of the Departmental guidance cannot be ascertained.

iv.   *Charges for optional extras*

With the introduction, in the state sector, of defined statutory curricular provision, it has become possible to make a legal distinction between such provision, which must be provided without charge to pupils, and "optional extras" in respect of which a "regulated charge" may be made.[2] Optional extras include music tuition (for a pupil or groups of up to four pupils) and fees for entry for examinations for which a pupil has not been prepared by the school. Parents can also be charged for the cost of materials used in school work which the parent wishes to keep or wishes his/her child to have.[3] In general, no charge

---

[96] See *The Observer*, April 21, 1991.

[97] *The Times*, April 29, 1991.

[98] A copy was kindly supplied to the author by P. Liell, solicitor.

[99] See ERA 1988, ss.17–19, *op. cit.* See also *supra* (n.79).

[1] See DES Circular 14/91 (1991) para. 6. The guidance suggests that if the parents indicate within a reasonable time (seven days) an intention to appeal it would be unreasonable to administer the tests until the appeal has been decided. The appeal lies to the governing body in the first instance: ERA 1988 s.19(7).

[2] "A regulated charge shall not exceed the cost of the provision of the optional extra": ERA 1988, s.109(5). The general restriction is contained in s.106(2). See also DES Circular 2/89 *Charges for School Activities*. For a table showing in full the provision that may or may not be charged for, see N. Harris *et al.*, *The Legal Context of Teaching* (1992) pp. 132–134.

[3] ERA 1988, s.118(3).

can be made for any education provided for registered pupils during school hours, including provision relating to an examination for which a school is preparing a pupil.[4] Charges may be made for provision on school trips where more than half of the time away occurs outside school hours or, in the case of board and lodging, where at least one night is spent away from home.[5] If the parents are in receipt of income support or family credit, however, the charge for board and lodging on a residential trip must be remitted in full.[6]

Although most provision, and any transport incidental to it, will have to be provided free, parents may be invited to make *voluntary* contributions.[7] Any such invitation must make it clear to parents that they have a choice over contributing and that their children will not be treated differently in relation to such provision.[8] Thus if there were insufficient contributions to finance the activity it would have to be cancelled rather than provided only to those pupils whose parents had paid a contribution. Permitted charges may not be made until the LEA and/or governors have prepared a statement of charging policy and policy on remission of charges.[9] Competition between schools may encourage some head teachers and governors to see the provision of optional extras as increasing their school's market appeal, and they will have the incentive of being able to cover their costs.[10]

v. *Examination entry*

Examination entry is another subject of particular concern to parents. Although the law requires schools to enter pupils for examinations for which they have been prepared by the school, this general rule can be overridden.[11] The governing body can refuse entry to the examination if there is an "educational" reason for doing so. Such a decision would be difficult to challenge, although a complaint could be pursued under the local curriculum complaints procedure and, thereafter, taken to the Secretary of State via sections 68 or 99 of the EA 1944 (see below). Parents themselves can block their child's examination entry via a written request. This right highlights the private-public dichotomy in the law in this field, in the sense that the public interest may well

---

[4] *Ibid.* s.106(2) and (4). If the pupil fails "without good reason" (this does not include simple failure on academic grounds) to meet any examination requirement the examination fee can be recovered from the parent: s.108(1) and (2).
[5] ERA 1988, ss.106(9) and (10) and 107(3).
[6] ERA 1988, s.110(3).
[7] ERA 1988, s.118(1).
[8] s.118(2).
[9] s.110(2). The creation of the policy is mandatory: s.110(1).
[10] The relevant costs comprise teaching and non-teaching staff costs and the cost of providing materials, books, instruments or other equipment: s.109(6)–(8).
[11] ERA 1988, s.117(1) and (2).

demand that a pupil should sit the examination if there is a chance s/he will thereby obtain a qualification. Furthermore, it ignores the child's interest in taking the examination. A concerned party, including the child him/herself, may however be able to obtain a specific issue order on this matter under the Children Act 1989.

Choice under the secular curriculum also has important gender and racial dimensions. These are considered in sections (d) and (e) below.

(d) Choice and gender

The treatment of gender in schools forms an important element in the "affective" or "hidden" curriculum which is so central to the socialising role of schools, as noted above. The success of the education system in inculcating values which are supportive of gender equality may be limited by a number of factors. Perhaps the principal one is home influence. As Anderson notes, "unless the home reinforces the school's notions of gender equality, children . . . are likely to grow up with many of the old stereotyped views and expectations, whatever the ethos and practices of the school."[12] A further factor is said to be the continuing domination of men in senior positions in schools and in teaching subjects in which girls have traditionally been unrepresented at GCSE and A level, such as physics, mathematics and craft, design and technology.[13] These are said to lead to lower expectations of girls than boys by teachers, especially in these subjects, and to reinforcement of traditional notions of the "passivity" of women and "assertiveness" of males.[14] In fact, male and female teachers alike can sometimes be guilty of covert discrimination.[15]

The law, in the form of the SDA 1975, provides the basis for formal equality. The Act proscribes sex discrimination, and provides remedies,[16] not only in relation to admission to school, but also in relation to access to the "benefits, facilities and services" provided and in the context of discipline, including exclusion from school (see

---

[12] B. Anderson, "The Gender Dimension of Home-School Relations," in F. Macleod (ed.) *Parents and Schools: the Contemporary Challenge* (1989) at p. 55.

[13] *Ibid.*

[14] D. Milman and K. de Gama, "Sexual Discrimination in Education: One Step Forward, Two Steps Back?" (1989) *Journal of Social Welfare Law* at pp. 8 and 20.

[15] S. Miles and C. Middleton, "Girls' Education in the Balance: the ERA and Inequality," in M. Flude and M. Hammer *The Education Reform Act 1988: Its Origins and Implications* (1990) at pp. 191–192.

[16] The Equal Opportunities Commission can investigate and issue recommendations or a non-discrimination notice (ss.57, 60 and 67). Alternatively, a complainant may pursue a claim (under ss.22 and 23) for damages in the county court, where High Court remedies are available: ss.62 and 66. A complaint may also be made to the Secretary of State under ss.68 or 99 of the EA 1944.

above).[17] In one case, the Equal Opportunities Commission informed a North Wales comprehensive school that it had been in breach of the Act by sending a boy home from school for wearing an ear-stud, as girls had not been disciplined in such circumstances. In another case, threatened legal action by boys at a comprehensive school in Dorset, who were excluded from school for wearing earrings, resulted in a climb-down by the head teacher and governors following legal advice.[18] In one Bromley school it was not possible for an entire class to move up a year, and a small number of pupils were selected to remain behind in their present year. All those selected were girls. This decision was declared illegal by the county court.[19]

It is clear that girls and boys should have equality of access to all subjects. There was, therefore, unlawful discrimination by one LEA in relation to the restricted opportunities in its schools for girls to take craft design and technology and for boys to take home economics.[20] However, separate facilities for boys and girls would not constitute a breach of the Act, provided those facilities were equal.

Duties under the Act rest with the LEA or governing body, or the proprietor of an independent school, as the "responsible body."[21] There is also a general duty on LEAs to secure that there is no sex discrimination in relation to the facilities provided by them.[22]

There are reasons to believe that the introduction of the National Curriculum under the ERA 1988 might help to promote gender equality in the field of education. First, subjects not traditionally studied by girls, such as mathematics and science, will be compulsory to age 16, ensuring considerably increased female participation.[23] Secondly, it is argued that the system of attainment targets and testing will encourage schools to treat girls on an equal footing to boys and, given that results may be published, to aim for higher levels of attainment among *all* pupils.[24] However, it is also argued that the

---

[17] SDA 1975, ss.22 and 23.

[18] *The Times*, January 9, 1993. The LEA commented that in future girls might have to be allowed to wear trousers and boys permitted shoulder length hair.

[19] *Debell, Sevket and Teh* v. *London Borough of Bromley* (Bromley County Court, 12 November 1984), reported in Liell and Saunders, *Law of Education* (9th edn.), F31.

[20] Equal Opportunities Commission, *Formal Investigation Report West Glamorgan Schools* (1988).

[21] *Ibid.* s.22, as amended.

[22] *Ibid.* s.25; see *Equal Opportunities Commission* v. *Birmingham City Council* [1989] 1 All E.R. 769, discussed at *supra* p. 119.

[23] It is argued that this could help women in the labour market in relation to employments where qualifications or subjects traditionally taken mostly by boys are favoured: A. Morris and S. Nott, *Working Women and the Law* (1991) pp. 71 and 209 n.4.

[24] Miles and Middleton, *op. cit.*, pp. 191–192.

trend towards a reduced role for LEAs and greater school autonomy will undermine the efforts made by local authorities to promote gender equality in schools, although the School Curriculum Assessment Council and OFSTED may be able to pursue equality initiatives which compensate for this to some extent. It is also argued that unless the structural factors which reinforce gender inequality in the classroom are tackled, genuine equality of opportunity will not arise.[25]

(e) Choice, race and religion

The 1976 Race Relations Act's protection is confined to groups whose historical development, distinct traditions and geographical origins mark them out as an ethnic as opposed to a religious group.[26] But issues of race and religion are often inextricably linked, as in the question of voluntary aided status for Muslim or Jewish schools, discussed in Chapter 4, and in the law governing collective worship and religious education in state schools. The question of the right to wear religious insignia or ethnic or religious dress in school highlights further the inter-relationship between race and religion in this field.

There is an apparent contradiction in the presence of religious education and, more especially, collective worship, in state schools in a secular state, although most parents seem to want it.[26a] However, once it is decided that they should be present, the question of how to accommodate freedom of expression of all religions in a multi-cultural society arises.[27] The approach in the United States has been to prohibit inculcation of all religious values in the schools system, under the Establishment Clause of the First Amendment to the Constitution. Cases have established that, for example, there is a violation of the Constitution if Bible readings (other than those occurring for the purposes of objective secular instruction) or recitation of the Lord's prayer are permitted.[28] In *Abingdon School District v. Schempp*,[29] a religious service in a school was unconstitutional despite the establishment of a parental right of withdrawal from it. Providing for a period of meditation and voluntary prayer has also been held to be unconstitutional.[30]

---

[25] *Ibid.*

[26] *Mandla* v. *Dowell Lee* [1983] 1 All E.R. 1062; *C.R.E.* v. *Dutton* (1989) I.R.L.R. 8; and *The Crown Suppliers (PSA)* v. *Dawkins* (1993) *The Times*, February 4 (C.A.).

[26a] 70 per cent. of parents, according to one survey: *The Independent* Sept. 6, 1993.

[27] For interesting discussion of how this question has been addressed and resolved by the *Conseil d'Etat* in France, see J. Bell, "Religious observance in secular schools: a French solution" (1990) 2(3) *Education and the Law* 121.

[28] *Engel* v. *Vitale* 370 U.S. 421 (1962); *Abingdon School District* v. *Schempp* 374 U.S. 203 (1963).

[29] *Supra.*

[30] *Wallace* v. *Jaffree* 105 S. Ct. 2479 (1985). See B. Levin, "The United States of America" in I. K. Birch and I. Richter (eds.) *School Law* (1990) at p. 25.

In England and Wales, a dual system of voluntary (denominational) schools and county schools was established under the EA 1944. But, as noted earlier, provision for religious education and collective worship in *all* state schools continued under this legislation. The question of parental choice and the content of these religious elements of schooling has become important in our increasingly multi-cultural society (or at least a pluralistic society, in which all ethnic groups may claim to have an equal stake in the education system, even if the voice of minority groups is often largely ignored[31]). Limited rights of choice have long been available. Parents were given the right to withdraw their children from religious instruction and/or collective worship in schools under the Elementary Education Act 1870.[32] This right was preserved under the EA 1944 and may now be found in the ERA 1988, which also continues the right of a parent to cause the child to receive RE away from school premises.[33] In one research study it was discovered that 14 per cent. of parents with children at county schools and 22 per cent. with children at denominational schools were unaware of the right of withdrawal.[34] It cannot be a condition of entry to a maintained school that a child attends, or refrains from attending, any Sunday school or place of worship.[35] Teachers also have a right to refuse to participate in collective worship.[36]

Although the law continues to require that religious education should be non-denominational (it must not be given "by means of any catechism or formulary which is distinctive of any religious denomination"[37]), section 8(3) of the ERA 1988 provides that all religious syllabuses must "reflect the fact that the religious traditions in Great Britain are in the main Christian whilst taking account of the teaching and practices of other principal religions represented in Great Britain." This provision has attracted the criticism that it serves to marginalise non-Christian religious/ethnic groups in society.[38] It is rather curious to find a statutory provision that seeks to justify itself by reference to facts ("the religious traditions in Great Britain are in the main Christian"). Poulter suggests that parity between religions, which would leave Christianity with perhaps only one-sixth of the RE syllabus, might not

---

[31] On the meaning of "multi-cultural society" and its relevance to the education system, see E. Hulmes, *Education and Cultural Diversity* (1989) pp. 12–18.

[32] s.7(1) and (2).

[33] ERA 1988, s.9(3) and (4).

[34] Public Attitude Surveys Ltd., *Parental Awareness of School Education April–July 1989* (1989) Table 50, p. 27.

[35] ERA 1988, s.9(1).

[36] EA 1944, s.30 and EA 1993 ss.143–145.

[37] EA 1944, s.26(1).

[38] See J. Hardy and C. Vieler-Porter, "Race, Schooling and the 1988 Education Reform Act," in M. Flude and M. Hammer *op. cit.* at pp. 173–185.

have been the most realistic formula and that in any event there will be room for differences between local syllabuses.[39] The National Curriculum Council regarded the law as requiring that more than 50 per cent. of the content of the agreed syllabus should be devoted to Christianity but reported that very few local syllabuses showed the balance between religions or gave great prominence to Christianity.[40] Local syllabuses reflected the concern during the 1980s to develop syllabuses that promoted the concept of multi-cultural education through religious neutrality. Since the enactment of the 1988 Act, such syllabuses have come under attack, with in some cases threatened legal action by parents demanding compliance with the law giving pre-eminence to Christianity. At the same time, many teachers and head teachers have condemned the disunity which they consider the legislation is producing and which they have been striving to prevent.[41]

Even more controversial than the law on RE has been the requirement, resulting from a House of Lords amendment proposed by Baroness Cox, that collective worship at county schools "shall be wholly or mainly of a broadly Christian character," which means it must "reflect the broad traditions of Christian belief," whilst remaining non-denominational.[42] This requirement applies to "most" acts of collective worship, which has been interpreted as meaning that only 51 per cent. of acts have to be of a Christian character.[43] It has been suggested that this, plus the fact that acts have to be only "broadly" Christian, gives plenty of scope for the continuation of the widespread practice of multi-faith school assemblies.[44] Furthermore, the 1988 Act gives a school the right to apply to the SACRE for modification or lifting of the requirement as to Christian collective worship if it considers this desirable in the light of the pupils' ages, aptitude, family backgrounds and other factors.[45] Although there have been complaints from ethnic minority groups about the pre-eminence given to Christianity, the right given to schools to apply to the SACRE can result in changes. For example, if more than 50 per cent. of pupils are Muslims, the SACRE could agree to predominantly Muslim collective worship.[46]

---

[39] S. Poulter, "The religious education provisions of the Education Reform Act 1988" (1990) 2(1) Education and the Law 1.
[40] See *The Independent*, March 11, 1993.
[41] See "Heads fear religious strife in schools" *The Guardian*, February 28, 1989.
[42] ERA 1988, s.7(1)–(3). See DES Circular 3/89 *The Education Reform Act 1988: Religious Education and Collective Worship* (1989).
[43] S. Poulter (1990) *op. cit* p. 5.
[44] *Ibid.*
[45] See ERA 1988, ss.7(4) and (5) and 12(1). As at April 1993, 253 county schools had had determinations granted under s.12(1): H.L. Debs, Vol. 545, col. 328 (April 27, 1993).
[46] See *T.E.S.* October 4, 1991. See also S. Poulter, *Asian Traditions and English Law* (1990) p. 85.

The continuing multi-culturalist policy towards the curriculum by schools and LEAs in parts of the country with large ethnic minority populations has provoked a campaign by the Parental Alliance for Choice in Education (PACE) to ensure that Christian pupils can take part in truly "Christian" collective worship within the terms of the Act.[47] One such complaint occurred in relation to a middle school which claimed to be offering multi-faith collective worship that was nevertheless broadly Christian within the terms of the Act.[48] Only 34 per cent. of the pupils at the middle school came from a Christian family background. Of the rest, 41 per cent. were Muslim and 16 per cent. were Hindu. When the complaint was rejected at both stages of the local formal complaints procedure, the parents and PACE referred it to the Secretary of State, who found no illegality or unreasonableness. The DFE's statement explained that Secretary of State concluded that the pupils' family backgrounds did warrant the approach adopted by the school. It had also been complained that there was no worship *per se* but rather promotion of equal respect for all faiths and cultures. But the DFE's statement suggested that:

> "To constitute worship as normally defined in common English parlance, the courts would be likely to judge that collective worship in schools must in some sense reflect something special or separate from ordinary school activities; that it should be concerned with reverence or veneration being paid to a being or power regarded as supernatural or divine; and that the pupil, at his or her level, should be capable of perceiving this ... It follows that collective worship must be distinct from parts of an assembly as deal solely with secular matters, though an act of collective worship could be incorporated within assembly."

Again the school's practice conformed to this pattern. The lengths to which the DFE has had to go to explain its understanding of the law highlights the difficulty in interpreting it satisfactorily. No doubt the courts will be called upon to rule on the matter; judicial guidance would be welcome.

Any dis-unity resulting from widened religious divisions as a result of this legislation could be damaging to schools. But it seems likely that where such dis-unity is threatened schools may simply prefer to break the ERA 1988.[49] The law in this field has traditionally sought to

---

[47] See "Legal challenge on school worship likely," *Education* August 30, 1991. A further case, in Manchester, is reported in *Education*, August 14, 1992.

[48] This complaint is reported in detail in N. Harris, *Complaints About Schooling: The Role of Section 23 of the Education Reform Act 1988* (1992) pp. 94–97.

[49] See Poulter *op. cit.* p. 10.

promote racial and ethnic harmony, and it has been suggested that the above provisions of the ERA 1988 are in a sense a step backwards.[50] With signs that racial tension has been mounting in some schools in recent years, illustrated most graphically by the murder at one school in Manchester (see the MacDonald Report *Murder in the Playground* (1989)), it has become even more important to adopt an effective (but also sensitive) anti-racist approach. But as in the case of gender equality, the reduced role of LEAs may undermine anti-racism initiatives, often taken in furtherance of local authorities' broad duty to carry out their functions in a way that will promote racial harmony.[51] Nevertheless, schools have been encouraged to continue to promote racial harmony and equal opportunities through cross-curricular aspects of the "whole curriculum,"[52] and the Commission for Racial Equality issued a *Code of Practice for the Elimination of Racial Discrimination* in 1989, with a foreword by the Education Secretary.

The principal aspects of the curriculum relevant to the RRA 1976[53] are, with the exception of discipline (which was discussed above), the way that pupils are assessed and the type of provision offered. The CRE's Code warns against the use of racially discriminatory language by teachers or the adoption of different expectations for one racial group as opposed to another.[54] The greatest conflict is likely to occur over dress, although there have also been complaints about choice of language — either the medium in which subjects are taught[55] or the choice of modern language under the National Curriculum.[56] Indirect discrimination through enforcement of school rules on uniform or dress would only be lawful if "justifiable,"[57] for example on safety grounds. In *Mandla* v. *Dowell Lee*[58] the head teacher had excluded the pupil, a Sikh, because his parents insisted that the boy be allowed to wear a turban for school (which was contrary to the school rules on uniform and dress). The

---

[50] See W.H. Taylor, "Multi-cultural Education in the 'White Highlands' after the 1988 Education Reform Act" *New Community* 16(3) 369–378.

[51] RRA 1976, s.71.

[52] See DES, *National Curriculum: From Policy to Practice* (1989) para. 3.8.

[53] ss.17–19, which mirror ss.22, 23 and 25 of the SDA 1975 (*supra*).

[54] For example, see P. Foster, *Policy and Practice in Multicultural and Anti-Racist Education* (1990) p. 174.

[55] See S. Poulter, *English Law and Ethnic Minority Customs* (1986) p. 177. Following the *'Belgian Linguistics'* case *supra* (p. 194 n.13), it is doubtful that a complaint under the European Convention on Human Rights could be successful on this ground.

[56] A range of languages (including Arabic, Bengali, Gujerati, Hebrew, Hindi and Urdu) may be offered as foundation subjects provided one of the prescribed European languages is also available on the curriculum: Education (National Curriculum) (Modern Foreign Languages) Order 1989 SI 1989 No.825.

[57] RRA 1976, s.1(1)(*b*)(ii). See S. Poulter, *Asian Traditions and English Law* (1990) p. 91.

[58] [1983] 1 All E.R. 1062. See also p. 141 *supra*.

court was not convinced that the school's policy of seeking to down-play cultural differences in the interests of racial harmony justified the head teacher's decision. The court also confirmed that the action or decision would have to be justifiable irrespective of the child's race. In another dispute, resolved before the matter came to court, a school in Altrincham refused to permit two Muslim girls to wear head scarves, for religious reasons, at school. The ban was probably unlawful, but the school governors eventually agreed to the request on the condition that the scarves were in school's colour (navy blue).

Although conflict on matters of race, religion and parental choice has arisen on a number of occasions in recent years, there have been so far suprisingly few complaints under the RRA 1976 concerning the content of education, either by complainants themselves[59] or by the Commission for Racial Equality.[60]

(f) Special educational needs: participation and redress

i. *Introduction*

Children with special educational needs often face a difficult and uncertain future, and the education system has a vital role to play in maximising their potential. In this field, the involvement of parents in their children's education is accepted to be of considerable importance. Nevertheless, the opportunities for effective participation and redress have proved limited in practice, although the EA 1993 offers some important improvements. In general the focus is on the child and his or her needs and on parental responsibility in the promotion of the child's educational development.

But recently there has been a more consumerist tone. For example, the 1992 White Paper argued that "we must allow the mothers and fathers of children with special educational needs to play as full a part in the decisions about their child's education and to express preference for a particular special or ordinary school from within the maintained sector as any other parent."[61] The intention seems, in part, to be that parents of children with special educational needs should be able to join other parents as consumers within the education system. This is emphasised by the expressed commitment (now given legal effect under the EA 1993) "to provide clear and sensible avenues of appeal for parents who are not satisfied with the decisions made about their child" and to

---

[59] The complaint would lie to a designated county court under s.57 or, in the case of breach of s.19, to the Secretary of State.

[60] The C.R.E can carry out a formal investigation under s.48 and thereafter issue a non-discrimination notice under s.58 (apart from in s.19 cases).

[61] *Choice and Diversity*, para. 1.53.

enable special schools to control their own budgets and opt out of local authority control in common with other schools.[62]

The 1993 Act has consolidated and amended the law on special educational needs previously contained in the EA 1981.[63] The 1981 Act was intended to reverse the marginalisation of children with special educational needs in the education system. The Warnock Committee[64] estimated that many children, approximately one fifth of all school pupils, had learning difficulties of one sort or another. By seeking to replace the prevailing concepts of handicap and sub-normality with one of "learning difficulty," and by placing an emphasis on integration rather than segregation, the 1981 Act sought both to de-stigmatise special needs in the educational context and provide a basis for a coherent approach. Such coherence was sought to be achieved by establishing legally prescribed procedures in which special needs would be assessed and provided for. It was also to be achieved by emphasising a multi-professional basis for the assessment and amelioration of learning difficulties, a process continued under the Children Act 1989, which aims for a co-ordinated support network.[65] Deficiencies in inter-agency co-operation and co-ordination have remained a problem, however.[66]

A coherent approach also demands the involvement of parents in decisions concerning their child's education. As will be shown, the rights provided by the 1981 Act have proved inadequate in several respects, and efforts have been made, via the EA 1993, to strengthen them.

---

[62] *Ibid.* paras 1.15 and 9.7. Provision for special schools to become GM is to be made via regulations (see s.186). It is not clear from the 1993 Act whether a parental ballot will be required.

[63] This part of the chapter assumes that the EA 1993 is in force in place of (most of) the EA 1981. Changes made by the EA 1993 are noted at appropriate places. In fact, the framework in the EA 1981 may continue until September 1994, when the new appeals system is planned to come into operation.

[64] *Special Educational Needs* (1978) (Cmnd 7212).

[65] Note that the Children Act 1989 has required co-operation between education, social services and health authorities in assessing and meeting these children's needs; but the duty in s.27(4) of that Act has been replaced under the EA 1993 (s.166)—see n.66 below. The 1989 Act also makes provision for day care for children in need: see Children Act 1989, s.17. A social services department may assess a child's needs in conjunction with an assessment of the child's special educational needs: Children Act 1989, Sched. 2 para. 3.

[66] House of Commons, Education, Science and the Arts Committee, Session 1986/87 *Third Report, Special Educational Needs: Implementation of the Education Act 1981* Vol. 1 HC201–1 (1987). C. M. Lyon, *The Implications of the Children Act 1989 on Children and Young People with Severe Learning Difficulties* (1991) pp. 9–10. See also *Report by the Local Government Ombudsman, Complaint No. 91/A/2899* (May 24, 1993). Against L. B. Richmond upon Thames. To combat some of these difficulties the EA 1993 now imposes fresh duties of co-operation and empowers the stipulation of time limits within which help must be given to the LEA: EA 1993, s.166 (see also s.161(3)).

ii. *When does a child have special educational needs?*

The extensive litigation in this field is not surprising given the way that special educational needs and provision are defined in the legislation. A child has special educational needs if he has "a learning difficulty which calls for special educational provision to be made for him."[67] Learning difficulty is defined in sub-s.(2) in an imprecise and relativistic way. One form of learning difficulty is where a child "has a significantly greater difficulty in learning than the majority of children of his age."[68] Inevitably, there are wide variations in the way that LEAs apply this definition in practice. The second form of "learning difficulty" arises where a child "has a disability which either prevents or hinders him from making use of the educational facilities of a kind generally provided in schools, within the area of the [LEA] concerned, for children of his age."[69] Even here, there is considerable scope for interpretation. A child who is under the age of five, but who might be expected to fall within either of these definitions when he reaches that age, if special educational provision were not made for him, also has a learning difficulty.[70] "Special educational provision" is defined, in relation to a child aged two or over, as "educational provision which is additional to, or otherwise different from, the educational provision made generally for children of his age in schools maintained by the [LEA] concerned."[71] The combined effect of these provisions is that the question of whether or not a child has a special educational needs depends not so much on the child's specific needs considered in isolation, but rather on the appropriateness or otherwise of existing provision.

The Education Select Committee found that there were variations from one LEA to another in the extent of special educational needs and the provision in respect of them.[72] Such variation is not surprising in view of the wide scope for interpretation left by the statutory definitions. But at least some areas of uncertainty have been cleared up by the courts. In *R* v. *Hampshire County Council ex p. J*[73] a highly intelligent boy aged 13 and a half, J, suffered from dyslexia which affected his capacity for continuous reading, spelling and essay writing.

---

[67] EA 1993, s. 156(1).

[68] s. 156(2)(*a*).

[69] s. 156(2)(*b*).

[70] s. 156(2)(*c*).

[71] s. 156(4)(*a*).Note that any educational provision made for a child aged under two is special educational provision: s. 156(4)(*b*).

[72] *Supra* (n.66), para 24.

[73] (1985) 84 L.G.R. 547. For authoritative discussion of the treatment of dyslexia in the context of the 1981 Act, see H. Chasty and J. Friel, *Children with Special Needs: Assessment, Law and Practice* (1991).

He was depressed and frustrated by his inabilities. The LEA considered
that his difficulties did not preclude him from following "a normal
mainstream curriculum suited to pupils of his age" and proposed to
place him at a comprehensive school. His mother wanted the boy to
attend a named independent special school, as recommended by a
doctor. The LEA refused to make a grant to cover the cost of his
education at the school. Moreover, the authority decided that, in the
light of an assessment, J did not have a learning difficulty and his needs
were not such that it should determine the special educational provision
that should be made for him. But Taylor J. said he found that,
irrespective of J's intelligence, the boy's dyslexia "would appear to give
him significantly greater difficulty in learning than the majority of
children of his age." Taylor J. clearly considered that dyslexia could
constitute a "disability" for the purposes of the Act. Although the
dyslexia did not prevent J from making use of the educational facilities,
it clearly "hindered him."[74] The LEA had also argued that provision
made for a person who was dyslexic, such as a special unit, might not
amount to "special educational provision" if the provision was generally
available to children in the LEA's schools. But Taylor J. rejected this
interpretation.

The Select Committee reported that some combined health and
educational needs were not considered to be adequately catered for in
the definition of special educational needs in the 1981 Act. Speech
difficulty was cited as a specific example.[75] In *R v. Oxfordshire Education
Authority ex p. W*[76] the Divisional Court refused to find "irrational" a
decision by the LEA that speech therapy required by a nine year old boy
who was "severely speech impaired" was not special educational
provision. The Court (May L.J. and McCowan J.) accepted the LEA's
argument that the 1981 Act had been drafted with knowledge of the reorganisation of the health service in 1974, which unified speech therapy
services under the NHS. It was not until the Court of Appeal
considered this question in *R v. Lancashire County Council ex p. CM*[77]
that it became clear that a need for speech therapy is almost always
going to be a special educational need requiring special educational
provision (although this is still a matter to be considered by the LEA on
a case by case basis). The Court of Appeal harboured "grave doubts"
about whether *ex p. W* had been correctly decided. Even though speech
therapists were outside the LEA's direct employ, the authority was
nevertheless required to arrange for speech therapy services to be

---

[74] At p. 555.
[75] *Supra* (n.66), para 25.
[76] (1986) *The Times*, November 12.
[77] [1989] 2 F.L.R. 279.

administered to the child in question. However, in practice there are constraining factors, not least the shortage of speech therapists,[78] which may be a factor outside the control of the LEA.

The concept of "learning difficulty" has become well-established. It is now also found in the provisions governing the responsibilities of LEAs and the Further Education Funding Councils in the provision of further education.[79]

iii. *Where should the child be educated?*

There are now 20,000 fewer children with special educational needs being educated in special schools than ten years ago,[80] although there are marked inconsistencies between LEAs.[81] The overall reduction suggests that LEAs have generally complied with their duties concerning integration of children with special educational needs into the mainstream. A proposal for school league tables to show the numbers of pupils with special educational needs at each school was rejected because M.P.s felt that these pupils would be marginalised and that it would work against the concept of integration.[82] Since the 1981 Act was introduced in 1983 the principle of integration has increasingly been acted upon; but its practice remains contentious within the teaching profession and LEAs.

The principle of integration is built into the legislation in several ways. First, there is a general principle that provided certain conditions are met, a child with special educational needs must be educated in an ordinary school "unless that is incompatible with the wishes of the parent."[83] The relevant conditions are that educating the child in an ordinary school will be compatible with (a) his receiving the special provision that his learning difficulty calls for; (b) the provision of efficient education for the children with whom he shall be educated; and (c) the efficient use of resources.[84] Secondly, there is a duty to ensure, subject to the same conditions (a)–(c) above and provided it is reasonably practicable, that each child with special educational needs "engages in the activities of the school together with children who do not have special educational needs."[85] The general principle of

---

[78] House of Commons Education (Etc.) Committee *op. cit.* paras. 44 and 45.
[79] EA 1944 s.41(8)–(10), substituted by FHEA 1992 s.11; FHEA 1992 s.4.
[80] DES, *Education Statistics for the United Kingdom 1991* (1992) Table 17. Less than 1.5 per cent. of the school population attends special schools.
[81] Audit Commission/HMI, *Getting in on the Act — Provision for Pupils with Special Educational Needs — the National Picture* (1992) para. 56.
[82] Official Report, House of Commons Standing Committee F, cols. 421–433, January 14, 1992.
[83] EA 1993, s.160(1).
[84] s.161(2).
[85] s.161(4).

integration would seem to apply even where a child is excepted from the National Curriculum, or where the National Curriculum is modified in his or her case, under sections 18 or 19 of the ERA 1988.[86] This is reinforced by the Government's policy that all children, including those with special educational needs, should have the opportunity of benefiting from the National Curriculum — something on which schools seem to be making quite good progress.[87] The National Curriculum Council has emphasised that the duty, in ERA section 1(2), to provide a "balanced and broadly based curriculum" which promotes children's development and helps prepare them for adult life (see above), applies to *all* children.[88] It is the duty of the governing body of the school (or LEA in the case of a nursery school) to ensure that a child identified as having special educational needs receives appropriate provision.[89]

Parents of children with special educational needs often have very strong feelings over the question of which school will offer the best environment for their child. For example, research has shown that over one-third of parents with children at special schools want to change their child's school.[90] Parents may now express a preference for a school to be named in a special needs statement, and their request has to be complied with unless either the school is unsuitable having regard to the child's age, ability and aptitude, or the child's attendance at the school would not be compatible with the provision of efficient education for the other children or the efficient use of resources.[91] Requests are not handled in the same way as in general choice of school cases (see Chapter 5) but rather as part of the process of enabling parents to influence and challenge the content of statements, in which special educational provision is among the matters that has to be spelt out. There is a right of appeal to the newly created Special Educational Needs Tribunal, discussed below.[92]

For children with severe learning difficulties, it is often the case that an appropriate education will only be available in a highly specialised

---

[86] These relate to provision set out in statements of special educational needs (s.18) and temporary exception from all or part of the National Curriculum in the case of a child whose special educational needs are being assessed (s.19 and the Education (National Curriculum) (Temporary Exceptions for Individual Pupils) Regulations 1989 SI 1989 No. 1181): see above p. 219, n. 81. Many teachers are opposed to disapplication of the National Curriculum in the case of special needs pupils: National Curriculum Council, *Special Needs and The National Curriculum* (1993) p. 2.

[87] HMI, *National Curriculum and Special Needs* (1991).

[88] See National Curriculum Council, *A Curriculum for All* (1989).

[89] EA 1993, s.161(1)(a).

[90] Audit Commission/HMI *op. cit.* para. 63. Only 11 per cent. of parents with statemented children at ordinary schools wanted a different school.

[91] EA 1993, Sched. 10 para 3.

[92] *Ibid.* para. 8(3).

environment — at a maintained special school, or an independent school, as in *ex p. J* above, or *not* at a school. If an LEA considers that all or part of a child's education should be provided otherwise than at a school, it can, after consulting with the parent, make appropriate arrangements.[93] Moreover LEAs can also arrange for a child to be educated outside England and Wales.[94]

Disputes between parents and LEAs sometimes arise over the question of whether a child's needs can be met adequately in an ordinary school. If the parents consider that the child should be educated at an independent (perhaps residential school) at the LEA's expense they may face LEA opposition. This occurred in *R. v. Mid-Glamorgan County Council ex p. Greig*,[95] where the LEA had insisted that a boy with special educational needs due to mental disability could receive an appropriate education in an ordinary comprehensive school. His parents had wanted him to attend an independent boarding school. The fact that the parents' legal action was brought several years after the boy had started attending the comprehensive school did not improve their prospects, but the real difficulty lay in establishing that the LEA had acted *ultra vires*. Even though Simon Brown J. considered that "a very strong case for funded boarding education had in fact been made out," he concluded that it did not follow from this that the LEA's decision was to be regarded as *ultra vires*. Even if a residential school might have provided the best environment, this did not mean that the comprehensive school was unsuitable. (As Slade L.J. had said in an earlier special needs case, *R. v. Surrey County Council ex p. H*,[96] "there is no question of Parliament having placed the local authority under an obligation to provide such a Utopian system, or to educate [the child] to his or her maximum potential.") Moreover, no challenge founded on alleged irrationality could be sustained on the facts of the case. Finally, Simon Brown J. said that the court could not substitute its decision for that of the LEA. It is clear that the courts are in any event reluctant to interfere where a statute provides an avenue of redress, a view affirmed in *ex p. Greig*.[97] A similar basis for non-interference was identified by the High Court in respect of a wardship application by parents who wanted their child to remain at a comprehensive school rather than being sent by the LEA to a special school and sought to prevent his special educational needs from being assessed by the authority.[98]

---

[93] s.163.

[94] s.164. This provision, first introduced under the C.A. 1989, was known as the "Peto" clause because it enabled LEAs to pay for children to attend the Peto Institute in Hungary which provides conductive education for pupils with cerebral palsy.

[95] (1988) *The Independent*, June 1; CO/756/86 *Lexis*.

[96] (1985) 83 L.G.R. 219, at p. 235.

[97] See above p. 35 for discussion of this general principle.

[98] *Re D* (1988) 86 L.G.R. 442, *per* Woolf L.J. at p. 457. The court's approach was consistent with that adopted in several cases in the 1980s involving wardship

—*cont. on next page*

If an LEA decides that a child with special educational needs should be educated in an independent school, it has powers under section 190 of the EA 1993 and section 6 of the Education (Miscellaneous) Provisions Act 1953 to pay the fees and, where relevant, meet board and lodging charges. Of course, as *ex p. H* and *ex p. Greig* (above) confirmed, the LEA would not necessarily be acting unlawfully by refusing to pay for a child to attend such a school, even where it is accepted that the education provided there would be best for him or her. Even where a social services department, acting under its duty under the Children Act 1989 towards a child "in need,"[99] considers that the child should be educated at an independent boarding school, the LEA's general duty under the 1989 Act to assist the social services department in the exercise of its statutory functions may not, in itself, mean that the LEA must comply with a request to meet the fees etc.

As indicated earlier, special education duties are also owed to children of pre-school age. The Department of Health's guidance on the Children Act 1989 states that, generally, integration into mainstream day care for the under-fives is the best approach.[1]

iv. *Identification and assessment of needs*

In some cases, schools and parents will become aware that a child may have special educational needs when so informed by the health services.[2] But in any event, there is a duty both at the LEA and school level to identify pupils who have special educational needs.[3] In most cases children with special educational needs will be identified by teachers as a result of routine monitoring of pupils or via National Curriculum assessments.

Of course, the precise nature and degree of special educational needs can only be determined properly through assessment. Non-statutory

---

[98]—*cont. from previous page*
applications where local authorities were exercising powers and duties with regard to children in care — in particular *A* v. *Liverpool City Council* [1982] A.C. 363; *In re W (A Minor) (Wardship Jurisdiction)* [1985] A.C. 791; and *Re Y* [1987] 1 F.L.R. 229.
[99] Children Act 1989, s.17 and Sched. 2 Part 1.
[1] Department of Health, *The Children Act 1989 Guidance and Regulations: Vol. 2 — Family Support, Day Care and Educational Provision for Young Children* (1991) para. 6.8.
[2] On the duties of health authorities and NHS Trusts in these cases, see EA 1993, s.176 (applies only to children aged under five). Where a child under the age of two and his/her parent believes that the child has special educational needs the parent can require the LEA to carry out an assessment: EA 1993, s.175. The assessment may be carried out "in such a manner as the [LEA] considers appropriate": *ibid.*
[3] EA 1993, ss.161(1) and 165(1). For a case in which the LEA failed to identify and assess a child's special educational needs, which was found to be maladministration causing injustice, see *Local Government Ombudsman Report on Investigation No.90/B/2031 Against Cambridgeshire County Council* (November 10, 1992).

assessment arrangements in respect of special educational needs are a matter for the school or the LEA to determine. Formal assessments on the other hand must be carried out under the procedure prescribed by the EA 1993, in which there is a clear attempt to promote parental involvement. It should be noted that a parent who is concerned about his or her child's progress at school could invoke the right in sections 172 or 173 of the Act to request an assessment or re-assessment. Prior to the 1993 Act the LEA could refuse to comply if the request was "unreasonable" (in the case of a non-statemented child) or assessment would be "inappropriate" (in the case of a statemented child).[4] The 1993 Act has shifted the onus onto the LEA to make the assessment, if one has not been made within six months prior to the request and is considered "necessary." It has also given parents a right of appeal where the LEA refuses to comply with the request.[5] The governing body of a GM school can also now request an assessment of a child.[6]

Assessment procedure begins with the service of a notice on a parent or guardian informing him or her of the proposal to assess the child, the name of an officer of the LEA from whom further advice may be obtained, and the right to make representations and submit written evidence within a stipulated period of not less than 29 days from service of the notice.[7] Once the period of notice has expired, the LEA must proceed to assess the child if it considers that, after taking into account representations and evidence submitted in response to the notice, the child has, or probably has, special educational needs and it is necessary for the authority to determine required special educational provision.[8] Regulations to be made under the 1993 Act will prescribe new time limits for the carrying out of the assessment and will continue to require that advice from a variety of professional sources is sought by the LEA.[9] LEAs will also have to have regard to the Code of Practice to be issued by the Secretary of State (see EA 1993, s.157).

Once the assessment process is in motion it is extremely difficult for the parent to resist it. Indeed, it is an offence for a parent not to comply with the requirements of a notice requiring the child to be examined at a stipulated place and time.[10] Other provisions aim for a

---

[4] EA 1981, s.9. See *R* v. *Surrey County Council ex p. B* (1991) January 11, *Lexis* CO 1127/90.

[5] EA 1993, ss.172(3) and 173(2). The Act has also removed the exemption from the requirement to assess children who were already receiving special educational treatment prior to April 1983, when the 1981 Act came into force (applied in *R* v. *Newham L.B.C. ex p. D* [1992] 1 F.L.R. 395).

[6] EA 1993, s.174.

[7] *Ibid.* s.167.

[8] *Ibid.* subs. (3).

[9] See Sched. 9 paras. 2 and 3.

[10] *Ibid.* para 5.

more gentle encouragement of parental involvement — for example by
giving the parent a right to attend the examination of the child and/or
submit information.[11] But it seems that insufficient weight tends to be
given to parents' views in the assessment process and that there are "still
situations in which parents feel their contribution . . . to be insufficient
or ineffective."[12] DES Circulars and the White Paper (*Choice and
Diversity*) have re-emphasised the need for parents to be seen as
"partners" in the assessment process, but the language and complexity
of the procedures continue to operate as barriers.

v. Statements

Following assessment, the LEA must make and maintain a
statement of the child's special educational needs where it considers "it
is necessary . . . to determine the special educational provision" that the
child's needs demand.[13] Parents may exercise a right of appeal if the
LEA decides not to make a statement (see below). If a statement is
made, it must be in the prescribed form,[14] setting out, in separate
sections, the advice from various professionals which is being taken into
account. The parents are entitled to receive a copy of the proposed
statement, make representations, meet with officials and receive the
LEA's decision on whether to proceed with the statement.[15] As
indicated above, the parents also have a right to express a preference for
a school to be named in the statement. They also have right of appeal in
respect of any part of the proposed provision (see below). Once the
statement is made, the LEA must ensure that the specified special
educational provision is made unless the parents have made other
suitable arrangements.[16]

---

[11] *Ibid.* para 4.
[12] House of Commons Education Select Committee *op. cit.*, para 16, and see also Same,
Third Report, Session 1992–93 *Meeting Special Educational Needs; Statements of Needs and
Provision* H.C. 287—I (1993) para. 49.
[13] EA 1993, s.168(1). The LEA need not arrange for this provision if the parents have
made suitable arrangements: s.168(5).
[14] Sched. 10, and regulations to be made in place of S.I. 1993 No. 29.
[15] Sched. 10 paras 2 and 4. Failure to consult parents over the proposed statement
contributed to maladministration and injustice in one case: *Report by the Local
Government Ombudsman Complaint No.89/A/2987 Against I.L.E.A.* (May 12, 1992).
[16] EA 1993, s.168(5)(*a*). In one case where the LEA failed for two years to provide the
additional teaching support specified in the statement there was maladministration and
injustice; compensation of £1,200 was ordered: *Report by Local Government Ombudsman
Complaints 90/A/3266 and 92/A/1580 Against L.B. Lambeth and I.L.E.A.* (August 17,
1992). For a case involving maladministration in changing schooling arrangements
contrary to the statement, see *Report by the Local Government Ombudsman Complaint
89/A/1972 Against the London Borough of Ealing* (August 14, 1991) and *Report by Local
Government Ombudsman Complaint No.91/A/0294 Against Kent County Council* (November
19, 1992). Note that an LEA-maintained or GM school (including a GM special
school) named in the statement must admit the child: s.168(5)(*b*).

The strictness of the requirements relating to the form of, and procedure concerning, statements was reinforced by the decision in *R. v. Secretary of State for Education and Science ex p. E (a minor)*.[17] Here a statement had been made in respect of E, a boy aged 13, who had learning difficulties as a result of dyslexia and discalcula. Part II of the statement, which dealt with his needs, referred to his difficulty with literacy and numeracy skills. But Part III, which covered the special educational provision to be made for his needs, referred only to the literacy difficulties. The necessary special education in respect of the numeracy problems, it was argued, could be determined by the school itself and so did not need to be included in specific terms in Part III of the statement. This argument was rejected by the High Court and the Court of Appeal. It was held that the LEA was required to specify and make special educational provision for the child in respect of each of the special educational needs which had been identified in Part II of the statement, particularly in view of the degree of detail contemplated by the regulations governing the form and content of statements.[18] But in *R. v. Hereford and Worcester County Council ex p. P*[19] it was held that it was not necessary to set out in full the terms and conditions under which any *non*-educational provision specified in a statement (in Part V) was to be made. All that was required was that "the general nature of the provision" should be specified. In the instant case the provision in question was transport between school and home. The parents were clearly unhappy with the arrangements, under which the child, who was aged five and had Down's syndrome, spent one hour travelling each way and had to be strapped in throughout the journey. McCullough J. said that the LEA was under no obligation to specify in the statement the maximum duration of the journey.

Hannon predicted that the 1981 Act would enable LEAs "to draw the line between the 'statemented' and the 'unstatemented' where they please,"[20] and the Court of Appeal's decision in *R. v. Secretary of State for Education and Science ex p. E (a minor)*[21] has borne out this view. Here the LEA considered that a 13 year old girl who was a slow learner attending an ordinary school did not need a statement. Her parents, having sought expert opinion, felt that the girl would be better off in

---

[17] [1992] 1 F.L.R. 377.

[18] It was held that the LEA was obliged to set out the provision in Part III in detail, referring to the curriculum and time to be spent in relation to different subjects, so that teachers would know precisely what would be required.

[19] (1992) *The Times*, March 13. See also *Report by the Local Government Ombudsman Complaint No. 89/C/0269 Against Calderdale Metropolitan Borough Council*.

[20] V. Hannon, "The Education Act 1981: New Rights and Duties in Special Education" (1982) *Journal of Social Welfare Law* 275 at p. 284.

[21] [1988] 1 F.L.R. 72.

an independent special school. The Court upheld the LEA's power not to determine the special educational provision that should be made for the child, drawing an important distinction: a child may simply have special educational needs, or, alternatively, may have needs that are such that the LEA may be of the opinion that it should determine the necessary special educational provision to be made — "not special needs *simpliciter*, but special needs that satisfy a further condition" (*per* Nicholls L.J.[22]). The parents had argued that because the school had taken a decision to include the child in a remedial class, the special educational provision for her had already been determined, so a statement should follow. But the Court rejected this argument. Dillon L.J. said that where the LEA leaves it to the school to decide on the provision that should be made, the LEA is not itself making a determination of provision, so a statement is not necessary.[23] LEAs' wide discretion over whether or not to make a statement was confirmed by the Court of Appeal decision in *R. v. Isle of Wight County Council ex p. S.*[24] The Court held that even though the LEA had made a draft statement it was entitled not to formalise it if it changed its mind about the necessity for a statement.

In view of the wide discretion resting with LEAs concerning statementing, it comes as no surprise that there is a considerable variation between them in the proportion of children who are made the subject of a statement. In the authority with the highest proportion a child is 100 times more likely to be statemented than in the authority with the lowest.[25] This divergence surely cannot be attributed to local social and economic circumstances alone and seems to flow from differences in the interpretation of the Act.[26] For example, in one LEA, officers developed a practice of not statementing children attending mainstream schools, which the Local Government Ombudsman said amounted to maladministration.[27] One of the main aims of the new Code of Practice, to which LEAs and others will have to have regard (EA 1993, s.157), is to ensure "a larger degree of material consistency in the making of assessments and statements."[28]

---

[22] At p. 82.
[23] At pp. 79–80.
[24] (1992) *The Times* November 2 (C.A.).
[25] House of Commons Education (Etc.) Committee *op. cit.*, para 33.
[26] Audit Commission/HMI *supra.* (n.81) para 21.
[27] *Local Government Ombudsman Report Complaint No. 90/A/3300 Against East Sussex County Council* (August 17, 1992).
[28] H.L., Debs, Vol. 545, col. 489 (April 29, 1993) *per* Baroness Blatch. But note that "The Code will not impose duties. It will offer practical guidance ... It will deal with matters that are not susceptible to hard and fast rules, matters where an element of judgment is always required": *ibid.* at col. 486.

National figures show successive annual increases in the proportion of pupils with statements. In 1989, LEAs held statements of special educational needs in respect of 138,679 pupils, or 1.8 per cent. of the school population. By 1991 this figure had risen to 168,000 or 2.1 per cent. of schoolchildren.[29]

LEAs are required to review a statement annually,[30] to ensure that provision is appropriate to the child's needs. They may amend, or cease to maintain, a statement, in which case parents generally have similar rights to be informed of proposed changes, make representations and appeal.[31]

Concern has been expressed about the amount of time taken to complete the assessment and statementing of children.[32] DES Circular 22/89 recommended a maximum of six months for preparation of a draft statement. The 1993 Act now enables time limits to be prescribed for each stage of the procedure (see Schedules 9 and 10). It is expected that parents might be able to sue for breach of statutory duty in respect of delays[33] (to add to their right to have the matter referred to the Local Ombudsman if the delay is alleged to have resulted from maladministration[34]).

---

[29] Audit Commission/HMI, *Getting In On The Act—Provision for Pupils with Special Educational Needs—the National Picture* (1992) paras. 4 and 33. The House of Commons Education Select Committee (1993, *supra* n.12) has called for fewer statements (para. 32).

[30] EA 1993 s.172(5)(b). A failure to review a boy's statement annually was maladministration giving rise to injustice: *Report by Local Ombudsman Complaint 91/A/0294 Against Kent County Council* (November 19, 1992).

[31] EA 1993 Sched. 10 paras 10 and 11. Appeal will lie to the SENT from Sept 1994 (see below).

[32] DFE, *Special Educational Needs — Access to the System: A Consultation Paper* (1992) para. 13.

[33] *Ibid.* para. 15.

[34] See, *e.g. Reports by the Local Government Ombudsman — Complaint No. 90/C/2397 Against Oldham Metropolitan Borough Council* (October 22, 1991) (delay in carrying out formal assessment due to boycott of posts was maladministration and injustice — LEA could have recruited outside assistance); — *Complaint No. 90/A/2257 Against Kent County Council* (January 27, 1992) (preparation and issue of a draft statement took eight and a half months; this was excessive delay, was maladministration and caused injustice); — *Complaint 90/A/2248 Against East Sussex County Council* (June 15, 1992) (general undue delays in assessment and statementing); — *Complaint No. 91/C/0353 Against Derbyshire C.C.* (March 4, 1993) (draft statement took 13 months to prepare — excessive delay, maladministration and injustice); — *Complaint No. 91/A/3614 Against L.B. Lewisham* (March 15, 1993) (22 months to produce the draft statement — result as in *Derbyshire* complaint); — *Complaint No. 91/B/0208 Against Bedfordshire LEA* (May 25, 1993) (28 months taken to issue final statement — result as in *Derbyshire* case); — *Complaint No. 90/B/1778 Against Lincolnshire C.C.* (April 30, 1993) (Delay in completing assessment; £12,500 compensation). See also *Complaints Nos. 90/B/2279, 91/A/2103, 92/B/0219* and *92/B/0031.*

vi.   *Reform of the appeals system*

From September 1994 there will be a new appeals system. At present, appeals in respect of the content of statements currently lie to a local appeal committee and then to the Secretary of State.[35] Others (on decisions not to make a statement) lie direct to the Secretary of State, who may only direct the LEA to re-consider its case.[36] The number of appeals to the Secretary of State more than trebled between 1984–1991 and, despite the small numbers (only 160 in total in 1991), it takes between 6–12 months before the appeals are determined.[37] With new rights of appeal — over refusal to re-assess a pupil, a decision to cease to maintain a statement and the school named in a statement — it was clear that reform was necessary. The DFE concluded that the existing arrangements failed to "meet parents' legitimate expectations of a clear, timely and effective means of redress for their grievances."[38]

Under the new appeals system, all appeals in special educational needs cases will lie to the Special Educational Needs Tribunal (SENT).[39] The SENT, which will be under the supervision of the Council on Tribunals, is to have a legally qualified chairperson appointed by the Lord Chancellor, and two other members appointed by the Secretary of State. No qualifications for the lay members are specified in the Act but may be prescribed by regulation.[40] The Government has confirmed that each tribunal will include a member with experience and expertise in the field of special educational needs and another with experience of local government.[41]

The SENTs will operate on a regional basis under a national President. As the Code of Practice (made under s. 158 of the 1993 Act) will indicate the kinds of factors to which LEAs should have regard when making decisions on statements and in respect of other matters, it obviously makes sense for it to be taken into account by the SENT; indeed there is a statutory duty for the tribunal to do so where the Code is relevant (EA 1993, section 157(3)). Further appeal, on a point of law only, will lie to the High Court (see EA 1993, section 181(2).

The introduction of a new system of redress in special needs cases is sorely needed. If the existing arrangements are satisfactory, why is it that 120 applications for judicial review in such cases were made in 1992?[42] The minister has said that the new system will aim to be

---

[35] EA 1981, s.8; but see *R* v. *Clwyd County Council ex p. A* (1992) *The Times*, August 26.
[36] *Ibid.* s.5(6)–(8).
[37] Audit Commission/HMI *op. cit.* para. 37.
[38] DFE *supra* (n.32) para. 21.
[39] See EA 1993, ss.169(2), 170'(1) 172'(3) and 173(2) and Sched. 10 paras. 8 and 11.
[40] EA 1993, s.178(2).
[41] Official Report, House of Commons Standing Committee E, col. 1168, January 28, 1993, Mr. T. Boswell M.P. (Under-Secretary of State).
[42] *Ibid.* col. 1177, Mrs A. Campbell M.P.; and *T.E.S.*, January 15, 1993.

"friendly to parents and suitable for the swift prosecution of justice."[43] Regulations will lay down detailed rules of procedure (see section 180). In referring to "discovery of documents" and "award of costs," the Act gives the impression that the procedure could be quite formal, despite the expressed intention that the tribunals will offer a degree of informality.[44] The Government resisted an attempted amendment to extend Legal Aid eligibility to SENT proceedings, which had aimed to combat the LEA's inbuilt advantage over parents in such a context. The concern that legally qualified chairmanship of SENTs will contribute to a court-like atmosphere[45] must be offset by the need for such chairmanship highlighted by firm evidence of procedural irregularities and deficiencies in lay-chaired local education appeal committees (see p. 156 above). Nevertheless, given the fact that few of the lawyer chairmen and women will initially have real experience of the law governing special educational needs, it will clearly be important that at least one of the members has expertise in that field and that proper training is provided. So far as swiftness is concerned, the Government has said that the procedural rules will ensure that the tribunal "will have strict time targets."[46] This should be of considerable benefit in a field where delay is undoubtedly detrimental to the children concerned. However, there is the danger that because of the considerable amount of evidence which will have to be assembled and considered, including the various professionals' reports, there may be frequent occasions when postponement or adjournment may be necessary.

(g) Local arrangements under ERA 1988 for complaints about schooling

i. *Introduction*

Local arrangements for the investigation of complaints about the way an LEA or school is discharging its legal obligations concerning the curriculum and related matters came into operation on September 1, 1989. According to the Minister, the procedures are intended to provide "a constitutional safeguard" for education consumers, enabling parents and others "to have any complaints considered carefully and effectively at local level ... and quickly."[47] Redress of grievance is one of the principal elements in the Government's *Citizen's Charter,* and as noted in

---

[43] *Supra.* n.41, col. 1182.
[44] *Ibid.* col. 1173. The regulations may also make provision for taxation of costs, in the county court.
[45] *Ibid.* col. 1178.
[46] *Ibid.* col. 1181.
[47] Official Report of Commons Standing Committee J, the Education Reform Bill, col. 429, January 12, 1988, Angela Rumbold M.P.

Chapter 1 the Government has said that "all public services . . . should have clear and well-publicised complaints procedures."[48] Funded research by the author into the section 23 procedures aimed to assess the extent to which the local arrangements matched up to the objectives established by the Government for them (above).[49] Some of the main findings are discussed below.

ii. *The scope of the section 23 procedures*

Section 23 does not specify who may use the local complaints procedures. As complaint to the Secretary of State, which might follow on from pursuance of a complaint under section 23, may be made by "any person"[50] or "any person interested,"[51] it would be appropriate to regard section 23 as similarly available. The Government has stated that the section 23 procedures should be considered to be available to "parents and others."[52] But there is no specific mention of child complainants, although the terms of the section do not preclude investigation of complaints by children. In contrast, the Children Act 1989 gives children a statutory right to complain in respect of social services provision.[53] The National Consumer Council has called for a similar right for children aged 16 or over in respect of education complaints.[54]

The section 23 procedures apply only to education provided in county schools, voluntary schools and special schools not established in a hospital.[55] Governors of GM schools are required to operate similar procedures.[56]

No complaint about a matter within the remit of section 23 may be entertained by the Secretary of State under his general complaints jurisdiction unless and until it has been pursued under the local procedure. Section 23 covers complaints that a:

> [local education] authority, or the governing body of any . . . school . . .
> (a) have acted or are proposing to act unreasonably with respect to the exercise of any power conferred or the performance of any duty imposed on them by or under—

---

[48] H.M. Government, *The Citizen's Charter* (1991) Cm 1599, p. 42.
[49] N. Harris, *Complaints About Schooling: The Role of Section 23 of the Education Reform Act 1988* (1992). The research was funded by the Nuffield Foundation.
[50] EA 1944, s.68.
[51] *Ibid.* s.99(1).
[52] See DES Circular 1/89 *Education Reform Act 1988: Local Arrangements for the Consideration of Complaints* (1989).
[53] Children Act 1989, s.26.
[54] National Consumer Council, *When Things Go Wrong At School: Grievance Procedures in the Education Service* (1992).
[55] ERA 1988, s.23(1).
[56] EA 1993 Sched. 6 para. 7(2).

(i)   any provision of this Chapter; or
(ii) any other enactment relating to the curriculum for, or
      religious worship in, maintained schools other than
      grant-maintained schools; or
(b)   have failed to discharge any such duty.

On the face of it, the section applies only to complaints about governing bodies and LEAs, and not to those about individual teachers or head teachers. That is certainly the way in which the DES (now the DFE) has interpreted it.[57] It is true that, as explained above, governing bodies have wide-ranging curricular responsibilities. But within the policy framework established by the LEA and governing body, the determination and organisation of the secular curriculum is, as noted above, the responsibility of the head teacher. Moreover, classroom teachers are involved on a day to day basis in securing the fulfilment of the school's curricular responsibilities. From the complaints which were examined in the course of the research it was clear that many had concerned, one way or another, the conduct of an individual teacher. In almost every case the complaint had been treated as admissable, probably incorrectly under the present law — as for example in the case of the prosletysing teacher who used morning assembly to preach his own religious ideas, and, in another case, where the parent complained about science teaching methods and unsatisfactory marking of homework.

The Department's guidance[58] on the responsibilities and powers in respect of which complaints may be entertained is rather superficial. For example, it makes no reference to LEAs' and governors' powers (as opposed to duties). In the light of this, it was not surprising that the survey of 25 LEAs and 36 governing bodies revealed widely differing interpretations of the scope of the section.[59]

iii.   *Awareness of the procedures*

The Commission for Local Administration in England recommends that local complaints systems should be "easily accessible and conspicuous to users of services."[60] However, nearly 60 per cent. of the 440 parents in the author's survey said that they were unaware of the existence of the local section 23 complaints machinery. The most obvious reason for this ignorance is the inadequate distribution of information. For example, although the law requires all school prospectuses to refer to the

---

[57] DES Circular 1/89 *op. cit.* para. 10.
[58] *Ibid.* para. 11.
[59] See N. Harris, *Complaints About Schooling op. cit.* at pp. 41–45.
[60] Commission for Local Administration in England, *Devising a Complaints System* (1992).

procedures,[61] only 20 out of 98 prospectuses which were examined in the course of the research mentioned them. Furthermore, a survey of 20 local public libraries around the country revealed that *none* had copies of the local procedure even though most of the procedure documents stated that copies could be found there. The *Parent's Charter* (1991) makes a brief reference to a parent's right of complaint about the school curriculum. However, even though, according to the DFE, seven million copies of the *Charter* were distributed, only 35 per cent. of parents in the survey had received a copy, and not all had read it.

iv. *The subject of complaints*

Among the trends which the official figures for 1989–92 appear to reveal are that concerns about RE and collective worship have diminished but dissatisfaction with the National Curriculum, especially testing, has grown (see Table).

Formal section 23 complaints by subject 1989–92

Number of recorded complaints

Subject	1989–90	1990–91	1991–92
National Curriculum	10	8	11
Exception from the National Curriculum[a]	5	19	32
Religious education	5	6	3
Collective worship	10	10	0
Resources for the curriculum	14	3	2
Other aspects of the curriculum[b]	28	20	14
Other s.23 matters[c]	17	9	11
TOTAL	89[d]	75	73

Notes:

a. Most of these complaints were by parents who wanted their children excepted from National Curriculum testing; 14 were in one LEA in 1990–91 and 28 in another LEA in 1991–92.

---

[61] The Education (School Curriculum and Related Information) Regulations 1989 SI 1989 No. 954, as amended, and the Education (School Information) (England) Regulations 1993 SI 1993 No. 1502. (The Welsh regs. were not available at the time of going to press.)

b.   In 1990–91 these included four complaints about sex education and three concerning entry for GCSE.

c.   In 1990–91 these included three complaints about incompetence or unfairness of the head teacher (even though complaints about head teachers strictly lie outside the scope of s.23).

d.   The individual figures add up to 89, but 88 is the total stated by the DFE.

What is striking above all about these figures is the small number of complaints overall. (Indeed, formal complaints occurred in only 30 per cent. of LEAs in 1991–92). There are a number of possible explanations for this. In part it may be the effect of ignorance of the procedures on the part of parents, which was noted above. It may also be attributable to the resolution of most complaints at the informal stage. Another factor could be a belief among potential complainants that complaining would not achieve a positive outcome; in the survey, one third of the parents who were unwilling to approach their LEA over a complaint cited this as their reason. This is linked to the broader issue of individual parents' willingness to assert their rights as 'consumers.' An overwhelming majority of parents in the survey said that they would, in principle at least, be willing to complain if dissatisfied with their child's education (412 out of 440 questioned). But if they really did have a grievance, might not some parents be afraid to stir up trouble for their child or, as indicated, be deterred by pessimism about the likely outcome? Finally it could be that almost every parent in the land is satisfied with his or her child's education — the simplest, but least plausible, explanation.

v.   *How the procedures work*

Aside from the need for DFE approval, the procedures are unregulated. There is no national code of practice.

The guidance issued by the Commission on Local Administration in England[62] also states that Local complaints procedures should be clear, simple, easily accessible, speedy, well publicised, name an initial first point of contact, be in three distinct stages (one informal followed by two formal), involve the keeping of records at all stages and ensure that the complainant is kept well-informed throughout. These general principles are in the main reflected in the section 23 procedures currently in operation. However, the procedures are silent on a number of issues, such as how and by whom a complaint will be investigated.

---

[62] *Op. cit.*

All the procedures have three stages. Stage 1 is an informal stage, in which complaints lie to the head teacher. Such complaints tend not to be recorded. It is the view of the majority of LEAs that because the informal approach generally results in resolution of the problem the formal stages (stages 2 and 3) under section 23 are having little impact. This is borne out by the relatively small number of complaints reaching the formal stages according to DFE national statistics (see below).

The procedure documents all state that formal complaints must be in writing. This contrasts with complaints under the Children Act 1989, where there is the option of making a complaint orally.[63] At stage 2, the complaint will be referred to the governing body. The complaint will be investigated by the governors themselves, although the precise manner of investigation is not clear. From the cases examined by the author it would appear that the head teacher and subject co-ordinator are generally asked to produce statements prior to the hearing of the complaint. These are sent to complainants. The panel that hears the complaint generally consists of three, five or seven governors; sometimes the entire governing body is convened. There is no requirement for there to be an independent member of the panel. The head teacher generally attends the hearing and, given his or her close relationship with the governors (he or she is, after all, generally a member of the governing body), the complainant is undoubtedly at a disadvantage. Complainants can be represented, however, although in none of the cases examined had there had been legal representation. The procedure is intended to be inquisitorial, although some of the procedure documents refer to the opportunity for "cross-examination" by the complainant. The complaint is generally heard on school premises.

Of only 68 section 23 complaints reaching governing bodies in 1991–92, just 6 were upheld (17 were still under consideration). At the next stage (stage 3), LEAs heard 26 complaints, of which only one was upheld.[64]

A formal complaint will reach the LEA at stage 3 either direct from the informal stage, if it lies against the LEA only, or otherwise via the governing body (stage 2). The LEA's designated complaints officer will cause the complaint to be investigated, usually by a member of the authority's inspection and advisory service. For example, in one case which concerned a complaint (which was rejected) that the content of a reading book for 11 year olds was risqué, the LEA's principal adviser for English evaluated the book. Given the fact that complaints reaching

---

[63] The local authority must cause the complaint to be recorded in writing and sent to the complainant for approval: Representations Procedure (Children) Regs. 1991, SI 1991 No. 894, reg. 4(2).

[64] DFE statistics, based on annual returns from LEAs, supplied to the author.

stage 3 may be about the LEA, there is surely a strong case for a more independent investigation. There is also a lack of independence in the constitution of the complaints panel responsible for adjudication of complaints at stage 3, which usually consists of three LEA members. In practice they tend to be drawn from the members of school admissions and school exclusions appeal committees.[65] In contrast, under the Children Act 1989 procedures the complaints panel must always have at least one independent member.[66]

The procedure documents generally provide for the complainant's right to attend, make representations and be represented, and (in cases proceeding from stage 2) the governing body's right to be represented and put their view. They also state that the complainant should be informed of the decision plus reasons as soon as possible. In most of the cases covered by the research fairly complete reasons were given; but in a small number of cases the statement of reasons was extremely terse. Most of the cases which had progressed to stage 3 were disposed of in the region of 8–10 weeks. However, some took significantly longer — in one case almost six months.

Despite the importance attached by both the UN Convention on the Rights of the Child and the Children Act 1989 to eliciting the views of children in various forms of proceedings (see pp. 21–22), there is no evidence that this is done in section 23 complaints cases. (See, for example, the case brought by the parents of a 14 year old girl concerning a school's policy of compulsory sex education, noted above.)

vi. *Remedying a complaint*
No provision is made for the legal enforcement of any recommendations arising out of the upholding of a complaint, other than via further complaint to the Secretary of State under sections 68 or 99 of the EA 1944.

5. CONCLUSION

It is clear that when it comes to the content of education, parents, as consumers, have few rights of choice over the 'product' and only limited opportunities for more general involvement. Means of redress have been extended, however, although they continue to be of variable effectiveness.

Consumer choice has been limited as a result of an unprecedented degree of central regulation of the school curriculum, which has created

---

[65] These are constituted, for both of these purposes, under the EA 1980, Sched. 2.
[66] Representations Procedure (Children) Regs. *op. cit.* reg. 8(3).

greater uniformity of content. The Government's attempt to introduce greater diversity of school type does little to disguise that fact (although opportunities for some degree of specialisation are now being expanded). It has been argued that the kind of market system being introduced in the education system "will only offer some people a choice of supplier; it will not offer people a choice between distinctly different types of education."[67] Even the choice between the kind of curriculum being provided in state and independent sectors is becoming less pronounced, as ministers use their powers to push for more "traditional" teaching methods and curriculum content in the state sector and as many independent schools decide to follow the National Curriculum.[68]

Of course, extending choice into the classroom would be extremely problematic. Choice would have to be limited by the resources available and organisational constraints. More importantly, it cannot be assumed that parents would necessarily make the best choices for their children: "many parents' expectations of school are shaped by their own experience of having been pupils themselves. Sometimes that experience bears little resemblance to the ethos of a modern British . . . school."[69] Nevertheless, it is accepted that parental involvement in the curriculum may be highly beneficial to the child.[70]

A fundamental question that has to be asked is how far should the private interest of parents in respect of their children prevail over the public interest, which ostensibly the education system as a whole seeks to represent? Sayer presents the case of a girl who attended dance lessons in her school. The teacher received a request to exempt the girl from the lessons on religious grounds. The parents believed that dancing to music would "stir the passions dangerously." But the school did not want to set a precedent in respect of what was considered part of the common curriculum. By law the parents were only entitled to remove the child from religious education. The girl had reacted to the dance class with great enthusiasm. The parents were invited to school to discuss the problem and observe a dance lesson. Afterwards they persisted with their wish to have their daughter excepted. Despite the head teacher's conviction that the class was in the child's best interests, and his/her wariness about setting a precedent, the parents' request was

---

[67] J. Raven, "Equity in Diversity: The Problems Posed by Values — and their Resolution", in F. Macleod (ed.) *Parents and Schools: the Contemporary Challenge* (1989) at p. 76.

[68] See *The Guardian*, May 4, 1993.

[69] T. Bryans, "Parental Involvement in Primary Schools", in S. Wolfendale (ed.) *Parental Involvement* (1989) at p. 36.

[70] J. Sayer, "Facing Issues in Parents' Responsibility for Education", in S. Wolfendale (1989) *op. cit.* p. 125. See also S. Jowett *et al.*, *Building Bridges — Parental Involvement in Schools* (1991).

granted. Sayer concludes "even if the prime client is the child, the question remains whether access to a common curriculum is more important than being able to relate to school and home."[71] This implies that the case for greater parental choice and involvement rests not so much on a broadly consumerist notion but rather on the importance of promoting the child's interests. In other words, the public interest in the education and welfare of children can up to a point best be served by accommodating the private interest. But public and private interests can be extremely difficult to reconcile in this context. Part of the difficulty flows from the way that the education system seeks to apply a *common* set of values — over such matters as compulsory school attendance, discipline, sex education and even, to some extent, religious education and collective worship. As we have seen, regulation of the curriculum has aimed to foster some of these values — in recent years via ideologically-driven changes to the law, which exemplify what some see as the Government's "social and moral authoritarianism."[72]

The practical consequence of the increasing regulation of the curriculum has been considerable pressures on teachers, head teachers and governors. This has led to suggestions that the administrative burden imposed may be detrimental to the interests of pupils, because it is seen as detracting from the teaching process. It has also precipitated industrial action by teachers seeking to reassert their professional autonomy and claim the moral high ground, by arguing that they are acting in the best interests of schoolchildren.

[71] *Ibid.* p. 123.
[72] G. Whitty and I. Menter, "Lesson of Thatcherism: Education Policy in England and Wales 1979–1988" (1989) 16 *Journal of Law and Society* 42 at p. 52.

8

CONCLUSION: THE LIMITS OF CONSUMERISM IN THE EDUCATION SYSTEM

We have seen how the employment of regulation and fostering of consumerism have been used to transform the education system and the power relationships within it. This process of transformation began with the Education Act 1980, gathered momentum with the E(No 2)A 1986, ERA 1988 and EA 1993, but is still in some respects incomplete. The GM sector is still in its infancy. Some parts of the country, for example Wales and the North-East, have a mere scattering of GM schools. It may be several years before the new funding authorities, the extent of whose role locally is dependent on the progress of opting out, can make their mark on local schools provision other than in a limited number of LEA areas. Full implementation of the National Curriculum will not be complete until 1999, and there are still teething troubles (and several more fundamental problems) which are precipitating necessary changes. The higher education sector has been re-structured, but the funding and regulatory regime is still new and the Government's draft *Higher Education Charter*, which promises a further element of consumerism, has only recently been published. But the key constituents of the new education system in England and Wales are in place: schools and colleges with responsiblity for their own budgets and overall management control; a legal regime governing the provision and publication of information about schools, schooling and the collective achievements of pupils; the establishment of a quasi-market for education based on competition and, within limits, individual choice; a degree of 'consumer-citizenship' based, in part, on individual and collective participation in some areas of decision-making; centralised control of the content of school education and of many of the regulatory structures in all sectors, especially higher education; reduced teacher autonomy; and the abolition of the LEA near-monopoly of local publicly funded provision. It can be predicted that within a few years the pattern of institutional autonomy, consumer power and central control will seem as settled as the broad structure of the education system in the decades following the EA 1944.

Although consumerism has become a dominant underlying feature of the education system, it has not been given completely free rein. We have seen how the scope for individual and collective participation in decision-making tends in practice to be quite limited (the one major exception being decisions on school opt-outs, although even here the final decision rests with the Secretary of State). Furthermore, individual choice of school is a concept which has not been translated into legal reality. Although consumer choice is central to the policy of reducing 'producer domination' in relation to public services, the rights presently associated with it have not marked the kind of individualism that would be associated with a free market system.[1] This may of course be entirely just and appropriate. As Tweedie suggests, there is a case for arguing that "granting a right should not enshrine an individual interest as superior to the social programme's other concerns."[2] At the same time, proponents of market ideology see competition and the exercise of individual choice as making a substantial contribution to improved standards of educational provision, which is said to be to the greater public good.

But critics argue that the operation of choice and competition creates social division and inequality,[3] improving the 'life chances' of some, but at the expense of others. Open enrolment and LMS combine to allow successful schools to expand and less successful schools to go into decline, offering an inferior 'product' which some consumers, whether because of geographical location, sibling connection with the school or social disadvantage reflected in low educational attainment or inadequate 'culture capital,'[4] are forced to accept. This disadvantage is likely to prevail at whatever rate the market model is pursued and no matter what legal rights are offered to education consumers in general.[5] For example, parental choice in Scotland is said to have "led to the re-emergence of something resembling a two-tier system of secondary schooling in the big cities," with "a small number of rump schools located in the most deprived areas."[6] There is also clear evidence from

[1] See L. Bash, "Education Goes to Market," in L. Bash and D. Coulby, *The Education Reform Act 1988: Competition and Control* (1989) pp. 29–30.

[2] J. Tweedie, "Rights in Social Programmes: the Case of Parental Choice of School" [1986] P.L. 407, at pp. 434–435.

[3] G. Whitty and I. Menter, "Lessons of Thatcherism: Education Policy in England and Wales 1979–88" (1989) 16 *Journal of Law and Society* 42 at p. 49.

[4] "Culture capital" in this context has been defined as a parent's "knowledge of which schools are 'good', and the ability and professional contacts to manipulate and 'play' the educational system to (his/her) children's advantage": D. Reynolds, "Parents and the Left: Rethinking the Relationship," in F. Macleod (ed.), *Parents and Schools: The Contemporary Challenge* (1989) 165, at p. 170.

[5] P. Woods, "Parents as Consumer-Citizens," Conference Paper, University of North London, September 1992.

[6] M. Adler, *An Alternative Approach to Parental Choice* National Commission on Education Briefing No. 13 (1993) p. 3.

the United States of the inequalities and social division that can result from the operation of a policy of choice and competition in the education system.[7] The *Cleveland* case[8] in this country demonstrated that one of the forms of social division that can be engendered by parental choice of school is a form of "ethnic segregation."[9] David argues that "parental choice of education in Britain in the late 1980s, and early 1990s, was seen to take precedence over promoting racial or religious harmony."[10]

The trend towards greater consumerism in the schools system, facilitated by various consumer rights, has offered the promise of choice and participation to parents. But it should be appreciated that it is the product of a deliberate policy initiative designed to afford the Government a further means of regulating the education system, in pursuance of particular political and economic objectives.[11] Thus the establishment of performance indicators and publication of performance related information about schools may be a means to consumer empowerment and accountability to the consumer, but these mechanisms also provide a means of regulating the flow of resources into the system. If schools (or universities for that matter) fail to achieve the necessary performance standards, they may receive reduced resource allocations, on the basis of the lower levels of consumer demand they generate or their relative inefficiency. That is not to deny that consumer empowerment has real social significance or legal substance. There is little doubt that the so-called new "consumer democracy"[12] has produced greater political accountability, by opening up decision-making processes and giving greater access to information relating to what schools and other institutions are doing and how public money is being spent. Furthermore, extension of rights of redress has increased the scope for legal accountability, although there are still deficiencies (for example in relation to school complaints procedures and school admissions and exclusions appeals).

But there must be doubts about whether most of the types of consumer empowerment that are envisaged really touch upon the true concerns of parents. Indeed, it is unlikely that most parents think of

---

[7] W. Clune and J. Witte (eds.), *Choice and Control in American Education* Vols. *1 and 2* (1990).

[8] See Chap. 5 at pp. 141–145.

[9] M. Adler, *op. cit.*

[10] M. E. David, *Parents, Gender and Education Reform* (1993), p. 135.

[11] G. Whitty and I. Menter, *op. cit.* p. 45 state that one of these objectives is to "make the public sector behave more like the private sector."

[12] See D. Taylor, "Citizenship and Social Power" (1989) 9(2) *Critical Social Policy* 19 at p. 20 and S. Ranson, "From 1944 to 1988: Education, Citizenship and Democracy," in M. Flude and M. Hammer (eds.), *The Education Reform Act 1988: Its Origins and Implications* (1990), p. 1.

themselves as "consumers" (as recent research has confirmed[13]) and, perhaps more significantly, act as consumers.[14] Parents are, in general, content to accept what is provided, as long as their own children make satisfactory academic and social progress at school and are reasonably content there. If they want to become involved with their child's school and schooling it is most likely to be through home-school reading programmes, attending assemblies and meetings at school and, perhaps, through membership of the school's parent-teacher association.[15] Only a small minority of parents want to serve as school governors. Few have anything to do with decision-making once their child is located at a particular school, other than over giving permission for school trips or assisting in GCSE or 'A' level subject choice. Even the right of withdrawal from religious education or collective worship has traditionally been used by very few parents,[16] although, as shown in Chapter 7, not all parents are aware of this right. But that is not to say that the rights which are available to parents are unimportant. As Sutherland says:

> "[T]he great majority of parents do have ambitions for their children and hope to achieve a good standard of living, probably better than that of their parents, in a safe and harmonious world. Consequently, parents are taken to have the right to make decisions about the kind of education their children will receive."[17]

In areas such as school exclusion, special educational needs, the school curriculum and school selection, dissatisfied parents may (increasingly after obtaining legal advice[18]) want to influence or change decisions and may utilise the redress mechanisms which are available (although with

---

[13] A. West *et. al.*, *Choosing A Secondary School: The parents' and pupils' stories* (1993) pp. 38–39: "Parents were asked whether they saw themselves as 'consumers of education' ... Altogether, nearly two-thirds of the parents did *not* see themselves as consumers of education, whilst just over a quarter (28%) did."

[14] See T. Wragg, "Parent Power," in F. Macleod (ed.) *Parents and Schools: The Contemporary Challenge* (1989), pp. 123–132.

[15] See S. Jowett *et al.*, *Building Bridges: Parental Involvement in Schools* (1991). Parent teacher associations (PTAs) are represented nationally by a National Confederation (NCPTAs). As yet NCPTAs has not had a major influence as a consumer pressure group, but in May and June 1993 took the forceful step of balloting parents on National Curriculum tests.

[16] See A. Bradney, *Religions, Rights and Laws* (1993), p. 63 n.65.

[17] M. Sutherland, *Theory of Education* (1988), p. 64.

[18] The Advisory Centre for Education (ACE), established in the early 1970s, is a registered charity offering free advice on education rights to parents and others. The Education Law Association (ELAS), formed in 1991, represents lawyers and others working in this field. Its members hold regular meetings and circulate key court decisions, etc.

variable prospects of success). Similarly, collective action by parents is likely to be engendered by plans to close a school or make a significant change to its character — and rights in connection with opting out, extended under the EA 1993, may prove a popular option in such circumstances. Any opportunities for participation provide an element of public accountability in an increasingly fragmented system, where both institutional autonomy and central government control have grown significantly.

As noted in Chapter 1, it is the form of accountability achieved via individual consumer choice in the market place that has received most attention from the Government. By comparison, accountability to consumers collectively has in general been neglected. Traditionally there was some scope for political accountability as a result of there being a democratically elected local authority. But LEA involvement is being drastically reduced (especially with the introduction of government-appointed funding authorities), in part to undermine the vested interests of local authorities and counter their perceived economic inefficiency. Yet governing bodies, which have gained power largely at the expense of LEAs, can also represent vested interests and use resources inefficiently. In the case of GM schools, where there is no LEA involvement, the political and legal accountability of education providers becomes more problematic. Central government has important powers over governing bodies, and they have been extended under the EA 1993. But central government is generally seen to be remote from ordinary citizens, and the availability of such powers hardly constitutes consumer empowerment and a means to proper public accountability.

There are, in addition to the social inequalities referred to earlier, a number of fundamental problems with market-based accountability in the context of education. First, it depends on freedom of consumer choice: as we have seen, the law has not given it to parents, and parents would in any event regard their choice as constrained by social considerations once their children are settled at a particular school.[19] Secondly, it assumes high levels of awareness of and reaction to the school's overall performance, which may not always be the case in practice. Thirdly, there must be extreme sensitivity on the part of education producers to market forces and the ability to improve the quality and attractiveness of provision in response to consumer demand. It is true that schools lose resources if pupil numbers fall; this can affect head teachers' salaries and teachers' job security. But there must often be a resignation to an existing situation, borne out of a realisation that

---

[19] R. Hambleton and P. Hoggett refer to the "formidable" human and social costs of upheaval, which limit the use of the "exit" option — taking your business elsewhere: "Rethinking consumerism in public services" (1993) 3(2) *Consumer Policy Review* 103 at p. 106.

improvement may, assuming it lies within the power of the school itself, be achieved only gradually and that a damaged reputation is not repaired easily or swiftly.

A further point, related to some of the others, is that a market system is founded on the existence of a contract between consumer and supplier. It is not the task of this book to explain how to distinguish conceptually and practically between the private and public legal basis of accountability. What is, however, being suggested is that a contractual basis of accountability offers a different kind of legal accountability to that generally provided for by the public law and statutory remedies that currently operate in the state education field. The former, being based on a private legal relationship under a contract, implies the existence of binding obligations on both sides without a public element. However, for the most part (independent schools excepted) education is provided free and there is no legal contract. That is not to say that the development of some form of quasi-contractual basis to the provider-consumer relationship in the public sector of the schools system could not occur in the future. Indeed, it would be entirely consistent with the atomisation of the state education system if schools were free to develop individualised contracts. Alternatively, generally applicable implied terms could be laid down by law, with perhaps local modification. David reports that "the notion of a 'home-school contract of partnershp' has gained considerable currency in recent years as a way of specifying and clarifying different parent-teacher responsibilities."[20] Indeed, such a development has the support of both Conservative and Labour parties. Tomlinson, in showing developments in other European countries, presents examples of formal legal agreements on which such partnerships might be based.[21] This kind of development would represent a further move towards privatisation of the kind encompassed by the education 'voucher' concept, which is already embodied in the 'credit card' system developed under the "Futures" training programme (see Chapter 1) and could be extended to the schools sector if a more workable system than that considered in the early 1980s were to be devised.[22] There is also considerable political and consumer support for the introduction of formal statements of mutual obligations between higher education providers and consumers (see below).[23] In relation to the schools sector, the House of Commons

---

[20] M. E. David, *op. cit.*, pp. 155–156.
[21] S. Tomlinson, *Teachers and Parents: Home-School Partnership* (1991), cited in David *supra*. p. 156.
[22] See D. Green *et al.*, *Empowering the Parents* (1992).
[23] See in particular the proposed *Student Charter* (1993), published by the National Union of Students.

Education Select Committee recently recommended that there should be "a form of written contract to be negotiated between the school and the parents of a child with special educational needs which sets out what the child's needs are and the provision the school will make to meet them."[24] But although home-school contracts are seen principally as a way of securing the co-operation of parents in matters of discipline and support for their child's education, it is easy to see how the concept could be taken a stage further.

There would be some practical difficulty in establishing a failure by an education provider (a problem which has hindered the development of educational malpractice tort litigation in the United States[25]). There appear to have been few reported cases (but must have been quite a number of unreported cases) of suit by a parent in respect of breach of contract by a proprietor of an independent school. However, in one case[26] a parent, whose child was away from school contrary to school rules, was told that unless he returned the child that night the boy would not be re-admitted. When the school excluded the boy, the parent sued unsuccessfully for recovery of school fees. The court held that the right to enforce the school rules was an implied term of the contract between parents and the school. There is also a Scottish authority which holds that the contents of a college prospectus can form part of a contract between students and the institution.[27] In another case,[28] Cockburn C.J. held that there was an implied contract between a parent and a private school, the substance of which was that the latter would continue to provide education for the child so long as the child's conduct did not warrant his exclusion from school. In a much more recent (judicial review) case, Brooke J. said that a parent seeking a legal remedy in respect of his/her child's exclusion from an independent school would have to sue for breach of contract.[29]

---

[24] House of Commons Education Select Committee, Session 1992–93 Third Report *Meeting Special Educational Needs: Statements of Needs and Provision*, Vol. I, H.C. 287–I (1993) para. 46.

[25] See A. Wolfgarten, "Educational malpractice: a potential problem for LEAs or teachers" (1990) 2(4) *Education and the Law* 157.

[26] *Price* v. *Wilkins* (1888) 58 L.T. 680.

[27] *Cadell* v. *Balfour* (1898) S.Ct. 1138. Of course, the students in this case were fee-paying. It has been suggested that where students have their fees paid by a local authority the rule that consideration must move from the promisee is not invalidated: D. Farrington and F. Mattison, *Universities and the Law* (1990), p. 71, citing Cheshire, Fifoot and Furmston, *The Law of Contract* (11th ed. 1986) p. 74. On the existence of a contract between students and universities, see H.W.R. Wade "Judicial Control of Universities" (1969) 85 L.Q.R. 468, and J.F. Garner "Students — Contract or Status" (1974) 90 L.Q.R. 6.

[28] *Fitzgerald* v. *Northcote* (1865) 4 F&F 656.

[29] *R.* v. *Headmaster of Fernhill Manor School and Another ex p. Angela S. Brown* (1992) *The Times*, June 5—see p. 217 n.71 *supra*.

But there is the possibility that the introduction of a widespread risk of exposure to civil liability could present such a constraining influence as to damage educational opportunities as a whole. A court in the U.S. considered this possibility (in relation to tortious liability) to offer a public policy ground for refusing to uphold a negligence claim in a case where the plaintiff's action was based in part on alleged failure by the school authorities to place the student in a class working at, and using books and materials of, an appropriate level for his ability and aptitude.[30] Precisely the type of problem experienced by the student in this case is addressed by the National Union of Students' proposals for "learner agreements" between students and colleges and universities, concluded after negotiation between provider and consumer over what is the most appropriate form and level of study and which targets are realistically attainable by the student.[31] Breach of the agreement by the institution would give rise to a "right of redress."[32] Institutions would be liable if, for example, they attempted to a close a course that was uneconomic.

There would be a need to provide legal safeguards for individual consumers. But there also has to be a system of public accountability in operation to safeguard and balance the wider collective interests of the community against those of individual consumers. The need to defend these wider interests and achieve the broader social objective of effective universal educational provision,[33] in itself limits the scope for individualism and privatisation. The idea that a combination of the expression of individualism and provider self-regulation, moderated by an element of public participation, can achieve these objectives may be flawed. In the context of education, consumer choice alone cannot

---

[30] See, *e.g.* the remarks of Rattigan, Associate J., in *Peter W. v. San Francisco Unified School District* 60 Cal. App. 3d 814, 131 Cal. Rptr. 854 (1976).

[31] Some universities, such as Nottingham Trent and Sheffield Hallam, have already concluded "learner contracts": "Close eye on charter for universities," *The Times*, April 26, 1993. Learner contacts/agreements are implicitly endorsed in the DFE's draft *Higher Education Charter* (May 1993, para. 24). But the *Charter* provides information rather than proposing wholesale changes in the student-university relationship.

[32] *Supra* (n.23) pp. 12–13. The type of redress envisaged is not explained. This is a separate issue to redress in respect of decisions on students' academic performance, in relation to which the NUS call for rights of appeal (p. 16). On the present scope for redress in relation to academic decisions, see D. Farrington and F. Mattison, *op. cit.* pp. 72–75; see also *R. v. University of London Visitor ex p. Vijayantunga* [1989] 2 All E.R. 843 (C.A.) and *R. v. Manchester Metropolitan University ex p. Nolan* (1993) *The Independent* July 15 (Q.B.D.).

[33] See also Howells' discussion, in relation to the more traditional areas of consumerism concerned with the purchase and supply of consumer goods, of the "societal justice" basis for intervention in the private contractual sphere: G. Howells, "Contract Law: the Challenge for the Critical Consumer Lawyer" in T. Willelmson (ed.) *Perspectives on Critical Contract Law* (1993).

determine how resources are to be allocated, and the education system cannot respond to changes in the pattern of demand in quite the same way as producers of goods or services in the private commercial sector. There is a need for some form of overall central planning to ensure a measure of social justice. Central planning is also needed to ensure the most effective use of resources. This is, of course, recognised by the Government in its plans for rationalisation and distribution of school places by funding authorities, central government and even LEAs (under the EA 1993).

The Government itself has to control the overall flow of resources into the education system and regulate their distribution. In the exercise of this function, the Government is politically accountable to Parliament and the electorate. While in theory a completely free market system could operate to distribute educational services to users, and "notwithstanding the appeal of the voucher system to the right," there is a general acceptance by politicians on both sides of the political divide that "public services should continue to provide major private benefits," including education, and that the alternative would be too difficult or politically costly to attempt to justify to the electorate.[34]

For all these reasons, it may be that in the field of educational provision, the market model, structured by regulation and dependent on consumerism, has been taken as far as is realistically possible — both politically and practically. Nevertheless, the culture of consumerism, which the legislation has begun to create is likely to have a prevailing influence on the education system well into the next century. Moreover, it seems certain that, whatever political changes occur in the future, the rights of education consumers will continue to form a central element in the education system's legal structure. Real consumer empowerment, may, however, continue to prove elusive — disappointing all those who, rightly or wrongly, and sincerely or not, claim it to be a pancea for the inadequacies of the state education system.

---

[34] R. Rose, *Ordinary People in Public Policy — A Behavioural Analysis* (1989), p. 21.

INDEX